Building the Prison State

The Chicago Series in Law and Society

EDITED BY JOHN M. CONLEY AND LYNN MATHER

Also in the series:

Additional series titles follow index

Building the Prison State

*Race and the Politics of
Mass Incarceration*

HEATHER SCHOENFELD

THE UNIVERSITY OF CHICAGO PRESS   CHICAGO AND LONDON

The University of Chicago Press, Chicago 60637
The University of Chicago Press, Ltd., London
© 2018 by The University of Chicago
Published 2018
Printed in the United States of America

27 26 25 24 23 22 21 20 19 18   1 2 3 4 5

ISBN-13: 978-0-226-52096-4 (cloth)
ISBN-13: 978-0-226-52101-5 (paper)
ISBN-13: 978-0-226-52115-2 (e-book)
DOI: 10.7208/chicago/9780226521152.001.0001

Library of Congress Cataloging-in-Publication Data

Names: Schoenfeld, Heather, author.
Title: Building the prison state : race and the politics of mass incarceration /
    Heather Schoenfeld.
Other titles: Chicago series in law and society.
Description: Chicago ; London : The University of Chicago Press, 2018. |
    Series: The Chicago series in law and society
Identifiers: LCCN 2017030432 | ISBN 9780226520964 (cloth : alk. paper) |
    ISBN 9780226521015 (pbk. : alk. paper) | ISBN 9780226521152 (e-book)
Subjects: LCSH: Prisons—Florida. | Criminal justice, Administration of—Florida. |
    Crime and race—Florida. | Criminal law—Florida.
Classification: LCC HV9475.F6 S36 2018 | DDC 365/.9779—dc23
LC record available at https://lccn.loc.gov/2017030432

IN RECOGNITION OF THE MEN, WOMEN, AND FAMILIES WHO SHOULDER
THE BURDEN OF THE PRISON STATE.

Contents

Figures and Tables

CHAPTER ONE

A New Perspective on the Carceral State

Gradually, during the last decade, punishments for fractious criminals on the former chain gangs have been made less objectionable. First, the lash was abandoned. Then the solitary confinement cell, "the sweat box," the stocks . . . And last of all shackles . . . The only punishment now invoked is confinement in a regular cell with a restricted diet.—"No More Shackles for Convicts," *Atlanta Constitution*, July 17, 1938, C4.

In 2002, the Florida Department of Corrections built fifteen "dog cages" at Union Correctional Institution—the state's original prison. The cages are box-shaped, approximately ten square feet, with reinforced wire walls through which flow fresh air, sun, and other natural elements. The space between the wires is not big enough to put a hand or arm through. This is important because the dog cages are not used by dogs; they are used by prisoners segregated in "close management" for their two hours of recreation time per week—one prisoner per cage.[1] Close management units—found in five of Florida's seventy-two prisons—are Florida's version of the "supermax" prison.[2] It is a prison within the prison, aimed at controlling the behavior of prisoners who don't follow prison rules or are deemed too violent for the general population.[3] According to expert testimony in a 2003 legal challenge of close management practices in Florida, "except for the few hours a week during which they are taken to their exercise cages," prisoners in close management have "no meaningful out-of-cell activity," are "subjected to unreasonable property limits," and "denied opportunities to engage in the bare minimum . . . programming that would be necessary for them to remain cognitively alert and intellectually functional."[4] Because long-term confinement in solitary conditions can severely debilitate prisoners, many professionals, activists, and academics believe these practices amount to "legalized torture."[5] Yet, between 1970 and 2015, state and federal corrections departments increasingly turned to close management, administrative segregation, secure housing units, and supermax facilities—where prisoners "spend 22 to 24 hours a day locked in small, sometimes windowless, cells"—in order to maintain control of large and potentially violent prison populations.[6]

While close management and supermax prisons are contemporary phenomena, the problem of finding appropriate punishment within prisons is not new. In the early twentieth century, Florida prison captains put recalcitrant prisoners in outdoor six- by three-foot wooden "sweat boxes" for days at a time, with little food or water—a practice dramatized by Paul Newman as a Florida road camp prisoner in the classic movie *Cool Hand Luke*. Although consistent with early twentieth-century public acceptance of corporal punishment, the sweat box became "objectionable" by the late 1930s.[7] As prison administrators reorganized the state's punishing power over the twentieth century into a modern bureaucratic prison system, solitary confinement cells gradually replaced sweat boxes, and close management replaced traditional solitary confinement. At each turn, the choices made by prison administrators fit with prevailing political, social, and penal logics. Yet vestiges of past policies remained in each new innovation. Restrictive dehumanizing confinement persists.

The historical continuity between sweat boxes and dog cages demonstrates one of the central claims I make in this book—that when it comes to new public policy or institutional innovation, there is "no such thing as a clean historical slate."[8] To understand how we got to where we are today, we need to understand past policy choices and practices. Accordingly, I demonstrate that what appears to be a dramatic break between punishment philosophy and practice pre-1970 and post-1970, when incarceration rates began to rise, is actually a developmental process of change.[9] Our present systems of punishment and their relationship to society, politics, and the economy are predicated on past politics, past policy choices, and past institutional structures.

Underlying the similarity between sweat boxes and close management is one crucial difference that upends the comparison. Unlike the sweat boxes and chain gangs of the early twentieth century, penal practices in the contemporary era are highly regulated and bureaucratized. Instead of banning penal confinement that rejects human dignity, we have created rules and procedures to protect individuals from "arbitrary" state violence.[10] The courts have upheld the use of solitary confinement when prison administrators can show they have taken steps "intended to minimize the potentially harmful effects," including screening prisoners for mental health problems, adequately training staff on mental health, and providing a "full range" of mental health services and other limited programming for prisoners.[11] Human Rights Watch (HRW) testimony to Congress in 2012 exemplifies the emphasis on "proceduralism":

> International treaty bodies and human rights experts . . . have concluded that *depending on the specific conditions, the duration, and the prisoners on whom it is imposed*, solitary confinement may amount to cruel, inhuman, or degrading treatment that violates human rights. (emphasis added)[12]

HRW's critique is not presented in terms of the humanity of prisoners per se, but on the specific technicalities that make supermax confinement violate legal norms. The second claim I make in this book, therefore, builds on the work of scholars who analyze the proceduralist bent of criminal justice policy.[13] I argue that the relatively new regulation and bureaucratization of penal practices by corrections officials, legislators and the courts is part and parcel of the increase in the state's capacity to punish. As lawyers and the courts enforced protections for criminal suspects, defendants, and prisoners, legislators passed laws and budgets that drew more people into the criminal justice system. Ironically then, while the federal courts have deemed close management and other practices constitutional (where they probably would not sweat boxes), close management impacts far more people in 2016 than sweat boxes did 100 years prior.[14]

Measured by number of people incarcerated in jails and state and federal prisons per 100,000 general population, the incarceration rate soared from approximately 161 in 1972 to 760 in 2008 at the height of imprisonment.[15] This amounts to 1 in 100 adults or over 2,000,000 people confined in a U.S. jail or prison.[16] While incarceration rates decreased slightly between 2008 and 2016—as of 2014, the rate was 690 per 100,000—the United States still incarcerates more people per capita than any other industrialized nation, including Cuba (510 per 100,000), Russia (475), South Africa (294), and Brazil (274).[17] Given vast racial disparities in incarceration, in the post–civil rights era time spent in prison or jail has become a new marker of marginality and a new means of constituting racial and class divisions in the United States.[18]

In the course of the incarceration boom, the media, think tanks and academics have often noted the above statistics, but have given less attention to the growth of the state institutions that enable mass incarceration.

Political scientists use the idea of "state capacity" to help explain the differences in the development of social and economic policy and institutions across industrialized nations. The notion reflects the degree and character of state authority, administrative control, bureaucratic effectiveness, and financial resources.[19] In order for more than 5.3 million people to funnel through our correctional systems each year, the state needs certain capacity in place: enough police officers, courts, data management systems, criminal laws, and prison cells, to give just a few examples.[20]

I reframe the story of mass incarceration as a story of the dramatic increase in the state capacity to punish, what I refer to as *carceral capacity*. This reframing points to the importance of state actors' creation of new bureaucratic structures, new frontline and administrative positions, new staff training, and new protocols across the institutions of the criminal justice system—law enforcement, courts, and "corrections" (probation, prison, parole, and related sanctions). Some of these changes required legislative action, others bureaucratic initiative, but almost all required the commitment of taxpayers' dollars. Total spending on corrections by the federal and state governments quadrupled between 1980 and 2007 from $17.3 billion to $74.1 billion (in 2007 adjusted dollars).[21] In 2011, states spent one out of every fourteen general-fund dollars on corrections.[22] In some states with especially large prison populations, like California, spending on corrections comprises a larger share of the state budget than spending on higher education.[23]

The reframing of mass incarceration in terms of capacity also points to the importance of physical space. In the past forty years, states and the federal government built over 1,500 new prisons.[24] Each prison not only required concrete and steel, but hundreds of new state employees and systems in place to provide food, health care, and programming. Again, big states like California employ up toward 50,000 people in their corrections departments. As former Florida Department of Corrections secretary Harry Singletary explained to me, by the mid-1990s "corrections" had become a complicated business: "You have to change the way you look at corrections, because you are running a large food service operation. Three meals a day, 365 days, 90,000 prisoners, over 60 prisons. And you have to run it efficiently, effectively."[25] Since the 1970s, the federal courts have prohibited states from providing inadequate food service, from cramming growing numbers of prisoners into old prisons, and, maybe most importantly, from delivering substandard health care.[26] As a result, state policymakers had to choose how to comply with constitutional

FIGURE 1.1. Florida built-prison capacity, 2010. Credit: Florida Department of Corrections 2009–2010 Annual Report.

standards.[27] In the case of overcrowding challenges, they faced a clear choice: reduce the prison population or build more prisons. This leads to my third claim: Mass incarceration was not inevitable. We had to build prisons to make it happen. In the case of Florida, policymakers built 130 prisons between 1970 and 2010 (fig 1.1).

A Political Developmental Perspective on the Carceral State

This book answers how the United States became a nation of prisons and prisoners.[28] Or, put differently, how we came to devalue some lives to the point that we are willing to lock people behind bars and refer to them as "dogs." It demonstrates how partisan competition and racial conflict led to a series of political decisions to expand the state's capacity to punish, which created a governing ideology that elevated prisons and long prison sentences as *the* appropriate response to crime. The emergence of mass incarceration, however, is only the most visible part of what scholars are now calling the carceral state.[29] The carceral state refers to the network of people and institutions responsible for "mass social control," including the police, courts, jails/prisons, probation, and parole, but also other technologies such as legal financial obligations (fines, fees, and restitution orders) and other types of community sanctions (for criminal and sometimes noncriminal behavior). The carceral state, with its "reliance on mass incarceration and degrading punishment" ensnares more than 8 million people, or one in twenty-three adults, who are under some form of state control.[30] As political scientists Amy Lerman and Vesla Weaver write, the notion of the carceral state marks criminal justice as an "integral part of state activity . . . much like the term welfare state refers not only to cash aid, but to a system of social provision that is politically constructed through policies, social movements and institutions."[31]

By conceiving of punishment for criminal wrongdoing under a broader tent of social control, scholarship on the carceral state invokes some of the first sociologists of punishment, including Georg Rusche and Otto Kirchheimer, for whom "punishment is neither a simple consequence of crime, nor the reverse side of crime, . . . [but] must be understood as a social phenomenon freed from both its juristic concept and its social ends."[32] The sociological understanding of punishment frees us to look for the foundations of punishment in broad social structures.[33] Structural explanations for the development of mass incarceration in the United States emphasize the role of fundamental socioeconomic changes in the late twentieth century, including deindustrialization, generalized economic insecurity, and the marginalization of African Americans in the labor market.[34] While the exploration of broad socioeconomic changes is useful, it can occasionally take us too far afield from a fundamental truth about punishment in modern societies—that decisions to criminalize behavior and decisions about how to punish criminal behavior are made by our political representatives, bureaucrats, judges, and law enforcement. These are the people that make up "the state." Punishment and its designated role in crime control involve their choices about how to distribute social risk, public resources, and political power.

Political explanations for mass incarceration often hinge on shifts in

American politics—often at the national level—such as the collapse of the New Deal coalition, the dismantling of Jim Crow, the post-civil rights era partisan realignment, and the rise of neoliberal politics.[35] In one of the first books on the rise of mass incarceration, sociologist Katherine Beckett, for example, argues that national politicians' crime control rhetoric was part of conservatives' larger agenda to elevate social control over social welfare as a public priority. By framing "street crime" as a problem of "lack of control," conservatives reconstructed public conceptions of the poor in support of their agenda.[36] The vast majority of imprisonment, however, happens at the state level; thus, to really understand how these broad social, economic, and political changes produced the carceral state, we need to examine the choices of state actors and their impact on policy.

Building on state-level accounts of mass incarceration in Arizona, Texas, and California, this book takes the development of Florida's carceral state as its object of study.[37] As advocated by sociologist and legal scholar David Garland in his groundbreaking book, *The Culture of Control*, my analysis is grounded in a theory of historical change that is action-centered and problem-solving, "in which socially situated actors reproduce (or else transform) the structures that enable and constrain their actions."[38] I use a historical case study research design that traces Florida state actors' policy decisions that expanded carceral capacity—in particular its capacity to imprison criminal offenders (see appendix for details).[39] Not simply a historical narrative, this book attempts to uncover the complex reasons for people's decisions to expand carceral capacity. In order to understand eventual policy choices, I take my cue from historical institutionalist and American state development scholarship, which demonstrates how the preferences of state actors are shaped by various factors such as the political landscape, administrative capacity, and cultural discourses, rather than simple cost-benefit analyses.[40] Specifically, I look to how people define the policy problem, what their incentives are, and the potential solutions on the table by tracing changes to (1) shared meanings and "rationalized myths about the situation"; (2) political struggle and interest group activity; and (3) state capacities.[41]

Policy Feedback Effects

Shared meanings, political struggle, and state capacities are not just shaped by contemporaneous events, they are also constructed and constrained by

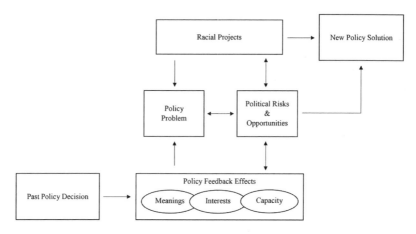

FIGURE I.2. A political developmental perspective.

the *forces of history*. In particular, past policy choices create what political sociologists and political scientists call "feedback effects."[42] Three
types of feedback effects are important to the story of carceral state development. First, *policy creates or institutionalizes meaning*. Past policies
provide discursive frameworks for state actors to conceptualize social categories, policy problems, and new agendas. Policies can also legitimize
certain meanings and ways of thinking, which can lead policymakers' to
readopt old policy solutions to fit new problems.[43] Second, *policy creates
politics*. This can work in a number of ways. Past policy decisions can
create spoils or motivations for certain state actors to mobilize; they can
provide new resources to particular interest groups; and they can create
niches for political or policy entrepreneurs.[44] Together with new discursive resources, new incentives and material resources can generate new
political coalitions or change the political playing field, giving politicians
new opportunities to win or lose.[45] Third, *policy creates new state capacities*. New bureaucratic capacity, new lines of authority, and new physical
resources expand lawmakers' options when solving new or reoccurring
problems. As Theda Skocpol wrote in her pioneering study of welfare
policy in the United States, "because of the official efforts made to implement new policies using new or existing administrative arrangements,
policies transform or expand the capacities of the state." In turn, policy
choices "change the administrative possibilities for official initiatives in
the future, and affect later prospects for policy implementation."[46] Quite

simply, certain policy options would be unthinkable if they had not been preceded by decisions that created state capacity. This process, what I call a political developmental perspective, is diagramed in figure 1.2.

Political Institutions

Shared meanings, political interests, and state capacities are also conditioned by *existing political and social institutions*—defined as "sets of formal and informal rules and procedures."[47] Comparative research and cross-national analyses of imprisonment rates suggest that political institutions mediate broad socioeconomic structural shifts leading to different policy choices.[48] For example, decentralized political and policymaking structures in the United States (in contrast to strong centralized state power in some Western European countries) shapes how policymakers evaluate the public's demand for harsh punishment.[49] Institutional explanations can help explain the relative rise of incarceration in the United States compared to other Western democracies that also experienced broad socioeconomic changes during this same period.[50]

Scholarship on punishment at the state level has also shown how differences in state political institutions and political culture mediate states' use of imprisonment.[51] In her comparative study, Vanessa Barker finds that the deliberative "democratic process" of Washington State, which "emphasizes citizen participation, discussion, compromise and self-governance," dampened a more punitive politics of crime control.[52] In contrast, Mona Lynch argues that Arizona's low level of civic engagement and conservative political culture led politicians to enact "symbolic, partisan-based" punitive crime control legislation.[53] As I will discuss in the pages ahead, the story of Florida is embedded in the particular bureaucratic and political arrangements of the state of Florida.

The importance of state particularities in carceral state development derives from U.S. federalism, which both allows for and limits unique state and local policymaking.[54] In theory, in the United States the Constitution gives states autonomy over certain areas of policymaking, some of which they, in turn, cede to local governments. In terms of crime control policy, local governments bear the responsibility for policing and processing criminal suspects. State governments usually run centralized court systems and corrections systems and establish criminal law and procedure— leading some observers to argue that the United States criminal justice system is actually fifty-one distinct systems.[55] The federal government's role is limited to enforcing violations of federal criminal law and providing support to state and local governments. At the same time, as Jonathan Simon notes, national politicians rely on their ability to "take drastic action against convicted wrongdoers" exactly because their power in other domains is limited.[56] As a consequence, over the twentieth century national politicians increasingly made promises to solve the "crime problem," which led to the "federalization" of crime control—where all levels of government enact "overlapping, uncoordinated, and simultaneous" policy.[57] Since federal policy (and policy rhetoric) cannot be easily ignored by state and local politicians, "national norms" began to "swamp state prerogatives" as the federal government became more proactive.[58]

The federalization of crime control policy also creates barriers between citizens and policymakers, influencing the types of policy problems and solutions policymakers actualize.[59] Research has consistently demonstrated that the best way to reduce crime over the long run is to invest in stable, healthy, and resourced families and communities. Policies that improve education and support labor market access, provide income support, counseling, health care, and intervention services for young children and their families reduce children's later offending.[60] Yet, as political scientist Lisa Miller demonstrates, the people who most need these types of investments and who understand the connections between poverty and crime have very limited access to federal and state policymakers. Instead, they petition local policymakers—who have the least resources to provide multifaceted community building and antipoverty solutions. On the other hand, state and federal policymakers are most likely to hear from law enforcement agencies, which have vastly different conceptions of how to reduce crime.[61]

To summarize so far, I approach the task of explaining the development of the carceral state through state actors' policy decisions that expanded the state's capacity to punish. Actors' decisions about what to do in a given scenario are predicated by past policy solutions and political institutions that influence shared meanings, political struggle, and state capacity, which in turn facilitates how actors define the policy problem, understand their political risks and opportunities, and formulate potential solutions. My perspective on the carceral state is political because it recognizes that within macro structures, political actors had choices about how to respond to policy problems and political circumstances. It is developmental in that the "crucial objects of study [policy choices] become the factors that set development along a particular path" and become the frameworks, the politics, and the capacities that guide future action.[62]

The Carceral State and the History of Race in the United States

So far I have laid out a path for explaining the development of the carceral state that centers policymakers' decisions as embedded in history and institutions. How does this perspective speak to the role of race? For anyone who studies criminal justice in the United States, the problem of the disproportionate arrest and incarceration of African Americans, and to a lesser extent Latinos, looms large. Sociologist Loïc Wacquant has argued that the prison (and the policies that put people there) are a means of racial control analogous to the urban ghetto, while legal scholar and activist Michelle Alexander has called the modern criminal justice system the "new Jim Crow." She argues that Supreme Court decisions and criminal justice policy have combined to create a new caste system in the United States: felons and former felons—disproportionately black and brown—are the new second-class citizens.[63]

It is undeniable that the contemporary penal order has deepened racial inequality—these effects have been well documented and are devastating for black families and communities.[64] The data support Alexander's argument that the carceral state functions as a "comprehensive system of racialized social control." I agree with her that "it is difficult to imagine a system better designed to create—rather than prevent—crime."[65] Because the system is so racialized, it is tempting, as Michael Tonry notes, to argue that "the criminal justice system treats American blacks so badly" because "deeper forces collude, almost as if directed by an invisible hand, to formulate laws, policies, and social practices that serve the interests of white Americans."[66] Yet, as a social scientist I hesitate to conclude that evidence that the system *functions* as means of controlling poor black people is sufficient for understanding how race or racism led to the development or persistence of the carceral state.[67] In addition, focusing only on racially disparate outcomes ignores the fact that "the United States would still have an incarceration crisis even if African Americans were sent to prison and jail at 'only' the rate at which whites in the United States are currently locked up."[68]

The analysis of race and racial politics in American political development provides a good starting point to build an account of the role of race in the development of the carceral state writ large. In effect, my analysis tries to make the "invisible hand" more discernable. I examine how race, like history and institutions, ultimately shaped policymakers' definition of policy problems, understandings of their political risks and opportunities, ideation of potential solutions, and, therefore, their decisions to increase carceral capacity. In the United States, race as a social category has been key to the way society is organized and ruled.[69] While the meanings attached to racial categories change over time, the United States' distinct history—of slavery, Jim Crow, and the civil rights movement—played a significant role in shaping the emergent state.[70] For example, Robert Lieberman demonstrates that during the New Deal, the interests of white Southern political representatives in maintaining white supremacy influenced political decisions about the initial design of New Deal social policy. In turn, these policy choices structured the provision of government benefits, creating new racial distinctions in politics and society.[71] The conceptualization of the carceral state, like the welfare state, helps us think about the ways that race, racism, and racial hierarchies shaped (and continue to shape) how the state choses to define and punish criminal offending.

The standard causal narrative on race and the carceral state can be briefly summarized as follows: in order to appeal to white voters' anti-black prejudice, conservative politicians promised punitive crime control policies, which, because of structural disadvantage based on race, led to a disproportionate number of African Americans behind bars. As Katherine Beckett argues, "the racialization of American politics created fertile soil for the creation and mobilization of the crime issue."[72] This narrative often begins in the 1960s, when conservative opponents to black civil rights strategically linked racial discord to crime, capitalizing on white voters' feelings that the liberal policies of the civil rights movement had gone too far. The crime control issue allowed conservatives to oppose civil rights policies without being explicitly racist.[73] From the 1960s through the 1980s the Republican Party used the proffered link between black protest and crime to capture white voters who were leaving the national Democratic Party in part because of their racial resentments.[74] Crime patterns and criminal justice policies (such as the focus on black youth) then reinforced historical stereotypes linking black Americans to crime.[75] A large body of psychological research finds that even today people unconsciously harbor bias against African Americans in part because of associational links between criminality and blackness.[76] Racial resentment of government efforts to integrate African Americans into social and political life also continues to be related to support for punitive crime policy.[77] Lawrence Bobo and Victor Thompson, who have pioneered much of this research, conclude that "a significant portion of the public appetite for harsh crime policies had its roots. . . . in the prevailing and deeply troubling cultural legacy of anti-black racism in America."[78] Harsh crime control policies, particularly those aimed at drugs and violent crime, in turn predictably impact black Americans disproportionately.[79] Furthermore, white empathy for those affected is "weak and uncommon."[80]

While white racial resentment and indifference are undeniably important to the rise of the carceral state, the above narrative glosses over some historical details worth considering. First, as Naomi Murakawa has recently uncovered, national policymakers' preoccupation with "law and order" began at least as early as the Truman administration and developed as a way to address white violence (often sanctioned by local police) against African Americans. Even through the 1980s Murakawa shows that criminal justice reform policies meant to *ameliorate racial inequality* sometimes had the unintended consequence of strengthening the state's coercive capacity to the detriment of racial minorities.[81] Second, conservative politicians did not uniformly support punitive policies. In fact, conservative Republicans in many Southern states were strongly opposed to building new prisons in the 1970s and early 1980s because of the expense it would incur. Third, liberal politicians also supported punitive policies. President Johnson strongly supported equipping police departments to suppress black urban youth's expression of frustration.[82] Democrats had firm control of the California legislature in the 1980s as that state's prison population tripled.[83] And the nation's first Democratic president in a dozen years and the majority-Democratic Congress enacted the Violent Crime Control and Law Enforcement Act of 1994—the largest federal anticrime bill in history.[84]

Rather than exclusively thinking of race in terms of racial resentment (conscious or not) and its influence on politics, I take a more diffuse approach consistent with Eduardo Bonilla-Silva's idea of "racialized social systems," or societies in which economic, political, social, and ideological institutions are partially structured by the placement of actors in racial categories.[85] In order to help make more concrete what is arguably a complex phenomenon, as part of the political development perspective I use the theoretical construct of *racial projects* to specify how racial divisions have shaped penal policy. My thinking about racial projects and how they influence policy builds on Michael Omi and Howard Winant's work on the process of racial formation, Desmond King and Rogers Smith's work on racial politics, and Robert Lieberman's work on the historical role of race in American political development. *Racial projects are collective actors' response to historic racial hierarchies guided by their shared beliefs and commitments around the meanings of race and racial inequality*. For Omi and Winant, racial projects are "an interpretation . . . of racial dynamics and an effort to reorganize and redistribute resources along particular racial lines."[86] Omi and Winant are primarily concerned with the racial politics of everyday life and the transformation of racial ideology. For King and Smith, American political development can be classified into conflicting "racial orders," which illuminates how political alliances shaped by race impact the struggle for control of governing institutions.[87] I am mainly concerned with explaining policy choices—which requires considering *both* policymakers' racial ideologies and their political incentives and alliances.

Racial projects denote purposeful actions in response to ongoing racial dynamics. Sometimes they rise to the level of a social movement, but not always; yet they are not passive either.[88] As they promote particular understandings of race and strategies to breakdown or sustain racial hierarchies, racial projects conflict and shift over time. Similarly, racial projects do not emerge anew, but rather stem from previous contexts.[89] To understand the conflict between racial projects in one era, we must understand the racial dynamics of the preceding era, because even as racial projects change, they do not wholesale replace previous commitments.[90] Yet while multiple racial projects usually exist, a dominant racial project often emerges and can be discerned by its strength in common discourse and the political power of its adherents.

In summary, a political developmental perspective on the carceral state examines shifting racial projects, past policy solutions, and political institutions in order to understand the development of shared meanings, political conflict, and state capacities that led to accumulating collective policy preferences to expand carceral capacity.[91] By contextualizing actors' definitions of the policy problem, their perceptions of political opportunities and risks, and their policy options in the wider racial, social, and political context, I provide a comprehensive picture of the development of the carceral state.

Why Florida?

The carceral state is not without variation, internal contradictions, and alternative rationales for criminal sanctioning.[92] In fact, each state in the United States has distinct criminal laws and procedures and criminal jus-

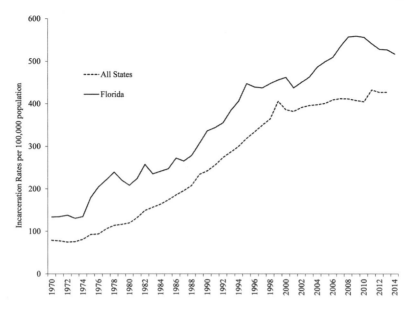

FIGURE 1.3. Florida and United States incarceration rates, 1970–2014. Source: Census Bureau Statistical Abstracts, 1970–1977. Bureau of Justice Statistics, 1978–2014 generated using the Corrections Statistical Analysis Tool (CSAT)–Prisoners at www.bjs.gov.

tice policies that result in varying carceral institutions, levels of incarceration, and patterns of growth.[93] Many state differences, however, can loosely be grouped by region. By 2014, Northeastern states (Massachusetts, Maine, Rhode Island) and Minnesota, with strong progressive roots, provided the highest levels of rehabilitative services for prisoners and had the lowest numbers of sentenced prisoners under state jurisdiction (below 240 per 100,000 residents). Southern states (Louisiana, Oklahoma, Alabama, Texas, Mississippi) and Arizona, with strong punitive traditions, had the lowest levels of funding for prisoner services and the highest imprisonment rates (approximately 600–700 per 100,000 residents). Southern border states such as Florida (fig. 1.3), Kentucky, and Missouri had slightly lower imprisonment rates (approximately 500–600 per 100,000). California significantly reduced its prison population after 2010, and other Western states (Wyoming, Alaska, Colorado, Oregon) have consistently trailed behind Southern states (300–400 per 100,000 residents); Midwestern and Mid-Atlantic states fall between the West and the Northeast.[94] The regional differences can also be dramatized by political rhetoric on crime at the height of public concern about crime, which in places like

Minnesota included the "humanity" of violent criminals, and in places like Texas focused on how quickly politicians could get violent criminals "off the street."[95]

This book focuses on Florida, arguably the most important Sunbelt state in national politics at the turn of the twenty-first century, when the inconclusive 2000 presidential election results went before the Supreme Court. Florida voters have chosen the winning presidential candidate in all but one election cycle since 1976. While Florida is not an average or typical state, in many ways it exemplifies the contemporary carceral state. Florida incarcerates the third largest number of prisoners, behind California and Texas, and its imprisonment rate falls just below high-imprisonment Southern states (at 513 per 100,000 residents in 2014).[96] Florida's crime policy and rhetoric have been more punitive than those of most states. For example, the state has the largest number of juveniles held in adult prisons and the most prisoners sentenced to life without parole. As of 2016, it had the second highest population of prisoners on death row and had carried out the fourth most executions since 1976 (behind Texas, Oklahoma, and Virginia).[97] Florida also has one of "the most punishing and restrictive criminal disenfranchisement laws," which in 2016 barred 1.6 million residents from voting.[98] Yet Florida officials tend not to be as stridently punitive as Texas or Arizona (which boasts the likes of Maricopa County sheriff Joe Arpaio, the professed "toughest sheriff" in the United States.)

Case studies of punishment in large Sunbelt states, including California, Arizona, Texas, and Florida are particularly important because their rapid population growth since the 1950s created both unique problems for their prison systems and increasing influence over national and presidential politics.[99] As a result, the penal policy solutions adopted by Sunbelt states were more likely to be incorporated into national policy agendas, which then helped diffuse these policies to other states. Prison overcrowding in Florida, Texas, Arizona, and California (and resulting court orders) led senators and congressional representatives from those states to introduce and lobby for two of the defining pieces of federal penal policy in the 1990s: "truth-in-sentencing incentive grants," which provided prison construction resources to states that increased time served in prison, and the Prison Litigation Reform Act, which severely curtailed prisoners' access to the courts.[100]

In addition, unique criminal justice policies and practices in Florida have set legal precedents that have shaped carceral state policy across the country. In 1961, a Panama City judge denied Clarence Earl Gideon's request for an attorney during his trial for breaking and entering. Gideon, a white uneducated repeat petty offender, represented himself during his trial and was convicted and sentenced to five years in state prison. At the time, states did not have to appoint counsel for indigent felony defendants. The vast majority of the 8,000 state prisoners in Florida had no legal representation at the time of conviction. In 1963, in *Gideon v. Wainwright*, the Supreme Court established a constitutional right for legal representation for those accused of felony crimes.[101]

In 1985, at the start of the War on Drugs, two Broward County sheriff's officers boarded a bus in Fort Lauderdale bound for Atlanta to search for illegal drugs. Although they had no reason to suspect him, the officers asked Terrance Bostick, a twenty-eight-year-old black man, for permission to search his luggage. "Bostick complied, somewhat inexplicably, because upon opening the bag, the officers found a pound of cocaine."[102] Bostick argued that the officers violated his Fourth Amendment right against "unreasonable searches and seizures," and the Florida Supreme Court agreed, finding that "a reasonable passenger in his situation would not have felt free to leave the bus to avoid questioning by the police." In 1991, the Supreme Court reversed.[103] Combined with a later Supreme Court decision that police do not have to inform people of their right to refuse searches, *Florida v. Bostick* has shaped police-citizen encounters across the country and facilitated a no-holds-barred approach to policing poor urban neighborhoods.[104]

In 2003, Terrance Graham, a sixteen-year-old black teenager from one of "Jacksonville's poor neighborhoods," was convicted of robbing a restaurant where an accomplice severely beat the manager. The judge sentenced Graham to one year in jail and three years on probation. The following year Graham was arrested for a home invasion robbery, and while that crime did not result in a new conviction, the judge sentenced Graham to life without parole for violating his probation.[105] In 2010 the Supreme Court overturned his sentence, ruling that life sentences without the possibility of parole (LWOP) for juvenile offenders who committed crimes in which no one was killed violated the Eighth Amendment's ban on cruel and unusual punishment. Of the 129 juvenile offenders with LWOP sentences that the Court identified, 77 were in the state of Florida.[106]

In 2012, Florida again became the center of national and international attention when George Zimmerman, a neighborhood watch volunteer, invoked Florida's stand your ground law in the shooting death of Trayvon Martin, a black seventeen-year-old unarmed teenager, who was walking to his girlfriend's house.[107] The 2005 law, written by the American Legislative

Exchange Council (ALEC), lobbied for by the National Rifle Association (NRA), and passed overwhelmingly by the Florida legislature, allows people to use deadly force without the duty to retreat if they believe they are at risk of "great bodily harm." In addition, the law provides immunity from criminal prosecution and civil action for those who use "such force" and prohibits police from making an arrest unless they find probable cause that the use of force was outside the bounds of the law.[108] After critical attention by protesters, the media, and the Department of Justice, the state of Florida tried Zimmerman for second-degree murder, but a jury acquitted him of all charges. Despite calls to amend the law, a version of stand your ground is now on the books in thirty states.[109]

It is not a coincidence that most of these stories are about young black men. Like in other states, African Americans are significantly overrepresented in Florida's criminal justice system.[110] Black Americans make up approximately 15 percent of Florida's population, but are consistently half of the prison population. At the height of the War on Drugs in the early 1990s, 60 percent of the prison population was black. Yet, it may strike some as strange that the racial narrative I tell about Florida is mainly a black and white one. After all, in the 2010 census, 22 percent of Floridians considered themselves "of Hispanic or Latino origin," making up the third-highest Hispanic population in the country. The Hispanic population of Florida is approximately 30 percent of Cuban descent, 30 percent of Puerto Rican descent, 15 percent of Mexican descent, and 25 percent of other Central and South American descent. Miami-Dade County, where 65 percent of the population is of Hispanic origin, has the largest population of Cuban-, Colombian-, Honduran-, and Peruvian-origin groups of any county in the United States.[111] Yet, tellingly, the Florida Department of Law Enforcement, the Florida courts, and the Department of Corrections do not keep data on Hispanic origin. When I visited Florida prisons in 2007, "prisoner counts" in each tier were clearly marked "black" and "white." It is like ethnographer Phil Goodman found in his study of California prisons, where "Hispanic" is a designated category, but for the purpose of housing classification officers state they do not "do Asian here."[112] Well, the Florida criminal justice system doesn't "do Hispanic."[113]

As I hope will be clear in the following pages, this is because the Florida carceral state developed out of white supremacist institutions designed to subjugate African Americans. Policymakers' commitments and reactions to black-white racial hierarchies thus shaped policy decisions around crime control and punishment. Furthermore, despite their large percentage in the general population, Hispanics' political power in the state is concentrated in three large urban counties and fragmented by ethnicity—Miami-Dade (Cuban American), Orange County (Puerto Rican), and Broward County (Central and South American origin)—where Cuban Americans tend to vote for Republican candidates and non-Cubans for Democrats.[114] A narrative of racial politics at the local level in these three areas would be quite different from the state-level story I tell. The black population, in contrast, is spread throughout the state (although with the highest percentages in the North and in urban areas, such as Jacksonville, Tampa, and Fort Lauderdale) and has shaped the development of political identities across the twentieth century—including those of Cuban Americans. At the state level, Cuban-American political power has been consequential but not determinative. Cuban-American power within state government is greater than that of other Hispanic origin populations because of their longer history in the state, their higher socioeconomic status, and their unique position as the only Latino group whose unsanctioned migration to the United States is not criminalized (and in fact given U.S. support).[115] In the late 1990s, Cuban-American voters in Florida helped Republicans takeover the statehouse and legislature. While occasionally Cuban-American policymakers break with their white Republican colleagues on issues that impact South or urban Florida, they have tended to support Republican initiatives at the state level—including proposals to crack down on illegal immigrants.[116] Thus while Cuban-American voters helped Florida become a Republican state earlier than it would have otherwise, the experience of Georgia, its Northern neighbor, suggests that Florida would have moved to the right regardless.

Explaining the Rise of the Carceral State

This book argues that over the second half of the twentieth century, racial projects and partisan competition led to politicians' decisions to expand the state's *carceral capacity* or the resources dedicated to detecting, apprehending, processing, and punishing people deemed criminal. In turn, carceral capacity empowered new punitively oriented interest groups, fostered the political dominance of a *carceral ethos*, and justified the continual expansion of the carceral state. The carceral ethos, comparable to David Garland's "culture of control" or Jonathan Simon's "governing through crime," is a political ideology that says it is better to sacrifice the liberty of a criminal offender than risk the victimization of just one person; that offenders are expendable and unredeemable; that criminal offenders should be incarcerated for long prison terms regardless of the costs to the state; and, perhaps most importantly, that voters will reward politicians that uphold these tenets and penalize those who do not. The story of Florida supports this argument and contributes to the understanding of the development of the carceral state in at least four key regards.

First, the case of penal development in Florida demonstrates that we need to take a fresh look at the role of "state capacity" in the rise of the carceral state.[117] Welfare state scholars have long acknowledged that the components of state capacity, such as clear bureaucratic hierarchies, administrator autonomy, and dedicated resources help state actors realize their goals. However, punishment scholars have not fully considered state capacity in the context of the agencies that implement the coercive force of the state—police, courts, probationary services, and prisons.[118] And yet, coercive and disciplinary capacity is central to state power.

Centering the issue of state capacity de-emphasizes other popular explanations for mass incarceration. One common explanation for punishment trends is that *our ideas about the goals of criminal punishment changed* as criminal justice professionals, policymakers and the public became fed up with the failure of the state to rehabilitate criminals. A range of scholarship points to Robert Martinson's 1974 "What works in correctional treatment?" article, which journalists soon dubbed "nothing works," as a turning point in both liberal and conservative discourse on punishment.[119] But as David Garland points out, this "assault" on the idea that the penal system could treat criminal offenders did not predetermine what ideas would replace the rehabilitative model.[120] Nor was the critique of rehabilitation rock solid. Martinson himself offered a more qualified version of his findings, and as Garland mentions, "there was a whole stock of responses available to defenders of the status quo that could have been used to fend off criticism."[121] Furthermore, in many states, particularly in the South and Southwest, rehabilitation's grip on punishment policy and practices was tenuous and fleeting.[122] At the same time, the story of Florida reveals that the demise of the rehabilitative ideal is overstated.[123] Only in 1992 did Florida legislators change the official justification for criminal sentencing to "punishment."

Centering the notion of capacity also helps clarify why another common explanation, *the politicization of crime control*, was so consequential for the development of the carceral state.[124] Many scholars note that beginning in the 1960s political rhetoric and partisan conflict increasingly centered on issues of crime and punishment.[125] However, *what changed after 1970* in the United States was not only beliefs about punishment or partisan politics but, more importantly, state capacity to arrest, convict, and imprison. As Marie Gottschalk demonstrates in *The Prison and the Gallows*, national politicians used anticrime campaigns as political fodder since the colonial period. The difference is that earlier appeals against crime (or vice) were largely symbolic, as the federal government lacked policing or punishment capacity. Over time however, "as each campaign receded, the institutions it created did not necessarily disappear. Rather, the institutional capacity of the government expanded."[126] Key to this expansion was a series of federal policies in the 1960s and 1970s that invested in carceral capacity through the Law Enforcement Assistance Administration (LEAA). Appropriations to LEAA, which provided grants to state and local entities, grew exponentially from $10 million in 1965 to $800 million in 1976. By 1981, LEAA had "funded roughly 80,000 crime control projects . . . amounting to . . . roughly $25 billion in today's [2016] dollars."[127] As suggested by a political developmental perspective, each of these investments in carceral capacity changed policy problems, political incentives, and policy options for state and federal lawmakers, thus continuously reinforcing the politicization of crime control over the twentieth century.

I tell the story of the expansion of carceral capacity at the state level by focusing primarily, although not exclusively, on Florida's capacity to imprison. Florida's policies and practices were actually quite punitive in the first half of the twentieth century, but they did not affect a large number of people. In 1900, the state held less than 800 prisoners—a rate of 149 per 100,000 people. By 1950, the state incarcerated a little fewer than 4,000 people—at a rate of 143 per 100,000. When making crime control decisions before the 1970s, policymakers assumed a *lack of* state capacity in terms of bureaucratic, financial, and human resources. Beginning in the civil rights era, however, a combination of reformist and anticrime initiatives spurred state and federal spending on policing, criminal courts, and prisons—investments that became crucial to fashioning the carceral state. And by the 1980s policymakers and administrators had much more leeway to demand carceral resources in order to solve ongoing problems (such as prison overcrowding). In fact, the story of Florida demonstrates that *only after state legislators abandoned their fiscal conservatism in the late 1980s* and began to build prisons could the use of crime for political gain really take off.[128] That is, prison capacity fueled the politics of crime, not vice versa.

Second, the story of Florida provides an ideal case to examine the interaction of national and subnational policy and politics in creating the carceral state. Given that most criminal punishment is meted out at the state or local level, we need to uncover distinct state policies and processes— which may or may not mimic those at the national level. For example, it makes sense to talk about the mid-twentieth-century racialization of politics on a national level (and its eventual effect on crime control policy), but in Southern states, and especially Florida, with its increasing population of moderate voters, the racialized nature of state politics actually *decreased* between 1950 and 1980.[129] At the same time, in a federal system, state policies and politics are not completely independent from national politics and federal policy.

Federalization of crime control is consequential for state penal policy-making in a variety of ways.[130] National crime control discourse sets the boundaries of political debate at the state level and can spur state politicians' use of crime as political fodder, ultimately helping to change state political dynamics. In addition, federal crime control policy, including federal funding and administrative directives, creates new problems, ideas, and capacities for state policymakers, bureaucrats, and interest groups. Because state and local governments have multiple priorities and are constrained by the need to balance their budgets, federal money is of particular importance for building criminal justice capacity and directing the nature of that capacity. Finally, complementing Mona Lynch's analysis of Arizona punishment and Robert Perkinson's work on Texas, the story of Florida highlights the destabilizing nature of federal court intervention into state prison systems and its long-term impact on the politics of crime. I argue that court decisions become frameworks for action, problems to solve, and opportunities for political gain for state actors and other interested parties.

Third, a close analysis of Florida political actors, politics, and policy contributes to current debates about the role of crime, media, and public opinion in fostering politicians' support for punitive policies.[131] For some scholars, the rise in crime rates between 1960 and the 1990s must be central to any analysis of the development of the carceral state. David Garland, for example, argues that the rise of crime created a general vulnerability or "ontological insecurity" that caused people to see themselves as "victims" (even if they had a low risk of actual victimization), and therefore politicians needed to respond.[132] More recent scholarship demonstrates that high levels of crime—and particularly violent crime—in this period tracked the public's concern about crime, suggesting that their concern was not unfounded.[133] Political scientist Peter Enns persuasively demonstrates that public punitiveness rose fairly consistently between the late 1960s and early 1990s, at which point it began declining. Scholarship also finds that media, and especially television news media, misrepresent the reality of crime, thereby helping to make the "crime problem" salient and in need of punitive solutions. Research finds that local TV news and cable news disproportionately cover violent crime, overrepresent black offenders, focus on extreme cases, and ignore corporate crime. In addition, the news media tend to frame crime as individual failings rather than as symptoms of larger social pathologies, such as poverty or inequality.[134] Combined with politicians' institutional vulnerability to the public's fear of crime, high crime salience can lead lawmakers to enact punitive crime control policy rather than more redistributive measures that could reduce crime.[135]

Alternatively, other scholars argue that actual levels of crime are unrelated to the salience of crime in both the public and political realms, thus explaining how incarceration rates increased steadily even as crime rates fluctuated.[136] Some even question whether crime rates actually rose in the 1960s and 1970s, since it is plausible that the dramatic increase in the state's capacity to both arrest individuals and keep track of statistics overstated the change in actual offending.[137] Scholars also debate the extent to which the media's depiction of crime versus the actual experience of crime contributed to "the salience of crime as an issue on the agenda of public discourse" or the extent to which it shaped the public's support for punitive policy.[138] Some research even suggests that the "increase in public punitiveness" is itself a myth, finding that the public has neither become dramatically more punitive through recent decades nor rejected rehabilitative approaches to crime control.[139] Finally, many argue that rather than actual crime or public fear of crime, politicians generate the salience of the "crime problem" themselves.[140] Loïc Wacquant, for example, argues that politicians blamed crime for the rise in social insecurity that was actually caused by economic deregulation, fragmentation of wage labor, and economic inequality.[141] In turn, political rhetoric on crime heightens public concern and support for punitive responses.

My findings on Florida strike a balance between the above competing positions: crime, media coverage, and public opinion are not irrelevant, but neither did they dictate political responses. While I do not track Floridians' opinions on crime, I consider politicians' perceptions of public sentiment (whether accurate or not). I find that politicians recognized public puni-tiveness (often through media accounts), but at times they made choices to activate those sentiments, while in other instances they purposely worked to tame them. In the early 1990s, I find that law enforcement and victims effectively used the media to communicate their interpretation of the crime problem and appropriate solutions. In turn, as prior research has found, the media's reliance on law enforcement officials' narratives influenced policymakers' understandings of the "crime problem" and made certain solutions "unthinkable."[142] Thus, the influence of public punitiveness was, if anything, indirect and mediated by political incentives.

The Florida story demonstrates that rising crime rates in the 1960s were more directly significant because they propelled federal lawmakers to provide states with federal resources to build new state capacities—particularly among law enforcement. In large part this solution linked (or reinforced the perceived link) between public concern about crime and concern about political and racial unrest. For state policymakers, however, the need to address crime ran alongside their interest in "modernizing" all state functions and processes—including those that were racially discrimi-natory. At the same time, the record demonstrates that progressive Florida Democrats perceived political value in being "tough on crime." However, while "tough" rhetorically, legislative policy solutions (when they could agree on them) were tepid. In fact, unlike the "long range master plan" to build over sixteen federal prisons in the 1970s (discovered in the archives by historian Elizabeth Hinton), Florida policymakers had little desire to increase the rate at which they put people behind bars.[143] In the early 1980s, as the public's faith in the criminal justice system waned, Florida policy-makers tried to find ways to appease the public without making costly in-vestments in the criminal justice system. By the late 1980s, partisan poli-tics and the federal courts' intervention in prison overcrowding, not rising crime rates, led Florida policymakers to abandon fiscal conservatism in order to build prisons. "Crime" became salient yet again with media and social movement actors' spotlight the "early release" of prisoners in the early 1990s, prompting politicians to "do something." In the second half of the 1990s, the perceived political utility of crime politics sustained fur-ther punitive policy choices—even as crime rates decreased. In the twenty-first century, the decline in violent crime and the salience of crime more generally has created the possibility for a reform movement (which, in turn, has actively publicized public support for rehabilitative policies).[144]

Fourth, my analysis of Florida contributes to scholarship about race, crime, and punishment by providing new terrain to explore the complex role of race in shaping the carceral state. I move beyond an analysis of racial discrimination *within* the criminal justice system to an investigation of *how* and *why* state actors chose policies that treat those targeted and labeled as "criminal offenders," disproportionately black and brown, as dispensable. To understand the severity of criminal punishment, we must grapple with the history of racial subordination in the United States, which created the context and the impetus for decisions to increase the capacity to punish.[145] The story of penal policy and politics in Florida is inseparable from the evolution of and responses to "the Negro question": from the project to maintain white supremacy, to ameliorate racial inequality, to adequately "represent" black Americans, to colorblindness.[146] The story of Florida demonstrates that at every key moment in the buildup of carceral capacity, *racial projects* shaped how legislators and advocates understood the policy problem, their political interests, and the potential solutions. The racial projects framework contributes to a growing body of scholarship that investigates how racial politics and structural political inequality, writ large, facilitated not just white conservatives' promotion of the carceral ethos, but black and white liberal complicity in building carceral capacity. For example, Naomi Murakawa argues that liberal Democrats' crime control ideology since the 1940s fostered notions of black criminality and provided much of the foundation for national crime control policy.[147] Similarly, Elizabeth Hinton argues that a theory of "racial pathology" informed the development of War on Poverty programs, which established the initial infrastructure for police surveillance and punitive responses to crime.[148] In a somewhat different vein, Marie Gottschalk argues that widening economic inequalities *among* African Americans reduced incentives for elite African American leaders to address the plight of the black poor.[149] Relatedly, Michael Fortner finds that many black leaders in New York supported the punitive Rockefeller Drug Laws in the early 1970s.[150]

The story of Florida demonstrates that in the early twentieth century, the racial project for white supremacy led to a decentralized and underfunded "criminal justice system." As the white supremacist racial project came into conflict with the project for racial equality in the civil rights era, white liberals in Florida used national resources to modernize and expand what Murakawa calls the "carceral machinery."[151] The conflict between racial projects also led to what I call the "paradox of prison conditions litigation," where despite the intentions of civil rights lawyers to reduce the use of incarceration, legislators complied with a federal court order to end overcrowding by instituting a massive prison construction program in the late 1980s.[152] Coming at the same time as the intensification of the War on Drugs, the historical record from Florida supports Doris Marie Provine's characterization of that time; namely, that policymakers knew their choices would impact "a poor, largely black, often addicted population."[153] Yet the story of Florida also highlights moments where black legislators, once the drug hysteria had calmed down, worked to change the conversation about the need for prisons. The shift toward the project of racial representation, however, ironically limited the political power of black legislators even as their numbers increased in the legislature, because they ceded more political territory to white (and Cuban American) Republicans. As Florida became a battleground between Republicans and Democrats, white Democrats abandoned the project for racial equality and embraced the carceral ethos. Furthermore, Republicans' politics of fear and white Democrats' complicity hinged on "shared understandings" about the need to protect white crime victims and the worthlessness of young black men.[154] More recently, the colorblind racial project has precluded state policymakers' attention to the disparate impact of the carceral state on black Floridians.

Outline of the Book

The following chapters elaborate the complex political development of the carceral state in Florida between 1954 and 2016. In order to explain key penal policy choices over a sixty-year period, the chapters flow chronologically. Within chapters, the story weaves back and forth between national political and policy trends and how they filtered through the specific partisan context and political arrangements in Florida. Following a political developmental perspective, each chapter builds on previous chapters by demonstrating how prior policy decisions created new meanings, new political interests and new state capacities that conditioned subsequent choices to build carceral capacity. While developmental, the story I tell is not inevitable; I highlight the moments where policymakers could have made different choices.

I begin the story in the 1950s so that I can adequately explore and explain the nuances of the more proximate decisions implicated in the development of the carceral state. However, punishment policy and practice in Florida's first hundred years, when the state went from a sparsely populated territory with scarce infrastructure to a booming vacation destination with the makings of a modern bureaucratic state, created policy feedback effects that set the stage for the expansion of carceral capacity.[155] Similar to other Southern states, forced labor, racial violence, and Jim Crow segregation are central to that history.[156] Specifically, the project to maintain white supremacy in all areas of life led to the criminalization of black Floridians and decentralized, harsh, and underresourced institutions of criminal punishment.[157]

In chapter 2, I demonstrate how the racialized neglect of criminal justice institutions by state legislators, or conversely, their interest in prisons as political spoils, shaped state punishment in the civil rights era between 1954 and 1970. I describe how national politics and policy interacted with racial conflicts on the ground to create a large-scale effort to modernize and invest in the criminal justice system. I argue that *penal modernization* at the state level changed policymakers' ideas about the state versus local nature of crime control and the criminal justice system's role in addressing the problem of crime. I describe how Florida criminal justice planners spent Law Enforcement Assistance Administration grants. Following the money demonstrates that penal modernization significantly enhanced law enforcement capacity to arrest and process criminal offenders. In addition, it created victims' organizations and empowered law enforcement professional associations, who would later come to shape how policymakers viewed the crime problem.

In chapter 3, I cover the decade of the 1970s, including the development of prison overcrowding, the origins of prison reform litigation, legislators' initial resistance, and the negotiation of an overcrowding settlement agreement between the state and the prisoners' lawyers. My description situates the litigation within the project for racial equality and the larger penal modernization effort, demonstrating how prison administrators welcomed the litigation as a tool to force the legislature to adequately fund corrections. I also closely examine the legal language of the court decisions that opened the door for state policymakers to comply by building prison capacity rather than reducing incarceration.

In chapter 4, I cover the unintended consequences of prison litigation in the "age of Reagan" between 1980 and 1991. I demonstrate that policymakers initially attempted to comply with the court through sentencing reform that reduced the use of prison and the length of prison stays. However, increased pressure from the federal courts, the War on Drugs, and the changing partisan landscape undermined their efforts. The new Republican governor used past policy solutions and the racially charged moment of concern about crime and drugs to change legislators' understandings of their political risks and opportunities—such that building prisons became the preferred solution, despite the monetary costs. I argue that the dynamics and timing of Florida policymakers' embrace of new prisons counters arguments that actual crime rates or constituents' punitive sentiments caused policymakers' punitive choices.

In chapter 5, I describe a crucial turning point in the development of the carceral state, the period between 1991 and 1995. I reveal how earlier policy decisions to reduce prison populations by releasing prisoners "early" created a new platform and rallying cry for law enforcement and white victims' rights activists, which in the context of increasing partisan competition created a bidding war over who could be "tougher on crime." Additionally, I address how the shift from a project of racial equality to a project of racial representation constrained black activists, whose communities bore the brunt of violent crime, from effectively countering punitive crime control solutions. I argue that the events of this period explain the origins of several key tenets of the carceral ethos, including the myth that anything that is good for criminal defendants is bad for victims and that prisons are necessary regardless of cost.[158]

In chapter 6, I cover the hold of the carceral ethos on politics and policy between 1996 and 2008—even as crime rates began to fall. I first describe the carceral ethos by looking at the effort to bring chain gangs back to Florida. I argue that lawmakers' previous decisions to build prisons allowed governors and legislators to use "tough justice" to gain political capital, which helped Republicans take over the state legislature and governor's office in the late 1990s. Once in charge, a few key Republican legislators and state prosecutors were able to drive changes to sentencing policy. Yet, I also detail the efforts of Republican crime control policy entrepreneurs who did not fit the conservative mold. In addition, I explain how black legislators, now in the political minority, worked to soften the impact of sentencing enhancements likely to disproportionately impact black youth. Finally, using an analysis of crime, conviction, and incarceration rates, I demonstrate that as crime rates decreased, changes in sentencing policy and prosecutorial practice put an increasing number of offenders at risk of imprisonment.

In chapter 7, I explore the longer-term consequences of the carceral ethos. Covering the years between 2008 and 2016, what some have called the "beginning of the end of mass incarceration," I describe the rise of a conservative movement for penal reform and the resurgence of unconstitutional prison conditions.[159] I argue that these developments are linked by new antigovernment populist politics, built on racial resentments, which have created new political incentives to reduce funding for public institutions (including prisons). I describe the contestation over reform strategies, which included debate over the merits of prison privatization. I end by examining the constraints placed on reform efforts, including the persistence of the carceral ethos, the complexity of penal policy after years of expansion, and the entrenched interests created by the growth of carceral capacity.

In the final chapter, I rearticulate a political developmental perspective on the carceral state and summarize the story of Florida. I then discuss the implications of the Florida story for our understanding of the causes of the carceral state. I conclude by reflecting on the broader lessons for decarceration efforts and the need for a new *just* ethos to guide punishment policy and practice.

CHAPTER TWO

Penal Modernization in the Civil Rights Era, 1954–1970

If the color line can only be maintained at the cost of adverse national publicity, a weakened school system, decreased business confidence . . . then that is the price that many people in North Florida are willing to pay. South Florida . . . may not favor desegregation but is certainly not willing to make every sacrifice to avoid it.—Hugh Douglas Price, *The Negro and Southern Politics*, 1957[1]

So long as disregard of national law rules the southern scene, national power must make itself directly felt.—Erwin N. Griswold, United States Commission on Civil Rights, 1965[2]

Each episode of racial violence, from Emmett Till to the use of explosives against black activists, became modernizing moments that propelled demands for federal civil rights protection via enhanced criminal justice.—Naomi Murakawa, *The First Civil Right*, 2014[3]

Like the rest of the country, Florida experienced profound changes during the civil rights era. Together, the federal courts, civil rights organizations, and committed citizens challenged, and forever changed, traditional customs, long-standing organizational practices, and political arrangements based on the second-class status of African Americans. Their collective response to historical racial hierarchies, what I am calling a racial project, was based on a belief in the inherent dignity of all people and the right to equal access and equal protection of the law. However, they faced concerted and often violent resistance from people committed to the racial project for white supremacy. Florida's population growth and demographic changes appreciably altered the dynamics of the conflict between racial projects in the state. Between 1950 and 1970 the population of Florida grew from 2.8 million to 6.8 million. This included hundreds of thousands of Cubans who resettled in Miami and Dade County, Midwesterners who settled in southwest Florida, and retirees, who by 1970 made

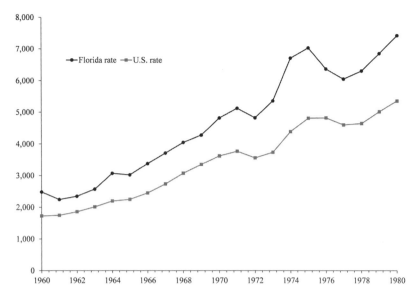

FIGURE 2.1. Property crime rates, 1960–1980.

up 15 percent of the state population.[4] As political scientist Hugh Douglas Price suggested in 1957, the shift in population centers from the rural North to the urban South had a profound effect on racial politics and policy in the state. New legislators from South Florida sought to rid the state of its racialized past and update its governing structures to respond to the opportunities and problems associated with population growth, including the rise in crime rates (see figs. 2.1 and 2.2). As part of this undertaking, over the 1960s and 1970s Florida policymakers engaged in a process of *penal modernization*, by which I mean the creation of modern criminal justice bureaucracies (policing, courts, and corrections) with hierarchical positions, merit-based hiring, professional and trained staff, the ability for self-reflection and reporting through the collection and use of data, updated facilities, and procedures that allowed for the coordination and diffusion of penal programs and policies across agencies and jurisdictions.

In this chapter, I demonstrate that Florida's penal modernization effort was not simply a response to rising crime rates. Instead, penal modernization was part of a larger state modernizing project that ensued from the political conflict between the old racial project for white supremacy and the new racial project for racial equality. In addition, I show how federal government policies and resources aided penal modernization on the

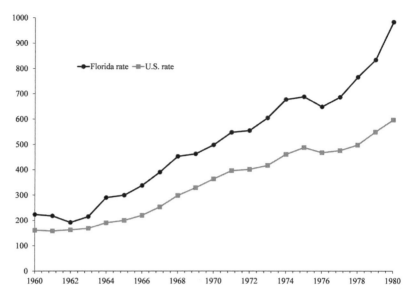

FIGURE 2.2. Violent crime rates, 1960–1980.

ground in Florida and created new criminal justice system capacity. While penal modernization included new progressive programs, ultimately, it created many of the necessary bedrocks from which the carceral state grew.

The events of the 1960s and 1970s in Florida complicate the usual narrative of race and criminal justice in this period. Instead of arguing that "law and order" policies represented a white backlash to the 1964 Civil Rights Act, the black power movement, and urban rebellions, I expand upon new histories of this era by Elizabeth Hinton and Naomi Murakawa, who argue that liberal efforts to address racial inequality also led to federal intervention in crime control.[5] In fact, many on both the left and the right supported new federal resources for state and local law enforcement through the Law Enforcement Assistance Act of 1965, which established the Office of Law Enforcement Assistance (OLEA), and the Omnibus Crime Control and Safe Streets Act of 1968, which established the Law Enforcement Assistance Administration (LEAA). Both federal agencies provided grants to states, cities, and criminal justice agencies to "assist . . . in reducing the incidence of crime" and "increase the effectiveness, fairness, and coordination of law enforcement and criminal justice systems."[6] According to Murakawa, while conservatives positioned federal law enforcement assistance as a means to strike a "neutral middle" between the lawlessness of civil rights protesters and the lawlessness of the Ku Klux Klan, liberals saw investments in law enforcement as complementary to the civil rights movement. In particular, liberals believed that professional and modern police agencies could counteract the long-acknowledged "brutality, corruption, and unbridled power of local criminal justice" and white "lawless violence" that plagued African American communities.[7] Murakawa's account doesn't deny that conservative opponents to the Civil Rights Act strategically linked racial discord to crime in order to appeal to white voters, as Vesla Weaver convincingly argues.[8] Nor does it ignore federal officials' decision to respond to urban uprisings by black citizens by equipping local police, as Hinton demonstrates.[9] Instead, it highlights that liberal Democrats responded with their own crime control agenda not only because they feared a political backlash; they also had their own reasons for advocating a federal role in criminal justice—in part as a tool in the project for racial equality.

In fact, in one of the first analyses of the politics of the war on crime, published in 1981, political scientists Thomas Cronin, Tania Cronin, and Michael Milakovich begin by writing, "This is a complicated story, rich in paradoxes, ironies, and dilemmas."[10] I explore how liberal ideology and policy contributed to federal intervention in state and local crime control, but it was conservatives' politicization of crime in the 1968 election cycle that brought "law and order" to "the center of loud and bitter national debate."[11] In fact, the Johnson administration quickly lost control of the original Safe Streets Act proposal. In the end, a small group of Republicans and a few Southern conservative Democrats rewrote the Crime Control Act. The new version replaced direct funding to large cities with block grants to states, emphasized funds for riot control, police equipment, and manpower rather than innovation and research, authorized wiretapping, and diluted the influence of Ramsey Clark, the new liberal attorney general.[12] While Congress initially appropriated $63 million for LEAA for fiscal year 1969, appropriations grew dramatically under the Nixon administration. By 1976, LEAA distributions to state and local governments reached a high of $800 million.[13]

Scholars have argued that the federal investment in criminal justice fueled the development of the carceral state.[14] In an essay on the legacy of LEAA, Weaver contends that "a decade of sustained infusion of federal dollars into underfunded law enforcement agencies" created new state capacities, policy precedents, and newly organized interests that forever changed the path of the emergent criminal justice system.[15] Yet empirical research on the long-term impact of LEAA has been sparse.[16] In her 2016 book, *From the War on Poverty to the War on Crime*, historian Elizabeth Hinton details LEAA spending for police strike forces and sting operations, juvenile justice programs aimed at low-income black youth, prison construction, and anticrime public housing fortification. Her analysis clearly demonstrates how the 1970s war on crime created policy rationales that set the stage for the federal policies that brought about mass incarceration in the Reagan era.[17]

The story of Florida highlights the neglected role of states and state decision-makers in Murakawa and Hinton's accounts. I demonstrate that the national conversation on "law and order" reflected *state* politicians' confrontations with literal and rhetorical fights over civil rights.[18] The federal policy response in turn accelerated state reformers' ongoing efforts to modernize and thereby rid the state from vestiges of its racial past. Specifically, federal policy gave Florida reformers the needed resources and political power to modernize law enforcement, courts, and corrections. In turn, penal modernization changed ideas about the federal and state (vs. local) role in crime control, significantly increased the ability of the state to arrest and process those deemed "criminal," and created new interest groups that reinforced the role of criminal justice in addressing crime. Together, the effects of federal and state investments in Florida's criminal justice system during the 1970s changed the course of subsequent state policy.

To demonstrate how the conflict over racial projects is connected to penal modernization and the growth of carceral capacity in Florida, this chapter weaves back and forth between political developments, the events of the civil rights movement, and reforms in Florida's criminal justice system. In the first section I provide the context of the conflict in Florida between new and old racial projects through a discussion of the struggle between the state legislature and Governor LeRoy Collins between 1954 and 1960. The conflict speaks to the interventionist role of the federal government on behalf of civil rights and the ways in which racial projects shaped seemingly unrelated penal policy. I then tell the story of the civil rights protests in St. Augustine in order to demonstrate one way that the conflict between racial projects highlighted the problems with local law enforcement and created the model for a "neutral" state police force. The second section examines the origins of penal modernization in Florida and how it fit into a larger project of state modernization that was embedded in political struggle and racial conflict. To do this I show how reformers drew on federal resources to develop new hiring and training requirements for police, create new state-level criminal justice bureaucracies, and implement new standards for corrections agencies.

To provide more systematic evidence of increased carceral capacity, the third section tracks how Florida agencies spent federal grants for criminal justice improvement between 1969 and 1979. Across policing, courts, and corrections, I demonstrate the growth in funding levels and numbers of employees, human capital in terms of training and professional organization, data and management systems, and new organizational units. The funding patterns further reveal both the priorities and the limits of penal modernization in Florida. I then discuss how penal modernization in the civil rights era created feedback effects that laid the foundation for the rise of the carceral state.

Racial Conflict as a Precursor to Penal Modernization

Tourists and migrants streamed to Florida over the 1950s as news spread of sunshine, low taxes, and cheap land. Yet as Florida political historians write, "Florida had become a modern, urban state, but it still had a 'horse and buggy' government."[19] The lack of a modern governing structure began to create holes in the image Florida officials and residents wanted to portray. The election of LeRoy Collins as governor in 1954 represented a significant shift in Florida politics. For the first time, the citizens of South and urban Florida, not those in the rural north, elected the governor. Collins, a former state representative from Tallahassee, was a political insider, but he represented a new future for Florida and promised to modernize government and work in partnership with private business for the benefit of the state.[20] He ran against Acting Governor Charley E. Johns, a long-standing state senator who had his political base in white rural North Florida and lived in Bradford County—the home of Florida State Prison. After his defeat, Johns returned to the Senate and began to rally opposition to Collins. The struggle between Collins and the northern rural "pork choppers" who dominated the legislature represented the underlying conflict between old and new racial projects and played out in the reaction to *Brown v. Board of Education of Topeka*, attempts to reapportion the legislature, and a battle over prison reform.

The Supreme Court's *Brown* decision in 1954 and its subsequent decision in 1955 led to the first conflict of the Collins administration. While both Collins and Johns opposed integrating schools, Collins's response was more moderate than that of the majority of the legislature, who stridently opposed integration. The reaction of Florida officials to *Brown* linked integration to crime and punishment in three ways. First, like other Southern state officials, the legislature saw the Supreme Court's decision as a crime against the autonomy of Florida and a "threat to the rights of the people of Florida."[21] Florida attorney general Richard W. Ervin put up the first line of defense against integration, arguing in front of the Supreme Court for "effective gradual adjustment" that would take into account "local problems" (such as white resistance to integration).[22] Second, in the public debate over the implementation of *Brown*, legislators argued that integration would cause "crime." As Senator John Rawls from Jackson County (on the border with Georgia) declared:

> The integration of the white and Negro races in the public schools . . . would tend to encourage the reprehensible, unnatural, abominable, abhorrent . . . and revolting practice of miscegenation which . . . both in conscience and by the law [is] a criminal offense.[23]

Third, Florida state and local officials supported a 1957 Florida Supreme Court decision that the *process* of integration would cause "violence" and "critical disruption."[24]

Although Collins managed to thwart a series of proposals that would have outwardly preserved segregation, in 1956 the legislature passed what would become one of the first "pupil placement statutes" in the South.[25] The following year, along with other Southern states, the Florida legislature passed its "interposition resolution," which found Supreme Court rulings "null and void" when related to the states' "power to regulate labor, criminal proceedings, public education, and to operate racially separate public schools and other facilities." A lone voice of moderation, Governor Collins attached a note to the resolution that read,

> Not only will I not condone "interposition" as so many have sought me to do, I decry it as an evil thing, whipped up by the demagogues and carried on the hot and erratic winds of passion, prejudice, and hysteria. If history judges me right this day, I want it known that I did my best to avert this blot.[26]

Importantly, in light of the concurrent civil rights bus boycott in Tallahassee, the legislature also saw fit to enact a series of laws that increased the powers of the state to "suppress disorder."[27]

A related source of political conflict during Governor Collins's tenure was his and South Florida legislators' attempt at legislative reapportionment. In 1955, the six largest Florida counties contained over half of the state's population but elected only one-fifth of the House and one-sixth of the Senate.[28] Collins had campaigned on the issue, yet he faced significant opposition from the pork choppers, who "recognized how critical the reapportionment issue was to their efforts to preserve the state's racial customs."[29] The fight over reapportionment became so contentious that it engendered "attempts (often quite successful) to emasculate the governor's proposals on such matters as the allocation of additional funds to purchase highway rights of way, race relations, changes in certain regulatory bodies, and administrative reorganization," including the reorganization of the state's prisons.[30]

Of the state institutions that made Florida look "backward," state prisons—decentralized, patronage-based, and underfunded—increasingly seemed egregious to non-Southern sensibilities.[31] Similar to other Southern states, after the Civil War, Florida legislators had adopted convict leasing as way for pre- and post-Reconstruction officials to provide cheap labor for the state economy, while controlling newly freed and enfranchised black laborers.[32] During this time Florida legislators likewise passed a series of "black codes" that criminalized the behavior of black men and women so that white county judges and sheriffs could conspire with employers to secure a steady supply of black convict laborers.[33] When Florida finally abolished convict leasing in 1919, legislators fashioned a new system of state punishment out of the old: they established a State Convict Road Force, which required minimal financial investment and kept prison operations at the local level. Just as in earlier private convict camps, disciplinary measures included chaining prisoners in leg irons during work, requiring them to spend days in a sweat box, and underfeeding them. At the same time, the legislature began to slowly invest in a state prison farm at Raiford in north central Florida as a facility for convicts unable to work on the roads (including women).[34] Over the next few decades, Raiford, in no small part due to the labor of prisoners, transformed from a "ramshackle wooden prison farm into a concrete and steel maximum-security prison."[35] By 1950, Florida's state punishment "system" looked like an amalgam of the industrial prisons of the North and the road work chain gangs and prison farms of the South. Conditions and length of confinement were severe: boys as young as fourteen were housed in adult facilities; girls and women lived with men; defendants were routinely sentenced to long prison terms for low-level crimes, such as breaking and entering and forgery. Sweat boxes had gone out of style, but leg shackles and guards with rifles kept prisoners in check.[36] While prison administrators in the North experimented with programs designed to reform, superintendents in Florida struggled to fund the basic necessities of confinement—such as housing, food, and medical care. The lack of funding was directly related to assumptions that prisons should be self-sustaining through prisoner labor, which in turn was tied to assumptions about the racial composition of the prison population and the stereotype of African American criminality.[37]

In 1956, the problem of the state prisons came to a head when white prisoners at Raiford began rioting because of poor conditions. After finding severe overcrowding (with 2,300 prisoners, it was 750 over design capacity) and harsh disciplinary measures, the Senate Prisons and Convicts Committee recommended building a maximum-security building, expanding parole and probation staff, and adding on to road prisons and the one women's prison.[38] Governor Collins, however, was ready for more fundamental changes to the prison system, and with the help of the Board of Commissioners of State Institutions (which included all seven of the elected executive officers of the state), pushed through a reorganization, establishing a centralized Division of Corrections. To lead the new bureaucracy, the board followed the recommendation of the Federal Bureau of Prisons, hiring Richard O. Culver, a former warden in the federal system, as director.[39] Culver began with an aggressive agenda to create a professional corrections staff and root out archaic practices, such as using black prisoners as "house boys," prohibiting prisoners from writing letters to their families, and the use of "inmate trusties" as guards.[40]

However, northern rural legislators and their allies were unwilling to cede their power over the prison system to an outside reformer or upset the racial status quo. Senator Johns, in particular, had many constituents who worked as prison guards whose livelihoods were threatened by Culver's plans for serious reform, thus undermining Johns's own political power.[41] An incident of prisoner abuse by guards in 1958 gave Johns and the legislature an opportunity to reassert their control over the prison system. Investigators of the abuse reported that

> prisoners were handcuffed and shackled to the bars in standing and sitting positions for periods of 72 hours long at a time; they were forced to strip naked; they were tear gassed separately and in groups; they were hosed with high pressure

water hoses on their naked bodies and particularly in their private parts which became swollen and inflamed; they were kept on a bread and water diet . . .[42]

When the charges of abuse surfaced in the news, Culver, initially supported by the board and Governor Collins, blamed the abuse on the superintendent's refusal to accept new rules and hierarchies, and his inability to fire (or train) incompetent staff.[43] In fact, the governor received numerous letters from around the country in support of Culver, and newspapers within Florida wrote that Culver's "hands were tied" by the legislature, "who put political patronage above the job at hand."[44] However, the Senate threatened to withhold appropriations if Culver was not fired. And Governor Collins, about to make his last push for reapportionment, could not risk losing more political support from the Senate. In April 1959, Culver resigned, stating he lacked the support of both the board and the legislature.[45]

Similar to their ability to block school desegregation and reapportionment, northern legislators were able to thwart attempts at penal reform. In their desire to maintain the status quo, legislators rebuked modern governance and federal court intervention. Yet ironically, by linking *Brown* with potential crime and disorder, they ultimately strengthened the coercive power of the state, which was then used to control *white resistance* to civil rights protests. In addition, *Brown* became a cultural reference point for conservative Floridians. For the next few decades, elite response to federal interference in local affairs, even when not related to racial equality, would be shaped by the "audacity" of the Supreme Court in *Brown*. In fact, when a federal court indicted the guards involved in the abuse at Raiford in 1959, both the public and politicians ardently fought what they viewed as "politically inspired" federal interference.[46]

The Struggle for Racial Justice in St. Augustine, 1963–1965

Black Floridians and their allies fought for racial equality at the lunch counters, in the schools, and on the streets of Tallahassee, Jacksonville, Miami, and Tampa.[47] But the civil rights campaign in St. Augustine, a small city and vacation destination on the northeast coast of Florida, captured the greatest national attention due to the involvement of the Southern Christian Leadership Conference (SCLC) and Dr. Martin Luther King Jr.[48] The campaign in St. Augustine also prompted some of the greatest resistance and violence from white citizens in the South.[49] Importantly, the violent reaction by white residents and Ku Klux Klan members to civil rights protests highlighted the role of sheriffs, police officers, and the courts in maintaining white supremacy. In addition, the unequal treatment of black protesters by local law enforcement brought attention to long-standing structural problems of Southern law enforcement, which had been historically decentralized, underfunded, and unprofessional. The story of St. Augustine, therefore, highlights how racial conflict prompted state officials' penal modernization efforts, including the creation of a centralized, professional state police force.

Organized by Robert Hayling, advisor to the youth council of the local NAACP chapter, small-scale demonstrations in St. Augustine began in June 1963, shortly after the murder of Medgar Evers in Mississippi. Initial demands included open civil service exams for city positions, the desegregation of city-owned facilities, and the establishment of a biracial committee to facilitate the desegregation of private facilities.[50] Denying protesters' demands, city officials reacted by arresting seven black youth during a sit-in. When four of the arrestees refused to comply with the judge's order to refrain from future demonstrations, they were transferred to Florida's juvenile reform schools. Later, a federal court review of their cases found that "the customary procedure with respect to juveniles in Florida charged with misdemeanors is to release them to parents' custody to await trial . . . Their detention without bond or release was an arbitrary and capricious act of harassment and cruel and unusual punishment."[51] Over the course of the protests in St. Augustine in 1963 and 1964, police arrested a total of 234 juveniles, many of whom were held without bail.[52]

In September 1963, city police officers, who had recently acquired dogs and cattle prods, and sheriff's deputies, who were known for their pro-Klan sentiments, attacked and arrested civil rights marchers in the first mass demonstrations in St. Augustine.[53] Shortly after reports of a gun battle between white and black youth later that fall, Governor Cecil Farris Bryant, a conservative Democrat who had replaced Governor Collins on a prosegregation platform in 1961, responded to the St. Augustine mayor's request for help by sending thirteen state highway patrol officers to supplement law enforcement in the city.

As local black citizens continued their protests into 1964, they were aided by the intervention of the SCLC and the elevation of St. Augustine to a national campaign (with the arrests of the mother of the Massachusetts governor and 287 others).[54] This only increased resistance by city officials, who linked protests to crime, communism, and outside agitators, and by white reactionaries, who stepped up their efforts to intimidate civil rights protesters and black citizens. Peaceful marches through town were met with fists, clubs, and tire irons.[55] Local law enforcement became instrumental in the resistance effort: even as the police decreased their attacks on protesters, they did not attempt to stop white segregationists' attacks. In fact, they were more likely to arrest protesters than the white attackers.[56] Evidence also points to collusion between local police, sheriffs, judges, and segregationist groups.[57]

By the time Dr. King asked the federal government for assistance in May 1964, Governor Bryant had called in additional highway patrol reinforcements twice. To help avoid federal interference, the governor was willing to challenge local officials. Invoking the new state power enacted in response to *Brown*, he placed all local law enforcement in St. Augustine under state control. In addition, he created a "special police force" comprising officers from five of the nine state agencies with the authority to bear arms, including the highway patrol and the Florida Sheriffs' Bureau. To help the efforts of his new police force, the governor invoked "powers granted him in times of emergency by the legislature" and banned all future marches and demonstrations in the St. Augustine area (an action that was later struck down in federal court). Although Bryant called "civil disobedience . . . a crass violation of law, clothed in other language," by the end of June he had assigned 230 state troopers to the police force, which was effective in holding back white violence with police dogs and tear gas.[58]

Although protests, tension, and violence continued throughout the summer of 1964, they were mitigated by the signing of the Civil Rights Act in early July and the subsequent departure of SCLC from St. Augustine.[59] Civil rights organizations began using the act to challenge shop owners and others in court, rather than in the streets. With a sympathetic federal judge, local businesses were eventually forced to open their doors to everyone in lieu of large fines.[60] The crisis calmed down so significantly that by the end of August, Governor Bryant recalled all of the state police from the area. The following summer, even the county sheriff began discouraging violence, stating that "regardless of the individual likes or dislikes concerning the passage of the Civil Rights Act, it is now the law of the land and we must live with it."[61] Along with this, police and sheriffs began more serious attempts to arrest and prosecute white offenders who attacked black citizens. Finally, in December 1965, a federal judge dismissed remaining charges against four hundred demonstrators in the 1964 protests.[62]

The course of the events in St. Augustine had two important feedback effects that influenced policy decisions and politics moving forward. First, the conflict in St. Augustine highlighted the role of local law enforcement in maintaining the racial status quo. Representatives of SCLC and St. Augustine's black citizens repeatedly testified in federal court about local law enforcement's failure to protect them. On more than one occasion, judges questioned the local sheriff and police chief about their officers' ties to the Klan and their qualifications more generally.[63] Second, Governor Bryant's actions set a precedent for new centralized police powers and caused state and local officials to rethink their assumptions about the local nature of crime control. Bringing together law enforcement agents from existing state units, Governor Bryant created the model for a new state law enforcement bureaucracy. Together, the recognition of the racialized nature of local law enforcement and the idea of a new role for the state provided reformers with a framework for "modernizing" the state criminal justice system.

State Politics and Penal Modernization

The conflict between racial projects at the statehouse and in St. Augustine (and other cities) led to the beginning of a penal modernization effort by state legislators, bureaucrats, and interest groups. Accordingly, when Congress appropriated $22 million under the Law Enforcement Assistance Act of 1965 to provide three years of grants to local law enforcement agencies for "modern training, organization, and equipment," they were entering into a conversation that was already happening in Florida.[64] Just as law enforcement funding drew support from the left and the right in Congress, penal modernization addressed both liberal and conservative concerns in the context of Florida's quickly changing political environment.

Three political developments in Florida were particularly important in shaping penal modernization. First, between 1962 and 1967, a series of Supreme Court decisions established the "one person, one vote" representation rule, which forced the Florida legislature to change its districting system to better represent the population. The changes began shifting power from the rural north to the urban and suburban areas, represented by a new group of "young, aggressive, reform-minded lawmakers."[65] With the help of a reformist attorney general, these lawmakers set about the gigantic task of modernizing state governance, including the state's law enforcement agencies.

Second, the statewide opposition to racial integration began to weaken with the Voting Rights Act of 1965.[66] In 1964, Haydon Burns, the former mayor of Jacksonville, campaigned on an "anti-integration image" and overwhelmingly defeated Robert King High, the popular mayor of Miami in the Democratic primary.[67] Yet in 1966, High, who openly supported desegregation and civil rights, beat Burns in the Democratic primary run-off. Although High's win would have normally secured the governor's mansion, in their desire to maintain white supremacy, Burns supporters backed the Republican candidate Claude Kirk rather than High. Thus the political moderation of Florida voters led to the election of the first Republican governor since Reconstruction.

Third, the shift in state political power resulted in the appointment of new criminal justice bureaucrats with stronger ties to national networks engaged in criminal justice reform. Reformist bureaucrats then waged their own battles by drawing on federal resources in order to modernize from within. All three political changes signaled the rise in dominance of the project for racial equality and created the possibility for modernizing efforts around police professionalization, state criminal justice bureaucracies, and, once again, the Division of Corrections. Federal funds from the 1965 Law Enforcement Assistant Act and the 1968 Crime Control and Safe Streets Act provided further momentum for penal modernization and helped to shape its content.

New Standards for Law Enforcement

Responsible for distributing funds under the Law Enforcement Assistant Act, U.S. Attorney General Nicholas Katzenbach asked states to convene committees to "find ways to halt the increase in crime, to enhance the security of persons and property, to deal effectively with criminal offenders, and to insure fairness throughout the criminal process."[68] In September 1966, Florida attorney general Earl Faircloth appointed twenty members to the Florida State Committee on Law Enforcement and the Administration of Justice in order to apply for federal grants to develop a plan.[69] Elected in 1964, Faircloth was active in Miami politics (in 1956, he founded the Florida Committee for Fair Apportionment) and was part of the group of reformers who headed to Tallahassee to between 1964 and 1967. The overarching goal of the reformers was to address the "problems of growth and progress" through modernization.[70] As Chesterfield Smith, the president of the Florida Bar Association and chair of the Constitutional Revision Commission, told legislators in January 1967:

> in my judgement, the State of Florida is poorly prepared to meet the responsibilities which have been entrusted to it. A modern constitution is the first and necessary step to qualify for that confidence . . . Florida must modernize its legislative process . . . ; it must reorganize its executive branch; it must simplify its Courts structure; it must reorganize its tax system; it must maintain adequate planning and resource agencies.[71]

Reformers saw constitutional revision as necessary step toward fixing malapportionment and developing effective public policy, including crime control policy. At the start of the 1967 legislative session, the conservative Democratic Senate president spoke to the "great occurrence of crime" throughout the nation and in Florida, adding, "if we can consider legislation that will give us a better Constitution and enforcement of the laws of this state, we will make a great contribution in this particular cause, for it benefits our growth to apprehend those who are destroying our society and our moral climate."[72]

Yet, in part because of the opportunity for federal money, the more progressive Democrats, along with their moderate Republican allies, were able to define the goals and strategies for penal modernization. To chair the committee, Attorney General Faircloth appointed Charles Jay Hardee Jr., a well-respected liberal trial lawyer from Tampa who had worked to promote nondiscriminatory jury selection in Florida courts.[73] The committee, made up of business owners and lawyers, state agency heads, law enforcement representatives, university professors, and legislators, quickly realized that evaluating the state's law enforcement needs was a "herculean job" because "Florida, as most of her sister states, had provided police services to its citizens on a piecemeal, overlapping, disjointed and fragmented basis."[74] The committee's investigation into local policing was led by Representative Murray Dubbin, a Democrat from Dade County and one of the state's first two Jewish legislators. In 1965, Dubbin had worked with Dade County police chiefs to establish a legislative subcommittee on police training.[75] Statewide law enforcement associations, including the Fraternal Order of Police, had long supported better and standardized recruitment and training practices because they realized that raising the "caliber of men involved in law enforcement work" would increase the public's respect for the profession.[76] In addition, as the best-trained police in the state, Miami-area police felt that smaller departments' unprofessional conduct made their interactions with minority groups more difficult.[77]

The committee commissioned a comprehensive survey of the state's approximately three hundred municipal police agencies in order to provide information about law enforcement's "most pressing problems." The survey responses revealed the absence of coordinated recruitment programs, a systemic lack of training, low pay and few benefits, a wide variation in pay (both within metropolitan areas and between different regions of the state), the use of volunteers as officers, no citizen complaint procedures, a gross underrepresentation of black and female officers, and a lack of interest in improving police-community relationships with black citizens.[78] The lack of recruitment programs (except in the few large urban departments), in particular, meant that local law enforcement departments hired officers through word of mouth and without regard to qualifications—leading to the perpetuation of racist attitudes within policing.

For the 1967 legislative session, the committee proposed a Police Standards Council tasked with creating higher standards and training requirements for local law enforcement across the state. Specifically, the Police Standards Council Act required that new police officers be at least twenty-one years old, have a high school or equivalent diploma, not have been convicted of a felony or certain misdemeanors, and complete a police training program.[79] Although representatives of rural and small cities lobbied to make the council's training program voluntary, both progressive and moderate legislators, including newly elected Republicans from urban and suburban areas, supported the legislation. Moderate legislators believed that new law enforcement requirements would make "our forces against crime more effective."[80] As House Speaker Ralph Turlington told his colleagues:

> The time has come for the Legislature to explore all facets of law enforcement at the city, county and state levels. . . . Foremost among our endeavors to strengthen the arm of law enforcement is the need to upgrade training and pay of the officers who are the soldiers in the field in the battle against crime.[81]

More progressive legislators linked police training with the struggle for racial equality. Speaking about the need for police professionalization,

Attorney General Faircloth explained his rationale: "We can't have that equal chance that was the dream of our ancestors or forefathers, unless we have public order."[82]

Minimally funded by the state, the council, comprising the attorney general, state bureaucrats, and sheriffs and police chiefs, counted on a grant from the Ford Foundation to develop a two-hundred-hour minimum training requirement for all law enforcement officers in the state.[83] The council developed the training curriculum, trained the instructors, and worked with junior colleges and other institutions to offer the required training. By 1970, forty-three institutions offered the certified basic training program and all but the smallest police agencies were in compliance with the training requirement and new standards for hiring.[84] In addition, the council received an Office of Law Enforcement Assistance (OLEA) grant in 1968 to develop models for voluntary in-service training, associate degree law enforcement programs, and the first BA-degree program in police science in Florida.[85] Importantly, the council also ran training conferences to increase the effectiveness of law enforcement professional associations, including the Florida Sheriffs Association, the Fraternal Order of Police, and the Florida Peace Officers Association. The capacity of universities and community colleges to train new recruits and provide new educational programs was enhanced by the Crime Control and Safe Streets Act of 1968, which established the Law Enforcement Education Program (LEEP). Between 1969 and 1979, the Law Enforcement Assistance Administration (LEAA) provided over $18 million in LEEP grants to approximately forty Florida community colleges for scholarships to law enforcement personnel.[86]

New State Law Enforcement Bureaucracies

In August 1968, the Florida State Committee on Law Enforcement and Administration of Justice wrote that "the past nineteen months have seen positive action that for the first time places the State of Florida alongside local communities in a combined effort against crime and juvenile delinquency."[87] In addition to the Police Standards Council, the 1967 legislature created the Florida Bureau of Law Enforcement (later renamed Florida Department of Law Enforcement or FDLE) and the Division of Youth Services. The former was the first statewide agency with authority to investigate and arrest for violations of the law in every county in Florida. The latter combined "a sprawling collection of agencies and courts with little official relationship . . . separated by lack of communication, diverse policies, petty bickering and personal idiosyncrasy."[88] In contrast to critiques that LEAA funding primarily went toward local riot control in the late 1960s, the establishment of these bureaucracies highlight the role of subnational political and social dynamics in shaping the content of criminal justice reform.[89] In Florida the first state-level law enforcement bureaucracy originally focused on organized crime—not suppressing social protest.

Governor Kirk's tenure covered the turbulent years between 1967 and 1970, including riots in Tampa in 1967, Miami in 1968, and Jacksonville in 1969. Yet his time in office was more consumed by his privately funded war on organized crime and vice in South Florida.[90] Carried out by a private police force headed by the Wackenhut Corporation, Kirk's war on crime also targeted Democratic officials.[91] In order to gut the Wackenhut program, the legislature adopted the committee's recommendation to establish a centralized law enforcement agency with statewide authority. As Attorney General Faircloth explained, to effectively fight criminals who cross county lines, a state law enforcement agency can't ask "permission" of the county sheriff.[92] Using the model of Governor Bryant's Special Police Force, the legislature created the FDLE under the attorney general's office; it absorbed the Sheriffs Bureau and the Narcotics Division of the State Board of Health.[93]

Originally staffed with forty agents and fourteen support staff and a budget of $1.5 million, FDLE, along with the committee, lobbied for additional staffing, equipment, and funding in order to "properly conduct and coordinate a state-side campaign against organized crime, narcotics and other vices that contaminate our streets."[94] The FDLE's focus on organized crime likely represented both the reality of crime in Florida— the FDLE later concluding that members of fourteen of the twenty-seven known mafia families lived at least part-time in Florida—and political "crime control theater."[95] Both Governor Kirk and Attorney General Faircloth wanted to be able to claim victories against organized crime in South Florida. The FDLE immediately joined the efforts of the Department of Justice Organized Crime Strike Force to root out the mafia in Miami—likely providing on-the-job training to new FDLE agents.[96] Using LEAA grants, in 1970 the FDLE established an Inter-American and Caribbean Intelligence Group to facilitate cooperation between law enforcement in Florida, Puerto Rico, and the Virgin Islands and a Statewide Organized Crime Intelligence Unit with twenty-two agents and four specialized attorneys.[97] By 1970, the legislature significantly increased FDLE's budget to approximately $5.6 million for 340 positions.[98] And over the next four years, the FDLE received an addition $1 million from LEAA to support expanding its crime intelligence gathering and organized crime prosecution capabilities to areas outside of South Florida.[99]

Louie Wainwright and Corrections Modernization

The beginning of "modernization" in Florida's Division of Corrections came from an unlikely source—a young, self-educated former prison guard from Bradford County (the home of Florida State Prison) who was widely considered one of the "good old boys." Appointed by Governor Bryant as secretary of the Division of Corrections in 1962, over the next two decades Louie Wainwright drew on national resources and ideas and his position within state politics to modernize and upgrade the division.[100] Appointed because he was an insider who would continue to "move the whole system forward," Wainwright "wanted to . . . have some continuity in staff, get the rehabilitation function working, and treat people decently." He explains that at the time the prevailing attitude among Florida's corrections staff was,

> "They are convicts and you treat them like convicts and you don't worry about what happens to them after they get out." I had a totally different concept. I thought we ought to put as much responsibility on them as we could, to make them realize that they were part of the community . . . and they ought to be given a chance to overcome the problems they had.[101]

The notion of rehabilitation, foreign less than a decade earlier in Florida, was gaining currency among a few corrections staff who became involved in the American Correctional Association (ACA) during R. O. Culver's tenure in the late 1950s. By 1965, Wainwright and four other Florida administrators had been elected to ACA positions, and their rhetoric suggested this national orientation:[102]

> Florida must expand its programs of academic education, vocational training, religious training, and other modern concepts which help to change attitudes and prepare the offender to re-enter society as a contributing tax-paying citizen.[103]

Wainwright's modernization effort included attempts to professionalize prison staff, to provide education opportunities to *all* prisoners, and to implement standards for prison and jail conditions.

Wainwright's biggest challenge was to professionalize the staff. In the early 1960s corrections officers and supervisors had worked in the same prisons for decades and were resistant to new structures of authority, new rehabilitation priorities, and new job duties. New recruits were friends or allies of local officials or current employees. While his power was limited, Wainwright encouraged division employees to join the ACA or attend newly available training courses in exchange for his promise to seek higher salaries and benefits from the legislature.[104] And in 1963, the legislature passed the state's first gasoline tax in order to implement a five-day work week for road prison employees.[105] Between 1961 and 1967, corrections officers' salaries increased by 25 percent across the board.[106]

In addition, Wainwright utilized new notions about standards for corrections officers—in terms of education and temperament—in order to refuse to transfer or promote political hires.[107] Writing in 1967 that "the job cannot be done merely keeping prisoners confined; there must be rapport and respect between the officer and the inmate if the statutory assignment of rehabilitation is to be fulfilled," Wainwright began recruiting college students, paraprofessionals, and those with social work degrees as "correctional classification counselors."[108] In line with a new national emphasis on "correctional manpower and training," Wainwright also focused on increasing educational opportunities for officers, as "the job requires intelligence above the level of the prisoners whose rehabilitation they are working toward."[109]

To facilitate employee education, the division developed a relationship with Florida State University's department of criminology, which offered on-site classes for corrections officers. It also applied for and received funding from LEAA for a new training institute—which graduated the first class from its five-week training program in April 1969.[110] Finally in 1974, at Wainwright's urging, the legislature established a Correctional Standards Council, along the lines of the Police Standards Council established eight years prior, which developed uniform minimum standards for the employment and training of corrections officers, approved minimum curricular requirements for schools, issued certificates, and researched salaries.[111]

Wainwright also worked to increase educational opportunities for prisoners. When he became director, educational opportunities for prisoners were starkly divided by race.[112] The content and rationale for classes was similarly shaped by assumptions about race. The 1961 biennial report noted, for example, that "basic education" for black prisoners "greatly assists the discharged prisoners in comprehending and coping with their environment"; while primary, intermediate, and secondary education for white prisoners "affords the prisoners an opportunity to learn a skilled trade."[113] Given legislators' acceptance of racial segregation, in order to gain support for the expansion of education and training programming, division administrators worked to portray the new Division of Corrections as a primarily "white" institution, attempting to disassociate the state prisons from black prisoners. The biennial reports of the Division of Corrections in the 1960s show the incorporation of pictures of prisoners that significantly overrepresent white prisoners. For example, in the 1963–1964 report, out of fifteen pictures, eleven depicted only white prisoners, compared to three pictures with all black prisoners and one picture of an integrated church scene, even though at the time 49 percent of state prisoners were black. In addition, the types of activities that engaged white and black prisoners in the pictures differed: white prisoners were pictured in classrooms, in "hobby shops," and in vocational training; black prisoners were pictured working at construction sites and playing sports.

Yet by mid-1966, the division had hired its first coordinator of education and thirty-eight full-time certified teachers, spread out across all the major institutions. At the road prisons, where educational programming had been nonexistent, the division now boasted sixty-five teachers through the various county adult education programs. By the end of 1967, almost all of the facilities were desegregated, including the education programs.[114] By 1972 the division's biennial report could claim 220 education staff, 3,700 prisoners enrolled in primary and secondary classes, and another 700 in college classes; and that "correctional education is now generally accepted to be an integral part of the total rehabilitation process for changing deviant behavior."[115]

Finally, over the course of the 1960s Wainwright worked to upgrade the standards for jail facilities across the state. Throughout the 1960s the governor's office was flooded with letters registering complaints about county jail conditions.[116] In addition, the incarceration of civil rights leaders and protesters brought national attention to the condition of jails in Florida and other Southern states. During the St. Augustine conflict a federal judge found that the St. Johns County sheriff subjected demonstrators to "more than cruel and unusual punishment" that included long stretches outside in the heat and storms, inadequate and exposed toilet facilities, and the use of sweat boxes.[117] Technically, the Division of Corrections had been given the authority to inspect county jails in 1957, but it was limited to *asking* county sheriffs to suspend antiquated practices such as the use of "inmate turnkeys."[118] Not able to convince the legislature to override county sheriffs, in 1967 Wainwright lobbied to shorten the number of months offenders could be sentenced to county jail from twenty-four to twelve by arguing that rehabilitation was not possible in the county jails.[119] And in 1971 Wainwright successfully lobbied for a law allowing the division to appeal to the U.S. District Court for an injunction to close a facility if not up to standards set by the division.[120]

Penal Modernization and State Capacity

In *Governing through Crime*, one of the key texts on the rise of the carceral state, Jonathan Simon argues that the Omnibus Crime Control and Safe Streets Act of 1968 was the "foundational" and quintessential piece of legislation for the modern "war on crime."[121] Subsequent scholarship argues that the law helped build the carceral machinery we live with today.[122] As a massive piece of legislation that represented multiple interests and agendas, it was no doubt the model for federal punitive crime control policies, including the Juvenile Justice and Delinquency Prevention Act of 1974, the Anti-Drug Abuse Acts of the late 1980s, and the Violent Crime Control and Law Enforcement Act of 1994. Previous scholarship has also emphasized how the Crime Control Act, in particular through its establishment of the Law Enforcement Assistance Administration (LEAA) to provide grants to states and local agencies, created new criminal justice bureaucracies and interest groups. Vesla Weaver finds, for example, that the number of criminal justice associations in the United States quadrupled between 1959 and 1979.[123] This surge was not altogether unexpected by observers at the time. Writing in 1975 that LEAA created "a natural clientele," including all those "who benefit, or are likely to benefit, from LEAA funds," one analyst noted that the active support of this clientele created a self-referential validation process. When LEAA came under attack from members of Congress, LEAA administrators used clients' claims to argue that its programs were extremely popular.[124] Together, new interest groups and LEAA thus reinforced attention to crime and criminal justice, sustaining congressional interest.[125] As I discuss below and is highlighted by Marie Gottschalk, LEAA in fact *directly funded* capacity building for associations in ways that wedded interest groups to law enforcement prerogatives. For example, in part because of the federal funding structure for rape crisis and battered women's shelters in the

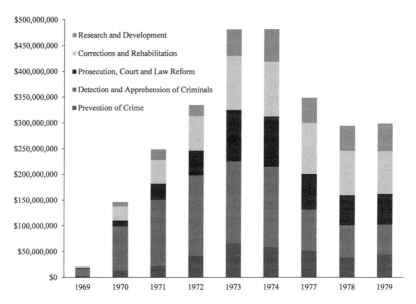

FIGURE 2.3. LEAA action grants to states by category. Source: LEAA Annual Reports 1969–1979, excludes "Other" funding; funding category data not available for 1975 and 1976. Action grants do not include planning or education grants.

1970s, women's organizations came to "myopically" focus on the criminalization of rape and domestic violence, as opposed to social and economic equality—what is now termed "carceral feminism" by many scholars.[126]

Almost all of the policy analyses of LEAA describe it as an example of the worst of modern bureaucracy: its objectives were both complex and ambiguous, its strategies procedural rather than substantive, and its authority weak.[127] As a crime fighting tool, LEAA failed: crime rates continued to rise over the 1970s and early 1980s.[128] In fact, the organization was shrouded in controversy throughout its brief existence. Initially criticized for allocating too much funding to law enforcement—and in particular to "riot control" and equipment purchases (some from military contractors)—advocates for each criminal justice component (prevention, policing, courts, and corrections) eventually managed to claim their piece of the pie. The act was amended five times over the course of the 1970s—each successive revision providing state planning agencies with more directives for allocating criminal justice dollars. As figure 2.3 illustrates, by 1979 LEAA almost evenly divided allocations between crime prevention, police, courts, corrections, and research and development.[129]

However, as an impetus for creating, upgrading, and centralizing state and local criminal justice institutions that could process criminal offenders, LEAA was a resounding success. Between 1969 and 1979, LEAA granted $6.7 billion to state and local agencies in seven categories: planning; education; crime prevention; detection and apprehension of criminals; prosecution, court, and law reform; corrections and rehabilitation; and research and development. While LEAA funds at their peak in 1976 accounted for 5 to 12 percent of state and local criminal justice budgets, this percentage understates LEAA's impact, as LEAA funds also incentivized state spending and were concentrated in particular areas, such as local policing.[130] This was of course one of the goals of LEAA: "As the Federal outlays come to make up a larger fraction of the resources for local police departments, the programs they underwrite can be expected to constitute a strategic force for change in local law enforcement in the 1970s."[131] Yet, not only did local police departments change—they grew in manpower. In fact, later studies demonstrated that police growth was primarily related to available resources and the racial composition of the municipality—not actual crime rates.[132] In addition, the structure of allocations emphasized "innovative programs" with the idea that state and local governments would continue to fund successful programs. At least one retrospective report estimated that this occurred for 85 percent of eligible programs.[133] Yet, as Elizabeth Hinton demonstrates, a thoroughly racialized understanding of criminal behavior determined what programs LEAA funded or replicated. For example, Hinton argues that while Office of Juvenile Justice grants to programs targeting white youth employed rehabilitation, those targeting urban youth developed new means of surveillance and punishment (such as police patrol in urban schools). Even successful rehabilitation programs with black clientele were not replicated.[134]

Between 1969 and 1979, Florida received $198.6 million from LEAA—reaching a high of $29.4 million in 1976 (or $122 million in 2016 inflation-adjusted dollars). The aggregate amount, while significant, obscures the vast number of programs and agencies that received funding. In 1971, the Florida state planning agency (SPA) distributed $11 million in grants for 218 different programs run by state agencies, counties, city police departments, educational institutions, and two interest groups.[135] By 1980, as LEAA funding began to significantly decrease, the Florida SPA was still administering 550 active grants.[136] In this section, I utilize seven reports written by Florida SPA penal reformers between 1969 and 1980 to provide a window into the ways in which penal modernization increased state capacity in policing, criminal courts, and corrections. Required by LEAA of each state in order to receive funding, the reports detail Florida's criminal justice system, reformers' perceptions of its strengths and weaknesses, the SPA's plans for improvement, and how they spent federal dollars. In addition, I use ten LEAA annual reports to document the changing priorities of LEAA. The analysis of this data reveals that penal modernization in Florida emphasized (1) recruiting and training quality employees; (2) building data processing capabilities; and (3) establishing new units and procedures within and across criminal justice organizations. Together these activities and programs expanded the human and nonhuman capacity to process criminal offenders—essentially creating a "system" where one did not previously exist.

Policing

As described above, the largest perceived need in Florida was hiring and training qualified police officers for a growing population. Specifically, reformers expressed concern about the "substandard performance" of small police departments, which made up the majority of local police agencies in Florida.[137] By 1970, 58 percent of Florida's LEAA allocation went to law enforcement—representing approximately 13 percent of local police and sheriff expenditures.[138] More than half of this funding was for "upgrading personnel" through local and regional programs meant to encourage the selection and recruitment of "quality manpower." Examples of programs included a regional cadet program for college students, a regional training center to provide in-service training for small departments, specialized training on equipment and law, and training to personnel "to develop and upgrade their managerial skills."[139] In addition, urban police departments and large sheriff's departments applied separately to LEAA for their own training grants. This often included the hiring of "legal advisors" to train police officers, consult on legal issues, and maintain "a close liaison between line law enforcement and the prosecutor."[140] A 1975 survey of local police agencies found that 37 percent had dedicated training programs, 17 percent had planning unit personnel, and 14 percent had in-house legal advisors.[141] Between 1970 and 1976, the number of local police and sheriff personnel in the five largest metropolitan areas had doubled and nine thousand more officers had completed basic training.[142]

In addition to the lack of police training, the state had no reliable data on the crime problem or police departments' workload. Although the FDLE had begun to comply with the FBI's crime reporting program "despite severely limited resources" in 1967, the SPA used LEAA funding to move toward a statewide "criminal justice statistical system" that could provide the FBI's Uniform Crime Reports (UCR) with administrative and other baseline data.[143] Based on the experience of the FBI and states like California, Michigan, and New Jersey, reformers aimed to build a system "so that any law enforcement agency in Florida could quickly, easily, and privately exchange data, or search databases related to crime, criminals, and stolen property."[144] As a result of these new systems, by 1978 the SPA could report local police department statistics for number of calls for service, the type of response, disposition of illegal activity–type calls, and response times.

The availability of trained personnel and data allowed for a new emphasis on enhancing performance, cooperation, and efficiency with the aim of higher clearance rates (number of arrests per reported crime).[145] And in 1980 Florida signed on to replicate the LEAA-sponsored national Integrated Criminal Apprehension Program (ICAP), which was designed to "improve police operations through sophisticated crime analysis and investigative and management procedures."[146] The precursor to problem-oriented policing and Compstat, ICAP was first used in Florida by Duval County in order to more effectively manage police resources, and then replicated in sixteen other jurisdictions.[147] LEAA reported in 1979 that in ICAP jurisdictions patrol apprehensions increased by 31 percent and criminal filings by 18 percent.[148]

Police departments also used LEAA funds to organize their resources into multijurisdictional task forces dealing with specific crimes. As early as 1970, Miami-Dade County applied directly to LEAA for a discretionary grant for an Organized Crime Fighting Team Project which equipped six investigative teams to surveil for vice and narcotics crimes. Over the next four years, LEAA awarded the county $488,000 for its organized crime teams and another $430,000 for a Robbery Control Project and a Safe Street Unit to focus on high-crime areas.[149] As Hinton explains, these LEAA discretionary grants were used by LEAA administrators to focus on urban areas when the SPAs had other priorities. In 1972 Florida highlighted the LEAA-funded fifteen-man Broward County Narcotics and Dangerous Drugs Intelligence and Enforcement Unit, directed by the Broward County sheriff's office, noting that 75 percent of arrests by the unit were for "actual sale of narcotics rather than simple possession."[150] In 1973, the state planning agency allocated almost half of its "crime prevention and control" budget to a dozen local "tactical units" aimed at increasing the rate of apprehension for narcotics violations, robbery, and burglary.[151] By 1975, 73 of 219 surveyed local police agencies had narcotics units with an average of four full-time officers.[152] Yet as happened in Detroit, New York, and other cities, new aggressive policing strategies led to "widespread use of force" by police in African American neighborhoods.[153] In 1980 in Miami, a series of well-publicized incidents of police abuse and killings over the course of the decade eventually led to one of the worst urban uprisings of the post–civil rights era—1,100 arrested, $80 million in property damage, and 18 dead—including 3 white motorists pulled from their cars and beaten to death.[154]

Courts

By the early 1970s, Florida policymakers generally agreed that they needed to "completely reorganize [the state's] criminal court system."[155] The current judicial system was a relic of the 1885 Constitution plus "years of amendment, expansion and addition," such that counties had eight different types of lower courts with various jurisdictions.[156] In 1972 voters approved a constitutional amendment that "consolidated . . . the multitude of trial courts . . . , abolished the justice of the peace system and municipal courts, established a clear system for court administration, defined judicial rule-making authority," provided a mechanism to determine judicial needs, and created a public defender system.[157] While a study of court reform implementation in 1975 found that elected court clerks resisted administrative changes, the disparate court systems in sixty-seven counties eventually became a bureaucratized and unified state court system. The new system gave responsibility for misdemeanor case processing to the county courts and felony cases to twenty circuit courts covering from one to six counties. Each circuit also had an elected state's attorney and an elected public defender, each with the power to appoint assistants.

The process of reorganization required the state to commit substantial new resources to the court system. Between 1972 and 1979, state funding for the judiciary (including state's attorney and public defender offices) went from $29.9 million to $111.8 million.[158] LEAA funding supplemented this budget increase with grants for hiring and training court personnel, including professional managers (court administrators), judges, and law students.[159] The object of the spending was "to reduce the time necessary for the handling of cases, induce more effective decisions by judges in terms of disposition alternatives, and reduce the necessary involvement in

TABLE 2.1 **Increase in number of court professionals, 1971–1976**

	1971	1976	% increase
Circuit court judges	140	263	88
State's attorneys/assistant SAs	145	492	239
Public defenders	111	304	174

Source: Florida Governor's Council on Criminal Justice, "Florida's Comprehensive Plan 1971" (Tallahassee, 1971), 111, 154, 181; Florida Bureau of Criminal Justice Planning and Assistance, "Florida's 1978 State Comprehensive Plan for Criminal Justice Improvement," Courts (Tallahassee: Department of Administration, 1978), 107.

routine administrative matters by judges."[160] The number of judges, state's attorneys, and defense attorneys grew (see table 2.1); by 1978, Florida's report indicates a significant decrease in the number of days between arraignment and disposition.[161] The increase in efficiency can also be seen in the number of felony dispositions per filing in a given year. Between 1973 and 1975 the raw number of felony filings went up by 41 percent, and dispositions increased by 67 percent.[162]

The ability to process more cases (and know how many cases were processed) was also the result of investment in court data systems. The 1971 report noted the "total lack of an accurate and reliable database."[163] Over the course of the decade, LEAA funding helped the Office of the State Courts Administrator implement a Master Plan for Criminal Justice Information Systems.[164] In addition, LEAA aided the development of large counties' data systems.[165] Similar to crime and policing data, the 1978 report included data on filings and dispositions by crime type and by disposition type for the felony and county misdemeanor courts. In fact, the new data identified new problems for reform. The 1978 report, for example, problematizes the low numbers of "releases from secure detention after arrest" due to the lack of pretrial release programs and the slow application of new "release on recognizance" rules enacted during bail reform in the late 1960s. In addition, the report expresses concern about sentencing disparities across judicial circuits.[166]

LEAA funding also helped establish data management systems for the state's attorneys' offices. In 1971, the National District Attorneys Association (NDAA) used LEAA funding to establish a National Center for Prosecution Management aimed at improving management of prosecutors' offices by developing and disseminating standards, guidelines, and models.[167] The Florida Prosecuting Attorneys Association received a $54,000 grant to hire a state prosecutors' operations coordinator "to coordinate activities of 83 such offices throughout the state."[168] In 1973, the governor's office received an additional grant to fund a similar position in order to distribute NDAA national resources to state's attorney offices.[169] This later grew into a Prosecution Technical Assistance and Coordination Office (also funded by LEAA) aimed at keeping state's attorney offices advised of training opportunities, new techniques, vital legal decisions and laws, and "correct and effective administrative procedures," including written case screening guidelines.[170] In 1974 the Florida Prosecuting Attorneys Association received a $55,387 grant to "develop standardized prosecution management techniques."[171] Concurrently, LEAA's National Criminal Justice Information and Statistics Service developed the Prosecutors Management Information System (PROMIS), and in 1980, Florida used $1 million of its $17 million in awards to roll out the system statewide.[172]

Similar to police departments, state's attorney's offices also received LEAA grants to develop specialized units focused on specific crimes and offenders. In 1974, President Nixon announced a major effort to "take the hardened criminal out of circulation" and LEAA created a Career Criminal Program, which gave resources to prosecutors' offices to focus on repeat offenders in order to increase conviction rates and sentence length.[173] The first program in Florida—in Clearwater—received a discretionary grant directly from LEAA in 1975. Subsequently, the Florida SPA funded a career criminal unit in the 4th circuit (Duval County) with four dedicated attorneys and one investigator, writing in their 1978 report that 96 percent of the 430 repeat offenders prosecuted in 1976 received prison sentences.[174] Other counties also implemented the model with local funding.[175] And in 1977, the state expanded the program to four additional offices in "an effort to remove career criminals from society."[176]

Diversion and Rehabilitation

Although the language surrounding career criminals suggests an early "incapacitation" rationale, following the orientation of Corrections Secretary Wainwright, almost all of the LEAA resources allocated to "corrections" aimed to divert offenders from prison or provide them with treatment while confined in modified correctional settings.[177] Florida's reports to LEAA over the 1970s consistently relay its goal to reduce admissions to jails and prisons, which, as I detail in the next chapter, were seriously (and unconstitutionally) overcrowded. Because of this need (and the advocacy of corrections administrators), by the end of the decade Florida planners allocated 44 percent of LEAA action funds to corrections

TABLE 2.2 **Allocations for corrections and rehabilitation by Florida State Planning Agency, 1973**

Spending category	Allocation ($)	% of total allocations
Predetention/diversion	956,500	11
Treatment/community corrections	5,213,530	63
Postdetention/parole	262,500	3
Manpower development	950,000	11
Secure detention	300,000	4
Research & development	651,000	8

Source: Florida Governor's Council on Criminal Justice, "1973 Program Areas: LEAA Program, Part 'C' and 'E' Funds" (Tallahassee, 1973).

programs. Consistent with national corrections professionals' emphasis on community corrections, a very small percentage of the grants went towards constructing secure detention. Instead, the programs expanded front-end diversion (pretrial services and probation) and back-end treatment (parole, work release, and drug treatment). (This was true for both adults and juveniles. In this narrative I focus on the adult programs.)The breakdown of 1973 allocations provided in table 2.2 represents a typical pattern for corrections allocations.

In addition to localized pretrial intervention programs (often aimed at "drunks" and drug users), in 1975 LEAA funding helped establish a statewide pretrial services unit within the newly named and reorganized Department of Offender Rehabilitation (DOR), which absorbed probation and parole officers as employees. Each circuit court district included one or more intake and community service offices staffed by probation officers who conducted presentence investigations, recommended offenders for alternatives to incarceration, and "supervised and counseled" offenders placed on probation or parole.[178] In 1976 and 1977 LEAA grants totaling $1.2 million helped hire probation staff to expand a preadjudication program for first-time offenders to eleven more circuits.[179]

Other LEAA-funded probation programs included Probation and Restitution Centers, a residential program for property offenders "designed to improve . . . life skills and to develop responsibility" while making restitution to the victim.[180] In addition, probation offices worked with an expanding network of county-based alcohol and drug detox and treatment centers (many of which received LEAA allocations). In 1980, seventeen large treatment providers signed on to Florida's adoption of the Treatment Alternatives to Street Crime (TASC) program, developed by LEAA in

1972 as a "linkage" program that referred adjudicated offenders to treatment programs, "then monitor[ed] a client's progress . . . and report[ed] back to the criminal justice system."[181] Eleven of the seventeen treatment centers received LEAA support for the program (about $100,000 each) in 1980. At the same time, the department used LEAA funds to experiment with intensive parole services that increased the ratio of parole officers to parolees and expanded small prerelease facilities that aimed to "provide comprehensive guidance and counseling," group therapy, and work and study release, "which will best facilitate the individual's readjustment to society."[182] By 1980, the department boasted twenty-four community correctional centers and eight women's adjustment centers, which held approximately 11 percent of the state's adult inmate population.

Crime Prevention / Victim Services

Optimistic liberal observers hoped that greater federal assistance for crime control would accelerate changes "already under way in law enforcement," including the use of data, training, and a "larger role for rehabilitation and the prevention of crime."[183] While they were correct about the growth in capacity for data production, training, and rehabilitation, crime prevention created a unique challenge. As articulated in Florida's 1978 report:

> With few exceptions, *the objectives of crime control and crime prevention programs over the past few years in Florida have not been directed at specifically reducing the level of crimes, criminals or criminal activity.* Instead, project and program activity has been directed at improving and upgrading the efficiency and effectiveness of the criminal justice system and its components. This approach has indeed brought the criminal justice system up to an acceptable level of "readiness" . . . but at the same time, Florida recognizes that improvements in the police, court and correctional systems do not necessarily lead to reduced crime. [emphasis added][184]

Instead, the criminal justice planners admitted, real crime prevention required investments in housing, community development, employment, and other "ameliorative economic measures."[185] Although the funding categories in LEAA's reports always included a "crime prevention" category and represented 6 to 15 percent of action grant spending, the structure of LEAA precluded these types of investments. All along, LEAA was "evaluated on the basis of a demonstrable improvement in systems integration and in the improved capacity of the criminal justice system to respond"— not a reduction in crime.[186] Thus, "crime prevention" as defined by LEAA was limited to what could be accomplished through criminal justice system organizations and actors.

In LEAA's first four years, crime prevention funding prioritized programs to improve "community relations" with the idea that if people's (particularly racial minorities') interactions with the criminal justice system improved, they would have less reason to protest. The original Florida planning committee did not have a task force on crime prevention, but did have one on public information and community involvement, which advocated informing citizens about law enforcement's objectives and activities.[187] New victimization data that revealed that citizens did not report many crimes to the police further bolstered the perceived need for public awareness.[188] Crime prevention activities also included law enforcement efforts to inform citizens about how to keep themselves safe and protect their valuables.[189] For example, Florida's 1971 plan highlights the public's failure to lock their cars and banks' failure to require adequate information when cashing checks.[190]

In 1974 LEAA combined the disparate elements of its crime prevention priorities into a new Citizens Initiative aimed at increasing the confidence of citizens in the criminal justice system by serving their "needs" and "involving" them in process. Elaborating on its rationale, LEAA identified three types of target citizens: victims, witnesses, and jurors, "without whose active cooperation justice cannot be done."[191] Viewing "everyone" as "a potential victim," the Citizens Initiative also reframed public education programs as teaching citizens about their role in the system:

> The criminal's job is made easier by a public that appears to believe it is the duty of police alone to apprehend all of the suspects. . . . In reality, the police depend on citizens to help reduce criminal opportunities and to report those crimes that do occur. The courts depend on citizens to accept witness responsibilities readily and to serve as jurors when called. Corrections institutions depend on citizens to help reintegrate offenders into the community.[192]

In this vein, LEAA supported the National Sheriffs' Association's development of the Neighborhood Watch program, which emphasized self-help, crime reporting, and local organizing on behalf of potential victims. In Florida, LEAA helped establish crime prevention programs run by law enforcement and local citizens groups that educated the public about how to protect oneself and one's property. This included the popular Help Stop Crime program, in which a local law enforcement officer helps to organize and coordinate the activities of a citizens committee for crime prevention.[193] This too reinforced the idea that citizens need the state to protect them from criminal outsiders, rather than to build strong communities and opportunities.

Beginning in 1975, LEAA crime prevention funds increasingly went to victim programs, including "witness coordinator" positions in the prosecuting attorney's office in order to facilitate the relationship between victim/witnesses and law enforcement agencies.[194] Between 1975 and 1979, LEAA's support of victim/witness programs increased from $3 million to $50 million.[195] Florida's reports to LEAA demonstrate this shift in focus. The 1978 report lists fourteen victim programs in the state (seven for victims of sexual assault) run by both law enforcement and nonprofit organizations.[196] By 1980, the state had twenty-six active programs and had received a LEAA grant to establish the Florida Network of Victim/Witness Services as part of the State Bureau of Criminal Justice Assistance in order to: (1) advocate on behalf of victims; (2) conduct training and educational workshops and conferences; (3) enhance public awareness of victims' needs; and (4) coordinate a Victim Rights Week.[197]

Penal Modernization as a (Necessary) Precursor to the Carceral State

The familiar narrative of crime control policy in the civil rights era as a conservative political project and backlash to racial inclusion is complicated by the history at the state level. This chapter has demonstrated that crime control policy did grow out of racial unrest—but partly as a means to combat the use of law enforcement to subjugate black citizens. The story of St. Augustine typifies this development: the protests and reactions exposed the racism of local law enforcement and created embarrassing scenes of disorder and new justifications for federal or state intervention. As the major crime control policy of the 1960s and 1970s, penal modernization— the professionalization and bureaucratization of local police, courts, and corrections—needs to be understood as part of a larger state modernization project. State modernization, or the upgrading and creation of modern state bureaucracies and capacities, was especially a priority in Southern states, whose political systems had been hamstrung by the racial project for white supremacy. While Florida is unique among Southern states because of the strength of the white progressive reform bloc from South Florida, shrewd lawmakers across the South during this time period began to recognize their increasingly diverse electorate and the need to appeal to "the urbanized middle class" with state institutions able to stimulate economic growth.[198] To be clear, the Florida reformers profiled in this chapter were not civil rights activists—racial equality was not their foremost goal. But they were also not willing to let white supremacists handicap the state. As a consequence, they aligned themselves with the project for racial integration and equal participation. To modernize Florida, they had to wrest control from the racial hardliners and reform neglected state institutions.

The content of penal modernization, while guided by federal resources and national standards, varied by state and depended on the political context and reformers' priorities. Penal modernization included both rehabilitative and punitive aspects—both the creation of diversion programs for drug offenders and prosecutorial units for repeat offenders. In Florida, state lawmakers, bureaucrats, and criminal justice planners used federal resources to implement law enforcement training, create new criminal justice state bureaucracies, and develop new data and communication capabilities. In addition, taking cues from federal initiatives and national models, they expanded the criminal justice system into the realms of narcotics control, treatment and education, and victims' services. In fact, national standards and professional organizations became a way for Southern criminal justice professionals to separate themselves and their institutions from racialized, antiquated practices and the criticism they garnered.

As evidenced by the data on LEAA spending in Florida, penal modernization created at least four feedback effects that laid the foundation for the growth of the punitive carceral state. First, in contrast to programs of the Great Society that addressed crime through investments in social support systems, penal modernization planted crime control firmly within the criminal justice apparatus. In 1971, the federal government spent eight times as much on federal aid to states for criminal justice as it did for crime prevention via health and human services.[199] In 1973, when Congress debated where to locate a new Office of Juvenile Justice and Delinquency Prevention, the previous establishment of LEAA led to their decision to "treat delinquency as a crime control problem rather than a social welfare concern."[200] In the 1980s President Ronald Reagan and like-minded politicians would cement this focus through their rhetoric and policies.[201]

Although liberal state governors continued to address crime through state education and social welfare systems, when political rhetoric around crime and drugs reached new heights in the 1980s social support systems lost out in part because prior investments had placed "crime control and prevention" within the criminal justice system.

Second, just as the 1968 Omnibus Crime Control Act created precedent for future federal crime control initiatives, the events of this period solidified the role of the state and state actors in what had been a local enterprise. Although penal modernization included local governmental units, it was primarily a state-level project. On balance, the legislature supported reform more than the small conservative counties that most needed it. And in some cases, such as corrections, reform specifically meant wresting control away from local stakeholders and placing it in a centralized bureaucracy. The flow of federal money through state governments thus reinforced these impulses—furthering state politicians' sense of responsibility for finding solutions to the perceived and real rise of crime during the late 1960s and 1970s. As time went on, state governors, attorneys general, and legislators increasingly responded to crime by adjusting the levers within the criminal justice system available to them, including sentencing law and corrections policy.

Third, penal modernization created new constituencies that helped build the punitive carceral state. The wide net cast by LEAA created (or strengthened) new professional and special interest groups by incentivizing them to organize in order to advocate for grant money. Of particular importance, penal modernization spawned the victims' rights movement and strengthened law enforcement associations. As Marie Gottschalk has demonstrated with national victims groups, the Florida victims' organizations established by police, sheriffs, and prosecutors' offices across the state during this time paved the way for politically active and punitively oriented victims' organizations in later decades.[202] In fact, the underlying ethos that would define the victims movement during the height of mass incarceration—that programs for offenders come at the expense of victims—appeared in the penal modernization discourse. Florida's 1978 report notes that local victim services were disproportionately limited "when compared to state and local programs for offender rehabilitation, including the program that provides funds to a prisoner upon release."[203] Likewise, law enforcement officers created professional advocacy organizations during this period. In Florida, the state's attorneys (who were no longer allowed to earn outside income) put their energies into the Florida Prosecuting Attorneys Association; the county sheriffs organized the Florida Sheriffs Association; and a few Fraternal Order of Police lodges created the Florida Police Benevolent Association (a politically active law enforcement union). All three organizations continued to justify and lobby for state and local criminal justice expenditures when LEAA funding ran out.

Finally, and perhaps most obviously, penal modernization built the criminal justice infrastructure that allowed the system to process more criminal offenders—that is, it created new *carceral capacity*. Police departments, court administrators, and prosecutors' offices all created procedures that allowed for efficiency and uniformity across units and/or personnel. While this capacity undoubtedly increased the fairness of the system and created the opportunity for justice where there had been none before (for example in the implementation of a public defender system), it also significantly increased arrests and convictions. While the Department of Corrections attempted to deal with the resulting increase in admissions to prison by building less secure confinement options, the few state prisons became increasingly crowded. In turn, as I discuss in the next chapter, civil rights lawyers used the federal courts to compel the governor and legislators to increase resources and pass reform. However, when President Reagan began the War on Drugs in the 1980s, police, prosecutors, and courts had the specialized "task forces" in place to ramp up arrests and shuttle people through the system—further exacerbating prison overcrowding.

Prison Overcrowding and the Legal Challenge to Florida's Prison System, 1970–1980

A free democratic society cannot cage inmates like animals in a zoo or stack them like chattels in a warehouse.—District Court Judge Charles R. Scott, *Costello v. Wainwright*, 1975[1]

[Sustained prison litigation in the South is best explained by] the interaction between sympathetic judges and a set of advocates who saw a potential for urging change by lawsuit and had both resources to bring case after case and expertise to work effectively within the legal frameworks.—Margo Schlanger, *Michigan Law Review*, 1999[2]

By the end of the 1960s segregation in schools, public accommodations, and transportation had no legal leg to stand on. The Civil Rights Act, the Voting Rights Act, and the Fair Housing Act gave the federal government and civil rights advocates the right and the resources (although not unlimited) to push forward the racial project to remedy inequality across a range of institutions. At the same time, however, resistance to the goal of racial equality persisted and in some cases, emerged anew. Often referred to as a "backlash," white voters began to feel that the liberal policies of the civil rights movement had gone "too far" and they reversed course and, at the national level, supported more conservative candidates and policies under a new Republican Party coalition.[3] Over the course of the 1970s, the continuing conflict over racial projects shaped the ongoing penal modernization effort, including the legal movement for improving prison conditions.

As I discussed in the last chapter, Law Enforcement Assistance Administration (LEAA) grants initially aimed to upgrade policing. Although money eventually went to criminal courts and "corrections" systems, in the early 1970s prisons and jails—especially in the South—were overcrowded and underresourced. Thus, prison reform litigation in the federal courts became an important impetus for improving conditions in the nation's prisons and jails.[4] By 1983, prisons under court order housed 42 percent of the nation's state prisoners.[5] Comprehensive accounts of prison conditions litigation in Texas, Arkansas, Alabama, and elsewhere chronicle the broad array of improvements in prison health care, nutrition and diet, access to justice, and safety.[6] Some of the greatest progress occurred in Southern states where penal systems—historically based on hard labor, racial subjugation, and self-sufficiency—were brutal, neglected, and racialized.[7] Of the ten states where the entire correctional system was placed under court order, six were in the South.[8] Just as the project for racial equality led to federal policy that supported penal modernization, it similarly prompted federal litigation that helped modernize and upgrade prison and jail facilities. In their account of 1970s prison litigation, Malcolm Feeley and Edward Rubin argue that the civil rights movement paved the way for prison reform litigation by creating a larger role for the national government in the modern administrative state, a norm of equality across regions, and a new ethos of rights. Feeley and Rubin provocatively refer to prison reform litigation as "the last and least glorious battle of the Civil War" because it challenged egregious racialized practices in the South's prisons and jails.[9]

The widely acknowledged improvements in prison and jail conditions however, can also be viewed as a "double-edged sword."[10] As legal scholar Margo Schlanger wrote at the turn of the twenty-first century, "by promoting the comforting idea of the 'lawful prison,' the litigation movement may have smoothed the way for ever-harsher sentences and criminal policies and contributed to the current situation."[11] Recent scholarship, in fact, demonstrates that independent of other factors such as crime rates, state politics, and initial levels of overcrowding, prison conditions litigation between 1971 and 1996 both increased state spending on prisons and incarceration rates.[12] This finding is surprising given that, in general, prisoner rights advocates "had extraordinary high hopes that . . . [prison conditions] litigation, and in particular overcrowding litigation," would further a decarceration strategy.[13]

The story of prison conditions litigation in Florida helps explain this contradictory outcome by highlighting three previously neglected factors in the translation of prison reform court orders into public discourse and public policy. First, it demonstrates how the framing of court orders in terms of prison "capacity" shaped state officials' options for compliance.

Second, it stresses how political context shapes court compliance. In particular, the white supremacist racial project led to the continued influence of conservative legislators, the disinclination to spend state resources on the prison system, and the opposition to court interference in state affairs. Third, it reveals how reformist corrections bureaucrats used court orders to demand more resources for their departments. In Florida, the legislature's timid efforts led the Department of Corrections to take matters into its own hands—helping to craft an agreement that specified the square footage per inmate necessary for a safe prison system. Yet the final court-ordered consent decree, approved in 1980, only specified the goal—not the reforms to reach it—leaving the policy details to be hashed out by the legislature over the next few years.

I begin this chapter by addressing the wider political context and the ongoing conflict between racial projects—both nationally and in Florida—in which prison conditions litigation unfolded. I then locate the origins of the prison conditions litigation in Florida, *Costello v. Wainwright*, in the project for racial equality. Next, I situate the problem of prison overcrowding within the penal modernization effort. I then examine the language of the court's injunction in *Costello*, arguing that this language shaped future compliance efforts. In the following sections, I recount the reactions of state politicians and Department of Corrections bureaucrats to the court's injunction and how they reached a settlement agreement with the prisoners' lawyers. Finally, in the last section of the chapter I highlight how racial projects shaped key actors' decisions regarding prison conditions litigation. In chapter 4, I detail the process of compliance over the course of the 1980s, which ultimately led to an increase in Florida's prison capacity.

The 1970s Politics of Race

In the 1970s the federal courts seemed increasingly eager to take on institutional reform that addressed the legacy of racial subordination and violence. In the political sphere, however, the attempt to appeal to white voters reluctant to concede their privileged position shaped new political coalitions that *minimized racial inequality as a problem*.[14] The fight over civil rights for black Americans prompted many working-class white voters to leave the Democratic Party, cementing the end of the New Deal coalition that had prevailed since the age of Roosevelt.[15] Republican politicians' thinly veiled racist appeals then helped shift white voters toward conservative Republican candidates and policies.[16] A Nixon advisor later said of the 1968 presidential election that Nixon "emphasized that you have to face the fact that the whole problem is really the blacks. The key is to devise a system that recognizes this while not appearing to."[17]

When it came to national politics, Florida exemplified this partisan realignment. Before 1968 the national Democratic Party could rely upon support from over half of Florida's sixty-seven counties, yet by 1980 only one county consistently voted Democratic in national elections.[18] At the same time, Democratic partisan identification among African Americans doubled between 1960 and 1968.[19] This partisan realignment would sustain the election of Republican presidents in five out of the next six presidential elections. At the state level, however, newly enforced rights for African Americans had a different effect on politics. In some Southern states, including Florida, new black voters led to increasingly moderate political discourse as candidates attempted to pull them into political coalitions. During the 1960s all three Florida governors campaigned on a platform that decried racial integration and the Civil Rights Act. Yet by 1970, Democrat Reubin Askew, a former state senator from the Panhandle, won the governorship on a reform platform with a broad coalition of white and black voters from North and South Florida.[20] Although Governor Askew incorporated some crime control rhetoric during his governorship and campaigns, he mainly focused on "environmental reform, education, and honesty and integrity in government."[21] In addition, as discussed in chapter 2, he was part of a new generation of white Southern governors and legislators who advocated for equal rights and racial justice as a central component of their states' modernization process.[22]

Southern state legislatures also underwent significant political changes during this period after the Supreme Court pronounced the "one person, one vote" rule. The ruling forced state legislatures to reapportion and create single-member districts, leading to the first signs of a representative two-party system in Southern states.[23] Reapportionment in Florida drastically increased the number of seats allocated to South Florida and urban districts: the number of House seats allotted to Miami-Dade County, for example, went from three to twenty-two. In a special election in March 1967, Republicans from metropolitan areas (especially in South Florida) increased their seats in the House from ten to thirty-nine and in the Senate from two to twenty.[24] The resulting political realignment in both houses forced rural and northern legislators to (at least initially) give up their leadership positions as heads of both chambers and of powerful committees.[25]

And as part of the apportionment reform, in 1968 Floridians adopted a new constitution that required annual legislative sessions and professional staffing for legislative committees.

At the same time, as scholarship on racial orders suggests, the project to sustain white privilege did not fully recede in Florida. The legacies of black disenfranchisement, malapportionment, and fights over racial segregation structured political institutions, norms, and assumptions about racialized groups of people.[26] Although representatives from urban areas (both Democrats and Republicans) now held a majority in the House, progressive Democrats were not quite a majority in the Democratic caucus, thus allowing for conservative Democrats to still assert influence. In the northern counties, "courthouse insiders" or long-time local officials, such as the county sheriff, who favored the old racial status quo, still had considerable sway over their legislative representatives.[27] Consequently, in 1975, northern conservative Democrats were able to win back leadership of the Senate by forging a coalition with more conservative Republicans. In their efforts against reform, conservative Democrats would deride the opposition as "liberals," a common epithet during the civil rights movement used to imply someone was a Communist and/or a proponent of racial integration.[28] While progressive Democrats, like Governor Askew, pushed for an activist government (to protect the environment, improve education, and update infrastructure), conservative Democrats continued to oppose increases in state spending and remained wary of state encroachment on local prerogatives. Finally, the legacy of *Brown v. Board of Education* also drove lawmakers' ongoing negative reactions to federal court "interference" in state affairs.

The Origins of Prison Conditions Litigation in Florida

As segregation and civil rights protests diminished, the network of civil rights lawyers who had spent much of the 1950s and 1960s challenging segregation and defending protesters against criminal charges began bringing other civil rights cases before sympathetic Southern federal judges.[29] Criminal defendants and inmates—potentially exposed to racial segregation, discrimination, and physical abuse—began to invoke their constitutional rights of equal protection, due process, and free speech.[30] Some of the first prisoner rights cases in Florida and nationally revolved around black prisoners' right to practice Islam and access religious materials.[31]

Early cases then gave way to systemic change efforts in prisons and jails.[32] By 1980, sociologist John Irwin found that prisoner's rights litigation had "altered" the "conception of the prisoner" from noncitizen and subhuman to "a citizen with temporarily reduced rights."[33]

Florida state prisoners learned the potential power of a federal court petition from the experience of Clarence Gideon, a Florida state prisoner whose petition to the Supreme Court became the basis to counsel in *Gideon v. Wainwright* in 1963.[34] Two other prisoners, Michael Costello, a white nineteen-year-old from Okaloosa, Florida, serving a life sentence for murder, and Roberto Celestineo filed similar complaints to the Federal District Court in Jacksonville claiming the conditions at Florida State Prison were tantamount to "cruel and unusual punishment."[35] The handwritten complaints landed on the desk of United States District Judge Charles R. Scott, who passed the complaints of Costello and Celestineo to his friend, civil rights lawyer Tobias Simon.

Judge Scott, nominated to the federal bench by Lyndon Johnson in 1966, was one of the active pro–civil rights judges in the South. He had written a number of desegregation orders—at one point Florida governor Claude Kirk even called for his impeachment.[36] In directing the course of *Costello*, Judge Scott drew on many of the doctrinal and procedural precedents established in desegregation cases. For example, citing *Carter v. West Feliciana School Board* (1970), he appointed a special master to help the court evaluate existing prison medical services. In addition, he assigned the United States as amicus curiae, in order to tap the resources of the Civil Rights Division of the Department of Justice.[37] Judge Scott also gave the DOJ rights of a party, which allowed them to participate actively in discovery, cross-examination, and oral arguments on behalf of the plaintiffs.

Toby Simon, an "eccentric" and well-respected Miami lawyer and graduate of Harvard Law School, was one of the few whites in a network of Southern civil rights lawyers supporting the desegregation movement.[38] His participation in the ongoing Civil Rights Law Institute in Warrenton, Virginia (established by the NAACP Legal Defense Fund [LDF]), complemented his hands-on experience.[39] In the summer of 1963, as a staff attorney for the ACLU, Simon volunteered to represent Gideon, later writing about his experience in terms that pointed to the logic behind his commitment to protecting the rights of prisoners:

> It has become almost axiomatic that the great rights which are secured for all of us by the Bill of Rights are constantly tested and retested in the courts by the

people who live in the bottom of society's barrel. . . . Upon the shoulders of such persons are our great rights carried.[40]

A short time later, Simon worked with the LDF to defend Martin Luther King Jr. and supporters in St. Augustine.[41]

By the mid-1960s the Eighth Amendment's applicability to the states had been confirmed by the Supreme Court, and Simon, motivated to address continued racial disparities, turned his attention to death penalty cases.[42] At the time, the LDF had begun litigating cases where a rape conviction resulted in a death sentence—as 90 percent of all defendants given a death sentence for rape were black men accused of raping white women.[43] Hoping to stop executions in Florida, Simon creatively drew on the legal resources of the LDF to file a class action habeas corpus petition, and in 1967, he and co-counsel from LDF won a stay of execution for all fifty-four death row prisoners.[44] When Judge Scott vacated all of their death sentences five years later, after *Furman v. Georgia*, Scott's words signaled his respect for class action lawsuits: "This case demonstrates the point that justice may best be obtained by the utilization of such a procedural device [class action] and impliedly asserts that, absent such a device, a dogmatic rejection would have lent credence to the petitioners' position that 'they will be heard together or they will be electrocuted individually.'"[45]

In addition to legal developments, civil rights attorneys, judges, and prisoners drew on new resources for legal representation. In the early 1970s, the Office of Economic Opportunity (OEO) and the Florida Bar Association established Florida Legal Services, Inc., to respond to the legal needs of poor people.[46] And in 1972, with the goal of reducing prison violence, LEAA funded a three-year demonstration project to expand the provision of legal services to prisoners. The Florida Prison Project provided postconviction relief, representation at parole revocation hearings, and assistance with prisoners' pro se civil rights actions.[47] Private resources for prisoner legal assistance also increased in the early 1970s. As the civil rights movement turned toward more militant black activism, the private foundations that had funded many of the civil rights legal projects in the 1950s and 1960s looked for other projects to fund.[48] With the new resources, civil rights lawyers established local public interest law firms, many of which took on prison litigation.[49] The Edna McConnell Clark Foundation provided start-up funds for one of the first public interest law firms in the state—the Florida Justice Institute in Miami—which was later instrumental in statewide jail conditions litigation.[50] It also helped found the ACLU's National Prison Project, which became instrumental in prisoners' rights cases around the country.

Given their close working relationship, Judge Scott likely saw Toby Simon as a natural choice to further investigate Michael Costello's claims of inadequate medical care. Extending the successful framework from death penalty lawsuits, Simon (at the urging of Judge Scott) added over-crowding to the complaint, and Judge Scott certified it as a class action on February 22, 1973. The amended complaint sued Louie Wainwright, the director of the Florida Division of Corrections (later renamed the Florida Department of Corrections [FDOC]), for relief from overcrowding and inadequate medical care that caused "substantial harm to inmates in vio-lation of the Eighth Amendment prohibition against cruel and unusual punishment." The complaint asked the court to compel state officials to "re-distribute" or "reduce" the prison population in one of three ways: "either stem the influx of inmates . . . ; accelerate the discharge of quali-fied inmates . . . ; or allocate adequate funds and facilities to care for the ever-expanding inmate population."[51]

While the lawsuit did not directly challenge racial injustice—as de-plorable prison conditions impacted both black and white prisoners—it was part of the larger project for racial equality in at least three regards. First, as mentioned above, the key actors initiating the case—Simon and Judge Scott—were themselves motivated by concerns about racial in-equality, and in directing the course of *Costello*, they drew on their civil rights litigation experience. In a nod to the legacy of slavery, in his first order Judge Scott reproached the state, arguing that "a free democratic society cannot . . . stack [inmates] like chattels in a warehouse."[52] Second, racial inequality pervaded all state institutions in Florida, including the penal system. In their court filings, the plaintiffs repeatedly blamed the overcrowding on "governmental neglect," which was due to the legacy of racialized penal servitude in Florida and the dominance of northern rural segregationist legislators who opposed spending money on black prisoners.[53] Finally, this same legacy contributed to Florida's "highly con-servative criminal justice policy," which relied on "excessive use of im-prisonment by the courts."[54] Thus, while leasing state inmates to compa-nies for hard labor ended in Florida in 1919, the cultural assumptions and institutions that led to racialized government neglect were still in place. As Simon's statements later indicated, he hoped that the lawsuit would force state legislators to amend Florida's penal culture, beginning by re-leasing nonviolent offenders and reforming sentencing in order to divert offenders from prison.[55] Similar to the eradication of the death penalty and expanding social services for the poor, these measures stood to disproportionately benefit black offenders, who composed 55 percent of the prison population (compared to the less than 15 percent black population of the state).[56]

Simon's hope that the state would reduce the prison population was not unusual, as it fit within the orientation of the national corrections reform movement at the time. As discussed in chapter 2, the 1973 National Advisory Commission on Criminal Justice Standards and Goals recommended halting prison construction and using community sanctions instead of prison sentences for all but the worst offenders. It also aligned with the goals of Wainwright, who had advocated for a rehabilitative role for corrections and expanded the division's community corrections capacity since the early 1960s.

Prison Overcrowding and Penal Modernization

When Michael Costello wrote his petition in 1972, the Florida prison system was at a crossroads. Having spent the last decade modernizing the department, corrections administrators faced a significant overcrowding problem that jeopardized their progress. The state's population grew by two million over the decade, the reported incidence of violent and property crime kept rising, and new policing and court capacity guaranteed additional entrants into Florida's prisons. Between 1968 and 1972, the number of prisoners in the system had increased by 31 percent (45 percent for black prisoners and 18 percent for white prisoners).[57] Yet the state had only added three new prisons in the last decade. As a result, facilities designed to sleep less than 6,500 (eight correctional institutions, two community corrections centers, and fourteen road prisons) housed over 10,000 prisoners.[58]

As detailed in chapter 2, Florida, along with other Southern states, was in the midst of modernizing and standardizing its governing bodies, bureaucracies, court systems, and laws, which had come under external and internal scrutiny during the civil rights movement. Historically underfunded and neglected due to the project for white supremacy and the legacy of the convict lease system, the prison system was a prime target for modernization and standardization.[59] Wainwright had worked diligently to bring the division within the "modern trend of treatment" by emphasizing qualifications and adequate pay for staff, and education, counseling, and "other self-improvement activities" for prisoners.[60] However, overcrowding and outdated facilities threatened this priority: "if these challenges remain unmet," noted the division's 1972–1973 annual report, "they will constitute an extreme detriment to the resocialization process and lend credence to the familiar charge that we are 'warehousing' offenders."[61] Consequently, Wainwright embraced Simon's decision to add overcrowding to Costello's compliant, seeing it as a chance to use the court as leverage with state legislators.[62] In fact, a few years earlier, Wainwright, concerned about overcrowding, had applied for a LEAA grant to hire the American Justice Institute (AJI) to survey Florida's eight major correctional facilities "to the end of determining their appropriate bed capacities."[63] In its final report, the AJI not only recommended institutional capacities for each facility, but commented on the genesis of the overcrowding problem: "excessive use of imprisonment by the courts" on one hand, and "an extremely cautious use of parole by the [Parole] Commission" on the other.[64] Toby Simon later submitted the American Justice Institute report to the court in his application for an injunction. Judge Scott in turn selectively drew from the report in his order for injunctive relief.

While Wainwright had been clamoring for facility upgrades since the early 1960s, prison conditions were not on state legislators' radar until February 1971 (eight months before the Attica prisoner rebellion), when a weeklong riot at Florida State Prison involving clashes between white guards and black prisoners led to dozens of prisoner and officer injuries.[65] The AJI researchers later attributed the "race riot" to overcrowded conditions: "population pressures had resulted in the crowding of as many as 10 men into cells . . . it was these men who sparked the mutinous action."[66] Although some black prisoners' protests included charges of racism, they complained more broadly that the prison was "a slaughter house of human beings."[67] While a small local group of black activists in Tallahassee aided black prisoners' efforts to organize their demands, no other local civil rights organization publicly supported the prisoners. In fact, while prisoners in other states, such as New York and California, were organized on the inside and supported by advocacy groups on the outside, Florida lacked any prisoner rights organizations in either space.[68]

In his first address to the state legislature a few months after the riot, Governor Askew called for $10 million for new correctional institutions and the expansion of community corrections and parole.[69] He acknowledged underpaid corrections officers, lackluster prison medical care, and a lack of coordination between the FDOC and the Parole and Probation Commission. Again, consistent with national reform rhetoric, more progressive House Democrats wanted to "reduce the penetration of adult offenders into the correctional system" and "abate the use of large institutions" by including "corrections" in their reorganization of the unwieldy Department of Health and Human Services (renamed the Department of Health and Rehabilitative Services or HRS). They floated proposals to remove youthful offenders from the prison system, move parole field staff to HRS, and create diversion programs at "each point of criminal justice processing" in order.[70] Legislators not specifically concerned about the "rehabilitation" of criminals worried about outbreaks of violence in the prisons. As two former legislators recalled:

> We had three and four people staying in a cell made for one person at the main prison down in Raiford. So overcrowded conditions and the fact that correctional officers were terribly underpaid and qualifications were if you had a broad back and a weak mind and could hit somebody over the head with a baton, you qualified to be a prison guard . . . our correctional system was just a boiling pot ready to explode.[71]

> When I first started [as a state legislator] they had as many as twenty-six people in the big block cells. And if you [as a corrections officer] wanted to get home at night and see your family, you picked the biggest baddest son of a bitch there and he ran the block for you. . . . It was not unusual. Guys are screaming Hail Marys while someone is lining up to rape them.[72]

Yet despite the general awareness of problems in the prison system, state officials initially paid little attention to the widening of the *Costello* lawsuit from medical care to overcrowding. In fact, in the spring of 1973, when Simon asked the court to restrict the FDOC from accepting more prisoners into the system, Wainwright took it upon himself to do so before the court had a chance to respond. The following year, the division signed a pretrial stipulation essentially agreeing with the DOJ-funded medical survey, which found "gross systemic deficiencies in the delivery of adequate medical care to inmates," and acknowledging the fact that "severe overcrowding may be injurious to the physical and mental health of the Plaintiffs and such overcrowding should be eliminated."[73]

Yet without the state legislature's help, Wainwright's options to remedy the overcrowding were limited, and in early 1975, Governor Askew, facing a tough reelection campaign, had strictly forbidden more system closures. As a result, Judge Scott granted plaintiffs' motion for a preliminary injunction to close the prison system to additional prisoners. Finding that the system held three thousand more prisoners than was safe, he noted that "the [Division of Corrections] are operating the Florida Prison System in a manner which violates the constitutional rights of the inmates by denying them adequate medical care . . . [which has] been greatly exacerbated by extremely severe overcrowding . . . which the State of Florida has been unwilling to rectify."[74]

In the summer of 1974, the state's Department of Legal Affairs assigned the case to Bill Sherrill, a young lawyer in the department, who to this day remembers the date of the injunction—May 22, 1975. He recalled that Judge Scott's order hit the attorney general, legislators, and the governor, who had basically ignored earlier legal proceedings, like a "bombshell"—finally making them take notice.[75]

The Federal Court Steps In: The *Costello* Injunction

Judge Scott's 1975 injunction became both the legal and political cornerstone of the events that unfolded around *Costello*. As it guided state actors' interpretation of the case and helped shape their subsequent responses, the content of the injunctive order is essential for understanding the ultimate impact of *Costello*. Three aspects of the injunctive order guided the development of a settlement agreement four years later. First, the language of the injunction led to the interpretation of the problem as current unconstitutional conditions, rather than too many people in prison. Second, the substantive framework of the order focused on adequate "capacity," leaving room to either increase capacity or reduce prisoner populations. Third, the order assumed that the Division of Corrections (as the named defendant) was responsible for providing relief. Importantly, as I show in chapter 4, the subsequent translation of the agreement into policy within a changing political context effectively set parameters on legislators' and state officials' choices for solving the problem of prison overcrowding.

With the memory of the 1971 Attica prison uprising still fresh, the language of the injunction defined the problem as the immediate possibility of violence in overcrowded prisons. In his published decision, Judge Scott cited a series of experts and Secretary Wainwright, who all testified that the current level of overcrowding created unsanitary, unhealthy, and dangerous living conditions for prisoners.[76] This and other portions of the testimony were included in Judge Scott's decision:

Q (DEFENDANT'S COUNSEL): Dr. Walls, is it your opinion that the medical conditions, physical and psychological and psychiatric well-being of the inmates in the present overcrowded conditions at Lake Butler Reception and Medical Center [RMC] would be helped in any great way if inmates were ceased to be taken there or they held off taking any more inmates into the Reception Center at this time?

A (DR. FRANCIS G. WALLS, HEAD PSYCHIATRIST AT LAKE BUTLER RMC): I think so long as they leave 1,300 people there . . . and if that's going to continue, the tenseness is going to get much greater. It's not just a matter of closing the doors and say "Now we've got 700, open the door." We are going to have to arrive at an acceptable figure that can be handled satisfactorily from everyone's point of view. The over-worked staff are doing the best with what they have. The inmates are cooperating quite well, the vast majority, but I don't think there's one answer . . .

Q: You characterized the Reception Center as being a tinder box?

A: Yes.

Q: Would you amplify that.

A: Well, in actual fact, I think if the number of inmates got together and decided they're going to get out of this place, there's insufficient staff, custodial staff to stop them.

Q: You are referring then to the possibility of a riot?

A: Riotous situations are always on hand, at all times, and the guards are not armed. They are walking about there with their life in their hands just wearing slacks like I do.[77]

In his own visit to the Lake Butler RMC, Judge Scott found the state of the one-man cells where four prisoners slept "the most disturbing." He further noted that the "mounting surge of incoming inmates" had "substantially impaired" the division's "system of classification," contributing to "the proliferation of rapes, assaults and tension in general."[78] Judge Scott concluded that "there is a direct and immediate correlation between severe overcrowding . . . and the deprivation of minimally adequate health care" and the "violence within the prison system."[79]

The injunctive relief utilized the framework of "prison capacity"—specifically as it was used in the American Justice Institute's 1974 report—to require that the defendants "*reduce* the overall inmate population" to "emergency capacity" in five stages over one year and to "normal capacity" by December 1, 1976. As defined by the American Justice Institute:

> "Normal capacity" [is] that population which an institution can properly accommodate on an average daily basis. It represents that population which best utilizes the resources currently available. It should include some vacant beds, to accommodate population surges, and to allow for different classifications of inmates within institutional totals.
>
> "Maximal capacity" [is] the fullest possible use of the plant, given virtually unlimited program and staff resources.
>
> "Emergency capacity" [is] the population beyond which the institution must be considered *critically, and quite probably, dangerously overcrowded.* It includes every bed in the institution which it is judged can safely be occupied at times of peak populations either due to intermittent and unpredictable population surges or to emergency and temporary circumstances.[80]

Judge Scott specifically stated that the order was based on "capacity" rather than a fixed number, to motivate the "Division of Corrections to maintain its pertinacious program of developing further innovations to increase the capacity of the Florida penal system."[81] In addition, at the end of the order, Scott clarified the term "reduce" as not to limit the division's right to *increase* capacity by constructing or leasing additional facilities, "so long as the number of inmates above the so-called 'emergency capacity' is being reduced."[82] The timing of the order to reduce the prison population to "normal capacity" was further meant to coincide with the construction of two new prisons that would have the effect of increasing normal capacity by 2,110 bed spaces.[83]

Despite the plaintiffs' motion to add the Florida Probation and Parole Commission (FPPC) as a defendant,[84] the decision placed the primary responsibility for reducing the population to normal capacity on the FDOC. However, in elucidating the ways to reduce overcrowding, Judge Scott touched on a number of means explicitly *not* in Wainwright's control. In fact, Judge Scott's remedies relied on at least three other institutional actors: he suggested that the FPPC could accelerate granting of paroles; the courts could increase their use of pretrial intervention programs; or the State of Florida could "simply construct or lease additional facilities."[85] Interestingly, Judge Scott chose not to point to some very specific remedies offered by the AJI report, including increasing the age of youth who can be sent to prison (over 6 percent of admits were seventeen or younger);

developing short-term incarceration options (three to six months) for offenders "whose transgressions are largely the product of some immediate
compelling circumstance . . ."; or establishing a precommitment diagnos-
tic service to the courts, which had been shown to "divert a significant
number away from the prison system."[86]

While Scott essentially gave equal weight to ideas for *reducing the prison
population* (more gain-time or time off for good behavior, parole, or diversion) and *increasing prison capacity* (adding to facilities), technically,
Wainwright only had the authority to administer more gain-time and to find
ways of housing prisoners temporarily. Unlike the director of the Mississippi Division of Corrections, who was also under court order, he could not
spread prisoners around from one facility to another in order to comply—
the point of the order was that the *entire system* was overcrowded.[87]

The Legacy of *Brown* and the Politics of
Federal Court Intervention

Although the *Costello injunction* came in the midst of broad reform efforts
by the state government (in tax policy, court reform, and environmental
protection), because of state politics and the legacy of *Brown*, state officials did not immediately add prison reform to their priorities. Instead,
they attempted to simply stall the court's order.[88] Attorney General Robert
Shevin, who had built a reputation as a "law and order" attorney general
and planned to run for governor in 1977, realized the case could become a
political liability. He told his legal affairs staff that "in no uncertain terms"
would the state begin to release inmates.[89] However, the state could not
reasonably appeal the case on factual grounds, as FDOC officials had
conceded to the basic facts. Instead, the state appealed on procedural
grounds: arguing that because the injunction required Wainwright to close
prisons to new entrants in violation state law, the case needed to be heard
by a three-judge panel.[90] The delay tactic worked, and over the next two
years the case went all the way to the Supreme Court on the three-judge
issue. In March 1977, the Supreme Court upheld the original injunction.[91]

In the meantime, the legislature responded ambiguously with lofty mandates, small reforms, and more funding for additional prison capacity. Governor Askew approached the problem by proposing a balance between
building new prisons and finding alternatives to incarceration, such as probation and restitution centers, pretrial intervention programs, and new

uniform parole guidelines.[92] Similarly, Democrats from South Florida supported these proposals and a further emphasis on rehabilitation within the prisons. In fact, in 1975, they passed a short-lived symbolic name change from the "Division of Corrections" to the "Department of Offender Rehabilitation."[93]

However, Governor Askew was not immune to the contemporary politics of crime, and therefore publicly objected to any "wholesale discharge" of inmates.[94] In addition, the continued influence of northern rural legislators tempered any impulse for wholesale reform. Northern Democrats rejected spending additional resources on prisoners and, as a legacy of *Brown*, resented any federal court interference in state affairs.[95] As one house representative wrote to the Florida Sheriffs Association after a state highway patrol officer was killed by a recent parolee in 1975:

> I want you to know that I am in complete agreement with your position [that the release of inmates is causing an increase in crime]. . . . The Federal Courts have stepped in to legislate conditions in our jails and *once again* the rights of criminals are vastly superior to those of honest, hardworking, taxpaying, law obeying citizens. Unless a dramatic shake-up takes place in this country and the doctrine of "separation of powers" which was set forth in the Constitution of the United States by our forebearers [*sic*] is reinstated, we might as well sign a contract with the Hilton Hotel to come in and build and operate our penal system (if you can call it one). (emphasis added)[96]

As conservative northern Democrats controlled the two most powerful committees—Senate Appropriations and Rules—they exercised veto power over any proposals that were too costly or too reformist.[97] Still, while less than the governor and Wainwright asked for, between 1975 and 1979, the legislature appropriated approximately $94 million in capital funding for prison construction and expansion.[98] In addition, they passed measures to simplify gain-time laws, create objective parole guidelines, establish a sentencing guidelines study committee, and create more coordination mechanisms to deal with youthful offenders.[99] While these measures were only tangentially related to overcrowding, some legislators viewed them as necessary precursors to either slow admissions or increase releases from the prison system. As part of the penal modernization process, these measures worked to proceduralize the discretion of corrections administrators, parole commissioners, and judges, whose decisions were deemed "arbitrary and capricious."[100]

Department of Corrections Advocacy

By the late 1970s, penal modernization, which had upgraded the policing and court-processing capacity of the system, collided with the lack of space in state prisons. As a result, prison administrators faced a real dilemma. On the one hand, the legislature had expanded the role of the Department of Corrections to include a mandate to "identify, evaluate and treat behavioral disorders of adult offenders."[101] On the other hand, even though the legislature significantly increased the FDOC's budget, they never gave it enough resources to even remotely accomplish this goal. Then in 1974 prison commitments began to increase dramatically: the department reported that growth in the prison population during fiscal year 1974–1975 "was more than the total net gain of inmates for the past four years combined" (see figure 3.1).[102] As a result, in the late 1970s department administrators spent most of their time deciding where to put newly arriving prisoners. Dave Bachman, former assistant secretary of the FDOC, recalled,

> in those days . . . much of our time and energy went to finding bed space for the people who were being sent in. They [the legislature] hadn't yet figured out that when you send someone to prison you have to have a bed and a place for them to stay. In the early days, it was our problem. I mean I heard legislators say in open meetings, "What are you going to do with your prisoners?" Those are actually the words [they used]. I told them, "These are the state of Florida's prisoners."[103]

Realizing that they had no ability to stem the flow of prisoners, but would be held responsible anyway, Department of Corrections administrators became the biggest advocates for increasing capacity by building new institutions.[104] Using the American Justice Institute's recommendations for bed space, department research staff initially estimated that they would need 7,500 more bed spaces by July 1, 1977, to reach "normal capacity." As this projection was likely a nonstarter with the legislature, Joe Kresse, the Department of Administration's budget director and Governor Askew's right-hand man, initiated a new capacity survey.[105] The new survey relied on the same concepts of capacity as the injunctive order, but labeled them "design capacity" and "maximum capacity" in order to arrive at different numbers—reducing the estimated need by over two thousand bed spaces.[106]

The concepts of design and maximum capacity then became the frame-

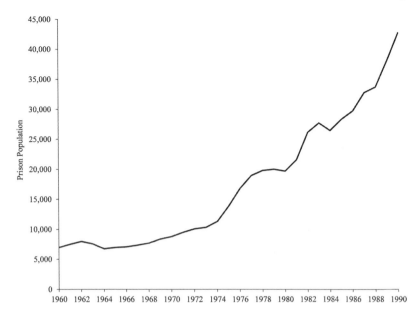

FIGURE 3.1. Florida prison population, 1960–1990. Source: Florida Department of Corrections Annual Reports, 1960–1990.

work for a settlement agreement reached almost three years later. In 1978 during depositions, the state shared the new capacity survey with Toby Simon. Bill Sherrill, who by then handled the case for the state as a private attorney, recalls Simon (whom he had great respect for) saying, "Great, this is what I've been wanting, you get an inventory and you budget these things and that will satisfy my needs." He also recalls that Simon instinctively liked Joe Kresse: "He had finally found someone [within state government] that he could trust." Rather than drawing on previous court decisions or prison experts, Simon and Kresse drew from their own experiences:

> Simon and Kresse sat down on my [hotel] bed and within an hour or two had worked out the settlement. Kresse's thesis for the settlement was that he had been in the Army and he had never had more than fifty-four square feet and it was nine-by-six; and you know you could put a double bunk in that and people could get out, and as long as they had other places they could go, but slept there at night, than that is okay as the minimum.[107]

And so, on the eve of the first day of trial in Jacksonville in May 1979, Simon and Kresse agreed upon a basis for a settlement.

The Costello Consent Decree

The final Overcrowding Settlement Agreement (OSA), reached by the parties to *Costello* in October 1979, stipulated that no individual prison should exceed maximum capacity (and may only be at maximum capacity for five days) and, most importantly, *that the inmate population of the entire system would not exceed "design capacity" plus one-third*. It defined "design capacity" as forty to ninety square feet per inmate in individual cells and no less than fifty-five square feet per inmate in dorms. "Maximum capacity" was defined as approximately 33 percent less space per inmate, with double bunking allowed along outer walls. In addition, the department agreed to no longer use three deteriorating buildings for housing prisoners. In exchange, the plaintiffs agreed to drop any liability claims. Judge Scott approved the agreement in February 1980 and gave the department *five and a half years* to comply with the consent decree.[108]

Although all parties signed the agreement and Judge Scott found it fair on balance, some national reformers felt that it gave the state too long to fix the problem. The ACLU's National Prison Project, the LDF, and U.S. Department of Justice called the settlement "premature" and objected to the allowance for double bunking, the unenforceable goals, and the lack of interim time periods.[109] In addition, a very small number of the plaintiff class (which then totaled 20,000 prisoners) further objected to the continued suffering of prisoners (even in new facilities) and called for additional facility closures.[110] However, Toby Simon thought that the timing was right: he "had a smell" that the Supreme Court was losing patience for prison cases and therefore comprehensive orders would be much harder to obtain.[111] As he told the court, while he had "given up the struggle to get the entire prison system down to design capacity,"

> I'm confident that from the point of views of the Plaintiffs in this matter while we have given, we have also gotten a great deal. We have gotten reductions. Most importantly, we have gotten an end to the litigation, and . . . the State of Florida can get about the business of attending to the reduction that has to be done in the elimination of certain prisons.[112]

At the same time Simon, who saw himself as a civil rights advocate, wanted to make sure that his clients understood and supported the agreement. Thus, over the court's winter break in December 1979 and January 1980, he visited eleven prisons to tour the facilities, met with prisoners, and answered their questions. He recounted an "exceedingly spirited" meeting with Michael Costello and seventy-seven other prisoners at Union Correctional Institution (formerly Florida State Prison), but felt he was able to make them understand the population "cap" required by the agreement would "eliminate excessive overcrowding."[113] Simon also may have felt comfortable because Kresse had convinced newly elected Governor Bob Graham to formally support the agreement. Governor Graham subsequently pledged to "exercise" his "authority and leadership" to implement its terms.[114] Thus Simon was hopeful that in contrast to the days when "there was no correlation between the number of people in prisons and the number of dollars that were being allocated by the Legislature to prison construction or to the number of people released by the Parole Commission," now the state of Florida, the legislature, and the Parole Commission would know their "obligations."[115]

However, similar to the injunctive order, the court did not provide any directives on how the department should fulfill the agreement. Instead, the court emphasized the responsibility not only of Secretary Wainwright, but of the governor and the legislature as well. Noting that the legislature had "provided very substantial increases in funding of the prison system," Judge Scott cited the increase in spending per year per inmate (from approximately $3,500 in 1972 to $7,500 for the 1981–82 fiscal year) and the construction of new facilities, approximately 2,200 more beds, at a cost of $141 million.[116]

For their part, state officials, while not being able to claim victory, had over five years to meet the terms of the order. Furthermore, they counted on being able to fund new construction based on maximum capacity, as "it would be like pulling teeth to get the legislature to fund at design capacity."[117] The agreement also freed up needed legal resources to fight other prison litigation, including the medical care component of *Costello*, a large suit challenging jail conditions across the state, and dozens of individual brutality cases.[118]

Department of Corrections administrators also benefited from the agreement in a number of ways. Not only did they now have the capacity surveys that they had always wanted, they had successfully convinced both sides to include nonbinding "administrative and operational goals" in the agreement. For example:

> Defendant promises to continue to plan for and attempt to provide dayroom space as a management goal. Defendant recognizes that inmates need recreational and social spaces during the evening hours when more closely confined

to dormitory buildings, and that dayrooms serve this important purpose. . . . Defendant will continue to seek similar funding, and will include dayroom space in proposed plans for future institutions.[119]

These goals of course went above and beyond any constitutional requirements, but could potentially provide the department with additional resources as they planned new facilities.

Since the OSA did not specify how the department or state should comply with the court order, Governor Graham appointed both Sherrill and Simon to a Governor's Advisory Committee on Corrections charged with developing legislative mechanisms to satisfy the requirements of the agreement.[120] Thus by 1980, legislators knew the state needed to initiate reforms that either *reduced the number of prisoners* behind bars or *increased the physical space* to incarcerate them. The question then became which goal to emphasize and the specific policies that could accomplish either of these objectives.

Racial Projects and Prison Litigation in Florida

As legal scholar Margo Schlanger has noted about prison conditions litigation generally, *Costello v. Wainwright* grew out of the new resources available to a network of civil rights movement lawyers and judges, including their personal training and experience, specific developments in civil rights law itself, and newly available financing for legal challenges to prisoner rights violations.[121] Yet *Costello*, and the reaction to *Costello*, was also tied to competing racial projects and the institutional legacy of those projects in Florida specifically. The actions and critical decisions of the key players during this time period, including Toby Simon, Judge Scott, and Louie Wainwright, can be traced to the project to remedy racial inequality. In contrast, the reluctance of the legislature to enact wholesale reform was grounded in the project to maintain white supremacy or, more specifically, resistance to *Brown v. Board of Education* and federal interference in the South during the civil rights movement. Importantly, racial projects shaped the decisions of these key actors in ways that created feedback effects on the development of subsequent penal policy.

Toby Simon, like other prisoner rights lawyers and activists in the early 1970s, was concerned with states' overreliance on confinement, the overrepresentation of African Americans in the criminal justice system, and the negligent treatment of prisoners. In a sense, both Simon and Judge Scott saw the federal courts as a means to force the State of Florida to finally adequately care for its state prison population, which was 55 percent black and had been neglected since the era of convict leasing. This history, therefore, shaped these legal activists' preferences and goals. Judge Scott, for example, defined the problem as one of underfunding of the prison system, rather than one of overincarceration. This informed his decision about the substantive framework for the injunction: that the department had to meet a general prison "capacity" in order to safely house prisoners. Later Judge Scott accepted the Overcrowding Settlement Agreement (OSA) because he saw increased state resources for the prison system as a positive sign of change in the state legislature.

For his part, Toby Simon was satisfied with a settlement agreement that required the state to stay within a more exact capacity framework. He believed (as it turns out, falsely) that the general fiscal conservatism of the state would push legislators to choose *to reduce the prison population* rather than expand prison capacity to meet these requirements. His satisfaction with the OSA was also partially determined by his (correct) perception that the courts had begun to back away from their support of civil rights initiatives, thus leading to diminished legal resources to address prison conditions. In fact, during this time Simon began working with the FDOC and the attorney general to create a new prisoner grievance system outside of the court-ordered reform that Simon hoped would help keep the prison system in check.[122] Yet Simon also expected that the new Democratic governor and his staff would carry out their responsibility to follow the law and protect prisoners' rights.

Wainwright's interests were similarly conditioned by the historic neglect of the prison system and his belief that all prisoners, regardless of race, had the ability to change and could become productive members of society.[123] As he was accustomed to fighting with the legislature for adequate resources, he embraced the *Costello* complaint and helped shape the settlement agreement, welcoming the chance to use the court as leverage with state legislators. He entered into a pretrial stipulation, welcomed Simon into the prisons, and negotiated with state officials to build new capacity. Since no prisoner rights or other civil rights activists mobilized on behalf of a decarceration agenda, the FDOC, as the "target population," could interpret the court's order based on its needs.[124] In combination with the capacity framework, this interpretation guided how the state would comply over the next decade.

The legislature was similarly structured and guided by racial commitments that influenced its reaction to the *Costello* litigation. First, while state voters engaged with a two-party system for the first time since Reconstruction, the long tenure of white northern Democratic legislators (because of black disenfranchisement) meant that they still could exert influence over the policy process.[125] Second, the idea that prisons should be self-sufficient and that black prisoners were not worthy of state resources still resonated with the fiscally conservative culture of the state.[126] Third, and perhaps most importantly, the legacy of *Brown v. Board of Education* and other civil rights era cases led legislators to bristle against any federal court intervention in state affairs. All three factors led the legislature to delay addressing the court case and opt for tangential reform that did not directly address overcrowding. During the 1980s their foot dragging would have a major impact on how legislators ultimately decided to resolve *Costello*.

The court-ordered consent decree in *Costello* marked a transition away from a period of great political transformation and state building in Florida. Between 1954 and 1980, the political structure and social hierarchies in Florida underwent major upheavals. Gone were the one-party system, the dominance of rural North Florida, and the exclusion of black voters.[127] Florida government became more professionalized, more centralized, and more committed to serving the needs of the entire state. In 1978, Floridians handily elected a "left of center" South Florida Democrat, Bob Graham, after he beat popular "law and order" attorney general Shevin in the Democratic primary in what David Colburn called "the largest political turnaround in modern Florida political history."[128] After the 1980 Census, Florida legislators redrew legislative districts, giving more political representation to black Floridians, South Florida, and the growing Republican Party. And while white Floridians had fought racial integration with fervor, it had become socially unacceptable for state leaders to tout racist ideology. Even locally, Florida counties made substantial progress desegregating their public schools.[129]

Relatedly, the status quo in Florida's penal system had been shaken to its core by the events of the last three decades. First, the progressive desire for modernization, professionalization, and centralization upended the long-standing tradition of patronage and local control. New resources from the federal government further incentivized reform—creating new correctional professional organizations, professional identities and bureaucratic structures that hadn't been possible before. Next, the federal courts weighed in, further creating impetus for change. Finally, the changing political context brought in new political and bureaucratic leadership that embraced reform. Thus, by 1980 a new penal system was on the horizon but had not yet taken shape.

Toby Simon, so instrumental in these changes, sadly did not live to observe the new system form. At age fifty-two, two years after signing the OSA, Simon passed away from cancer, leaving his name to live on in the Tobias Simon Pro Bono Service Award, given out each year by the chief justice of the Florida Supreme Court. Had he lived, Simon would have been surprised about the ultimate outcome of *Costello*, which would profoundly influence a new vision of crime control over the next two decades. Simon, Judge Scott, and maybe even Florida's attorney, Bill Sherrill, failed to appreciate that court orders drafted in one political context may be implemented in another. None of them anticipated how the capacity framework, fiscal conservatism, and FDOC advocacy would shape state officials' actions in the age of Reagan.

CHAPTER FOUR

The Unintended Consequences of Prison Litigation, 1980–1991

My own hope is that once the Federal Court enters a non-appealable order we will see the last of the new prisons built in this state. The system will begin to look at other remedies . . . because we know that if the prisons get overcrowded again . . . they will have to begin spending considerable sums of dollars for the construction of prisons. *And the legislature for the first time will be forced to make that choice.* For that reason, your honor, . . . we have signed it.—Tobias Simon, plaintiffs' lawyer, during the hearings for the Overcrowding Settlement Agreement, *Costello v. Wainwright*, 1979[1]

The corrections situation was unchangeable and immutable and you had to deal with it. *It really . . . wasn't a discretionary issue*; not dealing with it had . . . public safety consequences. So it wasn't a matter of joyfully pushing for more funding for corrections. It was a fact of life and a fact of the circumstances of that period of time.—John Mills (D. Gainesville), former speaker of the Florida House of Representatives, referring to decisions to build prisons in 1988[2]

In 1980, a National Institute of Justice report estimated that almost half of all state prisoners nationwide lived in overcrowded prisons. Southern states were the worst offenders: eight Southern states, including Florida, held 60 percent or more of their population in crowded facilities. Five Southern states, again including Florida, housed over 30 percent of their inmate population in "extreme crowding." As a result, judicial supervision of state prison facilities had become, in the words of the NIJ report, "a routine occurrence."[3] Building on the courts' protection of black Americans' civil rights in the 1960s and 1970s, prisoner rights lawyers and criminal justice reformers such as Toby Simon hoped that court oversight of prisons would force state legislators to improve prison conditions and, relatedly, reduce their reliance on incarceration. In the beginning of the 1980s, Florida policymakers agreed that they did not want to "build themselves out of" the prison overcrowding problem. They argued that (1) prisons were too costly—they required either raising taxes or sacrificing other state budget priorities; (2) prisons were difficult to "site" in appropriate areas—places close to prisoners' families and trained staff; and (3) prisons, of available criminal justice sanctions, were least likely to achieve the goal of rehabilitation. Accordingly, the legislature overwhelmingly passed corrections and sentencing reform meant to limit the growth of prison admissions and curb the need for prisons.

Yet by the end of the 1980s, with prison admissions soaring, Florida legislators reversed course and approved a massive investment in new prison capacity. This chapter answers why, less than ten years after Simon's statement, Florida officials decided to comply with the *Costello* Overcrowding Settlement Agreement (OSA) by building more prisons rather than finding alternatives to incarceration. In a very short time, Florida policymakers moved from what David Garland would call an "adaptive response," adjusting policy to fit within recognized state budgetary constraints, to an "expressive response," decrying crime while denying the limits of the state. I argue that the initial decision to institutionalize the *Costello* OSA in an "emergency release mechanism" and the court's robust enforcement of the *Costello* order during a racially charged moment of concern about crime and drugs led the new Republican governor to redefine the political costs and benefits of building prisons.

The paradox of prison conditions litigation in Florida, therefore, is that reform litigation on behalf of state prisoners aimed at reducing incarceration ultimately led to a massive increase in prison capacity. In a context where political actors wanted to be perceived as tough on crime, state officials who supported building prisons used the court order as a hammer to convince reluctant legislators. The outcome of prison overcrowding litigation in Florida thus highlights the indeterminate nature of legal action for institutional reform. Even when reformers win a settlement, implementation requires the translation of the court order into other institutional domains, including politics and social policy. The indeterminacy of court orders is particularly acute within a legal tradition that prioritizes negative rights, or in the case of prison conditions litigation, freedom from dangerous prison conditions.[4]

The story of Florida policymakers' change of heart on prisons provides evidence that building the carceral state was not inevitable: it was a developmental process that hinged on racial commitments and partisan politics. The dynamics and timing of Florida policymakers' shift suggests that their embrace of new prisons as a solution to overcrowding was due to a shift in perceived political opportunities and risks, rather than actual crime rates or constituents' punitive sentiments.[5] Importantly, the new political context in Florida was in large part a by-product of the national Republican Party's rhetoric around race, crime, and distrust of the state. Thus, the story of Florida unpacks the ways in which federal politics and policy during this period, and in particular the War on Drugs, actually contributed to mass incarceration. The view from the state level reveals how the federalization of crime control created both policy problems and political imperatives for state policymakers.

I begin the chapter by describing the national political context between 1980 and 1990 as it relates to crime control policy. My purpose in restating this history, previously described by other scholars, is to tie it directly to the actions of policymakers in Florida. Important to this history is how television and print news media racialized the crime and drug problem. I then follow the implementation of the *Costello* court order in two periods marked by a change in state partisan leadership and the onset of the War on Drugs. I first chronicle the period between 1980 and 1986, describing how legislators and corrections officials worked to lower prison admissions and prison populations through legislation that incorporated the work of various state committees. I then recount the drastic rise in prison admissions beginning in 1986 due to the War on Drugs. During the second period, from 1987 through 1991, legislators disavowed their fiscal conservatism and came to a consensus that, as the speaker of the Florida House later noted, they *had to* build prisons. I explain how the legacy of previous policy choices, increased federal court monitoring, and drastic increases in prison admissions for drug offenses created a heightened sense of crisis. In an attempt to differentiate himself from his Democratic predecessor, the new Republican governor worked to sell the idea of new prisons by framing the solution to the prison crisis as an either-or choice: legislators could *either* build new prisons *or* release criminals from prison. In a media and political environment shrouded with a racialized fear of crime and drugs, legislators decided to embark on a massive prison building program. Importantly, once legislators decided to fund new prisons, the Department of Corrections promoted prisons as economic development for rural communities dealing with deindustrialization and loss of farming. By 1991, these investments in carceral capacity led to the final settlement of *Costello*—over twenty years after the lawsuit began. In the final section I revisit arguments about the growth of the carceral state in the 1980s in light of my findings from Florida.

The Age of Reagan and the Racialized Politics of Crime Control

In the wake of the economic and social crises of the 1970s, including infla-
tion, escalating oil prices, unemployment, industrial stagnation, and rising
crime rates, a new conservative political coalition began to harness white
popular discontent that would eventually "knock the legs out from under
liberalism" and the national Democratic Party.[6] In particular, the Reagan
coalition blamed the welfare state for social ills and rearticulated the gains
of the project for racial equality as inappropriate and harmful demands
on the state.[7] Reagan argued that liberal protections of defendants' rights
that came about in the wake of the civil rights movement were to blame
for high levels of crime and the criminal justice system's inability to swiftly
and severely deal with criminal offenders.[8] While Presidents Ford and
Carter in some sense followed in Nixon's footsteps on crime control, Reagan more explicitly returned to Nixon's law and order political strategy.[9]
As sociologist John Hagan explains, "When Reagan ran for president in
1980, he leveraged the law and order reputation he had developed in California," once again propelling crime control to the forefront of national
public policy.[10] Reagan's rhetoric on crime intersected with his attempt to
appeal to Southern white voters. He gave his first campaign speech after
the Republican primary in the town of Philadelphia, Mississippi, where
the Ku Klux Klan had murdered three civil rights workers.

> The speech signaled sympathy for the legacy of states' rights and a disregard
> for the memory of the three university students who had lost their lives seeking
> voters' rights for southern blacks. This was an unsubtle message about states'
> rights and civil rights. The future president and his attorneys general made this
> kind of racially tinged messaging an accepted part of the age of Reagan.[11]

By resurrecting a states' rights and law and order message while emphasizing the poor performance of Democratic incumbent President Carter,
Reagan solidified the partisan realignment that had begun in the 1960s,
winning the election with 489 electoral votes (forty-four states).[12]

As president, Reagan needed to find a policy proposal that was consistent with conservative ideology, yet followed through on his promise to
protect society from criminals.[13] In 1982, calling drugs "an especially vicious
virus of crime," Reagan announced a War on Drugs, a coordinated effort
among thirty-three government agencies to wage a "planned, concerted

campaign." While the initial campaign was aimed at drug traffickers and included education, prevention, and detoxification for drug users, Reagan also set the tone for the future vilification of drug use by refusing to differentiate between drugs: "we're making no excuses for drugs—hard, soft, or otherwise. Drugs are bad, and we're going after them."[14] At the time, however, drug use was actually declining and public concern about drugs was very low. In fact, legal scholar Michael Tonry argues that given the data on drug use, "only the willfully blind could have failed to know that no war was needed."[15]

Unlike President Nixon's earlier War on Drugs, Reagan's announcement had an immediate impact on the financial resources and priorities of federal law enforcement agencies—which significantly expanded their partnerships with state and local governments to police drugs.[16] At the same time, a coalition of Senate Republicans and Democrats, headed by Strom Thurmond (R. South Carolina) and Senator Edward Kennedy (D. Massachusetts), spearheaded a crime bill that ultimately rivaled the 1968 Safe Streets Act in size and scope. The legislation further entrenched the federal government in "crime fighting activities" by expanding federal jurisdiction over various crimes, modifying asset forfeiture provisions, reversing or modifying prodefendant judicial opinions, and the "reinstatement of LEAA-like state and local anti-crime aid programs."[17] While House Democrats strongly opposed the bill, the Senate coalition secured passage of the 1984 Comprehensive Crime Control Act by attaching it to an appropriations package that ended a government shutdown.[18]

The War on Drugs

While federal crime control activity intensified and new resources for crime control began flowing to the states, crime and drugs did not capture the public imagination until the summer of 1986, when Leonard Bias, a college basketball star, died from heart complications related to a cocaine overdose. That same month *Newsweek* declared crack (a smokeable mixture of cocaine and baking soda) to be the biggest story since Vietnam and Watergate. In August, *Time Magazine* declared it the "issue of the year."[19] Seizing the opportunity to gain public support for their policies, Drug Enforcement Agency officials in the Reagan administration worked diligently to draw media attention to the "crack epidemic," crack-related violence, and the threat to white communities.[20] Similar to past drug scares, politicians from both parties began to invoke the "moral imperative to protect traditional American values" that crack threatened. In her sociolegal history of the War on Drugs, Doris Marie Provine notes that, as in the past, "suspicion of racial minorities and fearful assumptions about instant addiction and dangerous highs were essential parts of the message."[21]

Citing news media reports that characterized crack dealers as black men from the urban ghetto whose wares threatened white suburbia, Congress quickly and overwhelming passed the 1986 Anti-Drug Abuse Act, which increased penalties for federal drug crimes and enacted the infamous 100:1 weight ratio between powder and crack cocaine.[22] In addition, it authorized $1.7 billion for drug control and amended the Safe Streets Act of 1968 to include $230 million in grants to state and local police for narcotics enforcement.[23] Two years later, with the media still focused on the issue and few signs of success, Congress passed the 1988 Anti-Drug Abuse Act, which, most importantly for states and localities, created the Edward Byrne Drug Control and Systems Improvement Program, aimed at supporting multijurisdictional drug control efforts and other crime control programs.[24] Over the next four years, Congress appropriated $1.5 billion for the program.[25] In addition, Congress amended federal policy to allow police departments to keep a share of the money and property confiscated during drug investigations.[26]

The Triumph of National Crime Control Politics

Vice President George H. W. Bush's successful campaign for president in 1988, in which he portrayed Democratic opponent Massachusetts governor Michael Dukakis as soft on crime, cemented the perceived political advantages of the crime control issue. The Bush campaign capitalized on the crimes of William "Willie" Horton, a black convicted murder who assaulted and raped a white Maryland couple while on furlough from a Massachusetts prison. The details of the attack were horrific and became invaluable to the campaign. Bush's campaign manager at the time stated that "the Horton case is one of those gut issues that are value issues, particularly in the South . . . if we hammer at these over and over, we are going to win."[27] In Bush's first mention of the furlough program he linked it to the War on Drugs: "Is this [Dukakis] who we want to put in charge of our drug program? Is this who's going to get tough with the kingpins and break the cartels?"[28] While later analysis and commentary would link the success of the Willie Horton strategy to its implicit racial appeal—priming white voters' stereotypes about black criminality—the political takeaway was that voters would respond to charges that an opponent was soft on crime.[29]

Crime and drugs similarly came to be seen as a winning subject matter for the news media—an industry that became increasingly competitive over the 1980s with the advent of cable broadcasting and the proliferation of local news channels.[30] In their drive to maintain profits, media companies produced news that was increasingly "preoccupied with violent crimes committed by predatory strangers."[31] These news stories disproportionately portrayed black offenders in police custody and white female middle-class victims.[32] Along with episodic frames that attributed individual responsibility for crimes, local television news stories signaled that black people were prone to engage in violent crime and therefore less deserving of public aid.[33] Along with their coverage of politicians' calls for a war on drugs, the news media's framing of the crime problem helped to change public perceptions. Public polls showed that in the early 1980s most Americans identified unemployment and poverty as the main cause of crime, but by the end of the decade they blamed drugs.[34]

As will become clear, the triumph of national crime control politics had three important consequences for state lawmakers. First, new resources for the War on Drugs shifted the focus of urban police departments, driving up arrests, prosecutions, and admissions to state prison for drug offenses. Second, federal crime control politics and the media coverage of crime heightened the public's fear of crime and reactivated stereotypes that linked crime to African Americans, thus reinforcing punitive public attitudes. Third, as the Reagan coalition gained strength over the decade, state politicians increasingly viewed punitive crime control as a winning issue for Republicans, one that made Democrats vulnerable.[35] Republican politicians in Southern states, where the Republican Party was trying to carve out a place for itself, thus mimicked the national rhetoric on crime control—with important policy consequences.[36]

Implementing the Costello Consent Decree under Democrats, 1980–1986

The Florida gubernatorial campaign of 1978, characterized at the time as the "most media-oriented and expensive" to date, foretold a new era of crime control politics and media centrality in Florida and across the country.[37] State Senator Bob Graham, a lawyer with a family background in farming and ties to both North and South Florida, challenged Attorney General Robert Shevin in the Democratic primary. Although very similar to Shevin in terms of policy priorities (such as economic development, education, and the environment), Graham ultimately prevailed by running a more positive campaign that appealed to everyday working Floridians.[38] While state Republicans had gained some ground since the lackluster Kirk governorship, no big issue divided Florida Democrats (such as race had earlier), and Graham easily beat his Republican opponent.

Beginning almost immediately in his term as governor, Graham faced new media accounts of prison brutality and a series of prison overcrowding crises as defined by the *Costello* OSA. In response, Graham convened three task forces/committees, which ultimately recommended a series of front- and back-end reforms to the prison system. In 1983 the legislature enacted many of the recommendations into state law, including an "emergency release" mechanism meant to act as a safety valve to ensure that the prison population did not exceed legal capacity. Although the reforms aimed to reduce the prison population (and arguably could have, given enough time and resources), they did not work well enough to meet the capacity requirements set in the OSA, and the court stepped in to hasten the state's compliance. Ironically, however, the increased court monitoring along with the emergency release provision set the stage for the next administration's decision to resolve the problem by building prisons.

Reducing the Prison Population through
Sentencing Reforms and Release Mechanisms

The OSA stipulated that over the course of five years, the state would bring the prison population in line with the system's maximum capacity and close three antiquated housing units. In order to develop legislative mechanisms to satisfy the OSA, Graham appointed a Governor's Advisory Committee on Corrections, which included the prisoners' and the state's lawyers in *Costello*.[39] At the same time, citing public concern about the effectiveness of the criminal justice system, Graham also convened a Governor's Task Force on Criminal Justice Reform, chaired by the Florida Supreme Court chief justice and the attorney general, to study and propose changes to the state's entire criminal justice system.[40] Yet tasks forces and committees take time, so in the first two years after signing the OSA, nothing was incorporated into law that would reduce the prison population. In fact, in 1981 admissions to the Department of Corrections increased by an unprecedented

28 percent. Realizing that the department had "no control over the growth of the system and the cost of providing care and supervision for the increasing number of inmates," Louie Wainwright began to actively lobby Governor Graham for more prison beds.[41] In 1981 and 1982, however, Governor Graham and legislators, in part because of their alarm at recent revelations of brutality in the prisons, appropriated funds for just four hundred additional beds—less than 30 percent of what was needed just to keep up with state population growth.[42]

Wainwright, however, argued that the violence was due to the high turnover in corrections officers, who were significantly underpaid and overwhelmed. Facing the reality of negative attention from the press due to the ongoing revelations of violence, Wainwright used the media to make his case.[43] In 1982, after reading news articles where Wainwright openly admitted to levels of overcrowding in violation of the consent decree, Judge Scott ordered an immediate status report, which revealed that nineteen of the department's twenty-five institutions were operating above maximum capacity and that the department had built plywood temporary dormitories or "plywood tents" to house 320 inmates.[44] Judge Scott allowed the tents but warned the department not to be complacent and that "further recalcitrance in building adequate permanent facilities to house state prisoners will breed further woes for the defendants."[45]

Facing daunting estimates from the Graham administration of future prison costs, the newly apportioned legislature—including more African American and more Republican representatives—responded to the crisis in special legislative session by appropriating money for 1,640 temporary and 550 permanent prison beds, and 376 new probation and parole officers.[46] More importantly, the legislature convened a top-level bipartisan Corrections Overcrowding Task Force that included the attorney general, the secretary of corrections, the chairman of the Parole Commission and the chief justice of the Florida Supreme Court to recommend solutions to the overcrowding crisis.[47] In collaboration with the Governor's Advisory Committee, and taking into account the recommendations of the Governor's Task Force on Criminal Justice Reform, the new task force grappled with a longer-term solution to overcrowding. As it stood, in the summer of 1982, the Department of Corrections was still estimating that in order to comply with *Costello* by the end of June 1985, the state would need to build facilities to hold 5,500 more prisoners.[48]

Together the task forces recognized the public's fear of crime, their lack of faith in the criminal justice system, and their emerging punitive tone. Members of the Governor's Advisory Committee noted, for example, that "if the citizens of Florida were to vote today [September 2, 1982], they would likely vote to build more prisons than release inmates due to overcrowding."[49] Yet the overwhelming tone of the task forces' deliberations was concern with the *cost of incarceration*, and they began with the assumption that the state could not "continually build to match the current pace of admissions."[50] Attorney General Jim Smith, who sat on all three committees, concluded that "prison overcrowding is potentially the most expensive criminal justice problem facing the state" and that, despite public demands for punishment, legislators needed to create a system that balanced public safety with economy.[51] His principle detractor, state judge Ralph Nimmons, Jr., argued, however, that prisons were the price society had to pay "for the overly permissive attitudes which have acted as corrupting influences" leading to "a generation of people" who "never learned to respect . . . authority; never developed an appreciation for the rights of their fellow citizen; and never learned that every member of a free society must accept the consequences of his own acts." Yet, even Judge Nimmons could see that the Overcrowding Task Force was leaning toward finding ways to *control the level of imprisonment* rather than expanding capacity. He therefore advised that he would "rather see the State adjust its policies and programs at the 'other end of the sentence' instead of adopting a policy which would excuse a large category of felony offenders from the threat of imprisonment."[52]

The task force heard evidence of the lack of relationship between imprisonment and crime, and the success of alternatives to imprisonment, including probation, work release centers, pretrial intervention, and community-based sanctions. However, members reasoned that these schemes were underutilized because the public (and therefore publically elected judges) did not trust nonincarcerative sanctions to be punitive enough. For example, the probation expert on the task force argued that probation "is viewed as not doing anything *to* the offender or *for* the public."[53] Other experts discussed determinate sentencing guidelines as a way to control the prison population, noting, however, that evidence from California demonstrated a drastic increase, not a decrease, in prison admissions after the change to determinate sentencing.[54] Sentencing guidelines could, however, help to increase the public's faith in the system when combined with the abolition of parole, by providing set periods of incarceration that could be reduced only by gain-time. In fact, the experts agreed in part with Judge Nimmons that back-end mechanisms, such as early release programs, the liberal use of gain-time, work credits, and extended work release provided policymakers with the best tools for controlling prison populations.[55]

After eight months of meetings, testimony, and evidence, the task force settled on recommendations designed to: (1) respond to public concern by emphasizing the punitive nature of both incarceration and alternative sanctions; (2) control the prison population though both front-end and back-end solutions; and (3) create a means to predict and manage the need for additional prisons. To gain public support for their proposals, task force members worked to educate the public about the costs of Florida's prison system. Citing the often mentioned figure of $48,000 for one new prison bed, Senator Gerald Rehm (R. Dunedin) argued at a public forum that "the public needs to know that the economics of the prison system are going to break the state."[56] In fact, among the task force's recommendations was a public information campaign to build confidence in the criminal justice system.[57]

The recommendations were codified in the Correctional Reform Act of 1983, which received almost unanimous legislative support.[58] Finding that "state government can no longer afford an uncritical and continuing escalation in capital outlay for prison construction" and that "the effectiveness of incarceration . . . varies among . . . types of offenders and is not conclusively positive," the law put a cap on the incarceration rate of 275 per 100,000 and a goal to reduce the rate to 250 by the end of the decade. The act listed a dozen alternatives to state prison for court dispositions, including drug treatment and community service. In addition, it created a "punitive non-incarcerative sanction" called Community Control, which required closer supervision by probation officers for offenders who would have otherwise gone to prison. The primary reforms, however, were in sentencing and release policy. Similar to the federal government, the legislature abolished parole release, replacing it with a Sentencing Guidelines Commission charged with setting and reviewing guidelines every year.[59] The law specifically required the commission to take "correctional resources" and the "capacities of local and state correctional facilities" into consideration in developing the guidelines. In addition, it gave legislators the final say on changes to the guidelines.[60] Legislators responsible for drafting the 1983 legislation hoped that guidelines would "regulate the type of offenders who require incarceration . . . , reduce their average length of stay . . . [and] foster greater public and professional confidence due to the honesty of the new system."[61]

Yet the task force also understood the "necessary relationship between sentencing and legislatively funded prison capacity," and that guidelines, in and of themselves, would not adequately control judges' decisions—making additional statutory release mechanisms necessary.[62] To accomplish this, the act created a new gain-time schedule that essentially shortened sentences up to 50 percent as follows: basic gain-time (ten days per month served), incentive gain-time (twenty days per month), and meritorious gain-time (one to sixty days total), applied to all offenders sentenced after July 1, 1978, with the exception of those sentenced to mandatory minimums for firearms, drug trafficking, and capital murder.[63] The lynchpin of the 1983 legislative reforms, however, was an *emergency gain-time mechanism* to deal with crisis overcrowding, specifically developed by the *Costello* lawyers through the earlier appointed Governor's Advisory Committee on Corrections. The emergency release law required the Department of Corrections to send a letter to the governor when the prison system population came within two percentage points of system maximum capacity. Once verified by the governor, the law required the secretary of the department to call a state of emergency and to reward additional gain-time of up to thirty days, in five-day increments, to *all* inmates eligible to receive gain-time, until the system stabilized at 97 percent of system maximum capacity.[64]

Finally, the act required the Department of Corrections to develop a ten-year plan for prison siting and construction based on need estimates from a Criminal Justice Estimating Conference—a joint arm of the governor's office, the legislature, and the Department of Corrections. In addition, in response to complaints from Department of Corrections administrators that South Florida counties had not been willing to site prisons, the law stated that "it is desirable that inmates be confined in and released from institutions and facilities as close to their permanent residence or county of commitment as possible" and created a process by which the governor and cabinet could override counties' objections to locating a prison on county land.[65]

The Federal Court Intervenes

When Toby Simon, the prisoners' lawyer in *Costello*, passed away in early 1982, Judge Scott appointed William "Bill" Sheppard to represent the plaintiffs. A self-proclaimed workaholic, Sheppard was in a sense a protégé of Simon and an obvious choice to take on the case. In 1969, Sheppard, a graduate of University of Florida law school, had represented

Black Muslims in the Florida prison system in their suit for access to the Koran, appropriate meals, and a minister.[66] Shortly thereafter he founded the first racially integrated law firm in the state, which pursued housing discrimination, public accommodations, police brutality, and wrongful death cases.[67] Judge Scott appointed Sheppard to his first jail conditions case in 1974; and in 1979 Sheppard worked with the Florida Justice Institute and the National Prison Project to bring a class action suit against Wainwright for "inadequate medical, psychiatric and psychological care" and "grossly overcrowded living conditions" in the sixty-six county jails.[68] He was respected by Simon and Simon's law partner, Sharon Jacobs, who had consulted with Sheppard on the health care and food service agreements in *Costello* the previous year.[69] In fact, Sheppard credits Simon with teaching him "how to out-lawyer" the other party and inspiring him "to do what lawyers should do."[70]

Sheppard approached the case with new energy and less confidence that the state would live up to its promise. As the state's lawyer Bill Sherrill, a former classmate of Sheppard, stated at the time, he knew Shepard was going to "go for the jugular."[71] Sheppard realized that the overcrowding was "beyond the control" of the Department of Corrections, but he hoped that by staying on top of them he would force the state to either fund adequate prison space and health care or reduce the prison population.[72] When he learned that the department was using plywood tents to house prisoners he immediately filed a motion for a hearing to determine if the plywood buildings met constitutional standards.[73] After Judge Scott allowed the tents, Sheppard began closely monitoring the daily population in each facility, the location of the tents, and their safety.[74] As Wainwright also wanted the state to fund adequate capacity, he was not shy about reporting to the court when the system had exceeded maximum capacity.

Thus despite the fact that the prison population had decreased by about 1,200 prisoners with the imposition of the 1983 reforms, by the summer of 1985 on the effective date of the OSA, the department was neither in compliance with the overcrowding nor the health care agreement (which had been approved November 1981).[75] By this time, Judge Scott had passed away and the state showed no sign of finding a permanent solution to the space or health care crisis. In response, Sheppard asked Scott's successor, Judge Susan H. Black, to appoint a special master to enforce the court orders. Not willing to let the state drag its feet any longer and concerned about prisoner deaths due to substandard health care, Judge Black agreed, noting that "timely implementation" by Florida officials "would have avoided protracted litigation, cost and delay in the State's meeting its responsibilities to society."

> When [the first medical report was] filed, the report indicated problems and made recommendations. Time passed, and the defendants claimed compliance. The Court then ordered another survey to remeasure compliance, and the pattern was repeated. The Court is now ready to break the cycle and bring to an end this protracted litigation.[76]

By appointing a special master and a monitor, Judge Black hoped to conclude the case without further delay.[77]

Judge Black appointed Joseph Julin, former dean of the University of Michigan and Florida law schools, who was known as a "superlative negotiator," respected by lawyers and politicians alike.[78] From the bench Judge Black called him a "man of intelligence, ability, integrity, leadership and commitment to public service, and enormous energy and zeal."[79] Thus, Julin's appointment as special master represented a turning point in *Costello*; instead of petitioning the court, Bill Sheppard could now pick up the phone and call Julin when he perceived a lack of effort by the state of Florida. Julin arranged constant prison visits and hearings, requested report after report and threatened the state with the high costs of plaintiffs' demands. Bill Sheppard recalled,

> I think [at that point] everybody took it seriously. They [state officials] had no choice. . . . The special master asked me what I wanted—I said I wanted $35 million put in an account and they can only spend it for medical care. Stuff like that. . . . Julin was appointed . . . to clean this up, and enforce these settlement agreements. By God he did.[80]

Furthermore, the monitor, Bob Cullen, was able to go on site to all the department's institutions to verify the inventory of beds claimed by the department. Again, as recalled by Sheppard,

> You know we were dealing with stuff like, "Okay we have another four hundred beds here at New River." You go to New River and what you got? You got four hundred tents. So, we attacked the tent by getting at the heat. And we got heat experts who said that if you stay in this tent in this weather, your brain will boil . . . So we litigated every bed space.

As a result of this constant attention, Cullen uncovered contract beds in jails that were closed, double bunking in areas not allowed, and a series of units that he would later determine "uninhabitable" and therefore un-countable as "capacity."[81] As these reports came in, Sheppard filed dozens of notices of violations and motions for relief to the court often highlight-ing problems in specific prisons.[82]

Only three months after Julin's and Cullen's appointments in March 1986, Wainwright, in accordance with the state law, sent Governor Gra-ham a letter indicating that the prison population exceeded the 98 per-cent cap. In the middle of a tight campaign to become Florida's next U.S. senator and likely reluctant to tarnish his tough justice record, Gra-ham refused to verify the numbers or allow the state of emergency that would have triggered the release mechanism.[83] Instead, he pushed the leg-islature to increase the cap to 99 percent, provide additional funding for beds in jail facilities, and create a new release program that would allow inmates in minimum custody and good standing to be supervised in the community for the last three months of their sentence.[84] By mid-June, these measures—along with bed spaces in the plywood tents—brought the department below the new 99 percent cap by 144 inmates.[85]

In summary, despite the efforts of the legislature to reduce Florida's prison population, over the course of the Graham administration the prison population increased from 20,000 to just below 30,000. The growth was due in part to the growing state population, but the incarceration rate increased as well, from 212 inmates per 100,000 population in 1979 to 255 in 1986. Yet the department built only eight major facilities and six work camps or work release centers (less than 5,000 beds) during this same time period.[86] Furthermore, in the summer of 1985, it lost 1,367 beds due to the court-mandated closing of two facilities. According to a motion filed by the plaintiffs, inmates housed in these units were simply transferred to already full dormitories creating "wall to wall double bunks."[87] With the appointment of the special master and the monitor, it was clear to all in-volved that something was going to have to change. As the chairman of the Senate Appropriations Subcommittee stated at the time (in reference to the unconstitutional prison health care system), "This is one where the federal courts has a gun pointed at our heads. This is a price tag we don't know what it is yet, but whatever it is, it comes right off the top. We can't begin to deal with any other problems until we've resolved this."[88] Yet by the summer of 1986, the prison population had started to creep back up and the department told legislators that only 1,079 beds would come online in the following year.[89] That same year the crack cocaine frenzy hit and prison admissions jumped once again.

The Drug War Comes to Florida

One of the first targets of President Reagan's War on Drugs was actually South Florida: under the direction of Vice President George Bush, the Presidential Task Force on South Florida began to interdict drugs coming into the state in 1981 and was used as a model for expansion to twelve cities around the country in 1982.[90] By mid-1983, the combined task forces had produced 1,150 federal indictments for drug offenses.[91] In Florida, however, state court prosecutions for drug offenses grew only slightly before 1985. This all changed in the summer of 1986, with the media discovery of crack cocaine and a renewed political attention to fighting drug crime on both the national and state levels.

The practice of smoking freebase cocaine had been popular among Miami's upper class since the early 1980s.[92] Although it was portrayed in the media as potentially harmful, it was thought to be a problem of those with money and one that could be overcome with drug treatment.[93] By the fall of 1985, however, South Florida newspapers began reporting the existence of cocaine rocks, crime sprees caused by coked-out burglars, and freebasing—a method of "injecting [cocaine] into your brain without a needle" that was no longer just for the rich.[94] In fact, the term "crack" did not appear in the lead paragraph of any *Miami Herald* news article until 1986, when Leonard Bias died of a cocaine overdose (figure 4.1). In in the midst of a campaign against Republican Paula Hawkins, the self-styled "general in the War on Drugs" for U.S. Senate, Governor Graham responded by calling for a "crack cocaine action plan."[95] Declaring that "the distribution and usage of 'crack' cocaine . . . has become a major statewide problem," Graham brought together his top policy advisors to develop a series of short-term initiatives.[96] Although Graham's initiatives focused equally on preventing drug use through education and treatment and sanctioning drug use and sales through law enforcement efforts, over the next few years media attention blaming crack for an increase in violence reinforced the perceived need for increased arrests and confinement.[97]

As a result of the new federal and state emphasis on drug enforcement, arrests in Florida for sale and possession of cocaine jumped in 1986 by 30 percent. The focus on cocaine, and specifically crack cocaine, had a

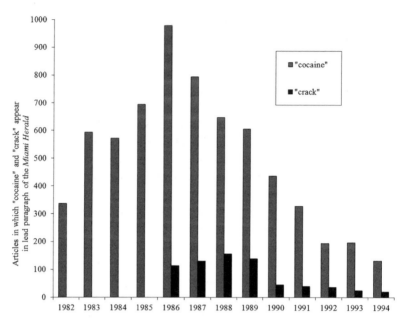

FIGURE 4.1. Media coverage of cocaine, 1982–1994. Source: NewsBank Inc., Access Word News search.

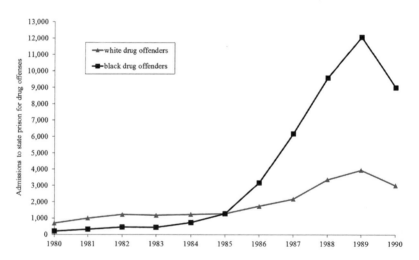

FIGURE 4.2. Prison admissions for drugs by race, 1980–1990. Source: Florida Department of Corrections Annual Reports, 1980–1990.

disproportionate impact on black offenders: arrests of black drug offenders increased by 78 percent and only by 7 percent for white drug offenders. The increased enforcement and prosecution of cocaine offenses led to a jump in prison admissions: from fiscal year 1985/86 to fiscal year 1986/87, prison admissions increased by 7,400 offenders. Almost half of this increase was due to the increase in admissions for drug crimes. The following year, prison admissions increased by another 9,000 offenders. By fiscal year 1989/90, drug offenders made up 36 percent of prison admissions. In that year alone, over 5,000 black defendants received state prison time for *drug possession*. Over three years, the number of black Floridians admitted to prison for drug crimes increased by 850 percent, while admissions for white drug offenders increased by 210 percent (see figure 4.2).

Legal Compliance under Republicans during the War on Drugs, 1987–1991

In November 1986, Florida voters elected a Republican governor for only the second time since 1884. Although only recently switching to the Republican Party, Bob Martinez, the Cuban-American former mayor of Tampa, ran on a platform similar to the national Republican Party and banked on the popularity of President Reagan, who had won 65 percent of Floridians' votes in 1984.[98] While gubernatorial candidates on both sides of the aisle "offered competing promises to get tough on criminals," Martinez's endorsement by President Reagan gave him added credentials for the fight against crime.[99] The shift to a more conservative political climate in Florida and the national preoccupation with crime and drugs changed the course of the state's compliance with *Costello*. Just when the federal court increased its pressure on the state to finally solve prison overcrowding, prison admissions skyrocketed because of the War on Drugs. Yet because Martinez wanted to retain his tough-on-crime reputation, his preferred policy solution was not to reduce the prison population, but to build more prisons. To do this, however, he had to convince legislators to abandon their concerns about the costs of prisons and the goals of the Correctional Reform Act they had passed just four years prior. Four factors contributed to Martinez's eventual success. First, the prior institutionalization of the Overcrowding Settlement Agreement in an emergency release mechanism led to the common (but mistaken) understanding—perpetuated by both the media and legislators—that the court order *required the state to release inmates* if it didn't have enough prison space. Second, as was the case nationally, racialized media coverage of drugs and crime increased, but in Florida, the media *linked crime to inmates who had been released early* because of the emergency release law. Together, these factors helped Martinez strategically redefine the prison crisis from a problem of the high cost of prisons to a problem of court-ordered prisoner releases. Third, because of policy changes and advocacy by the Department of Corrections, rural county officials in North Florida began to think of prison building as economic development. And Fourth, Dukakis's loss reinforced Democrats' desire to look tough on crime after a recently released African American convicted felon killed two Florida law enforcement officers. As a result, most legislators recalculated the political risks of building prisons and reinterpreted building prisons as their "only" option, voting to embark on the largest expansion of the state's prison capacity to date.

The Republican Response to Prison Overcrowding

The increased drug arrests and admissions to prison drastically exacerbated the existing prison overcrowding crisis. The newly appointed secretary of corrections, Richard Dugger, a career prison warden, recalls that in 1987 he "inherited the inevitability of having to release inmates" from Wainwright.[100] Dugger discovered that the department had already gone over budget due to the continuing unprecedented number of prison admissions. Warning Governor Martinez that he did not have enough operating revenue to finish out the fiscal year and that the prison population would soon be above 99 percent capacity again, Dugger suggested that the 1983 emergency release law be revised to exclude more inmates from compulsory release. Martinez acted quickly, calling a special legislative session on February 4, 1987, to consider "appropriating the funds necessary . . . in response to the unexpected increase in the inmate population . . . [and] authorizing [the department] to grant a limited amount of administrative gain-time to a restricted class of inmates based on the nature of [their] offenses . . . in order to maintain the inmate population . . . at or below legal capacity."[101] In his memo to lawmakers justifying the session, Martinez stated that Judge Black was "rapidly losing patience" and that the plywood tents ordered by Governor Graham were becoming "increasingly unacceptable" with the district court.[102]

The governor's final proposal, adopted by the legislature in only one day, called for $25.6 million in operating funds for FDOC, $6.5 million for temporary and new beds, and a new administrative gain-time mechanism triggered by the governor's acknowledgment of the secretary's certification that the prison population had reached 98 percent of capacity.[103] Instead of *requiring* the FDOC to credit *all* inmates with five-day increments of gain-time, the new law *allowed* the FDOC to grant up to sixty days of administrative gain-time to all inmates with positive work evaluations, program participation, and/or behavior adjustment, except those serving mandatory minimum terms for drug crimes, firearm possession, and capital offenses. Sex offenders who had not received treatment and those sentenced as habitual offenders were also ineligible.[104]

Redefining the Prison Crisis

Administrative gain-time and the new beds—including contracted jail beds, tent beds, and beds in converted industry buildings—brought the department into temporary compliance. The question remained, however, as to a permanent solution to overcrowding. Although in favor of some alternatives to incarceration, Governor Martinez adopted the position of the Department of Corrections that building capacity was the best way to finally comply with the *Costello* lawsuit. As Secretary Dugger stated at the time, prison admissions had gone up to such an extent that "it's difficult to conceive that we're going to build one institution too many."[105] The difficulty, rather, lay in convincing a fiscally conservative legislature, who perceived that their constituents opposed funding prisons, to spend millions of dollars on prison construction and operation.[106] As Lieutenant Governor Bobby Brantley, who headed the administration's effort to persuade the legislature, explained,

> It is a hard thing [funding prisons] because . . . you've got educational needs and [constituents] don't want to . . . spend all this money on prisoners, because the public, they'll tell you real quick, "Oh yeah, do what Governor Graham did, put 'em in tents." I mean they'd bury 'em all if it was up to the public. But, yeah, we had to do it . . . there's just not a whole lot more than anybody's been able to come up with . . . other than lock 'em up.[107]

Brantley's task was aided by the emergence of a common understanding of *Costello* that "under the terms of the federal court order, inmates must be released early when a population cap is reached."[108] As the Department of Corrections began to rely upon the release mechanism to control the population, newspaper articles quoted judges, prosecutors, and defense attorneys worried about offenders returning to the community faster than expected. Rightly or wrongly, the media blamed the early release mechanisms passed by the legislature, who then blamed the federal courts. For instance, the *St. Petersburg Times* quoted one North Florida Democratic lawmaker who said, "I don't like letting them out on administrative gain-time at all, but we've got to go by the federal guidelines until we build enough prisons to hold them."[109] While this understanding conflated the legislative emergency release mechanism with the court order to end overcrowding (which allowed reducing the prison population through any means), the Martinez administration used it as a strategy to gain legislative approval for prison construction. In effect, they used the threat of early releases to persuade legislators to fund prisons. The governor's office even sent state legislators (and local officials) lists of offenders from their districts who would be released if the state didn't build more prisons. Lieutenant Governor Brantley later recalled, "I mean we actually did this: 'here's a list of the people that are . . . going to be appearing in the neighborhood near you' . . . and yeah, it just wasn't a good prospect to not [build prisons]."[110]

Of course, the legislature did have other options, but none were as radical or as guaranteed to end the overcrowding. Some South Florida Democrats initially argued, for example, that Florida relied too heavily on incarceration and that the proposed budget lacked resources for programs such as drug treatment.[111] Randy Berg of the Florida Justice Institute, a public law firm in Miami and a supporter of the *Costello* litigation, spent considerable energy arguing that taxpayers should not build more prisons as "Florida is already hard on crime" and "prison does not reduce future criminal behavior of non-violent offenders." He cited alternatives already in use (but not to their full extent) such as probation, restitution, community control, community service, and work release.[112] This argument, however, didn't convince many legislators, because "if somebody gets killed because you don't have a [prison] bed . . . [or] the Federal Court tells you to release [a criminal offender] and they kill someone the next night, that's not very good."[113]

In fact, this is exactly what happened. Despite new restrictions on potential releasees, in the winter of 1988 a repeat offender named Charlie Street, who had only served half of his prison sentence, killed two Miami police officers. Calling the incident "Florida's Willie Horton," the *Miami Herald* wrote in the tone typical of the day:

> Numbness is the first reaction to the murders of Metro Police Officers Rich-
> ard Boles and David Strzalkowski. Then, as the story unfolds, the shock gives
> way to rage. Screaming rage. Rage that cracks the veneer of civilization from
> one end of urban South Florida to the other. How could these two fine, dedi-
> cated police officers be dead, allegedly at the hands of a career criminal, an
> attempted murderer just 10 days out of state prison . . . ?[114]

Although the media most directly blamed Governor Martinez, legislators
felt the need to express their outrage by vowing to "build more prisons
to make room for more criminals."[115] The Charlie Street incident thus solidified legislators' understanding of the problem not as too many people
in prison, but as the risk of too many people being released from prison
because of the court order.

Quick Construction and Prisons as Economic Development

Once legislators reinterpreted the problem, a few practical issues still
needed to be addressed. Namely, where to put the new prisons, how to
build them at the lowest cost to the state, and how to construct them
quickly enough to accommodate the incoming population. To address the
first problem Secretary Dugger discontinued the state's previous policy,
which emphasized building facilities in the regions where most prisoners
came from—South Florida. Recalling conversations with Martinez from
that time, Dugger asserted, "My Governor doesn't care [where prisons get
built], all we want to know is that we are going to build them wherever we
can and wherever it is the cheapest."[116] To find the cheapest land, the department put advertisements in North Florida local newspapers and developed brochures advertising the safety and economic benefit of prisons
for the community, including jobs and a multiplier effect of employees'
salaries (see figure 4.3). In addition, the department advertised inmate
work crews, which, according to Representative Al Lawson (D. Tallahassee), turned out to be a good selling point:

> A lot of things in the county that they had to pay for, they no longer had to
> pay for anymore. . . . [In] Liberty and Calhoun [Counties] I could take you to
> numerous projects that were [built by prisoners]. [County officials] were able
> then to see prisoners in South Florida that had electronic skills, computer skills,
> electrical engineers, and so forth and move them into these prison facilities so
> they could benefit the community.[117]

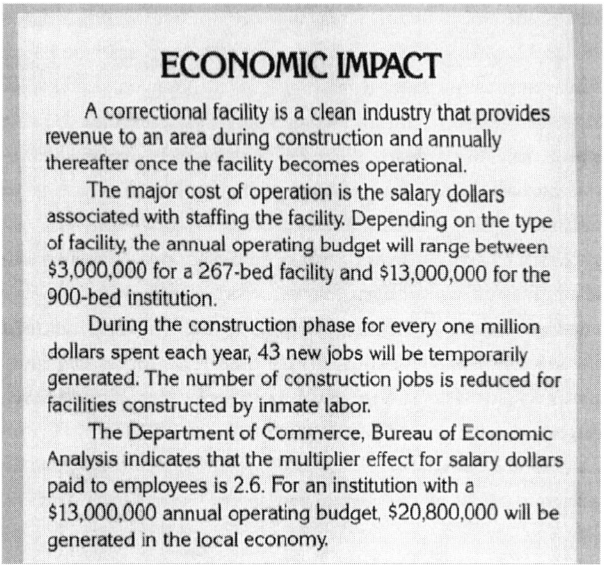

ECONOMIC IMPACT

A correctional facility is a clean industry that provides revenue to an area during construction and annually thereafter once the facility becomes operational.

The major cost of operation is the salary dollars associated with staffing the facility. Depending on the type of facility, the annual operating budget will range between $3,000,000 for a 267-bed facility and $13,000,000 for the 900-bed institution.

During the construction phase for every one million dollars spent each year, 43 new jobs will be temporarily generated. The number of construction jobs is reduced for facilities constructed by inmate labor.

The Department of Commerce, Bureau of Economic Analysis indicates that the multiplier effect for salary dollars paid to employees is 2.6. For an institution with a $13,000,000 annual operating budget, $20,800,000 will be generated in the local economy.

FIGURE 4.3. Florida prison siting brochure, 1990. Source: Florida Department of Corrections, "Siting of New Correctional Facilities" 1990, Courtesy of the State Archives of Florida.

Legislators and county officials, faced with struggling rural economies, quickly became enamored by the economic potential of prisons. For many state legislators, the rationale for building a prison in their district was simple:

> Well, we needed a prison and I figured if it was going to be somewhere we ought to get some advantage out of it. . . . [It] was always recognized [as] a good clean industry, no smokestacks, employed a lot of people. [Later] the chamber [of commerce] saw it as economic development.[118]

For others, especially black legislators in North Florida, it was a more challenging decision. Then-Representative Lawson, one of the nine new black representatives elected in 1981, explains that the commissioners from several different counties asked him how to obtain a prison. Yet it was a very difficult issue for him because part of his district was heavily African American:

> They [his black constituents] really didn't like the fact that Florida was going to have a mass building prison program. . . . It was a difficult task because, on one

hand, I had people here that really wanted these facilities and then on the other hand, we have people saying we don't need this . . . dominating our budget.[119]

In the end, many North and Central Florida legislators lobbied the department to put prisons in their districts. "It became a bidding war," with the department choosing to put prisons in the community that gave it the most incentives (free land, infrastructure, etc.).[120] Representative Robert Trammell (D. Marianna) recalled of his North Florida colleagues,

> We had a lot of influence back then on what happened ultimately in the legislative process. And it was historical thing . . . So that's kind of . . . intertwined with this . . . prison situation. We were able to fill up our counties with them as much as we wanted because we had that influence on the total process.[121]

As Secretary Dugger complained, "They put me in the middle sometimes trying to choose you or you. [But] actually we needed all of them, [I told them] 'just be patient, we will get to you too.' "[122]

In addition to finding prison sites, Secretary Dugger took responsibility for "building prisons in the quickest, least expensive way possible."[123] To accomplish this, the department abandoned ongoing efforts to expand smaller community-based institutions and instead used in-house architects and engineers to develop two simple eight to nine hundred–bed prototype prisons: one a single-cell institution that would be built by contract labor and the second a "quick construction" dormitory-style institution that could be built almost entirely with inmate and staff labor.[124] The quick construction facilities included six to seven dormitories, a mess hall, a confinement building, and an academic/vocational building. The dormitories were designed in two seventy-bed pods with a control room in the middle, two day rooms, and two sets of showers/bathrooms (see figure 4.4). Instead of a wall surrounding the prison, inmates installed high fences with razor ribbon. Even the guard tower in the center of the facility was designed and built in-house.

Doubling the Prison Capacity

Governor Martinez's successful reframing of the prison crisis and the Department of Corrections' advertising strategy led Republicans and North Florida Democrats to reassess their previous opposition to building prisons. Yet even relatively liberal Democrats, such as John Mills, the speaker

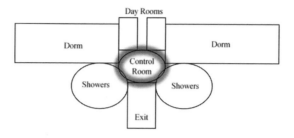

FIGURE 4.4. Layout of prototype prison dormitory. Source: Field notes March 22, 2007.

of the House from Gainesville, believed the urgency of the moment ne-
cessitated building more prisons:

> I think there was some looking ahead, but it was more viewed as this is what
> we have to do and *there really are no other options* and trying to work with the
> department and work with the governor and others to meet what was a situa-
> tion that had backed up.[125]

As a result, between 1987 and 1991 Florida embarked on what would later
be called "an aggressive prison construction program": the legislature appropriated 27,087 prison bed spaces or the equivalent of twenty-seven
new prisons—six times what had been appropriated in the previous five
years.[126]

The legislature's willingness to forgo its earlier commitment to hold
down corrections spending is highlighted by its concurrent passage of new
mandatory penalties and restrictions on gain-time for certain offenders.[127]
In 1988, after the Charlie Street incident, the legislature unanimously
passed a new "habitual offender" law, created new mandatory minimum
sentences for offenders with two prior violent felonies, and made them
ineligible for gain-time. In addition, the law allowed judges to sentence
offenders who had formerly required a nonprison sanction under the new
sentencing guidelines to prison for up to twenty-two months.[128] The Sentencing Guidelines Commission, still under orders to take prison capacity
into account, responded by essentially throwing up their hands. Writing
in their 1989 report that they were troubled by "the mixed signals arising
from 1988 legislation regarding the statewide sentencing guidelines," they
noted that "before a revised guidelines format can effectively divert nonviolent and non-serious offenders, policy determinations must be made

as to the type of offender to be considered for diversion and the types of alternative sanctions to be utilized."[129]

Despite the commitment to building new prisons quickly, soaring prison admissions led the Department of Corrections to continue to rely on a modified emergency release mechanism in order to comply with *Costello*. In 1988, the legislature replaced administrative gain-time with "provisional credits," which allowed for up to ninety days to be subtracted from the sentence of eligible inmates when the prison population reached 97.5 percent of capacity. It became so common it was referred to as "computer release."[130] Combined with the generous gain-time schedule enacted in 1983, average time served decreased to less than 35 percent of court-imposed sentences.[131] By the end of the decade, overcrowded prisons in Florida had gained national attention, with the *New York Times* reporting in the summer of 1989 that for every prisoner the Florida Department of Corrections accepted, it had to release one.[132] Importantly (for the long term), the legislature built new prisons without generating any new sources of revenue: Governor Martinez worked to pass a new tax on services, but after a media and lobbying campaign by the Association of National Advertisers, the legislature repealed the tax, opting for an increase in the sales tax instead.[133]

The Final Settlement

The efforts by the Department of Corrections and newly elected Democratic governor Lawton Chiles finally brought the state into compliance. In May 1991, the parties to *Costello* entered into an agreement with the governor and the state legislature to resolve the case. The first part of the agreement concerned the stability, independence, and power of a newly created medical oversight agency, the Correctional Medical Authority (CMA). Developed by Special Master Dean Julin and passed by the legislature in 1986, the CMA was an independent agency funded by the state designed to replace the court in its role as monitor. The second part of the agreement required that the legislature enact a law requiring that the prison system population remain below design capacity plus one-third.[134] The parties then asked the special master to draft a report and recommendation based on the agreement that would provide a framework for case dismissal.[135] The special master's report, issued in October 1992, found that actions prior to Dugger's appointment as secretary in 1987 "would support a finding of failure of compliance." Since then, however, Dugger's actions supported a "conclusion of a good faith effort to comply."

These actions include not only removal from bed inventory of questionable actual housing units and of certain jail and other beds which did not exist but also the promulgation . . . of criteria by which the Department will determine bed capacity.[136]

The report further noted that the compliance had been "maintained long enough" that future noncompliance was unlikely. Finally, it found that the governor and legislature had fulfilled the commitments of the May 1991 agreement. As a result, Julin recommended that the court vacate all previous orders, terminate the responsibilities of the special master, the monitor, and plaintiffs' counsel, and declare the case closed.

As the case had now spanned twenty years, the final case settlement was welcomed by Judge Black, the department, the state, and even the plaintiffs.[137] Although Bill Sheppard found closure a hard judgment call, he reasoned that he had gotten more from the deal with the state than he would have from a court ruling:

> I didn't have faith in the system. [But] I love Lawton Chiles and [Lieutenant Governor] Buddy Mackay. I had a great deal of admiration for them. I guess I thought that maybe the system would work. And that the statutes that were passed would be in place for some time . . . I was satisfied that we had done everything that we could. When they said, we will put it in the statute, I said, fine, put it in the statute and when you get it done come back and talk to me, and they did that. I guess I was more hopeful that it would last.[138]

From the state's perspective, the court orders had "micromanaged the operation of the prisons," and proving compliance (especially with the health care standards) had been time-consuming and difficult.[139] According to the lead attorney for the state litigation team, who took over the case in 1989, "when I took over as counsel of the litigation team, my instructions were to terminate the case. To do everything in my power to terminate the case. And we did that."[140]

On March 30, 1993, after hearing direct assurances from Lieutenant Governor MacKay and the new secretary of corrections that the state remained committed to an independent Correctional Medical Authority and a prison population below 133 percent of capacity, Judge Black issued her opinion and order granting final judgment in *Costello*.[141] While legislators and newspapers around the state hailed the decision, many Floridians still resented the court's "interference" in state affairs. One citizen wrote to the *St. Petersburg Times* after reading an article praising improvements in Florida's prisons:

> Costello's lawyer or lawyers, various federal judges and their law clerks, and the ACLU interfered with and changed Florida's prison system at great expense to the taxpayers of Florida . . . In other words, the subsidized legal community brought about the unwanted and unwelcomed change, and the overtaxed and crime-vulnerable citizen paid an enormous monetary and social price.[142]

Reacting to this public sentiment, in the summer of 1993 two Republican Florida congressmen, Charles Canady (12th District) and Bill McCollum (8th District), with the support of their respective county sheriffs, introduced the Prison Litigation Relief Act, which aimed to "limit judicial interference in the management of the nation's prisons and jails." Congress eventually adopted their ideas, along with proposed provisions introduced by Arizona senator John Kyle, in the Prison Litigation Reform Act of 1995, which drastically reduced the number of federal claims filed by prisoners and prevented new legitimate claims from being heard.[143]

Building Prison Capacity in the 1980s

Across the country, state imprisonment rates more than doubled over the 1980s. The story of Florida prison policy during this decade demonstrates how federalism, proceduralism, and partisan politics intervened in the racial project to challenge punishment practices, ultimately leading to policymakers' decision to dramatically expand carceral capacity. As I demonstrated in chapter 3, prison conditions litigation grew out of the civil rights movement and the project for racial equality. Civil rights lawyers expected prison litigation to improve prison conditions while at the same time challenge the utility of imprisonment. And in fact, legislators in the early 1980s attempted to comply with the court order by limiting admissions to prison and lowering the incarceration rate. Yet the nexus of Reagan's focus on crime and drugs and state partisan politics profoundly changed the direction of state-level prison policy. When prison admissions began to soar because of the War on Drugs, judicial supervision forced legislators to make a choice, just as Toby Simon had hoped it would, but at a rather unfortunate time. Influenced by the law-and-order politics and ideology of the Reagan coalition, insurgent Republicans in places like

Florida, Arizona, and Texas abandoned their fiscal conservatism and led the charge for more prisons.[144]

Importantly, the historical details of this period demonstrate that this shift took *political work* that relied on the racialized fear of crime and drugs. In order to overcome legislators' reservations about prison costs, appropriate prison sites, and their rehabilitative limitations, Governor Martinez used the threat of early releases to change legislators' understandings of the political costs of *not* building prisons. In his recollection of the 1980s, Dave Bachman, the former Florida Department of Corrections assistant secretary, captures how legal intervention on the side of prisoners ultimately helped Martinez and the FDOC change legislators' willingness to expand prison capacity:

> [The Overcrowding Settlement Agreement] helped us tremendously, because we finally had some standards. We wanted that. . . . So we developed through that, housing standards—maximum capacity beyond which we wouldn't be able to go without violating the *Costello* agreement. That then gave us the hammer we needed to go to the legislature and say "Look, we are within two percentage points of being in contempt of court, we got to build more beds, or we are going to have to trigger this release mechanism," and nobody wanted to do that, so they said "We'll give you money for more beds."[145]

To sweeten the deal, Governor Martinez's administration promoted prisons in rural North Florida counties as economic development, which, as Ruth Gilmore argues in the case of California, provided a "prison fix" to the restructuring of rural economies.[146]

While the specifics of the above narrative are unique to Florida, they reveal some of the mechanisms by which federalism and the federalization of crime control policy contributed to the growth of carceral capacity across states. First, federal crime control policy, in this case the War on Drugs, created new problems for states that they might not have otherwise faced. While the forces behind police and prosecutors' choices during the early War on Drugs have not been studied, it is unlikely that drug arrests and prosecutions would have increased as much or as quickly as they did without the national uproar over crack and federal incentives for drug arrests. Since the criminal justice system is interconnected, more arrests and prosecutions led to more admissions to prison.[147] The timing of the War on Drugs thus created particular difficulties, as prisons across the country were already overcrowded. Second, federal discourse and politics limit the "thinkable" solutions to state problems. Given both the discursive link between drug use and crime and Governor Dukakis's political vulnerability because of just one released offender, releasing even nonviolent drug offenders turned into a potentially significant political liability. As will become increasingly important in the 1990s, the political liability of being "soft-on-crime" was in part due to a racialized notion that the state could not be trusted to protect the (white) public because it was too concerned about ensuring fair treatment of minority groups. While legislators in some states, such as California, had already committed to building prisons, the new politics of crime was enough to convince legislators in more fiscally conservative states to change their tune.

In addition, the story of prison conditions litigation in Florida highlights how proceduralism and the focus on freedom from coercion encouraged or, at the very least, did little to prevent the expansion of carceral capacity (especially as the federal courts became more conservative). Many socio-legal scholars argue that the legal liberal focus on procedural legal protections and process severely limit the impact of civil rights law.[148] In *Costello v. Wainwright* the court found that Florida prisoners had a right to be free from immediate physical violence brought about by overcrowding and inadequate medical attention. Yet when legislators changed their plan for compliance, this negative rights framing of the problem gave the court and prisoners' lawyers zero traction to insist that they reduce rather than expand the use of imprisonment. As at the onset of the case, the court was mainly concerned with the unnecessary loss of life inside a state prison, not the dignity of prisoners or the appropriateness of their sentences to prison.

Despite the structural constraints placed on legislators by federalism and proceduralism, the story of Florida during this period also highlights policymakers' ability to make different choices. For example, in the early 1980s all three task forces/committees acknowledged the punitive sentiments of the public. Yet members felt that the interests of the state would be better served by stabilizing prison growth and costs while attempting to pacify public punitiveness. They even sought to educate the public about the fiscal costs and trade-offs inherent in prison spending. While violent crime rates did increase between 1983 and 1988, violent crime rates had been increasing and high since the late 1970s. Yet legislators in the early 1980s were willing to go against perceived public demand and limit punitive policies.[149]

Similarly, prison overcrowding crises in the early 1980s were not particularly racialized. In their attempts to rein in prison spending, lawmakers in the early 1980s did not blame racial "others." Yet it is not as though

Floridians did not connect race and crime in the early 1980s. The deadliest riots since 1968 occurred in May 1980 in Liberty City, an African American section of Miami, after an all-white jury acquitted four white police officers for the deadly beating of a black motorist.[150] That same year over 125,000 Cubans arrived in Florida during the Mariel boatlift, including prison inmates and mental hospital patients.[151] The historical record suggests that state officials could have blamed Cuban and other immigrant criminals for taking up space in the prison system. In fact, in years past Florida officials frequently blamed the crime problem on non-Floridian migrants. Yet instead of tapping into racialized populist sentiment, in his 1980 address to the legislature Governor Graham cautioned that "we in the various state legislatures around the country did *a lot of talking* . . . about states' rights. But in the decade of the eighties we have to realize that states *also have responsibilities*" (emphasis added).[152] For new Florida Democrats these responsibilities included stewardship of public education, transportation, the environment, and a probusiness climate.

Finally, it is worth noting that the decline in the rehabilitative ideal played a negligible role in legislators' embrace of prisons. In Florida, the advent of punishment as a purpose for prison—giving a secondary role to rehabilitation—coincided with attempts *to reduce* the prison population. The change in thinking about rehabilitation was not, at least initially, that all criminal offenders were beyond redemption, but that "rehabilitation, as a focus for corrections" was logistically problematic.[153] The doubts about rehabilitation produced a more nuanced and ambiguous official rhetoric: rehabilitation could no longer be the official purpose of punishment but it was certainly appropriate for the correctional system to rehabilitate some offenders.[154] What worked, according to the rhetoric of the time, was certainty in punishment. Prison sentences should be short and certain, and be served in prisons that treated and housed inmates humanely. Under this philosophy, long incapacitative sentences should be reserved for those "who through repeated criminal activity, or through a single extremely serious act indicate they need to be kept from society for the benefit of both themselves and the public at large."[155]

Taken together, the above suggests that lawmakers' pivot on crime control in the late 1980s should be understood as an explicit response to changing partisan circumstances. Firmly in control of the statehouse and the legislature in the early 1980s, Democrats had no reason to emphasize crime or or to alienate black voters. Nor did the Republican minority, which also supported the 1983 reforms as fiscally responsible. Yet as national politicians and the media increasingly drew attention to crime and drugs, state-level Republicans hitched themselves onto Reagan's coattails by making crime and drugs a key part of their platform. The tactic was self-reinforcing: it generated public support for punitive policies, which was no doubt in part because it activated both implicit and explicit racial resentments and stereotypes. Democrats' choice to respond by emphasizing punitive solutions also constituted a partisan move to hold on to their position as Republicans gained ground.

In some sense the story of Florida in the 1980s is a perfect storm—a storm that could conceivably pass. But in this case, because of politicians' response, the storm left behind not only destruction (in the lives affected by drugs and prison), but also new policy and state capacity. Some of this capacity undoubtedly benefited state prisoners. Hanging on Bill Sheppard's office in 2007 was a letter from Michael Costello thanking him for bringing about vast improvements to life behind bars. Yet the storm also left in its wake a liberal gain-time policy, a statutory emergency release mechanism, twenty-seven new prisons, and new resources to fight the War on Drugs. Perhaps most importantly, it left a successful political strategy: promise to get tough on crime while attacking your opponent for letting criminals go free. When the storm blew over, as storms do, the new laws, capacity, and political strategies created feedback effects that, as I detail in the next chapter, created the carceral ethos that would guide us into the twenty-first century.

CHAPTER FIVE

The Politics of Early Release, 1991–1995

We need to be sure we are not brining minor offenders in the front door of our prisons and letting dangerous career criminals out the back.—Representative Willie Logan (Democrat, Opa-locka [Miami-Dade County]), 1991[1]

The immediate concern is to get these people off the streets now. I don't care if we build 3 million jail cells. We've got to solve the [crime] problem.—Neal Alper, vice president, Kendall Federation of Homeowners Associations [Miami-Dade County], 1993[2]

In 1992, the country elected a Democrat to the White House for only the second time since the 1960s. Two years later, Republicans took control of the Senate and House for the first time since 1953. The change in party control was not a blip; it represented a long-term shift in partisan loyalties and the ongoing transfer of political power from the north to the Sunbelt.[3] At the state level, Republicans contested once solidly Democratic Southern legislatures. Yet, what these changes would mean for prison growth was unclear. In 1990, the country was in a recession and fiscal conservatism was still a powerful political force. And at least some commentators were concerned about the states' buildup of prisons in the previous decade. Two prominent criminologists, James Austin and John Irwin, published a series of pamphlets called "It's about Time," detailing the costs and problems of "America's Imprisonment Binge." The pamphlets noted that the majority of sentences to prison were for nonviolent crimes, and they urged lawmakers to reconsider their use of incarceration.[4]

In Florida, lawmakers in the early 1990s were finally in a position to resolve the federal lawsuit on overcrowding and medical care in the prisons that had hung over the state for twenty years. The legislature had committed substantial new resources to prisons, enacted a release valve to guard against future overcrowding, and established an independent board responsible for overseeing prison health care. Early in 1993 the court agreed that Florida had met its obligations under the *Costello v. Wainwright* consent decree. The resolution of the *Costello* case should have, in theory, relieved some pressure on the state, allowing legislators, corrections administrators, and the public to take stock of the last dozen years and decide where to go from there. The decline of media and political attention to the War on Drugs also created an opportunity for legislators to move away from the excesses of the late 1980s and readopt an approach that reserved prison for violent offenders. Finally, legislators had a potential moral imperative to do so as the racial disparity created by the War on Drugs became increasingly clear.

In February 1990, the Sentencing Project released a study that found that one in four African American males age twenty to twenty-nine were either in prison, on probation, or on parole (compared to just 6 percent of white males the same age).[5] The report, publicized in *Time Magazine*, *USA Today*, and *U.S. News and World Report*, prompted Florida's and other states' officials to look into the racial disparities in their own criminal justice systems. One study found that 19 percent of black males between the ages of eighteen and thirty-four in Florida were in the custody of the state or county criminal justice system—more than double the number enrolled in college or university.[6] A year later, a commission convened by the first African American chief justice of the Florida Supreme Court recommended that the legislature repeal mandatory minimum and habitual offender laws after finding that the courts disproportionately applied them to African American offenders.[7]

As a consequence of these developments, the early 1990s marks a clear point when policymakers could have steered away from further investments in the carceral state. This chapter addresses why they didn't. An easy answer is high crime rates. Although property crime began declining in 1989, violent crime rates remained at relatively high levels throughout this period and had been increasing drastically since the early 1980s—especially in large urban areas, such as Miami, Tampa, and Ft. Lauderdale. However, given the expense of prisons, the economic recession, and the fiscal conservatism that dominated state politics, it is not evident why legislators would choose more prisons as a form of crime control.

A better, but more complex, explanation hinges on the feedback effects of earlier policy choices within an increasingly partisan political context. The policy choices to build prisons, release offenders before the expiration of their sentences, and undermine sentencing reform with new mandatory minimums created a new problem for legislators. In the early 1990s, released prisoners served only one-third of their original prison sentences. How this problem was defined (and its potential solutions), however, depended on the meanings, capacities, and interests created by prior policy. In particular, the early release policy and previous investments in prisons created a political opportunity for a new coalition of law enforcement and victims' rights groups to define the problem as "a lack of prisons" by arguing—again largely through the news media—that the state was protecting *criminals' rights* at the expense of *crime victims' right* to more prison space for criminal offenders. Given the growing black presence in prisons and the media attention to (primarily) white victims, the argument that pitted victims versus offenders was necessarily racialized. It was also a racialized notion of victims' rights. Despite the fact that black Floridians were overrepresented as crime victims, their voices were not part of the victims' rights movement in Florida. In fact, as noted below, black residents of high-crime areas had a different notion of rights—one that was not contrary to offenders' rights, but that would address the needs of the whole community. Yet the link between crime and early releases presented by the media provided law enforcement a privileged platform to advocate their preferred solution—more prisons to keep prisoners in prison for longer.

A counterframing of the problem, backed by many state-sponsored studies in the early 1990s, was that the admission of (disproportionately black) *nonviolent* criminals to the prison system and restrictions on early release for drug offenders forced the early release of *violent* offenders. However, this counterclaim to the need for more prisons, along with arguments highlighting the cost of prisons, faltered in new political context. First, demographic shifts in the state and a conservative shift of the electorate nationally gave Republicans a chance to compete for control of the state legislature for the first time since Reconstruction.[8] Accordingly, a new generation of Republican challengers emerged who appropriated crime victims' moral appeal to gain political advantage, arguing that Democrats' prison policies had sacrificed public safety and the rights of law-abiding citizens. Second, Democrats moved to the right and away from traditional liberal solutions to crime and the project for racial equality. In its place a racial project for racial representation emerged that, along with structural political inequities, could not address the criminalization of the drug problem and its impact on poor black communities. The new political context weakened Democrats' commitment to achieving alternatives to prison and compelled legislators and Democratic governor Lawton Chiles to support law enforcement's "lock 'em up" solution to the crime problem.

Importantly, policymakers' eventual embrace of prisons was predicated on their past investment in prison capacity. Legislators learned that they would not be punished in the polls for state spending on prisons, making each further investment in prisons seem less monumental than the last (and less of a political risk). In addition, the prior establishment of a Criminal Justice Estimating Conference created a mechanism for estimating needed prison beds given current flows into the system and policy goals, such as ending gain-time for prisoners. As a result, although some legislators initially tried to tweak the sentencing structure, lawmakers eventually redoubled their investments in prisons by retracting funding for education and health care—solidifying the grip of the carceral state for years ahead.

The story of Florida in this period helps to explain the political development of key aspects of the carceral ethos pointed out by prior scholarship. David Garland, for example, notes that the fear of crime rather than the objective reality of criminal victimization has "come to be regarded as a problem in and of itself."[9] Jonathan Simon characterizes penal policy in this era as a "zero-sum game in which any gain for prisoners or criminals is experienced as a loss for law enforcement and victims."[10] Zimring, Hawkins, and Kamin assert that policymakers increasingly viewed public sentiment on crime as the appropriate basis for penal policy.[11] The story of Florida in this period demonstrates how the news media and law enforcement advocates *constructed and disseminated* these meanings out of the legacy of the court intervention in penal policy and past policy choices. Joshua Page similarly finds that the California Correctional Peace Officers Association (CCPOA) essentially created and funded two victims' rights organizations to help secure support for their legislative priorities. Often through their representation in the media, the "CCPOA-allied victims' groups . . . provided a sympathetic face" to the association's campaigns for punitive penal policies.[12]

My analysis further highlights the news media's ability to set the political agenda by calling attention to particular issues and choosing which sources to cite. Katherine Beckett demonstrates how journalists' tendency to use official state sources for their stories helped produce a law and order framing of the drug problem in the 1980s (as opposed to a framing based on public health or lack of resources).[13] In turn, media framing

shapes what solutions constituents want to see from political representatives. In the early 1990s, Florida newspapers devoted significant space to
the problem of early releases. Yet, as Page finds in California, the mainstream news media in Florida gave voice to nascent white victims' rights
groups and their law enforcement supporters who advocated for more
prisons without looking for or presenting a countersolution. The victims'
rights framing went beyond crime per se, to connect antistate and anti–
federal intervention sentiments to "the fear that government authorities
will serve the interests of criminals" over law-abiding citizens.[14] Politicians
both implicitly and explicitly reinforced this framing by juxtaposing their
commitment to build prisons with their pledges to protect ordinary people against an overreaching government. By doing so, Florida lawmakers refashioned the thinly veiled racist arguments of Nixon, Reagan, and
others that state protection and support for black Americans came at the
expense of the well-being of white Americans.

I begin the chapter by describing the national political context in which
state politicians made decisions in the early 1990s. Of particular importance for the Democrats in charge in Tallahassee was the party's move
to distance itself from issues of concern to African American voters and
fashion a new tough-on-crime image. This section also covers the debate
within traditional civil rights organizations about the direction of the
civil rights movement—highlighting the emergence of the racial project
of racial representation. In the second section, I introduce the problem
of early releases, detailing the early media coverage and initial attempts
by Democrats, and in particular black Democrats, to revise sentencing
practices to stem the flow of drug offenders into prison. I then detail law
enforcement's efforts to organize victims in order to frame the problem of
early releases as a lack of prison space. In the third section I discuss how
the politics of early release prompted Governor Lawton Chiles to reverse
course on building more prisons. I also argue that Governor Chiles inadvertently exacerbated the politics of early release in his attempt to secure support for additional revenue streams for new prisons. In the fourth
section I discuss how black mobilization—primarily at the local level in
high-crime communities—could not counteract law enforcement's framing of the problem. This section highlights the racialized and gendered
framing of victim's rights. In the fifth section, I demonstrate how partisan
competition in 1994 and 1995 pushed Republicans and Democrats toward
a new political consensus on the need for more prisons, such that they
built thirty-eight new prison facilities in the space of a few years—even

as crime rates began to decline. In the final section I summarize my argument that the years between 1991 and 1995 mark a crucial turning point in the development of the carceral ethos and the carceral state in Florida.

Democratic Politics and Remaking the Project for Racial Equality

Florida policymakers' decisions in the early 1990s can be understood only in light of the emergence of rightward-leaning New Democrats, the Democratic Party's retreat from liberal Democratic policy solutions, and intensified partisan competition (at both the state and national level).[15] Epitomizing the New Democrats was former Arkansas governor Bill Clinton, whose presidential campaign, and subsequent victory, marked a shift for Democratic politics. Demographic changes continued to shift political power to the Sunbelt—by 1990 Sunbelt states represented 303 of 538 electoral votes, an increase of 30 from 1980.[16] In order to regain the votes of white working- and middle-class voters and challenge President George H. W. Bush, a Reaganesque drug warrior, Clinton sought to bolster his own (and the Democratic Party's) tough-on-crime credentials.[17] In 1992, Clinton's Southern roots, his choice of Al Gore as a running mate, and his decidedly moderate positions helped him win eight Sunbelt states that had gone to Bush in 1988. And in 1996, Clinton picked up Florida and Arizona as well.

With this political shift, two racial projects reemerged to take a dominant place within political and popular discourse. Instead of an explicit focus on racial inequality, the conversation turned to adequate *racial representation* and to a lesser extent *racial uplift*. Clinton, supposedly the country's "first black president," by all accounts believed in the virtues of racial equality, yet his group of centrist Democrats began to retreat from racial equality as a political goal.[18] As Paul Frymer writes about the 1992 presidential campaign:

> For the first time in almost three decades, [the Democratic Party platform in 1992] contained no mention of redressing racial injustice. Clinton's own policy platform . . . had only one reference to race, and this was to oppose the use of racial quotas as a remedy for employment and education inequality. A chapter entitled "Cities" did not mention the problems of inner cities or the continuing existence of de facto racial segregation, while the chapter on civil rights devoted more space to people with physical disabilities than to African Americans.[19]

As a presidential candidate, Clinton created a new image of a tough-on-crime Democrat: promising more policing, posing in pictures with "mostly black convicts providing the backdrop," and emphasizing his death penalty record as governor.[20] President Clinton's policy solutions once in office repudiated traditional Democratic policies around the project to fully incorporate black Americans into the country's economic, social, and political institutions.[21] Instead, his administration focused on universal social benefits such as health care and advocated social policies that resonated with white constituencies.[22] Responding to Clinton's call to pass a "strong, smart, tough crime bill," the majority-Democratic Congress enacted a crime bill in 1994 that expanded the number of federal crimes eligible for the death penalty, increased prison sentences for federal criminal offenders, and provided grants to states for more police, new prisons, and crime prevention programs.[23] Importantly, the impetus for federal subsidies for prisons came from Sunbelt state representatives from Texas, New Mexico, and Florida—all states with strong factions that wanted to build prisons to address violent crime and prison overcrowding.[24]

To maintain the support of his black constituencies and the Congressional Black Caucus while disavowing traditional civil rights remedies and rhetoric, President Clinton enthusiastically embraced a project of *racial representation*.[25] Gathering popularity since civil rights leaders began to be incorporated into partisan politics and fostered by the ethos of affirmative action, the project of racial representation sought to increase the representation of people of color in politics, education, business and the professions.[26] Representatives were thought to provide a voice for their communities and act as role models for future generations. The project of racial representation did not deny the problem of racial inequality, but argued that putting people of color in positions of power would help improve the lot of racial minorities more generally. President Clinton, for example, appointed an unprecedented number of African Americans, women, and other minorities to the cabinet, high-level administrative offices, and the judiciary.[27] The editorial board members of the *Miami Times*, Miami's black newspaper, like other black leaders, praised President Clinton's overtures:

> Not only are these not token appointments for obvious reasons but also they come from a leader who has learned in life's classroom the fundamental importance to America's well-being of treating all citizens as equals and giving all an opportunity to contribute to nation-building. With that background and the senior aides he is surrounding himself with, Mr. Clinton is ushering in a new era

of hope for all Americans and can be expected to set a tone of racial harmony and intolerance for bigotry that have been lacking for at least a dozen years in the national body politic.[28]

The move away from project of racial equality was also reflected in the discourse and actions of civil rights organizations at the national level. In some sense, the "capture" of the black vote by the Democratic Party and what some saw as stagnation in progress toward racial equality created a crisis in traditional civil rights organizations.[29] Although Jesse Jackson, the first African American presidential candidate, had exceeded expectations in the 1988 primary, he was snubbed for the vice presidential nomination. He went on to spearhead a coalition of black organizations in an attempt to define and reposition a "black agenda."[30] Some black activists talked of the need for a third party, while others espoused what could be termed a project of *racial uplift*, which in the spirit of Booker T. Washington posited that the solution to continued racial inequality was self-improvement by black individuals, families, and communities. For example, the press release announcing the "African American Summit '89" concluded with a punitive focus on the personal failings of black Americans:

> Finally, we shall address ourselves; we shall speak to our own community. The painful process of self-examination is long overdue. We are not a perfect people and those among us who continue to fail to meet the standards necessary to achieve freedom, progress and parity in this country must be exposed, isolated and reeducated.[31]

In the early 1990s, with membership plummeting, the NAACP also took a different direction. Under the leadership of Benjamin Chavis, the organization turned toward self-help and economic empowerment as a means to racial equality.[32] After he was let go in 1994, Chavis went on to lead the organization responsible for the Million Man March, which again encouraged black men to take "personal responsibility."[33]

As I will discuss below, the shift in dominant racial projects is also evidenced at the state and local level in Florida. The incorporation of racial uplift and racial representation made it increasingly difficult for black local community and state leaders to speak in one voice on issues of crime and justice. So while many Floridians were still concerned about racial equality and the trade-offs to more prisons, no one organized collective effort emerged to counter the claims of law enforcement. As a consequence of the lack of countermobilization, the shift in Democratic politics nationally, and the larger retreat from the project to remedy racial inequality, Democrats had few political incentives to oppose expanding carceral capacity.

Defining the Problem of Early Releases

As covered in chapter 4, Florida policymakers in the early 1980s had tried to rein in prison populations through a combination of sentencing guidelines and provisions to shorten time served, including an emergency release mechanism that required the Department of Corrections to release prisoners before the expiration of their sentences (in five-day increments) *if* the prison population neared court-ordered capacity limits. Yet the War on Drugs, which brought thousands of new drug offenders into the prisons, thwarted their efforts. And instead of addressing the influx of prisoners *into* the system, legislators built new prisons and relied upon the release mechanism to maintain compliance with the federal court. This decision to use early releases to manage the prison population created a media frenzy and political opportunity that shaped penal policy over the next decade.

In August 1989, the *Orlando Sentinel* ran a three-day, seven-article series on Florida's early release program.[34] Examining the records of almost 4,000 offenders released before the expiration of their sentence between February 1987 and March 1989, the *Sentinel* found that 950 had committed new crimes "within the period that they would still have been in prison if no early release credits had been given."[35] Over the next three days, the paper ran some of their pictures: 27 male offenders recently charged with murder, robbery, assault, sexual assault, lewd behavior, and theft. The pictured group were accused of some horrible and frightening crimes: the random murder of a businesswoman in the prime of her life, the molestation of a four-year-old, the dragging of an elderly women across a street in an attempt to grab her purse, and the holding up of bystanders with knives and guns for small sums of money. Yet a closer look at the numbers demonstrates that of the over 2,000 criminal charges against this group, 88 percent were for property or drug crimes. In tacit acknowledgment of the nonviolent nature of the crimes, the *Sentinel* writers emphasized the right to be free from *fear* rather than victimization:

> What the analysis cannot calculate are the hundreds of innocent people who are the victims of these so-called lesser crimes and the thousands of man-hours that police spend investigating crimes that should not have happened. "Now I'm just terrified to talk to anyone I don't know, and that isn't my nature," said

Kathy Mawer of Orlando a year after her purse was snatched by a stranger who stopped her to ask for directions. The stranger was Daniel Boone, a convicted purse snatcher who had been released from prison 85 days early despite repeated citations for violating prison rules. Within three weeks Boone had committed four new crimes.[36]

The *Sentinel* series directly connected these crimes with the *Costello* prison conditions case filed fifteen years prior. In addition to the early release policy instituted to keep the prison population under the court-ordered capacity limits, the state also maintained a system of automatic gain-time for prisoners, which allowed them to earn approximately one-third off their sentences. As a result by 1990, the majority of released prisoners were only serving approximately 36 percent of their prison sentences.[37] The *Sentinel* series framed the early release program as a gift to criminals:

> Though stripped of the right to vote, Florida prison inmates have reaped as much good favor from the state's elected leaders as any other special interest group over the past three years . . . "If the incarcerated population in Florida would have had a lobbyist, they couldn't have done any better than what the Legislature did," said Leonard Holton, director of the state Sentencing Guidelines Commission.[38]

Over the next five years, law enforcement and victims' advocates argued that this benefit to criminals came at the direct expense of victims and other law-abiding citizens.

Importantly, tucked into a chart in the *Sentinel* article was the source of the problem: "A steady stream of convicted cocaine dealers and users has created most of the pressure that forces Florida prison officials to dump other inmates onto the street early."[39] As chronicled in the last chapter, admissions to prison for drug offenses increased five-fold between 1986 and 1990. Due to drug law enforcement, by 1990 African Americans had become 60 percent of the state's inmate population—a marker of inequality that the state had not seen since the Jim Crow era. And yet during the heightened hysteria around drugs and crime, legislators chose to build more prisons and rely on early release policies, rather than find alternatives for drug offenders. As Al Lawson, an African American former state representative from Leon County, recalled,

> My thinking [about crime at the time] because the majority of the inmates were African Americans, my thinking was why do we need more prisons? Can we

rehabilitate? Can we get programs to keep some people out of prison? Are they getting fair hearings? . . . Many of us knew that we are locking up a lot of people that needed help. Drug-related help. . . . In a lot of the poorer communities, drugs were prevalent and so, as a result, we were overstocking prisons and not having room for more violent offenders. They needed to be in treatment. But that's the way the system responded.[40]

Despite this concern about treatment, legislators did not adequately fund treatment programs—leaving counties to pick up the slack. Thus even when urban counties established diversion programs (as was eventually done in Dade County under the direction of State's Attorney Janet Reno), only a small proportion of drug-addicted offenders could access treatment.[41] The growth in prison admissions had done little to alleviate crime in Florida. Violent crime rates increased by 32 percent between 1985 and their peak in 1990, although property crime rates began to decrease in 1989 (see figures 5.1 and 5.2). In addition, violent crime was concentrated in urban areas; the average violent crime rate for the most violent counties—Miami-Dade, Hillsborough, and Leon—was four times as high as the rest of Florida in the period between 1989 and 1994.

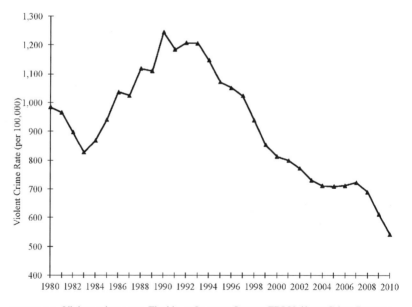

FIGURE 5.1. Violent crime rates, Florida, 1980–2010. Source: FBI Uniform Crime Reports.

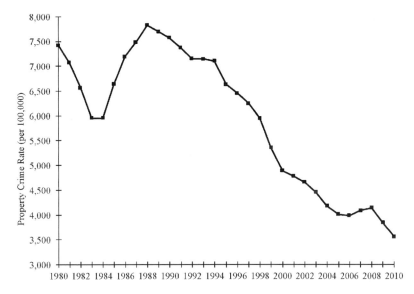

FIGURE 5.2. Property crime rates, Florida, 1980–2010. Source: FBI Uniform Crime Reports.

Early Release as an Overincarceration Problem

In response to the media attention on the early release policy, in November 1990 the legislature reactivated the nearly defunct parole board as the Control Release Authority, giving it the power to review which prisoners were eligible for control release. However, the system was still taking in too many people—making the "temporary" early release policy indispensable on an ongoing basis. According to a 1991 report by the House Committee on Criminal Justice, the continued need for early release—which everyone acknowledged was a public relations nightmare—was due to state's attorneys' increased use of habitual offender and mandatory minimum laws to prosecute low-risk offenders, who could have been placed in less restrictive alternatives to incarceration.[42] Because prisoners sentenced under habitual offender and mandatory minimum laws were *not eligible* for control release, the Department of Corrections was forced to release more violent offenders in order to admit nonviolent offenders.

In 1991 the legislature directed the Office of Economic and Demographic Research (EDR) and the Sentencing Guidelines Commission to suggest revisions to the sentencing guidelines in order to "make the best use of state prisons" and reserve prison space for violent criminals and repeat nonviolent criminals who had "demonstrated an inability to comply with less restrictive penalties." In addition, the revised guidelines were to take into account "present and future state prison resources."[43] *Both agencies recommended repealing habitual offender and mandatory minimum statutes and incorporating their intentions into a new system of structured sentencing guidelines.*[44] The new structure would allow the legislature to manipulate the points below which a prison sentence would *not* be an option in order to preserve prison space for the worst offenders.[45]

Recently elected, Governor Lawton Chiles, a Democrat and popular former United States senator, pledged his support to sentencing guideline revisions, writing in 1991 to Representative Willie Logan (D. Opa-locka), chair of a legislative task force on sentencing reform, "certainly in these times of severe budgetary constraints, I would encourage this group to view our State prison system as a scarce state resource that should be utilized for only those offenders who pose the greatest threat to our citizens."[46] Logan, the sixth black representative elected to the Florida House (in 1982) and former mayor of Opa-locka, an urban area in Miami-Dade County, specifically wanted the legislature to repeal the habitual offender statutes because of their disproportionate application to black offenders.[47] In 1992, Logan and Representative Elvin Martinez (D. Tampa), a public defender, incorporated the EDR/Sentencing Guidelines Commission recommendations in a proposal to revise the guidelines "to correlate with the number of [prison] beds projected."[48] Yet even after a compromise bill that tightened the habitual offender laws instead of repealing them and retained mandatory minimums for crimes against law enforcement, lobbying by law enforcement and a new victims' rights organization helped defeat the bill.[49]

Early Release as a Victim's Rights Problem

The new victims' organization, Stop Turning Out Prisoners (STOP), was the brainchild of Sheriff Charlie Wells and State's Attorney Earl Moreland of Manatee County (southwest Florida). Wells, who had been lobbying the legislature to build new prisons for years, decided to create a statewide organization along the lines of Mothers Against Drunk Driving (MADD) to convince the state legislature to end early release and pass a truth-in-sentencing law.[50]

> I was riding back from Tallahassee one evening with my wife, feeling about as low as you can feel . . . It was just flat rejection. That same day, a MADD

representative testified. I recalled the attention she received and the courteous treatment.[51]

The Florida Sheriffs Association (FSA) and the Florida Prosecuting Attorneys Association (FPAA) had been locked in a battle with the state legislature and the Department of Corrections since the early release policy went into effect in 1987. Early in 1990, the FSA challenged the early release policy in court, claiming that it was unconstitutional since only the governor could shorten prison sentences under Florida law.[52] The sheriffs had a direct stake in prison overcrowding. As the stewards of the county jails, when the state prisons released prisoners early, sheriffs saw increases in the number of offenders going through the county system. In a never-ending cycle, many county jails were overcrowded and had been (and could be) sued by the Department of Corrections to maintain adequate capacity. This created a headache for sheriffs who found themselves asking county voters for more funding for county jails.[53] Of course, sheriffs were also concerned about crime: just a few months prior to founding STOP, a Sarasota teenager was killed. Of the two young black men accused (their photos appeared in the news article announcing the charges), one had been released from prison early for an aggravated battery conviction (Sarasota is just south of Manatee County).[54]

The FPAA also sued the state to stop early releases and lobbied for more prison beds. The state's attorneys' complaint about the system went back to the early 1980s; they did not like the sentencing guidelines, insisting that they hindered their ability to their job.[55] But in later years this became conflated with their dislike of early release mechanisms.[56] Ed Austin, the Jacksonville state's attorney and spokesperson for the FPAA, called the guidelines a "computerized numbers game" and stated that the system worked only with "a real threat of jail and prison time."[57] In recalling those years, Austin emphasized the need for sufficient prison space:

> If you are going to maintain order . . . if you are prosecuting and you don't have an empty jail cell, everything you do is bluffing because none of these people do these diversionary things voluntarily.[58]

In addition, prosecutors were adamant about keeping the habitual offender laws intact, as they were "a tremendous tool in the negotiation of pleas."[59]

But the sheriffs and state's attorneys faced an uphill battle. The majority Democratic and fiscally conservative legislature had already committed

significant resources to build prisons in order to comply with the *Costello*
order and they faced declining state revenue because of the recession. To
counteract these concerns, Sheriff Wells and State's Attorney Moreland
conceived of STOP as a crime victims' organization with the understanding that, like MADD members, crime victims would be compelling to state
legislators. Wells and Moreland recruited the first active victim—a woman
whose sixteen-year-old son had been killed by a man with six prior convictions, released from prison because of gain-time. She joined Wells, Moreland, and Buddy Jacobs, the lobbyist for FPAA, on the executive board
of STOP. During STOP's first statewide meeting in May 1991, Wells and
Moreland emphasized four key framings that STOP members in chapters
across the state would later repeat.

1. The system protects criminals' rights at the expense of victims.
2. The way to keep violent criminals off the streets is to build more prisons and
   ensure that criminals serve their full sentences.
3. Citizens are willing to spend money to put violent criminals in prison.
4. It is less expensive to house prisoners than let them roam the streets.[60]

Wells then won election as chairman of the FSA and used his position as
a platform for STOP.[61] Recognizing that politicians would listen to "real
people who have been victims," Wells encouraged sheriffs and district attorneys across the state to reach the legislature and public by organizing
victims.[62]

State's attorneys and sheriffs took his advice and began to use the resources of their offices to organize local chapters. In particular, state's attorneys' victims assistance coordinators hosted meetings and organized
victims to lobby state government.[63] Newspaper reports on upcoming
local STOP meetings directed interested parties to contact their state's
attorney's office, and early articles chronicling STOP's activities quoted
law enforcement officers rather than citizen members.[64] Despite this institutional affiliation with law enforcement, the news media consistently
referred to STOP as a victim-run or citizen-led initiative. In 1992, Wells
recruited Kathleen Finnegan, a former assistant state's attorney who had
been shot by a repeat offender (the colleague with her was killed), as the
executive director of STOP. Finnegan, who gained national recognition
after appearing on the *Oprah Winfrey Show* in 1992, traveled around the
state speaking to new chapters, saying things such as "victims don't get
gain-time."[65] Finnegan became by far the most powerful spokeswoman for
this framing of victims' rights, later appearing on local and national news

broadcasts, including a *60 Minutes* segment called "Ten Will Get You Five."[66] Wells reported that by the end of 1992, STOP had eighteen chapters and five thousand members across the state (although I could only verify six chapters).[67]

Initially, STOP's primary tactic was to publicize cases where violent prisoners had been, or were about to be, released early. They would organize petition and letter-writing drives around specific early release cases—sometimes going to Control Release Authority hearings to object to an offender's release.[68] The news media's coverage of these cases often began with the victims' loss juxtaposed by the offender's gain. A *St. Petersburg Times* piece begins, for example, "The courts did little to compensate Jesse Nieves for the horror of his daughter's killing by a reckless hit-and-run driver." It goes on to say that the "man who caused the 3-year-old girl's death" had been released from prison after 8 months.[69] A *Bradenton Herald* article began,

> Julie was sexually abused for 13 years. She endured a traumatic trial four years ago while still a teen-ager to bring the man who abused her to justice. Wednesday, she got a surprise. The man who ruined her childhood . . . was being released from prison after serving 4 1/2 years of an 11-year sentence.[70]

STOP members also protested at the statehouse and outside prisons to call attention to the victims of prisoners released early. Excerpts from an April 1992 *Orlando Sentinel* article demonstrate how the prisoners-versus-victims frame translated to the solution of more prisons:

> Saturday at the reception center, a minimum-security prison in east Orange County, a small roped-off area contained 20 white crosses marking 20 imaginary graves. Each wooden marker bore the name of a relative killed by an early-release inmate. There were names like 19-year-old Leonard Reese, hit at 65 mph by a drunken driver . . . "Criminals who are repeat offenders should not be released early. *They have food, shelter and clothes on their backs. What do we have? We need to start protecting the victims,*" [Charlie] Reese [the victim's sister] said.
>
> [Orange-Osceola State's Attorney Lawson] Lamar said prison sentences are not long enough or tough enough. And he stressed a need for more money funneled into the prison system. *"We're not imprisoning the wrong people, we're not imprisoning enough people,"* Lamar said. "You've got to motivate people with fear if they're not motivated by ethics. The entire system of Florida has lost its bite." (emphasis added)[71]

Thus the notion that the state incarcerated *too few offenders* framed the argument against Representative Logan's 1992 proposed sentencing reform. In one of their first official policy actions, STOP, along with police, sheriffs, and district attorneys, campaigned against the proposal, arguing that it would put more criminals on the street *and* that the public was willing to spend the money for new prisons.[72] As the president of the Hillsborough County STOP chapter wrote in a letter to the editor:

> Our senators and representatives say, "Yes, it's a terrible problem, but our constituents do not want us to raise taxes, even for prisons." We at STOP cannot imagine who they have been talking to because that is not what we have learned from talking to the residents of Florida. . . . While our representatives worry about how to position themselves to get re-elected, our citizens are being shot, raped, robbed, maimed and preyed upon like sheep in a pen. Now with a vehicle like STOP in place to focus our anger in a positive direction, victims no longer have to "suck it up."[73]

As a result of this negative media attention and lobbying by law enforcement, the sentencing reform bills did not even make it to the House or Senate floor for a vote.[74]

Negotiating a Solution: Governor Chiles and the Safe Streets Initiative

The failure to pass sentencing reform in 1992 prompted the need for new emergency rules indicating which prisoners could be released early.[75] And in May 1992, papers across the state reported that "Florida prisoners convicted of manslaughter, aggravated battery, robbery, burglary, theft and some drug crimes may be considered for early release."[76] As fewer and fewer prisoners were available for early release to stabilize the prison population, those who were released served even shorter prison terms.[77] Local newspapers continued to run front-page stories with lists of released offenders having served between 11 and 40 percent of their sentences.[78] Thus, by the 1992 election the early releases of prisoners had become commonplace and law enforcement had perfected its argument that the state was protecting criminals' rights at the expense of crime victims' rights. In turn, law enforcement and victims' activism and media attention shaped Governor Chiles's approach to the early release problem, as the state's political winds continued to shift to the right.

In the 1992 election, Republicans picked up eight seats in the Florida House of Representatives to put them six seats away from parity. And in the Florida Senate, Republicans picked up a one-person majority. On the heels of a presidential campaign steeped in tough-on-crime promises, statewide media attention to crime, and Republican gains in Florida, Governor Chiles reversed his earlier position that prison should be considered a "scarce state resource" and proposed a Safe Streets Initiative that would eliminate the basic gain-time that reduced prisoners' sentences by one-third. To accommodate the resulting increase in the prison population, Chiles proposed building 21,000 prison beds over the next five years.[79] According to the *St. Petersburg Times*, the "price would be steep," putting Florida in debt for twenty to thirty years and ultimately costing $1.5 billion.[80] Governor Chiles realized that funding prison expansion with general revenue would come at the expense of his other priorities, including education and health insurance subsidies for the lower middle class. Consequently, his original proposal financed new prisons with state revenue bonds and a twenty-five-cent increase in the cigarette tax.

In his campaign to generate support for his cigarette tax increase, Governor Chiles inadvertently fed the politics of early release and the growing political clout of law enforcement and victims' rights advocates. As early as 1992, Chiles had proposed a public safety investment fund that would have collected a special tax from businesses to support criminal justice operations. Importantly, in order to drum up support for his proposal, Chiles sent personalized letters to law enforcement officials that capitalized on their frustration with early releases.[81] Later during his campaign for the cigarette tax, Chiles adopted former governor Martinez's tactic of mentioning specific offenders who were about to be released early.[82] In addition, he asked the Department of Corrections to study reoffending by released prisoners—and then used this to argue that "the state must act as quickly as possible to build new prisons to hold the most dangerous criminals and to expand alternatives to incarceration for the least dangerous ones."[83]

While Chiles ultimately hoped to revise sentencing guidelines to prioritize bed space for violent offenders, STOP and law enforcement did not make a distinction between violent criminals that needed to be in prison to protect society and nonviolent offenders who might be dealt with in a less expensive way. For example, as the legislators debated various versions of the Safe Streets Initiative, STOP and the Orange County sheriff and police officers protested the proposed early release of drug offenders and "less dangerous habitual offenders."[84] STOP representatives also stayed clear of nuanced arguments that left room for less costly alternatives to incarceration for some types of offenders. As Kathleen Finnegan stated, "I don't care how it gets paid for, I just want more beds."[85] STOP ultimately backed the governor's plan for a cigarette tax because it promised to buy the biggest number of beds to keep the most people off the streets.[86]

Legislators, however, were reluctant to commit to new taxes to fund prisons.[87] Urban Democrats initially supported what amounted to a regressive tax, because they realized prison funding would come at the expense of prevention programs, including education. But Republicans, who shared power in the Senate, were ideologically opposed to new taxes.[88] The other main point of contention was the habitual offender statute — the Senate wanted to keep it (and the support of the state's attorneys), but the Democrats in the House wanted to abolish it. Again, they cited the law's disproportionate impact on African Americans: of the prisoners sentenced as habitual offenders in prison as of June 30, 1992, 75 percent were black, 86 percent had committed nonviolent offenses, 36 percent had one or no prior commitments to prison, and 35 percent were serving sentences for a drug offense.[89] Prosecutors, however, insisted the law was necessary for keeping career criminals behind bars.

After months of negotiation and a failure to pass the Safe Streets Initiative in the regular session, Chiles took his campaign for the initiative on the road, attempting to build support from local constituencies who could press their legislators. Standing onstage with STOP members and law enforcement, Chiles stated that "innocent people pay the price" when the legislature refuses to build more prisons.[90] Chiles convened a special legislative session in May 1993 for the sole purpose of authorizing additional prison capacity, amending sentencing guidelines, and raising revenue. Representative Logan and other black legislators "delivered impassioned pleas" against the guideline changes (which did not abolish the habitual offender laws) and the lack of funding for treatment.[91] Yet the legislature passed the Safe Streets Initiative of 1994 (with very few no votes) noting that

> the people of this state have repeatedly voiced their concern about the early release of serious and violent felony offenders. . . . Lack of bed space to house felons sentenced in the state in unprecedented numbers has resulted in an undermining of corrections policy in the state so that punishment and rehabilitation now seem only incidental to other considerations.[92]

The final bill revised the sentencing guidelines structure along the lines of the 1992 proposal, taking into account new principles, including that the primary purpose of sentencing is to punish the offender and the use of incarceration is "prioritized toward offenders convicted of serious or repeat offenses" in order to "maximize finite capacities of correctional facilities."[93] In addition, the bill abolished basic gain-time and various mandatory minimum laws, tightened the habitual offender laws, and increased the capacity limit at which control release would be triggered from 97.5 to 99 percent.[94] Finally, it also created the Correctional Privatization Commission to facilitate contracts with private companies to construct and operate prisons in the state.[95]

Notably, *the final law did not require a dedicated funding source for prison operations.* Yet it included an "intent to adequately fund" prisons going forward. It also required that future changes to sentencing must demonstrate a "net zero sum impact on the overall prison population" unless the legislation contained a funding source to accommodate the change.[96] To pay for the required prison beds, the legislature appropriated $211 million from general revenue for 10,000 new prison beds (over the next five years). In addition, the new private prison contracts allowed the state to delay the construction costs of 2,300 beds at private facilities.[97] Governor Chiles was not happy with the funding plan (or the reduction from 21,000 to 12,300 new beds), but the new law allowed him to claim in the upcoming gubernatorial campaign that criminals would serve more prison time under his watch.

Black Mobilization, the Community as Victim, and the "Solution" of Racial Representation

While the 1993 Safe Streets Initiative can be seen as a compromise between Democratic legislators who favored deemphasizing incarceration for nonviolent offenders and Republicans who supported maintaining the state's option to incarcerate, more liberal Democrats clearly lost in their efforts repeal discriminatory sentencing laws and to secure new revenue sources for prison beds. As Democrats still had control of the state House and the governorship in 1993, this failure represented Democrats' growing ambivalence around crime control strategies in a changing political context. When Governor Chiles campaigned in 1990, he criticized Governor Martinez's overreliance on building prisons, promising to put more money into public education and diversion programs to keep nonviolent offenders out of prison.[98] His stance at the time was in line with the traditional liberal Democratic position that lowering crime rates in the long run required government investment in poor communities. However, his position had little traction—in part because of a lack of organized support (especially when compared to law enforcement) for alternative solutions to the crime problem.

Presumably a natural ally in the effort to divert more resources toward prevention and diversion, local civil rights activists could have attempted to counter the claims of law enforcement and white victims by arguing that early release policies were a result of the *unequal treatment of young black men* who bore the brunt of drug arrests, drug offense convictions, and mandatory minimum prison sentences. Yet while they recognized the disproportionate perils of drugs, crime, and prison on the lives of young black men, local black activists chose to focus on solutions that emphasized prevention through self-help, respect, and pride.[99] At public forums, representatives of black organizations spoke of young people's lack of self-control and moral compass, rather than state or federal policy.[100] For example, citing past disappointment in government efforts to produce racial equality, organizers of a local NAACP conference in 1990, "A Conference on Self: Making the Difference in My Community," specifically turned away from government solutions and instead pointed to church, community, and family as responsible for "ensuring that young blacks do not turn to crime" in the first place.[101] The Miami Urban League similarly stressed the ability of black families to solve their own problems. An article in Miami's black newspaper summarized the tough love approach of T. Willard Fair, the executive director of the Miami branch of the Urban League: "Social services were not, by themselves, the answer . . . The answer lay in the development of the child, with parenting skills an important ingredient also missing . . . [and] an inability [for young blacks] to 'manage disappointment.'"[102] The problem, in effect, was not stagnation in society's efforts to achieve racial equality, but parents and teachers' failure to teach values to black children.[103]

However, as evidenced in Representative Logan's efforts to reform discriminatory sentencing laws, the racial uplift rhetoric of local community organizations did not seep into black politics at the state level. Instead, African American state politicians focused their efforts on racial representation while continuing to advocate for better government services for their constituents.[104] When the Florida legislature began its process of redistricting in 1992 black legislators spearheaded an initiative to create four majority-black congressional districts. (Floridians had not sent an African American representative to Congress since Reconstruction.) The plan was welcomed by white and Cuban-American Republicans, who stood to gain from a "redistricting plan that . . . captured all blacks in a geographic area," therefore diluting Democrat strength in other districts.[105] The *Miami Times* saw the deal as an alliance with black legislator's "Latin counterparts," while white Republicans saw it as a chance to win control of the Florida legislature for the first time since Reconstruction.[106] Despite efforts by white Democrats to block the redistricting plan, black Democrats and Republicans prevailed. The new voting districts effectively created three "black" seats in the U.S. House of Representatives and an additional five in the state legislature.

Despite the shift toward projects of racial uplift and racial representation, many black activists and politicians continued to view broader issues of social welfare as explicitly linked to crime and black overrepresentation in the criminal justice system. Within the tough rhetoric on responsibility, for example, was the belief that the education system was failing black children. Education was seen by many as a way to prevent crime and black youth involvement in the criminal justice system. As Earl T. Shinhoster, the long-time director of the NAACP southeast region, stated at a conference in 1989: "If the community itself does not come together to address [education], then we will, in effect, be losing a whole other generation of human resources who are black, and who are going to be the wards of this state by way of our welfare rolls, by way of our prison systems."[107] In fact, the first black woman elected to the Florida Senate, Senator Carrie Meek, focused much of her political life on dropout prevention, literacy, and access to higher education for black students.[108]

Black community leaders' response to Governor Chiles's Safe Streets Act demonstrates how black urban communities' multiple, intersecting concerns around crime and justice made it difficult to coalesce around *one* framing of the crime problem. When the governor's office held a community meeting in the Miami area in May 1993 to elicit support for his Safe Streets proposal, black civic and church leaders gave Governor Chiles an earful about the quality of public education and the dysfunction of the social service system.[109] Yet leaders also complained about police brutality and urged Governor Chiles to provide more funding for police officer sensitivity training.[110] In addition, those in attendance felt that state officials' response to recent killings of white tourists in the North Miami area was disproportionate to the response given black victims of crime.[111] As Georgia Ayers, one of the members of a newly established Florida Commission for African American Affairs, commented after the killing of the sixth white foreign tourist in North Miami:

> We see these kinds of crimes all the time in this community and the governor isn't doing much about it, except in these type cases. Those who are concerned about the Black community feel that the Black community should be treated like to [*sic*] this incident that happened Friday. We should be treated with this kind of respect and concern 24 hours a day, 365 days a year, not just times like when this lady was killed.[112]

As the killings of white tourists continued—even bringing Oprah Winfrey to Miami in September 1993—community residents tried to reassert their victimization into the public conversation while making the point that the accused offenders were also sons, daughters, and community members:

> "What people don't realize is that it happens to people like me every day," said Cathey Hazelhurst, mother of [Recondall] Wiggins, who police say, drove the truck that rammed [the German tourist's] rental car before he was killed. "It could happen to me by someone like my son, yes. It doesn't matter who you are, it can happen."[113]

Likewise, the mayor of Miami, Xavier Suarez, insisted that "every single one of the 130 murders in our city are important."[114]

Notably, while Governor Chiles clearly heard these complaints in this instance, groups representing black urban interests were not organized at the state level and did not appear in the legislative record in debates about the Safe Streets Act. Nor did their complaints make it into the mainstream media, such as the *Miami Herald*. As Lisa Miller argues in her account of crime politics in Philadelphia, Pittsburgh, and at the state level in Pennsylvania, the complexity of the issues, scarce resources, and the fragmentation of the criminal justice system across three levels of government limit the ability of citizen and social service organizations to effectively advocate for their constituents' interests at the state level.[115] The Florida State Conference of the NAACP, for example, had no state field office and no paid staff.[116] Other community organizations, like the Urban League and People United to Lead the Struggle for Equality (PULSE), were oriented toward local advocacy and often engaged in multipronged approaches to stem crime and violence. For example, PULSE, a greater-Miami civic organization started in 1981 and primarily run by black church leaders, had been working in the community for years on a number of fronts: mobilizing the community to improve city services, monitoring complaints about the police, and pushing for more black law enforcement officers.[117] At the state level, Miller finds that only single-issue citizen organizations—such as victim advocates and the National Rifle Association—are represented, which significantly narrows the conversation about the problem of crime. As Miller notes, "broad based groups are rarely represented before the Pennsylvania legislature in any forum. They have no lobbyists, and they make up a tiny fraction of 'interested parties,' a minuscule portion of witnesses at hearings, and an almost imperceptible percentage of personal contacts with legislators."[118]

As a consequence of the "invisible black victim" in state-level policy debates,[119] and the move away from the project of racial equality, when Florida state officials *did* attempt to address the disproportionate number of young black men in the criminal justice system, they relied on the new dominant racial project, *black representation*, as the solution. As the Florida Commission for African American Affairs noted in its first report, to address the "'state of emergency' in the African American community as it pertains to crime and justice issues" the commission should work toward:

- Increasing the number of African Americans employed in the fields of law enforcement and the judiciary.
- Improvement in the relationship between community and law enforcement.
- Developing model juvenile prevention and intervention programs.[120]

Governor Chiles also adopted a racial representation strategy—going to great lengths to appoint African Americans as heads of the Florida Department of Corrections and a newly created Department of Juvenile Justice.[121]

Yet black law enforcement officials' positions did not allow them to advocate for the type of broad-based solutions to crime needed by black urban communities. Harry Singletary, the new secretary of the Department of Corrections, was outwardly critical of the disproportionate incarceration of young black men—actively giving talks, writing opinion pieces and speaking to the press—yet as he notes,

> You can use your bully pulpit to talk about overrepresentation. And you talk to the political people, newspapers, civic groups, black folks. I figured I had a

moral responsibility to do that. *I figured I could not stop my receipts [of pris-oners]*, but I could tell people what is going on and try to encourage them to do something differently. (emphasis added)[122]

Election Year Politics and the New Carceral Consensus

By 1994, the opportunity to reverse course on incarceration was quickly closing. Law enforcement and victims' groups had framed the problem of early release as not enough prison beds, rather than too many nonviolent offenders in the system. And while a plausible racial equality counter-frame existed, black community advocates' structural absence at the state level and competing racial projects made it less tenable. Furthermore, Florida's crime rate was widely reported as "the highest . . . of the 50 states" after a year of international media attention to the murder of foreign tourists.[123] As Republicans and the news media continued to promote the idea that anything good for offenders was bad for victims, Democrats felt increasingly compelled to follow the example of President Clinton, ignore the implications for racial equality, and embrace a tough-on-crime stance. The new carceral consensus was cemented by election year politics and increasing partisan competition. As Governor Chiles pointed out in his annual address to the state legislature in February 1994:

> We all know that this session is going to be dominated by crime. . . . It is an election year. We can spend our time and the people's money by engaging in demagoguery or posturing, or we can come together and work hard to produce answers that will help us unravel the tangle of violence which grips our state.[124]

And by the end of 1994 legislators had come to an answer: the way to address crime was to build more prisons and keep criminals behind bars for longer.

As Governor Chiles predicted, both of his Republican challengers for the governor's seat, Insurance Commissioner Tom Gallagher and Jeb Bush, proposed building more prisons.[125] Not to be outdone, Governor Chiles claimed that the "most important priority that faces us this ses-sion is protecting our people in their homes, in their neighborhoods, in their schools." He congratulated the legislature for passing a budget in 1993 that would allow prisoners to serve 75 percent of their sentences, but insisted that lawmakers could do more. In a nod to his more liberal supporters, Chiles balanced his call for three-strikes laws, boot camps, and fourteen thousand more prison beds with more preventative measures such as schools for at-risk kids and after-school programs.[126]

As the entire Florida House of Representatives and half the Florida Senate was up for reelection, Republicans saw the issue of early release and continuing high crime rates as a means to beat Governor Chiles and other Democratic opponents.[127] Even after the 1993 special session funded ten thousand more beds, early release still made headlines. This is partly because the public could not immediately see the impact of the new law (which abolished basic gain-time for new prison admits) on the practice of early releases. Thus, despite historic action by the legislature two months earlier, a new STOP member in Lake County's chapter claimed that *legislators had done nothing to stop the early release of prisoners.*[128] Another STOP member wrote in *the Orlando Sentinel* in August 1993,

> The citizens of Florida are tired of being victimized by criminals who should have been behind bars. We are disgusted that many Florida felons serve less than 15 percent of their sentences. We have had the highest crime rate in the nation for a decade. We need more prison beds and sentencing reform.[129]

Politicians and state administrators did not actively dispute this inaccurate statement.[130] Consequently, in December 1993, over 5,000 STOP members throughout the state approved a petition drive for a constitutional amendment that would require prisoners to serve at least 85 percent of their sentences. The STOP ballot initiative was supported by Republican U.S. senator Connie Mack, who stated that he "believed that the people of the state of Florida are so concerned about the crime problem, in essence saying it's got to stop, that they are prepared to do what is necessary to take criminals off the streets."[131]

As crime and early releases continued to draw media attention through the end of 1993, including the murders of tourists, law enforcement continued to push for prison beds as a solution to the high rate of violent crime. In January 1994, Ed Austin, a former state's attorney and the mayor of Jacksonville, organized a summit of the large city mayors and police chiefs from across the state who unanimously called for twenty-five thousand new prison beds and the abolition of sentencing guidelines.[132] Since it was an election year, local law enforcement, including sheriffs and state's attorneys, were given a wider platform from which to make their case. Organizations such as the Police Benevolent Association (PBA) (which represented corrections officers, sheriff deputies, and police officers) also took advantage of election year politics, pledging their support to candidates who favored more prisons and pay raises.[133]

Given the media attention, the lobbying efforts, and the need to appear to "do" something concrete in an election year, most legislators felt compelled to go along with plans for more prisons. For example, according to Representative Randy Mackey (D. Lake City), "when you look a correctional officer in the eye and have to push that button, it makes a big difference."[134] Another Democrat lamented,

> You can actually see the guy in handcuffs going to prison right away on your TV. The kid who's improving in education you won't see today, especially in the lower grades. You can't measure that until the guy completes his education and doesn't get into crime—and if he does good, nobody notices because that's what's expected.[135]

Even progressive Democrats who clearly saw the connection between social disadvantage and crime would eventually recommend building more prisons. In part, progressives ran up against the dominant criminology of the day in books such as James Q. Wilson and Richard Herrnstein's 1986 *Crime and Human Nature* (1986).[136] David Garland argues that this bestselling book was the most prominent example of a new "criminology of the other," which treats offenders as a "different species of threatening, violent individuals for whom we can have no sympathy and for whom there is no effective help."[137] It became common sense that at a certain point, offenders were beyond reform. As State Senator George Kirkpatrick (D. Gainesville) noted at the time: "If you look at the continuum of experiences that create juvenile criminals, they start at a very early age . . . If we fail in the education piece of this solution, then *we have no choice* but to spend whatever dollars it takes to build prisons" (emphasis added).[138] As a consequence, the bipartisan support for more prisons as the solution to crime and the perceived early release crisis negated concerns over their expense, their disparate impact on black offenders, and whether they would even have an impact on crime.

The only question was *how* to pay for them: those concerned about taking money away from "health, education, and economic development programs that have proven valuable in preventing criminal behavior" still wanted to devise a dedicated funding source for prisons; and those ideologically opposed to new taxes (as symbol of bigger government) wanted to fund prisons from general revenue.[139] The political culture and elderly demographic of Florida also contributed to a long-standing pay-as-you-go antitax mentality. As Representative Robert Trammell (D. Mariana) stated to a journalist at the time, "You don't have to be a Harvard economist to understand that if you run up the cost of something, money has to come from somewhere . . . but one thing I've learned, in the state of Florida you don't talk lightly about a tax increase."[140] As the Senate would not go along with issuing bonds or a tax increase, Governor Chiles and the less conservative House members accepted a compromise in May 1994 that approved funding for the construction of seventeen thousand beds at more than two dozen institutions from general revenue.[141] They did not reach an agreement on how to pay for the upcoming $250 million a year in operating costs.

Even without the 1994 appropriation, the 1993 prison funding brought approximately six thousand new beds online by the end of 1994.[142] The new beds, along with the deportation of illegal immigrants in the prison system and the new sentencing guidelines, allowed the Department of Corrections to terminate its use of control release in December 1994.[143] In making the announcement to the media Chiles stated, "We can keep a campaign promise today. We are ending early release. It's history. We . . . are in a position of saying to the people of Florida, 'We've heard your message. We are going to see that prisoners serve more of their time.' "[144] At the same time, Chiles hoped the state could finally move past its preoccupation with early release and building prisons: "Hopefully at some time . . . we'll say, 'Stop, slow down.' "[145]

Republicans and the 1995 STOP Legislation

Unfortunately, Governor Chiles's wish did not come to pass, in part because of his and fellow Democrats' earlier policy choices and political strategies. In particular, the choices to rely on early releases to stabilize the prison population, to match Republicans' calls for more prisons, and to empower law enforcement during the fight for increased resources created a political opportunity for new policy that privileged law enforcements' priorities and white victims' notion of rights. So although legislators had fulfilled their commitment to end early releases by passing new sentencing guidelines, ending gain-time, and funding twenty-thousand more prison beds, their actions did not slow down the politics of crime control. In fact, Republicans appropriated the arguments of law enforcement and victims in order to further their political ascent.

In the 1994 election, Governor Chiles barely retained his position against Jeb Bush, and Republicans took control of the Florida Senate and increased their presence in the House. Black Democrats also gained seats, but at the expense of accelerating the Republicans' political power.[146] Both Chiles and the Republicans interpreted the election results as a call for a government that returned, as Malcolm Feeley has noted, "to the basics."[147] In announcing his budget proposal for 1995, Chiles explained: "We're taking care of basic needs. . . . This budget reflects our top priorities. We will continue to make our streets safer, spend our tax dollars more efficiently and work to create stable, high-paying jobs."[148]

In July 1994, the Florida Supreme Court ruled against the proposed STOP ballot amendment, which would have required prisoners to serve 85 percent of their sentences.[149] In reality, by 1995 prisoners were already serving, on average, almost 60 percent of their sentences, and the change to the guidelines and the end of early releases promised to increase the average percentage of time served to 75 percent by 1996.[150] Yet Republicans took advantage of the court decision to dismiss this achievement. The Senate Criminal Justice Committee chairman, State Senator Locke Burt (R. Ormond Beach) told the press, "There's a significant difference between prisoners serving an average of 75 percent of their sentences and the STOP petition." And State Senator Charlie Crist (R. St. Petersburg) told newspapers, "I don't understand why the political leader of this state isn't committed to keeping criminals serving at least 85 percent of their sentences."[151]

Having been the minority party since Reconstruction, state Republicans were anxious to make their mark and deliver on campaign promises, including enacting truth in sentencing. Future governor and then state senator Charlie Crist, using his membership on the Senate Committee on Criminal Justice, quickly sponsored a bill that mimicked the STOP ballot initiative. He published an editorial in the *St. Petersburg Times* announcing his proposal:

> The residents of Florida are frightened and frustrated. They want the killings and robberies that dominate the news to stop. They are not asking too much, only to be safe in our communities. . . . And they want action. They want criminals who are sentenced to prison to stay locked up. . . . This is my No. 1 priority for the 1995 legislative session. . . . We have to send a clear and unmistakable message to criminals: If you commit a crime in Florida and you are convicted of a crime in Florida, Florida will punish you, and you will serve your time.[152]

Describing STOP as a "a citizen-led organization" (disguising its ties to law enforcement organizations), Crist invoked a populist anticourt and antigovernment sentiment to build support for the legislation:

> Hundreds of volunteers spent countless hours gathering signatures of support to place this on the ballot. . . . [But] the Florida Supreme Court threw it off the ballot. It has created tremendous frustration in the people of Florida. They were exercising the power of democracy to do something that needs to be done, that state government had failed to do. . . . Partly in response to the Supreme Court ruling, voters this year went to the polls in search of change. Tired of the old ways of doing things, they voted for those who would get the job done— and those who will put public safety above all else.[153]

The Senate quickly and unanimously passed the STOP bill in March as part of a four-bill crime package, which included new mandatory minimums for "career criminals" and increased penalties for crimes against the elderly.[154] By this point, Senate Democrats didn't just quietly demure, they also vigorously supported the bill. In fact, Ron Silver (D. North Miami Beach), who was also on the Senate Committee on Criminal Justice, publicly challenged House members to pass the STOP bill as quickly as possible.[155]

In April, the House overwhelmingly passed the bill, with critical support from House Republicans who had campaigned on truth in sentencing.[156] Objections came from a few Democrats concerned about the budgetary tradeoffs to prison building. Under current sentencing guidelines, the state had sufficiently appropriated prison beds to accommodate an estimated 77,900 prisoners that would be in the system by 2000. *The 85 percent requirement would again require more prison beds and an increase in operating expenses.*[157] As Representative Les Miller (D. Tampa) complained, "Where's the money to come from? It comes out of education, and it comes out of programs to take care of the elderly and the poor. We're going to have more prison beds than we have schools." Despite this sentiment, even Miller felt compelled to vote for most of the Republicans' crime package because of public support for tough justice.[158] As two North Florida Democratic legislators who were sympathetic to issues of over-incarceration explained,

> Some of [the 1995 crime legislation] I was very supportive of because as a politician little ladies and everyone else was very concerned about their safety. Your opposition would label you as a person not tough on crime. . . . So . . . as a

result, you end up getting trapped between a rock and a hard place. . . . You try to do all of the debate and put amendments . . . on bills to weaken some of the criminal justice issues, and then ending up having to vote for it because you are going to be the only person out there voting against it.[159]

I have had to push that button many times and when you have to go on the board and the whole world sees how you are voting, it puts legislators in a very difficult position. Because mandatory sentences on their face look very good. Are you against a strong criminal justice system? You can't [be]. That's like being against American apple pie.[160]

So despite their general opposition to mandatory minimums and other tough justice legislation, many House Democrats felt compelled to support these measures for fear of looking soft on crime.

Importantly, those close to the process acknowledged that *the decision to support the STOP initiative was made easier by the previous commitment to end early releases.* As Richard Stevens, the former director of the Criminal Justice Estimating Conference explained, once the legislature had funded over twenty-five thousand beds in the last two years, it was easier to make smaller prison bed commitments going forward:

The commitment to stop early release was a much bigger commitment than what it took to go to 85 [percent]. . . . The amount of [administrative gain-time and emergency release] credits that were being handed out were so enormous, the average percent of time served dropped so low, that once they eliminated early release, that was a much bigger step than actually going to the 85. . . . It seems like I remember the numbers as something like fifteen thousand additional beds were needed to make the 85 [percent]. That was not as overwhelming and undoable as it may have sounded like or seemed like [before stopping early release].[161]

While those sentenced under the 85 percent law would in reality serve less than one more year in prison, the popularity of the initiative and the political risks of not supporting it outweighed the relatively small fiscal cost of fifteen thousand additional beds. In fact, as part of the 1994 Crime Control Act, Florida received federal truth-in-sentencing and violent offender incarceration grants for almost half of the needed beds.[162]

Once again, the question became how to pay for the 1995 prison expansion. Governor Chiles wanted to issue bonds or levy new taxes for the $2 billion required over the next five years: "What I see happening is a prescription for disaster in the coming years for Florida."[163] As Ray Wilson, the staff director for the Senate Committee on Corrections, explained, new prisons were a direct trade-off with federal dollars for entitlement programs:

> It's pretty much axiomatic, if you want to drive crime control you have to use [state] money. If you use [state] money you can't match federal funds in social services or education. And that's one of the anomalies of intergovernmental revenue . . . if you want to lead in criminal justice you will trail in social services.[164]

Accordingly, when legislators proposed cutting Medicaid funding to help pay for prisons, Chiles argued that the cuts would result in the forfeiture of billions in federal dollars. These trade-offs were criticized by many working in health, education, and human services. The secretary of the Department of Health and Rehabilitative Services (HRS) was quoted in the *Miami Herald* as saying that the budget was really bad news for the poor: "They're writing all these laws and big checks for prisons and prison sentences. What they're really saying is: the poor will pay."[165] Representative Ben Graber (D. Coral Springs), a physician, was quoted as saying, "We've traded nursing home beds for prison beds, HRS workers for prison guards."[166] The chancellor of the state university system even pointed out that the state was spending more on prisoners than university students.[167] Despite these critiques, lawmakers voted to cut Medicaid funding by 4 percent. In addition, the legislature cut funds for welfare and social services by making the AFDC application procedure more difficult, reducing benefits for poor pregnant women and aid to county public health clinics, and laying off HRS employees.[168]

The Triumph of the Carceral State

The years between 1991 and 1995 mark a crucial point in the development of the carceral ethos and the carceral state in Florida. During these years, lawmakers moved from contestation over appropriate penal policy to a new consensus on the best way to deal with crime. While efforts to prevent crime and divert offenders from the system continued (or began) at the margins,[169] politicians from both sides of the aisle reached an agreement to incarcerate criminal offenders for long periods of time—regardless of the costs. Crucially, past policy choices created the rhetorical frameworks that facilitated the formation of new political alliances that advocated additional prison capacity. By choosing to regulate the prison population at the back door rather than address the number of offenders admitted to the system, legislators and previous Florida governors spawned early release as a potential political issue. In turn, early release opened up new opportunities for mobilization and persuasion—particularly for sheriffs and state's attorneys, who had been looking for a way to expand the state's prison capacity. In their framing, the federal courts' concern for prisoners' living conditions had trampled on victims' right to the long-term incarceration of criminals. By defining victims' rights in opposition to the rights of criminal defendants, law enforcement and crime victim organizations created the myth of the zero-sum game in penal policy—that anything that is good for criminal defendants is bad for victims.

This framing had clear racial and gendered overtones. Law enforcement and members of STOP were predominately white and the majority of prisoners were black. The media further depicted offenders as disproportionately black and brown men and victims as white females.[170] Thus, the message implicit in media representations and STOP advocacy was that the cost of protecting (white) crime victims was the *disposal* of (black) criminal offenders. But incapacitation through imprisonment was a *white* framing of victims' rights. Advocates for black communities that were disproportionately impacted by crime and drugs put forward a different notion of victimhood. To many of them, the whole community—including offenders—suffered from crime. And the community as victim had a right to better education, police protection, and programs that could rehabilitate young people. As T. Willard Fair, the president of the Miami Urban League, stated in 1993 after the murder of a tourist in the Miami area: "What I propose is for the community and the churches to help *re*-direct, re-focus and re-train our children, because you can't tell me that when a teen can purposely sit and devise a plan to attack and kill people that that cannot be redirected into something positive."[171] In this view, criminal offenders were not expendable, but salvageable. However, as Michael Fortner has demonstrated regarding New York in the 1970s, urban black residents did not speak with one voice (in the way that law enforcement did), with some also calling for stiffer penalties and mandatory jail time for those offenders who made the "whole community look bad."[172]

While both Democrats and Republicans in the Florida legislature had previously kept law enforcement at arm's length, the change in partisan context and continuing high rates of violent crime in the early 1990s led both parties to eventually jump onto the prison bandwagon. The influx of white middle-class residents to the suburbs and Cuban residents to South Florida and the concentration of black Democratic voters in fewer legislative districts gave Republicans the chance to win both houses of state government for the first time since Reconstruction. To gain political capital, state Republicans appropriated the issue of early releases and victims' rights and campaigned on the promise to make criminals serve their full sentences. In an attempt to stay competitive (both nationally and in Florida) Democrats moved to the right on traditional liberal issues, such as racial equality, welfare spending, and crime prevention. In part, this conservative shift was made possible by the capture of the black vote by the Democratic Party and it, in turn, changed the possibilities for racial justice advocates' rhetoric and strategy.[173] As Michelle Alexander has poignantly noted, "What is most striking about the civil rights community's response to the mass incarceration of people of color is the relative quiet."[174] In Florida, this absence was due to both the structure and the ideological orientation of civil rights organizations and urban community groups. Civil rights organizations were relatively weak at the state level, where policymakers made decisions to build prisons and lengthen time served. Ideologically, civil rights organizations retreated from advocating for state policies designed to foster racial equality and moved toward a racial project of self-empowerment and/or racial representation. The civil rights community's absence from the debate over penal policy and its lack of mobilization further weakened Democrats' incentives to resist the politics of early release or to deal with the thorny issue of black overrepresentation in the criminal justice system.[175]

As a consequence, state politicians developed a new political consensus. Despite the enormous costs, legislators made good on their promise to put more criminals behind bars by increasing the state's carceral capacity—appropriating more than $500 million to build twenty new prisons (including Florida's first three adult private prisons), seventeen work camps, and one work release facility—space for approximately twenty-five thousand more prisoners. Again, early decisions to expand prison capacity to resolve *Costello* paved the way for legislators' subsequent commitment. Yet as Secretary of Corrections Harry Singletary pointed out:

> The ongoing prison buildup comes at the expense of education. . . . Some of the things that will have a long range impact haven't been funded—education, drug treatment, child care, the things that will stem the growth of corrections. As

Secretary, I'm proud of what we did for corrections. But as a parent and citizen, we really didn't deal with some of the systemic and root causes.[176]

Legislators' decisions to trade social welfare dollars for prison cells were made in the context of extreme politicization of crime control policy, but they were no dummies. Legislators knew the state would be paying for prisons for years to come.[177] The story of Florida during this period suggests that "social welfare retrenchment" in the 1990s was partly a result of the growth in carceral capacity.[178] While social welfare spending in Florida, like in the rest of the South, has always been more meager than other states, this chapter demonstrates that legislators first made the decision to build prisons and then, because of aversion to new taxes, funded them at the expense of social services and education. Likewise, while private prison companies had active lobbyists and paid "researchers" who worked to sell private prisons to Florida state legislators, they were not an impetus for incarceration growth in Florida.[179] They, like sheriffs and state's attorneys, took advantage of an opportunity to promote their interests. As I demonstrate in the next chapter, legislators also benefitted politically in the short term: once they had committed to building prisons, they could continue to capitalize on the politics of crime and fear in order to accomplish their own agendas.

CHAPTER SIX

Republicans, Prosecutors, and the Carceral Ethos, 1995–2008

Decisions [were] made many years ago and by very responsive, and I have to tell you, very responsible people. And at the time they knew that this was a multigenerational commitment. When they put those [prisons] in the rural counties they knew that was going to be *the* economy. . . . And there was an accommodation reached, "I'll give you a career, you get out of my neighborhood." And that was an understanding. Everybody was comfortable with it. We're now entering the second generation of that . . . where the child that was born at the start of the prison population [boom] is now incarcerated.—Ray Wilson, former staff director of the Florida Senate Corrections Committee, May 2007[1]

B y the mid-1990s politicians across the political divide had come to a resounding consensus on a new set of assumptions to guide criminal justice policy and practice. As David Garland accurately describes, legislators decided "it is better to keep a known criminal locked up forever than to risk the life or property of another innocent victim. Their calculations are simple—the liberty interests of the prisoner are set at zero if his or her release might expose the public to avoidable danger, or require the responsible official to run any substantial political risk."[2] From the mid-1990s through the Great Recession of 2008—when some states began to rethink mass incarceration policies—this crime control script, which I refer to as the *carceral ethos*, guided politicians' policy choices.[3] Previous chapters explained the political development of the carceral ethos by looking at how past policy decisions created new meanings, state capacities, and interest groups who shaped subsequent policy options for lawmakers in a competitive partisan environment. In this chapter, I further interrogate the carceral ethos with its attending investments in carceral capacity and I examine the consequences for Florida politics and penal policy. Unlike Philip Goodman, Michelle Phelps, and Joshua Page, who argue that penal ideology and practice remained contested throughout this period, I find that the overriding political sentiment was, as one policy analyst noted, "the more prisons, the better."[4] To be sure, some key players such as corrections administrators, black legislators, and public defenders resisted policymakers' punitive choices, but even their contestation was circumscribed by the available punitive policy options. In this context, politicians defined new problems that could be solved with new sentencing enhancements and more prisons, thus deepening the grasp of the carceral state.

First and foremost, this chapter argues that investments in carceral capacity created the potential and the ability for lawmakers to, as Jonathan Simon states, "govern through crime," where legislators rationalized policy by claiming to protect (white) crime victims (or potential victims).[5] Whereas previous changes to sentencing laws aimed, at least in part, to address the early release crisis (which had largely subsided), once in charge, Republicans' crime control legislation increasingly became symbolic politics. In this vein, *political profiteers*, such as Governors Jeb Bush and Charlie Crist, pushed for rhetorically catchy sentencing enhancements that they could bank for their later campaigns. For some Republicans, such as Governor Bush, the turn to imprisonment was part of a larger neoliberal political project to retract the state more generally. Yet for other Republican *policy entrepreneurs*, imprisonment was part of a continuum of government programs needed to reduce the high rates of violent crime that still plagued their communities. While divergent in motive, both models of crime control policy put more offenders in prison for longer periods of time.

Second, I argue that the carceral ethos empowered public prosecutors as the voice both of the public and of victims. Similar to Joshua Page's argument that prison capacity created political opportunities for the California corrections officers' union, I demonstrate how the carceral ethos and the change in partisan control created an opportunity for the Florida Prosecuting Attorneys Association to rewrite the state's sentencing laws to emphasize prison time for low-level offenders.[6] Along with new mandatory minimum sentences for repeat offenders and for crimes where a gun was present, new sentencing policy increased the likelihood that convicted offenders received a prison, rather than nonprison, sentence.

Third, I argue that the structure of the state legislative process enabled political posturing around crime and the ability of Republicans to pass their crime control agenda. In particular, term limits, part-time legislators, and the committee structure facilitated what I refer to as *legislator-driven* crime control policy, where one *legislator-expert* becomes the point person for other lawmakers on a particular topic and thus is able to successfully guide their proposals through the legislative process. In other words, in a political context where policy decisions are based on short-term political viability rather than the long-term health of the state, a few policymakers can steer legislation in ways that sustain mass incarceration.

Finally, I argue that the move away from the project for racial equality and the racialization of crime and victimhood made it easier for white lawmakers and the public to accept the carceral ethos that offenders (adult and juvenile) were disposable and beyond salvaging. Yet it also made it difficult for black lawmakers and their allies to oppose harsh crime control policies. While black legislators were instrumental in abolishing mandatory minimum sentencing for many crimes in the early 1990s, their power to direct legislative policy drastically waned after the Republican takeover of the legislature, which, ironically, their presence helped facilitate. In addition, the move away from the project of racial equality toward racial representation limited the arguments that black legislators could make about the overrepresentation of black Floridians, and particularly black youth, in the criminal justice system.

Taken together, the arguments in this chapter demonstrate that Florida policymakers constructed the carceral state in the shadow of the earlier events, policies, and politics. In particular, they were guided by the memory of prison conditions litigation, early releases, and Charlie Street. I begin the chapter by describing the carceral ethos through the fight over "cushy" prison conditions and the return of chain gangs to the state. In the second section, I examine the consequences of the Republican takeover of the state legislature on crime control policy, including sentencing reforms supported by the Florida Prosecuting Attorneys Association. In the third section, I describe how the changing structure of the legislative process facilitated symbolic tough justice politics and policies. In the fourth section, I outline two models of Republican-led crime control initiatives: crime control as *political capital* represented by Governor Jeb Bush's 10-20-life proposal in 1999 and Governor Charlie Crist's Anti-Murder Bill in 2006; and crime control as *responsible policymaking* by policy entrepreneurs such as such as Representatives Victor Crist from Tampa and Alex Villalobos from greater Miami. In the fifth section, I address the resistance by and influence of black legislators. I conclude with an analysis of the consequences of the carceral ethos in an era of declining crime rates, including a growing prison population and the need for additional prisons.

Chain Gangs and the Call for Harsh Confinement

The renewed calls from Florida legislators for harsh confinement for prisoners in the mid-1990s help illustrate the scope of the carceral ethos. No longer was it enough to put criminals behind bars for more significant amounts of time; their time needed to be "hard." The notion that prisoners had it too easy and were being coddled while in prison was a legacy of the court cases meant to improve earlier unsafe prison conditions.[7] Politicians and victim advocates explicitly or implicitly contended that prison improvements came at the expense of regular people, victims, and states' rights and publicly promised to address the laxity of state prisons. Their initiatives, opposed by the secretary of the Department of Corrections and unsupported by any academic or professional experts, began the trend toward *legislator-driven* crime control policy, which was highly effective at making a name for ambitious politicians. In addition, by implicitly evoking images of black criminals, the return to harsh confinement reinforced the idea that, as the president of the Florida Police Chiefs Association, Kenneth R. Wagner, was quoted as saying, "There is a large group of people out there who are beyond salvaging."[8]

When State Senator Charlie Crist first introduced the STOP bill to increase time served to 85 percent of imposed prison sentences in 1995 (as detailed in chapter 5), he also stated that prisons in Florida were too "pleasant," put too much emphasis on "recreation" and "entertainment," and not enough on work.[9] As part of the 1995 legislation, Crist proposed a bill that required the Department of Corrections to develop a plan "for inmate labor wearing leg irons in chain-gang work groups."[10] Crist's proposal passed (with few objections) and earned him repeated mentions in newspapers across the state.[11] At the time, the *St. Petersburg Times*, the state's left-leaning newspaper, derided him as "Chain Gang Charlie." But "Crist welcomed that put-down and wore it with pride," helping to make the nickname stick.[12] Crist rejected the arguments of critics who found issue with "the spectacle of shackled men, most black, stirring images of slavery."[13] Florida had of course used chain gangs from the end of convict leasing up until the late 1940s; and prisoners continued to work under armed guards along the roads until the late 1960s. In fact, some former legislators had personal memories of the practice:

> I remember as a boy my father built roads and bridges for an American construction company. We lived in Ocala and I would go to work with him on

weekends and . . . they were working prisoners and they were in chains and they had on the striped suits. . . . Road contractors could contract with the state prisons for labor. And, of course, the prisoners weren't getting paid anything.[14]

While Alabama legislators reinstituted chain gangs on the condition that they reflect the racial makeup of the prison population, Crist did not support a similar provision in Florida.[15]

It fell to Florida Department of Corrections Secretary Harry Singletary, the first African American to lead the Department, to implement the chain gang policy. Appointed by Governor Chiles in 1991, Singletary served the entire eight years of Chiles's terms and enjoyed a close working relationship with him. Singletary's commitment to rehabilitation and humane prison conditions increasingly put him at odds with legislators and the public concerned with coddled prisoners. In a July 1994, *Correctional Compass* newsletter, Singletary cited two letters to the editor in the *Tallahassee Democrat* that advocated "making prison hell on earth." In response he wrote, "Today there are many who would have corrections professionals set aside constitutional guarantees in the name of justice and retribution. . . . We need to impress upon the public that the inmate's institutional environment is also our daily work environment."[16] Like other corrections professionals, Singletary opposed the use of chain gangs. However, he followed the law and developed a plan for "restricted labor squads" to be composed of prisoners who violated prison rules. He decided that the prisoners would not be chained to each other (as they were doing in Alabama at the time) and would work in crews of twenty or fewer, under the supervision of three correctional officers with guns. In November 1995, the first "chain gang" began its work in the Everglades under the watch of Senator Crist and numerous reporters.[17] Over the next year the department expanded the program to seven institutions and 140 prisoners (out of a population of 62,000). The restricted labor squads mainly worked on state property cleaning drainage ditches, picking up trash, maintaining holding ponds, and repairing fences and roads.

Senator Crist, unsatisfied with this arrangement, sponsored a bill in 1997 that would make the punishment more harsh.[18] To dramatize his intent, he carried chains into the Senate chamber (see figure 6.1). Representative Allen Trovillion, a Republican from a small town in rural Orange County who chaired the House Corrections Committee, recalled:

Chain Gang Charlie, you know he was always getting in front of the press . . . so he says, "We're gonna put the worst of the worst inmates out on there. We're

FIGURE 6.1. Senator Charlie Crist (R. St. Petersburg) makes a point by holding up chains while debating the chain gang bill on the Senate floor, April 24, 1997. AP Photo/Hugh Scoggins.

gonna have chain gangs. We're gonna have them chained together and they're gonna be on the highways where people can see them."[19]

While his bill passed the Senate Corrections Committee, Trovillion killed the bill in the House by arguing that it would be "terrible" for public safety. In addition, he reasoned that "Florida's had a chain gang law ever since way back. . . . so we didn't need another one."[20] At the time he told the press that chain gangs were counterproductive. Echoing the opinions of prisoners' rights advocates and corrections professionals, he added, "These people in prison are human beings. I want our inmates ready to go back into society."[21] Despite this setback, Crist was able to use his nickname and his support for chain gangs in his run for U.S. senator in 1998 against Bob Graham. Although he lost the race, the chain gang bills had made him one of the most well-known state senators: his campaign could "fly on press clippings."[22] He even ran campaign advertisements that used his Chain Gang Charlie nickname.

Prisoner access to televisions, weight equipment, air conditioning, and the privilege of smoking also became a source of political posturing in the mid-1990s. Legislators claimed that prisoners had *better* access to food, health care, and other amenities than "millions of law-abiding Floridians," and accordingly, these amenities, including "cable television and magic shows," were "unjustified for . . . lawbreakers."[23] To address this "discrepancy," legislators passed a broad law banning the department from using the Inmate Welfare Trust Fund to purchase "audio-visual or electronic equipment used primarily for recreational purposes."[24] Immediately before the law went into effect, Singletary ordered the purchase of new televisions from the fund, justifying his transgression by saying he was "being a good manager."[25] In 1996, the legislature sponsored bills to ban smoking by prisoners, penalize prisoners for filing frivolous lawsuits, and remove all weight-training equipment from prisons.[26] In support of these measures Representative Luis Rojas (R. Hialeah) invoked the fight over cable TV: "Here's a guy that can't afford health insurance. Here's a guy that can't afford cable TV. Yet people who are in prison, who committed crimes, can get these things. There are people in prison who get more basic commodities than people who are not in prison."[27] Yet as Al Shopp, the business and services director for the Police Benevolent Association (the labor union for corrections officers), told me, officers would rather have had legislators take away GED programming than TVs: "sometimes we think that [legislators] are too damn liberal for their own good, and other times we'd like to see them put more money into programs to assist us, but they're not."[28]

The political rhetoric over "plush" prisons prompted the Department of Corrections to use its annual report to address the "misconceptions" that prisoners have cable TVs and satellite dishes; spend all day lifting weights and playing basketball; eat better and have better health care than average citizens; and live in air-conditioned prisons. They clarified that over 75 percent of the able-bodied prisoner population have either a job or a program assignment; TV's are not purchased with public funds; "exercise and activity programs are security enhancements"; the state is required to provide appropriate levels of medical, dental, and mental health care to prisoners; and "only seven of the 55 major state prisons in Florida have air conditioning in the living areas, and many of these are located in South Florida."[29] In addition, the department commissioned a survey and posted the results on its website: "Some of these activities, which are often singled out . . . are not as distasteful to the public, press or Department staff as some believe." Most interestingly, they reported that while almost 90 percent of the public incorrectly believed that prisoners were housed in air-conditioned prisons, 67 percent thought they *should* have air conditioning.[30]

Republicans, Prosecutors, and Tough Justice

While the public might have expressed a more ambiguous stance on prisoner conditions than assumed by political leaders, Florida Republicans transformed Florida politics over the course of the 1990s in part through an unwavering commitment to the carceral ethos. In 1997, with Democrat Lawton Chiles as governor, Republicans took over both chambers of the state legislature for the first time since Reconstruction. By all accounts, it was a big deal. Helping them to get there, ironically, were black Democrats who worked with Republicans in 1992 to create more majority-minority state legislative and congressional districts. As expected, the number of black representatives increased, as did suburban Republican representatives.[31] The Republicans' newfound political power ushered in an era of tough justice, first, by empowering the Florida Prosecuting Attorneys Association (FPAA) to rewrite the state's sentencing structure to decrease the discretion of judges and increase prison time for offenders; second, by reconfiguring the expectations of legislative committee research to support the carceral ethos; and third, as the following section details, by enacting new symbolic sentencing enhancements and mandatory minimums.

The FPAA's main legislative agenda during the 1990s was the abolition of sentencing guidelines. During the debate over the 1995 STOP legislation, it argued that the guidelines were too lenient and didn't give judges enough discretion.[32] Brian Berkowitz, executive director of the Task Force on Criminal Justice that met between 1993 and 1995, recalled that Ed Austin, the former FPAA president and Jacksonville state's attorney, frequently came to task force meetings to insist that it took too many offenses for someone to be eligible for prison.[33] The state's attorney's fight against the guidelines led to a perception by newly elected members of the House and Senate Committees on Criminal Justice that the 1994 Sentencing Guidelines set the threshold for prison so high that serious offenders were not getting

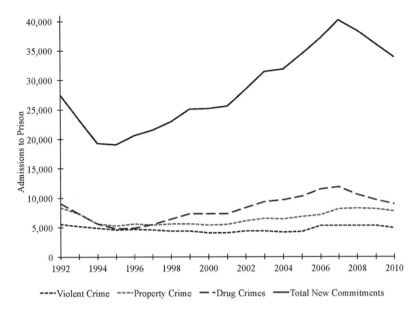

FIGURE 6.2. Prison admissions, 1992–2010. Source: Florida Department of Corrections Annual Reports.

prison time.[34] This was despite the fact that analyses of the cases sentenced under the 1994 guidelines demonstrated that it was not the guidelines, but judges, who sent fewer offenders to prison and issued shorter sentences than recommended by the guidelines.[35] Yet in 1995, the FPAA successfully lobbied for a bill that would raise the point values on a variety of crimes, thus pulling more offenders into the discretionary prison range and the range where a prison sentence was mandatory.[36]

By 1997, when the Republicans assumed control of the legislature, there were signs that the criminal justice system had regained some semblance of stability. Property and violent crime rates had been decreasing over the past five years; the 1994 sentencing guidelines had increased average time served to 70 percent of sentence imposed; and the dramatic increase in prison admissions had stopped as judges took advantage of new alternatives to incarceration (see figure 6.2). In the 1995/1996 fiscal year, the Department of Corrections had planned to construct an additional 9,079 beds, but only built 6,451—returning the unused construction funds to the state.[37] In March 1997, the *Tampa Tribune* reported "a 28 percent drop in the anticipated growth of the prison population over the next five years means the state has $2.2 billion to spend on other expenses in that period."[38] In theory, the Republicans could have taken credit for the drop in crime and increased prison terms. Instead, they—along with Democratic allies—doubled down on incarceration. Representative Victor Crist (R. Temple Terrace) argued, for example, that if beds were becoming available lawmakers should "tweak the sentencing guidelines to make sure career criminals are put away for a long time."[39]

The FPAA and the Florida Sheriffs Association seized the opportunity surrounding excess prison capacity to intensify their fight to abolish the sentencing guidelines.[40] Republicans, who had relied on prosecutors' support to get elected, welcomed the prosecutors' initiative as they began their effort to make their mark by reversing key Democrat-led legislation and remaking Democrat-led state agencies.[41] As Buddy Jacobs, the chief lobbyist for the FPAA, explained, the prosecuting attorneys worked with the House Crime and Punishment Committee to draft legislation:

> We never liked the sentencing guidelines and we worked very hard to get rid of them . . . We actually drafted [the Florida Criminal Punishment Code] . . . State Attorney Kathy Rundle from Miami spent a month with us in Tallahassee and we brought all the state attorneys up and we lobbied for that very hard.[42]

The bill proposed by the prosecuting attorneys completely abolished the guidelines and allowed judges to impose the statutory maximum penalty for any felony (five years for a third-degree felony, fifteen for second-degree felony, and thirty for a first-degree felony).[43] After concerns about sentencing disparities were raised by public defenders and black legislators, legislators amended the bill to allow judges to depart from the guidelines while keeping the sentencing structure intact in order to provide some means of assessing and comparing sentences across region, race, and other factors.[44] Despite this change, the two black members on the House Criminal Justice Appropriations Committee either voted against the bill (Kendrick Meek, D. Miami) or abstained (Willie Logan, D. Opa-locka).[45]

While some Democrats supported abolishing sentencing guidelines as a means of returning discretion to judges, the final bill was more proprosecutor than projudge.[46] The FPAA argued that judges did not treat drug cases seriously enough and that downward departures were too frequent and easy. Accordingly, their proposal created a "floor" (or minimum number of guideline points) under which a judge could not impose a nonprison sentence without written reasons.[47] The changes, therefore, gave judges discretion on one end (longer prison terms), but not the other (shorter or no prison term). Even the title, Criminal Punishment Code, was symbolic and important to the FPAA—both signaling the emphasis on punishment and allowing them to claim that they "got rid of sentencing guidelines."[48] In addition, the bill abolished the Sentencing Guidelines Commission, composed of circuit and county court judges, replacing it with a new Sentencing Reform Commission, composed of representatives from the FPAA, Florida Sheriffs Association, Public Defenders Association, the Florida Department of Law Enforcement (FDLE), and the Florida Police Chiefs Association. The Public Defenders Association lobbied against the bill:

> The pitch we [the Public Defenders Association] made to the Legislature in opposition was that there was a good reason why guidelines were first enacted. There were studies that showed disparity, racial and geographic. We needed uniformity in the state. The only response we got from the Legislature is "this is a different world now. If Miami wants different sentences than north Florida, that's OK." I stood up and told them [the Legislature] about these problems, but the State Attorney said "it's a good bill," so that was that.[49]

Judges, conceivably concerned about staying out of politics, did not come out for or against the legislation.[50]

The fiscal impact of the bill was officially recorded as an "indeterminate, but significant, increase in the prison population."[51] On the one hand, as lawmakers had intentionally given less weight to possession and sale of narcotics in the 1994 guidelines, the legislation would likely increase the number of drug offenders sent to prison. On the other hand, judges had been reluctant to impose longer sentences under the current guidelines. As in previous years, supporters of the Criminal Punishment Code drew on the legacy of early releases and the STOP campaign rhetoric to make the case that *cost didn't matter*. Recent events helped their cause: in March 1997, the Florida Supreme Court issued an opinion requiring the Department of Corrections to restore previously revoked provisional credits to violent prisoners who had lost them as the result of a 1992 opinion by Attorney General Butterworth.[52] The decision outraged lawmakers and law enforcement. Speaker of the House Daniel Webster was quoted in the *Tampa Tribune* saying that he wanted the early-release prisoners back behind bars if they so much as "spit on the sidewalk."[53] Lee County sheriff John McDougall publicly stated that tourists should avoid Florida because of the ruling.[54] Representatives Victor Crist and Adam Putnam (R. Lakeland) (who would go on to become a congressman and then

secretary of agriculture) immediately sponsored a Prison Releasee Reoffender Bill, mandating that those released from prison who committed a
violent crime within five years must serve 100 percent of their new sentences plus any gain-time previously taken off.[55] Unlike other habitual
offender laws already on the books, the bill gave even more power to prosecutors by mandating judges to impose the enhancement if the prosecutor seeks the "prison releasee reoffender" designation.[56] In explaining his
vote for the bill (which ultimately passed), Representative Tom Feeney
(R. Oviedo) stated that "unlike the Florida Supreme Court, we are more
concerned with the safety and protection of our citizens . . . than what is
convenient and comfortable for the violent criminals."[57]

When the Criminal Punishment Code came up for debate, the specter of the early 1990s helped Republicans get the bill through. In fact,
the trials of some of the defendants accused of killing tourists took place
in Tallahassee during the legislative session—drawing legislators' attention. As Victor Crist told the *Tampa Tribune*, "The general message is
we're going to be making Florida one of the safest places in the country."[58]
Many House Democrats, however, still argued that, although unknown,
the costs of the changes were too high—especially when the 1994 guidelines and the 85 percent mandate had not been given adequate time to
work. In addition, black legislators expressed concern that the new rules
would lead to an increase in sentencing disparity by race.[59] Twenty-eight
out of fifty-four Democrats voted against the final bill in the House, but
the Senate passed it unanimously.[60] Governor Chiles let the bill become
law without his signature, along with a law that required chemical castra-
tion of twice-convicted sex offenders.[61]

The Structure of Crime Control Policymaking

The success of crime control initiatives by prosecutors and Republicans
built on past policy decisions and, in turn, reinforced the carceral ethos,
allowing for further tough justice measures. As Frank Messersmith, a
lobbyist for the Florida Sheriffs Association, stated, "Florida progressed
from the habitual offender laws up to the really dramatic 10-20-life-type
things."[62] Importantly, however, changes to the structure of the legislature
and the legislative process during the 1990s also facilitated lawmakers'
ability to pass new tough justice legislation.

The biggest change in governing structure in the 1990s was Florida's
adoption of term limits for legislators—Florida now limits representatives

and senators to eight years in each office.[63] At the same time, over the course of the 1990s state public policy became increasing complex, making it unrealistic to expect part-time legislators to fully understand all the issues that came before them. As a result, legislators looked to one or two colleagues or lobbyists with particular expertise to guide their decisions in specific policy areas. Term limits also give legislators fewer years to enact their agenda—especially if they wanted to be elected to higher office. Combined with the structure of campaign financing, term limits gave legislators who wanted to focus on crime control legislation an advantage: compared to legislative committees related to banking, insurance, or commerce, which attract political action committee contributions for legislators, criminal justice and corrections are undesirable committee assignments.[64] As a result, legislators could easily obtain a criminal justice–related committee assignment from which they could promote their self-proclaimed expertise and agenda. Often these *legislative experts* had a background in law enforcement and were more likely to be former sheriffs or prosecutors than former defense attorneys.

In addition to term limits, the change in Republican leadership brought about changes to the legislative committee process. First, substantive legislative committees, such as the committees on corrections and criminal justice, began to move away from a legislative research model that allowed committee staffers to help define a research agenda and objectively lay out policy options for lawmakers.[65] They moved toward a model where policy options (and the staff presenting them) were based on ideology rather than empirical data. For example, House committees analyzed bills based on the following five "House Principles":

1. **Less Government**. Does the bill tend to reduce government regulations, size of government, or eliminate entitlements or unnecessary programs?
2. **Lower Taxes**. Does the bill promote individual responsibility in spending or reduce taxes or fees?
3. **Personal Responsibility**. Does the bill encourage responsible behavior by individuals and families and encourage them to provide for their own health, safety, education, moral fortitude, or general welfare?
4. **Individual Freedom**. Does the bill increase opportunities for individuals or families to decide, without hindrance or coercion from government, how to conduct their own lives and make personal choices?
5. **Stronger Families**. Does the bill enhance the traditional American family and its power to rear children without excessive interference from the government?[66]

As substantive committee chairs, legislator-experts were also more likely to hire staff with a similar law enforcement orientation. Victor Crist explained that when he took over from Elvin Martinez (D. Tampa) as chair of the House Criminal Justice Committee, he had to uproot the former staff because Martinez, himself a former defense attorney, had hired staff who were "only concerned about offender rights and due process."[67] As Amanda Cannon, the staff director for the Senate Criminal Justice Committee, explained, "We have to be very careful and we are very good about saying, well if you believe incapacitation works, you want to do this. If you don't believe incapacitation works, you want to do this."[68] This new model was tied to the rise of "fact-driven crime legislation" (as one committee staffer called it), where legislators wanted to know the specific facts of a notorious crime and how to fix the specific problem without looking at the big picture.

Second, as part of a growing anti-intellectualism among the Republican Party during this period, legislative committees became less likely to consider academic research and more likely to rely on law enforcement practitioner knowledge when considering policy options.[69] As Richard Stevens, the director of the Criminal Justice Estimating Conference (CJEC), explains, this decision to forgo research was directly related to the decision to build prisons as the solution to the crime problem:

> I remember the days when it was very common practice for the legislative committees to have Florida State University criminology professors come and testify before the committees. . . . It seems that there was more of an interest in research, the legislature sponsored more research themselves and they brought the academics in . . . that was more part of the standard operating procedure that these [policy options] were open questions. It sort of seems like at some point the answer to these questions was, "We just have to build more prisons." In the short term that might have been the case. . . . On the other hand, there doesn't seem to be that openness to asking questions and seeking various answers, or that there may be new answers out there that exist.[70]

As many of my interviewees explained, policymakers distrusted academics, viewing them as too liberal and therefore not objective, again putting more faith in law enforcement practitioners. One staffer told me that he wished there were some "intellectually honest" studies about what is behind the high incarceration rate, but that most people who study it have a political agenda.[71] Another said, "I will tell you right away, most of the academic work in this field is so liberally laced that most policymakers, even the black caucus and Democratic caucus, don't view it as credible."[72] The move away from academic expertise to practical expertise is vividly caught in an example from the debate around the cost of the 1997 Releasee Reoffender Act. Stevens explained:

> We went through and did an impact [analysis] as if everybody that was eligible would get that sentence. Well, one of the advocates of [the Releasee Reoffender Act] was a former prosecutor that was working at the time as a staff director for the House Criminal Justice Committee and said, "Well, wait a minute, in the criminal justice system the way this really works is that these guys plea bargain and if the sentence is absurd, if these people . . . had no violence in any of their history, then even though they committed a third-degree felony, they are not going to get this five-year sentence." We thought, what is going on here? You talk about truth in sentencing elsewhere, why is that not the case here?[73]

From then on, the CJEC attempted to approximate the extent to which mandatory minimum sentences were *actually* applied, deciding that going forward their projections would assume that "mandatory" laws would be applied only 50 percent of the time.

These changes in the legislative and committee process further gutted objective analysis of the crime problem and its solutions, allowing political posturing and campaign promises to *drive* the policy process. Governors and *legislator-experts* thus defined the criminal justice problem to be solved—the continued high rates of violent crime by persistent offenders—and the solutions considered—namely, more prison time. The reliance on law enforcement expertise then lowered cost estimates of tough justice solutions and increased their purported crime control benefit. In turn, legislators' assumption that their role was to enact the wishes of their most crime-weary constituents and that looking soft on crime was politically dangerous made it very difficult to vote no. This was true for both highly symbolic bills, such as chain gangs, and bills with more extensive impact, such as the CPC and new mandatory minimums.

Republican Crime Control Politics

By the end of the decade, Florida legislators had an agreed-upon crime control policy script. While a few Democrats and Republicans pushed

against the policy implications of the carceral ethos, Republican governors and legislators interested in passing new punitive crime control
policy measures had an advantage. Between 1998, when the new Criminal
Punishment Code went into effect, and 2008, the Florida legislature, like
many others across the nation, newly criminalized a host of behaviors and
passed a series of sentencing enhancements, new mandatory minimum
laws, and offender registration requirements, even as crime rates continued to fall. While some previous scholarship has argued that punitive
crime control policies are part of a cohesive neoliberal political project
to promote the market, retract the welfare state, and cultivate the trope
of individual responsibility, a close look at the individual players in crime
control policymaking in Florida during this period reveals a more diverse
set of ideologies complementing the carceral ethos.[74]

The data from Florida reveal two motivations behind Republican crime
control initiatives during this time period.[75] First, politically ambitious
politicians, what I call *political profiteers*, sponsored some initiatives as
"crime control theater" meant to garner political capital.[76] Governor Jeb
Bush and Governor Charlie Crist both used crime control to capture the
public attention in ways similar to other symbolic public policy issues such
as abortion or same-sex marriage.[77] While Governor Bush most strictly
adhered to the neoliberal view that "state government had become too
powerful and intrusive" and that the private sector would provide better
outcomes, he also "dramatically expanded the state's involvement in public
education," arguing that it was "too important to leave to educators" and
local communities.[78] Crist, who eventually ran for United States Senate as
an independent and then became a Democrat, seems to be the ultimate political profiteer with little ideological grounding.[79] Yet as political historian
David Colburn commented in 2007, "Crist also respects government and
those who work for it, a dramatic change from the Bush years . . . [and] . . .
the former governor's ideological extremism."[80]

Second, what I am calling *policy entrepreneurs* sponsored initiatives in
an attempt to solve a policy problem—whether it be violent crime in a
particular community or an inefficient criminal justice system. State legislators Victor Crist (R. Temple Terrace) and Alex Villalobos (R. Miami),
two of the most influential Republican crime control policy entrepreneurs,
strongly believed in the state's role—not just for crime control—but in
education, crime prevention, and community development. This model of
motivation is more consistent with a classic and positive understanding of
policymaking as collective puzzlement with imperfect information.[81] Yet

it is important to remember that even as these legislators aimed to be "responsible" policymakers, looking out for the long-term health of their communities, the prevailing carceral ethos shaped their understanding of the best policy solutions.

Jeb Bush and the 10-20-Life Campaign

The idea for 10-20-life originated in California in 1997 as ballot initiative proposed by Mike Reynolds, the architect of California's three-strikes law.[82] The initiative focused on gun crime, providing mandatory minimum sentences for gun possession (ten years), gun use (twenty years), and inflicting injury with a gun (life) while committing another serious felony. California governor Pete Wilson (D) signed the bill into law to counteract criticism from law enforcement after he vetoed gun control legislation that targeted manufacturers of cheap handguns. The National Rifle Association had used its considerable resources to lobby against the gun control measure. Justifying his decision, Governor Wilson stated,

> Not only does Senate Bill 500 [the gun control bill] fail to keep guns out of the hands of criminals, it will deprive law-abiding, legitimate gun users of the needed protection of handguns. . . . I am convinced that vigorous enforcement of the 10-20-Life law will provide the people of California with far more protection against gun violence.[83]

In Florida, Jeb Bush was facing a similar political problem in his run for governor in 1998. Although he was significantly ahead in the polls, Bush's opponent, Lieutenant Governor Buddy MacKay, was trying to close the gap using Bush's opposition to a popular gun control amendment on the ballot that gave counties the right to regulate sales at gun shows. In September, Bush announced his 10-20-life plan surrounded by thirty county sheriffs: "The message here is clear. Commit a crime with a gun, and you're done."[84] The next month the Bush campaign ran television advertisements claiming Bush to be tougher on crime than MacKay because he was "ready to put criminals away for 10-20-Life."[85]

After he won the election, Bush turned to State Representative Victor Crist, chair of the House Justice Council, to sponsor his 10-20-life proposal. Crist argued that 10-20-life would be a deterrent to gun crime and would take serious criminals of the streets. As he later explained to me, "If you are using a gun, you are already hardened."[86] The bill was supported by the Florida Sheriffs Association, the Police Benevolent Association, and individual victims. The only organization that testified against the bill was the Association for Criminal Defense Lawyers, which pointed out that under current law judges already had the option of the sentences mandated by the bill. While no one raised the point that violent crime was already decreasing, Representative Randy Ball (R. Brevard County), who was also considered a legislative expert on criminal justice, did express concern about the cost of a ten-year mandatory minimum for the most likely offenders. As a result, the House Committee on Crime and Punishment reduced the mandatory minimum to three years for those charged with possession of a gun during an aggravated assault and burglary.[87]

The strongest objections came from members of the black caucus (the Florida Conference of Black State Legislators) who correctly predicted a disproportionate impact on young black offenders.[88] First-year representative Frederica Wilson (D. Miami) expressed these concerns during a House Corrections Committee hearing as recorded in the minutes:

> Representative Frederica Wilson (D. Miami): "How is adding years to a prison sentence affecting the offender when he/she comes out?"
>
> Sheriff Perry [testifying at hearing] responded that every year incarcerated decreases the propensity to commit violent crime. He noted that the 30 year age mark is significant.
>
> Representative Wilson: "is there an age limit for the bill?"
>
> Representative Crist answered yes, 16 years old.
>
> Representative Wilson expressed concern about children who are in possession of guns.
>
> Sheriff Perry said that ages 17–25 are the most violent years of criminals.
>
> Representative Sally Heyman (D. North Miami Beach) (in an effort to refocus the discussion), said that this bill is a backdoor to gun control, not a rehabilitative bill. The purpose is to remove these dangerous people from society.[89]

When the bill reached the House floor, black members proposed other measures to reduce the impact of the bill, including an exemption for first-time offenders. They did manage two concessions—the applicable age was raised to eighteen years old, and a public service campaign around the initiative would start immediately and target areas where most gun crime occurred. In addition, Senator Daryl Jones (D. Miami) added to the reporting requirement for state's attorneys, specifying that they report

10-20-life prosecutions by age, gender, and race.[90] The final bill passed the House 108 to 11 and the Senate 39 to1. Of the twelve members opposed to the bill, only two were not African American (six black representatives and four black senators supported the bill).

Although the final bill had large price tag, the absence of the need for an immediate increase in prison beds helped garner support for the measure.[91] As the bill analysis for the governor acknowledged: "Currently, we have a 4,000 to 5,000 prison bed surplus, so that no new beds would need to be built. Given this prison bed surplus, the five year cost would be $34.6 million for the operation of newly filled beds."[92] In addition, lawmakers and law enforcement officials' continued concern over early release motivated their support of 10-20-life. For example, when I asked the lobbyist for the Florida Sheriffs Association about the FSA's rationale for supporting 10-20-life, he responded that offenders were "getting too much gain-time and . . . it just wasn't right." When I reminded him that 10-20-life focused on gun crime, he clarified,

> Well, in concert with 10-20-life was the big gain-time issue . . . so they were focused on those two things in concert. To curb the violent crime, "you do that bad crime with weapons, you are going to go away mandatory," and you are going to serve it, because you are not going to be able to get gain-time.[93]

As a result of this continued conflation with early release and the availability of prison beds, in the short term lawmakers could only lose by opposing 10-20-life, even if they were skeptical that it would bring about the deterrence it promised.[94]

Republican Policy Entrepreneurs and "Responsible" Crime Control Legislation

Both the political need to "create stricter gun control without affecting law abiding gun owners" and a neoliberal ideology against the "too powerful" and "too invasive" state motivated Jeb Bush's support for 10-20-life.[95] Yet some of the most influential legislators did not fit the mold of political profiteers, nor did they always conform to neoliberal ideology. Rather they are best described as policy entrepreneurs.[96] Former state senator Alex Villalobos, a former prosecutor and defense attorney, ran for state representative in 1992 because he believed that the criminal justice system was broken and that the people fixing it should be those who understood how the system worked. While he campaigned on truth in sentencing and sponsored the STOP legislation in the House, when he became chair of the Criminal Justice Appropriations Committee the following year, his main priority was to divert more money to prevention efforts, including funding schools for at-risk kids.[97] His efforts were blocked by the Senate: "God forbid we fund things that will keep kids out of prison. Apparently it is not Republican."[98] Yet he conceded that providing education for prisoners was not high on his constituents' list of priorities and believed the public should have some role in deciding corrections policy.[99] Villalobos's interest in mending the criminal justice system led him to occasionally support measures that lost him favor within the Republican Party.[100] For example, he supported a bill that would have required a unanimous jury to recommend a death sentence. When Villalobos ran for reelection in 2006, his opponent used this against him—running campaign ads showing Villalobos's picture next to Ted Bundy's.[101]

Yet as chair of the Criminal Justice Appropriations Committee, Villalobos supported 10-20-life after the modification that reduced gun possession crimes to a mandatory three years, even though he had doubts about removing more discretion from judges. He explained his support by emphasizing how the mandatory sentences targeted such serious crimes and noting that "the tide was going in that direction." Yet in the very next breath, he stated that mandatory minimums have gotten out of control: he agreed with the enhanced sentences for those caught selling drugs within one thousand feet of a school, but tells me that then lawmakers added churches, and then parks, and then "7-Eleven stores." Villalobos claimed he got a map and drew circles around each of those areas in his district, and said to his colleagues, "The only place where they will wind up selling cocaine is in front of my house."[102]

Finally, Villalobos was inconsistent in his deference to victims in crime legislation. In response to a campaign by Jimmy Ryce's mother (Jimmy was raped and murdered in 1995), Villalobos cosponsored the 1998 Jimmy Ryce Act, which allowed the state to indefinitely detain violent sexual predators after completing their sentences until they can prove they are rehabilitated. Yet he also pushed back against colleagues who privileged victims' role in the legislative process. For example, Villalobos opposed legislation to put cameras at intersections to catch people going through red lights because studies were inconclusive that they prevented accidents. He seemed bothered that his colleagues were swayed by testimony from "widows whose husbands were killed because of someone going through a red light."[103]

Former State Senator Victor Crist is another crime control policy entrepreneur. In the legislature, he focused on securing prison beds for violent offenders, but his goals were motivated by very different concerns than politicians like Jeb Bush or Charlie Crist. In fact, Victor Crist first ran for state representative to "brand" the blight in his community in order to foster support for community development. In 1990, he cofounded the University of South Florida Area Community Civic Association to revitalize the area north of the university in Hillsborough County—a suburban community adjacent to Tampa that had become what Crist called a "suburban ghetto." With about fifty thousand people in five square miles, a high percentage of young people, a crime rate above the state average, and high infant mortality, civic association leaders decided that the area was not being well represented at the state level. Crist ran as a Republican because it meant he wouldn't have to face anyone in the primary election. They didn't expect to win, but they wanted to "brand" their problems, so that whoever did win would be forced to engage with them.[104]

When he did win in 1992, Crist joined the house as a Republican with a "Democratic agenda" (that state government should help with neighborhood revitalization), and he claimed that neither party "wanted him."[105] As crime was the biggest issue facing the civic association, Crist worked to be appointed to all the various criminal justice and law enforcement committees in hopes of testing or implementing successful crime control policies. By doing this, he became the in-house authority on criminal justice issues. Consequently, when the Republicans took over in 1997, they chose him to lead the Justice Council.[106] One of his immediate goals was to create a separate Department of Juvenile Justice. However, he faced opposition from those within his party who wanted to move juvenile justice to the Department of Corrections. Crist fought against this (and prevailed) because he felt that a significant majority of juvenile offenders can be helped and that otherwise funding for prevention, intervention, and treatment would be lost to funding for prison beds.[107]

Thus, in "the best interests of the community," Crist supported rehabilitation for "those who should be and could be rehabilitated" and long confinement in prison for those who needed to be kept out of the community. To this latter end, in 1999 he sponsored a three-strikes law that he hoped would keep drug traffickers and "the violent criminals who continually victimize us, our neighbors, our elders and our law enforcement officers" of the streets.[108] Although the proposed bill followed other states' three-strikes laws in name, five of its six basic provisions had nothing to do with three strikes at all. In fact, the majority of the bill *reimposed* mandatory minimum sentences for assault on law enforcement and elderly persons and for drug traffickers (regardless of prior offenses) and second-time sexual batterers. In addition, it redefined prior offenses for the purposes of the habitual felony offender and the career criminal statutes, allowing all criminal charges sentenced on the same day to be counted in prior offense calculations. Yet, the three-strikes portion of the bill was more responsible than California's—although it provided lengthy mandatory minimums for three-strike offenders (five, fifteen, or thirty years or life depending on the felony degree), it specified that all three strikes had to be violent felonies. Additionally, the final bill reinstated the requirement that the three crimes had to be committed and adjudicated on separate dates.[109] Crist credited the black caucus with forcing these positive changes.[110] Despite this, nine of the fifteen black house members voted against the bill (along with six other Democrats from South Florida).[111]

The strong support for the bill was contradicted by predictions of its uselessness in combating violent crime. As the policy analysis of the bill for the governor stated, "With the exception of its mandatory sentences for drug crimes and crimes on law officers and elders . . . the bill's sentencing mandates are so similar to prior legislation that its capacity to be a new and different deterrent is questionable."[112] In fact, a 1998 report by RAND found that in the twenty-five states with three-strikes laws, there had been no appreciable impact on crime.[113] Yet the bill analysis for Florida's three-strikes law cited a report by the Office of the California Attorney General from 1996 that pointed to a $5 billion to $15 billion cost savings due to the reduction in crime associated with the three-strikes law.[114] When I challenged Crist about the seemingly symbolic nature of the law, he responded that if you ask any state's attorney or law enforcement official, they will tell you that three strikes is helping to keep the "10 percent of criminals that commit 90 percent of the crime" off the streets.[115]

Finally, similar to Villalobos, Victor Crist had reservations about victims' role in policymaking because they encourage legislating "emotionally versus practically." He offered Mothers Against Drunk Driving (MADD) as an example: MADD runs around yelling and freshman legislators who are looking for grassroots support and volunteers get close with them and feel beholden to their priorities. As a result, "you have people who have an alcohol problem and who aren't really dangerous unless they are behind the wheel drunk, who are spending years in prison."[116] Instead, Crist said that drunk driving should be "policed up front" in a way that prevents drunk people from getting in cars in the first place. "We just need them off the street, we do not need them wasting a prison bed that could go to a violent offender."[117]

Charlie Crist and the Anti-Murder Act

Very early in his political career, Charlie Crist had his sights on being a U.S. senator, maybe even president. As a politician who got his start in the 1990s, Crist learned early on the appropriate response to criminal acts and how to politically capitalize on them. His status as Chain Gang Charlie allowed his first failed run for U.S. senator in 1998, after which he ran for and won three statewide offices before trying again for a Senate seat in 2010. As governor between 2007 and 2010, Crist focused on lowering property taxes, improving public education, and protecting the environment. But to get to the governor's mansion, he relied heavily on a politics of crime and fear—in particular the fear of sexual predators. As both Loïc Wacquant and Marie Gottschalk have documented, since 2000 policymakers have increasingly passed a "punitive maze of laws and restrictions" aimed at sex offenders that "amount to a kind of ritual exile."[118] Wacquant argues that politicians turned to sex offenders as a "fresh motive" for the "repudiation of rehabilitation" and "vengeful retribution" when lower crime rates reduced the value of the racialized criminal in the public mind.[119] Three brutal murders of Florida girls in 2004 and 2005 that received national media attention motivated Crist's attention to crime.

In February 2004, Carlie Brucia, age eleven, was abducted as she was walking home in Sarasota. Caught on a security camera, the kidnapper was identified and led the FBI to her body four days later.

> Carlie was the archetype child victim of a stranger abduction: a [white] adolescent female who was raped then soon murdered. . . . The medical examiner said Carlie fought for her life. He found cuts and bruises on her arms, legs and left heel. She had struggled mightily in a losing battle with her attacker.[120]

The man accused (and later convicted) of her murder, Joseph P. Smith, was a drug addict with a long criminal record who was on probation for a drug offense. Two months before the murder, his probation officer had asked a judge to declare Smith in violation of his probation because he had not paid all his fines and court costs, but the judge declined.[121] In its later exposé on probation violations, the *St. Petersburg Times* began with words that harked back to Charlie Street: "When people learned about Joseph P. Smith's past, their sorrow turned to outrage."[122]

In February 2005, Jessica Lunsford, age nine, was taken from her family's mobile home in Citrus County by a convicted sex offender who lived across the street. Investigators found her body on March 19 and determined she had been raped and buried alive in the garbage bag in which she suffocated. Her killer had an extensive criminal record and had served time in prison for fondling a five-year-old child. Less than a month later, the Florida legislature proposed and eventually passed the Jessica Lunsford Act, which, among other things, broadened the criteria for registration as a sexual predator, made it a felony to harbor a sexual predator, and mandated lifetime electronic monitoring for defendants convicted of various sexual offenses.[123]

The third murder occurred in April 2005. Sarah Lunde, age thirteen, was strangled in her home in Hillsborough County by David Lee Onstott, a convicted rapist who was on probation after seven years in prison (he had been released in 2002). Onstott had previously dated Sarah's mother, who he had come to see the night of the murder. There were conflicting reports at the time about whether Onstott had properly registered as a sex offender.[124]

In response, in the 2005 legislative session then–Attorney General Crist proposed a new law that required probation violators convicted of a forcible felony to be jailed until a judge held a "danger-to-the-community" hearing. Crist advocated for the bill, dramatically named the Anti-Murder Act of 2005, with John Walsh, the host of *America's Most Wanted* and the father of Adam Walsh, whose 1981 murder inspired the Federal Sex Offender Registry.[125] Despite the recent killing of Sarah Lunde and significant legislative support, Republican leaders on the Justice Appropriations Committees, including now Senator Victor Crist, let the bills die in committee.[126] Unlike the case in previous crime control legislation, some judges also spoke out against the act arguing that "judges have to have discretion."[127] Others pointed out that the law would not have applied to the defendant charged in Carlie Brucia's murder because it excluded violations for not paying court costs.

Notwithstanding this opposition, Crist used the Anti-Murder Act as the centerpiece of his subsequent run for governor. In May 2005, John Walsh personally filed Crist's campaign papers.[128] Crist reproposed the Anti-Murder Act in the 2006 legislative session with some modifications designed to lower the cost estimate. Representative Joe Negron (R. Stuart), then a candidate for attorney general, sponsored the House version: "The list of qualifying offenses is much more modest. I tried to make those as limited to the serious felonies as possible."[129] In response to the *St. Petersburg Times* editorial board's claim that the legislation "would strip discretion from local judges and could unnecessarily burden the state's prisons," Crist responded in a letter to the editor reaffirming his commitment to the carceral ethos:

> A unanimous House apparently shares my view that putting hundreds of violent probation violators back in prison is something the state should be doing. . . . I strongly believe we must do everything we can to protect our citizens, especially our children, from violent criminals and sex offenders. The applicability of this law, had it been on the books before Joseph Smith took Carlie Brucia's life, can be debated. . . . *Getting even one potential killer off the street makes it a cost-effective proposition, not even considering its broader benefits to society.* (emphasis added)[130]

The Senate, however, never took up the bill. Citing a cost of $118 million a year by 2010, Senate president Tom Lee told reporters, "at the end of the day, it was just a question of how much money are we going to spend to grow the criminal justice infrastructure in our state in 2006?"[131]

On the campaign trail in the summer of 2006, Crist began vowing not to sign any other bills into law until the legislature passed the Anti-Murder Act. One *St. Petersburg Times* reporter noted that "Crist is making safety a signature issue at a time when violent crime in Florida is at its lowest point since the early 1970s. Polls show Floridians are more concerned about rising property insurance costs or the quality of their kids' schools. On the campaign trail, Crist refers to 'monsters' and 'creeps' who kidnap children."[132] Before the Republican primary, Crist ran television spots that highlighted his efforts as attorney general to reduce crime, his support from law enforcement groups, and his promise to "keep violent criminals behind bars."[133] With a huge fund-raising advantage from large corporate donors, Crist won the election with 52 percent of the vote.[134]

When Crist took office in January, however, he quickly backed away from his promise to "sign no other legislation." At the time, Florida voters were reeling from spiraling property taxes and homeowner's insurance premiums and, maybe as a result, Crist, as the self-proclaimed "people's governor," decided to respond by reaching across the aisle to find solutions.[135] Crist did not drop the Anti-Murder Bill, however. Two Crist supporters filed the 2005 version of the bill in the House and Senate, and Crist and his lieutenant governor took to the road to campaign for the bill in Jacksonville and Orlando, both cities that suffered from high violent crime rates. The same critiques surfaced from some Democrats and liberal commentators about the cost and the lack of discretion for judges. Yet this time, in addition to the carceral ethos that "you can't put a price tag on a human life," legislators were inclined to give the governor what he wanted as a sign of the goodwill he had shown them.[136] As the editorial board for the *Tampa Tribune* wrote, "While there's no pressing need for this anti-murder law, lawmakers should give the new governor his due and then get on with finding substantial solutions to the more pressing issues facing Florida: taxes, insurance, education, transportation and growth."[137]

As promised, on March 12, 2007, Crist signed the Anti-Murder Act— the official press release stated that it could have prevented the "the horrendous murders of children like Adam Walsh, Carlie Brucia, Jessica Lunsford, [and] Sarah Lunde."[138] Passed unanimously by the legislature, the bill created a new category, "violent felony offenders of special concern," who would now be jailed upon an allegation of a probation violation until a judge could make "a written finding as to whether the violent felony offender of special concern is a danger to the community."[139] If the judge determined that the violator was dangerous, the law required the judge to revoke probation or community control and sentence the offender to prison. The qualifying offenses included nonsex crimes such as attempted aggravated battery/assault, attempted robbery, and second-degree attempted burglary. The Criminal Justice Estimating Conference projected the need for 2,500 more prison beds at a cost of $270 million over the next five years; the Office of the State Courts Administrator projected that the bill required forty additional circuit court judges over the next three years; and legislative analysts recorded that the cost to local governments of jailing probation violators was "indeterminate but could be significant."[140]

The Limits of Black Resistance

The legislative history of 10-20-life, three-strikes, and the Anti-Murder Act provides a window into the role black legislators played in the tough justice initiatives of the late 1990s and early 2000s. While high crime rates put black legislators in a difficult position when it came to voting for crime control policy in the early 1990s, by the end of the decade, the clear negative impact of hyperincarceration on black families and communities led black legislators to almost unanimously oppose tough justice initiatives. At the same time, however, their power to direct legislative policy drastically waned after the Republican takeover of the legislature. As Ecitrym

LaMarr, executive director of the Florida Conference of Black State Legislators explained in 2007:

> When black elected state officials grow in one party or the other, the other party gains more leadership control. And so as the black caucus grew, the Democratic caucus shrank and the Republicans grew. And so every time we elected one or two more black elected officials, so did the Republicans, they elected more and more white Republicans and they took over the speaker's office, the Senate president, and ultimately the governor's office. So now that there's not thirteen [black legislators], but twenty-five, they are in a minority party.[141]

Furthermore, black legislators had no broad support network for their critiques of the justice system: civil rights organizations or other advocacy groups rarely stepped forward in debates on crime and punishment issues.[142] Finally, the carceral ethos along with the continuing shift away from the project of racial equality toward racial representation limited the types of arguments that black legislators and their supporters could make against tough justice initiatives. As a result, black legislators realized that they could not stop the momentum of tough justice legislation, so they often worked to amend bills at the margins in order to soften their impact.

By the year 2000, the dire warnings of critics from the previous decade had come to pass. A crisis of the young black male existed and it was nowhere more evident than within the stark racial disparities of the criminal justice system. In a report to the United States Commission on Civil Rights, Marc Mauer of the Sentencing Project wrote:

> A wealth of statistical information is now available to document what a walk through virtually any urban courthouse or state prison displays quite graphically. A courtroom observer in New York, Detroit, Atlanta, Los Angeles or any other major city will witness a sea of black and brown faces sitting at the defense table or shackled together on the bus transporting prisoners from the jail for court hearings.[143]

The report noted that African Americans constituted 49 percent of the country's prison population, compared to their 13 percent share of the overall population; on any given day 32 percent of black males age twenty through twenty-nine were under criminal justice supervision; and black male children had a 29 percent chance of spending time in prison during their lives, comparted to a 4 percent chance for white males. A similar report by the Leadership Conference on Civil Rights in 2000 warned that "the injustices of the criminal justice system threaten to render irrelevant fifty years of hard-fought civil rights progress."[144]

Occasionally, brief acknowledgment of these disparities appeared in legislative debates and discussion of tough justice initiatives in Florida. The initial bill analysis for three strikes, for example, cites a report on the effects of three strikes in California and notes that "combining the high probability of black male arrests and higher probability of being admitted to prison . . . [the bill] could have a greater impact upon black offenders than upon white offenders."[145] While this language implies that the legislation could conceivably *not* have this effect, it should be judged relative to the *lack* of language on the ability of tough justice legislation to *actually* reduce crime rates. Even when "deterrence" or "incapacitative" effects are mentioned, they are posed as "indeterminate" at best.[146]

More often, the race of offenders "taken off the streets" went unstated. For example, the bill analysis for 10-20-life states,

> The increased penalties in this bill should deter many potential offenders from committing crimes with guns. For those that are still committing violent crimes with guns, this legislation will take them off the streets for a long time. This legislation creates stricter gun control without effecting [*sic*] law abiding gun owners.[147]

Given the disproportionate gun violence among black youth in poor neighborhoods, however, the argument that 10-20-life is a gun control measure implied a tradeoff between gun ownership and black life. The rationale posits that the right to own a gun was more important than the life of a black victim of urban gun violence.

Yet black legislators struggled to make convincing arguments against tough justice laws under the frameworks of either of the two competing racial projects of the era. Specifically, the project of racial representation was challenged by a new commitment to a project for colorblindness. Adherents to the colorblind racial project believed that all racial classifications were problematic and opposed proactive state intervention in remedying racial inequality. Jeb Bush's statement during his 1994 campaign that he would do "nothing" to help black Floridians exemplified this view. As political historian David Colburn writes,

> When [Bush] was asked what he would do to help black Floridians, he responded, "probably nothing." In fairness to Bush, he had actually said: "It's

time to strive for a society where there's equality of opportunity, not equality of results. So I'm going to answer your question by saying, 'probably nothing.' "[148]

The project for racial representation, on the other hand, insisted that society and the state must proactively address racial inequality through race-conscious policies and programs.[149] The conflict between the two racial projects playout out repeatedly under Governor Bush beginning in 1999, when he abolished affirmative action in state hiring and higher education by executive action. In response, black legislators Senator Kendrick Meek (D. Miami) and Representative Tony Hill (D. Jacksonville) staged a sit-in at the state capitol that started a mass movement against Bush's actions.[150] African Americans leaders expressed pointed critiques that the governor did not care about black Floridians.[151]

While both factions agreed that intentional racial discrimination and offensive statements should not be tolerated, the concern that new mandatory minimum laws would exacerbate the problems faced by underprivileged black youth did not fit neatly into an acceptable framework of intentional discrimination. In fact, given the colorblind assumption that the law treats all people the same except in cases where intentional racial discrimination can be concretely shown, the argument that tough justice legislation disproportionately impacted black Floridians threatened to reinscribe stereotypes that black people were more prone to criminal activity. As a result, black legislators often relied on arguments about the "unintended" or "unknown" consequences of these laws without making specific reference to race.[152] The veiled disproportionate impact argument, however, fell flat in the face of law enforcement's argument that they police, prosecute, and detain criminals regardless of skin color and their commonsense contention that tough prison sentences would deter would-be offenders.

Furthermore, since legislators almost uniformly accepted the basic tenets of the carceral ethos (at least publicly), the problem of racially disparate outcomes could not be framed as a criminal justice system that was too harsh in general. Yet the two dominant racial projects limited the types of solutions imaginable to disparate impact claims. While many of the white legislators I interviewed explained the racial disparity by citing social disadvantage, they felt that their criminal justice policy decisions wouldn't change the fact that social disadvantage caused black people to commit disproportionately more crime.

I mean because how do you change that? I mean do you say "all right, we're going to set a quota and once we get . . . *x* number in the system then we're not

going to lock anymore of them up?" . . . I mean everything in life isn't fair . . .
It's just because a lot of your crimes are being committed by people that are
being raised in poverty situations. So I've always believed that if we do a better
job in education, helping people get jobs, and earn a living then that is probably
the best way to reduce your prison population. I mean once they're out there
committing the crimes, I don't expect the Department of Corrections to solve
those problems for society.[153]

In this former politician's mind, solutions based on taking stock of the
racialized outcomes of the criminal justice system presented no logical
solution. Yet by insisting that criminal laws are colorblind, the racialized basis of carceral ethos went unchallenged.

The continued unstated racialization of the criminal other became
clear in my discussions with legislators and legislative aides about the increasing number of white offenders who have gotten caught in the system. Thus while State Senator Victor Crist actively supported long prison
terms for drug dealers, he opposed these sentences for DUI offenders
because, as he told me, they are people like "you and me."[154] Remark-
ably, sex offenders are another category where the assumption about the
criminal other comes to light. Between 2003 and 2007, 65 percent of those
admitted to prison for sex offenses in Florida were white; of these, 70 percent had no prior prison commitments, and 60 percent were sentenced
for lewd or lascivious behavior.[155] Yet the average prison sentence for this
group was over seven years. While legislators are loath to say it publicly,
three of my interviewees expressed the idea that sex offender laws had
gone too far. These sentiments leave the impression that tough justice is
problematic or too cost-prohibitive only when it negatively impacts white
offenders, rather than the assumed black offender.

Despite their severe structural disadvantage, black legislators worked
to modify tough justice measures in order to soften their impact. In 1999,
for example, they not only restricted 10-20-life to adults, they argued that
the deterrence rationale was plausible only if people knew about the law.
Senator Frederica Wilson (D. Miami) negotiated funding for a public service campaign and a delayed start in order to roll out the campaign. When
the public service campaign didn't materialize, she and other black legislators began working with local organizations to create awareness about
the new law in their communities (figure 6.3).[156] However, the following
year Republicans sponsored a bill that mandated that prosecutors charge
sixteen- and seventeen-year-olds under the 10-20-life statute. The purported rationale for the bill was to "address the scenario in which an adult

FIGURE 6.3. 10-20-life billboard in Putnam County, Florida. Joel Gordon, 2007.

offender gives the gun used in the crime to a 16 year-old juvenile offender who is participating in a robbery . . . to avoid having the 10-20-life penalties imposed."[157] This time, black legislators refused to offer support for even a softer version of the proposal. Two Cuban-American Republican legislators from Miami pushed for a revision that required juveniles have a prior forcible felony, a firearm adjudication, or a prior incarceration in a juvenile facility to be sentenced under 10-20-life. In addition, the amended version allowed for prosecutorial discretion if "exceptional circumstances exist." It also required the DOC to "make every reasonable effort to ensure that any child 16 or 17 years of age . . . be completely separated such that there is no physical contact with adult offenders in the facility."[158] Despite these changes, eighteen black legislators (out of twenty) along with nine other Democrats opposed the final juvenile 10-20-life bill.[159]

Institutionalizing the Carceral Ethos in the Twenty-first Century

The events covered in this chapter further demonstrate the developmental process of carceral state building. The outcome of political fights and policy deliberations in the early 1990s—the 1994 sentencing guidelines, truth in sentencing, and building enough prisons to handle twenty-five thousand admissions per year—created significant feedback effects. First, they cemented the carceral ethos that criminal offenders should be incarcerated for long periods of time regardless of cost. Once lawmakers decided that prisons were the answer, expert opinion and academic research became unnecessary. Instead, the best policy became the policy that sounded good or made intuitive sense regardless of effectiveness. Instead of debates about how to stem early releases, reduce crime rates, or create alternatives to incarceration, dissent from the margins was limited to modifications meant to soften the blow. Second, they solidified tough justice as a means to gain political capital—especially for Republicans. Consistency and rationality were ignored for the sake of piling on punishments. By 2008, Florida statutes included a half-dozen different repeat offender laws and over one hundred different mandatory minimum sentences—on top of what was originally enacted as structured sentencing guidelines.[160] Third, they increased the physical capacity of the prison system. Surplus prison beds in the late 1990s (created by decreased admissions and prison building) enabled lawmakers' decisions to embrace prosecutors' demands to sentence more offenders to prison, for longer periods of time, and to enact "expressive justice" measures in order to further their own political goals. In fact, as legal scholar William Stuntz argued, the relationship between prosecutors and legislators was mutually beneficial—prosecutors received more discretion and in turn could use that discretion to blunt the impact of legislators' symbolic policies.[161]

   In turn, these effects created a new period of carceral growth between 1998 and 2010. Although crime rates continued to decline, incarceration rates in Florida grew. A decomposition analysis demonstrates how Florida's criminal justice system responded to declining crime rates and changes in sentencing policy (see appendix for methodology). Between 1998 and 2010, violent and property crime rates dropped by approximately 40 percent, arrests for drug offenses went down by 20 percent, and arrests for other offenses stayed flat. And yet incarceration rates increased, from approximately 442 to 538 per 100,000, representing another thirty-six thousand people in prison by 2010. For incarceration rates to increase while crime rates decline, other criminal justice components need to change, including police enforcement (measured by arrests per crime), prosecutors' decision to charge and ability to convict (measured by convictions per arrest), and judges and legislators' use of prison (measured by admissions to prison per conviction and expected length of time served) (table 6.1).

TABLE 6.1 **Offense, arrest, and felony conviction rates by crime type, 1998 and 2010**

Offense category	Offending rates (per 100,000)		Arrests per 100 offenses		Felony convictions per 100 arrests		Prison admissions per 100 convictions		Expected length of stay (years)	
	1998	2010	1998	2010	1998	2010	1998	2010	1998	2010
Violent	933	536	40.9	43.2	13.5	16.9	54.7	64.9	4.9	6.7
Property	5914	3521	16.1	19.6	31.2	40.2	12.5	15.1	2.5	2.4
Drug	903	746	–	–	35.2	31.2	12.5	21.0	1.8	2.0
Other	3629	3703	–	–	8.0	6.3	17.0	29.8	2.4	2.4
Total	5867	5371	–	–	16.3	15.1	15.4	22.6	3.0	2.9

Shaded cells designate increases between 1998 and 2010. Drug and "other" offending rates are based on arrests.
Source: Author calculation from United States Census Bureau, Florida Department of Law Enforcement (UCR reported offenses, arrests), Florida Courts Summary Reporting System (convictions), and Florida Department of Corrections (Prison admissions/population). See appendix for details.

TABLE 6.2 **Change in incarceration rate from 1998 to 2010 due to stages of criminal justice process**

Offense category	Crime	Arrest	Conviction	Prison admission	Expected time served	Change in incarceration rate
Violent	−58.0	4.4	20.9	19.5	45.7	32
Property	−38.0	12.0	19.7	18.6	−5.9	6
Drug	−12.7	0.0	−6.9	35.7	11.7	27
Other	2.4	0.0	−25.2	70.6	4.2	52
Total	−37.4	0.0	−29.7	174.3	−11.2	96
% contribution to absolute value of change	15	0	12	69	4	

Shaded cells designate positive values.
Source: Author calculation from United States Census Bureau, Florida Department of Law Enforcement (UCR reported offenses, arrests), Florida Courts Summary Reporting System (convictions), and Florida Department of Corrections (Prison admissions/population). See appendix for details.

In other words, had criminal justice processing stayed the same between 1998 and 2010, the decrease in crime would have reduced the incarceration rate about 40 points, for about twenty-five thousand fewer prisoners. Instead, as previous scholarship has noted, the criminal justice system adapted—continuing to fill prison beds.[162]

The decomposition analysis (see table 6.2) reveals that admissions to prison per conviction exerted the strongest upward pull on incarceration rates during this period: about 70 percent of the absolute value of change was due to the admissions stage.[163] This implies that the changes to the Criminal Punishment Code (CPC) had exactly the impact prosecutors intended: it put more people on the path to prison. This makes sense given that under the previous sentencing regime, offenders who scored between 34.8 and 52 (which depended on the seriousness of the current and prior offenses) fell into a "discretionary range" where judges could impose a prison or nonprison sentence. The CPC mandated a prison sentence for offenders who scored above 44. In fiscal year 1995–1996, only 19 percent of convicted felons in the discretionary range were sentenced to state prison.[164] While it is possible that the 2010 cohort of felons had more prior convictions which would increase their chances of a prison sentence, research comparing sentences under the 1994 guidelines and the CPC found "offenders sentenced under the CPC are 65 percent more likely to be incarcerated and receive sentences thirty-four months longer than those sentenced under the 1994 guidelines" holding individual-level characteristics constant.[165]

Using Uniform Crime Report definitions, the decomposition analysis also reveals that the CPC had the largest impact on drug and "other" offenders. While prison admissions per conviction increased the violent and property offense incarceration rate by about 19 people per 100,000, it increased the drug offense incarceration rate by almost twice that, and the "other" offense incarceration rate by almost four times that of violent crime. Thirty offenses comprise "other" offense admissions, but eight make up the majority (51 percent) of admissions: aggravated battery/assault and battery (14 percent), stolen property (11 percent), weapons (11 percent), lewd and lascivious behavior (8 percent), and fleeing a law enforcement officer (7 percent). Yet the bulk of the *increase* in admissions within the "other" category was for "other violent offenses," criminal justice process offenses, assault and battery, traffic offenses, abuse of children, fraud, and pollution and property damage.[166] The data suggest that changes to the conviction or admissions rate, rather than arrest rates, are primarily responsible for the increase.[167] For example, arrests for weapons offenses decreased between 1998 and 2010, but an increase in admissions per arrest, plus a slight increase in their estimated length of stay, put 2,000 more weapons offenders in prison than would have been the case if criminal justice processing had remained the same. Part of this growth is due to 10-20-life, which in 2010 accounted for almost 1,500 admissions, 13 percent of which received a sentence of twenty-five years or more.[168] Estimated length of stay also exhibited an upward pull on incarceration rates for violent and drug offenders. Time served increased most substantially for violent offenses, almost cancelling out the decrease in violent crime rates over the period.

As prison admissions grew, so did Florida's prison capacity. In 2000, the Department of Corrections highlighted that it had "enough prison beds to house its inmate population" of just over 71,000, having added 5,600 beds in the last three years (half of them in privately run facilities).[169] The very next year, the department went to the legislature to ask for an appropriation for "additional capacity through expansion and new construction." Between 2000 and 2008, the department budgets included $400 million to build, design, and plan for additional capacity. By the end of 2008, the prisoner population had reached one hundred thousand and the department had added one new large prison (Franklin), six new annexes to existing prisons (some as large as the original prison), fifteen work/boot camps, and three work release centers. In addition, in 2007 the department entered into a contract with GEO Group to house prisoners in a privately run 1,800-bed facility in Jackson County. As part of this expansion, the department added a half dozen new secure housing units at existing prisons.[170]

As the first decade of the twenty-first century came to a close, the physical markings of the carceral ethos literally dotted the Florida landscape. As I will detail in the next chapter, the presence of 146 correction facilities filled with over 100,000 prisoners—half of whom were black—had a myriad of consequences for the state and its citizens. It marked politics and policy, limiting the dynamics of what was possible as the state's fiscal circumstances changed. It required $2.08 billion in resources from the state, which, when added to spending on judicial and other criminal justice expenditures, accounted for 17 percent of the state's general revenue fund appropriation.[171] It created interest groups, including the 22,000 employees of the Department of Corrections and the dozens of communities in which prisons were located. For many Floridians, this carceral capacity made them feel safe and protected by their political leaders. For others, it made their communities less secure and their lives more unstable.[172] For the approximately 130,000 people who entered the state criminal justice system in 2010, many for the first time, the state's carceral capacity and the collateral consequences of felon status put their and their children's future in doubt.[173]

CHAPTER SEVEN

Recession-Era Colorblind Politics and the Challenge of Decarceration, 2008–2016

A 50-year-old mentally ill inmate at the Dade Correctional Institution . . . was pulled into the locked shower by prison guards . . . He was left there unattended for more than an hour as the narrow chamber filled with steam and water. When guards finally checked on prisoner 060954, he was on his back and dead. His skin was so burned that it had shriveled from his body.—Julie K. Brown, "Behind Bars, a Brutal and Unexplained Death," *Miami Herald*, May 22, 2014

We are spending billions of tax dollars locking people up and getting very little value on the dollar. Sixty-six percent of those incarcerated will be back within three years and we will have to pay for that, too.— Governor-Elect Rick Scott Law and Order Transition Team, January 2011[1]

In 2011, the United States Supreme Court reemerged from a long stretch of silence on prison conditions during the height of the prison boom. After Congress passed the Prison Litigation Reform Act in 1996, the number of civil rights wins for prisoners in the courts and the percentage of state prisons under court supervision drastically declined.[2] Yet in *Brown v. Plata*, the court sided with the prisoners of the California Department of Corrections, upholding a prison "population order" that required California to reduce its prison population by about forty thousand people. In the opinion, Justice Kennedy wrote that overcrowding had "overtaken the limited resources of prison staff; imposed demands well beyond the capacity of medical and mental health facilities; and created unsanitary and unsafe conditions [that made the provision of] medical care difficult or impossible to achieve."[3] The Court thus found that without a population order there was an unacceptable risk of continuing violations of the rights of sick and mentally ill prisoners.

While the California prison conditions litigation and ruling is the most well-known—in part because it impacts a prison system larger than that of New York, Georgia, and Ohio combined—the story of what has happened in California resonates with the experience of states all over the country. Between 2009 and 2015, another eleven states faced major lawsuits concerning overcrowding or medical care in their prison systems.[4] These cases often describe a shocking level of neglect and "serious, sometimes life-threatening failures to provide adequate health care to prisoners."[5] The complaints also contain allegations of notably unsanitary conditions of confinement. In *Boyd v. Godinez*, for example, Illinois prisoners claimed in 2013 that life in their overcrowded prison includes exposure to things like "raw sewage [that] overflows in the toilets and backs up in the showers [and the fact that] the entire facility, including the kitchen and dining hall, is infested with insects and vermin."[6] Other cases document violence in overcrowded facilities. In a case against the Alabama Department of Corrections that was settled in 2010, the harms to named plaintiffs include commonplace slashings and stabbings by inmates and assaults by officers.[7] Another handful of states faced Department of Justice investigations into abuse at the hands of staff in overcrowded and ill-managed facilities.[8]

As the scene painted by the quote at the beginning of the chapter graphically suggests, Florida prisons have not been exempt from these problems. In 2015, former state senator Paula Dockery (R. Polk County) offered a laundry list:

> A record number of inmate deaths, suspicious deaths not reported as such, claims of widespread prisoner abuse, drugs and contraband, investigator reports ignored, investigators intimidated and silenced, potential inspector general retaliation and cover-ups, four Department of Corrections secretaries in as many years, crumbling buildings, leaky roofs, dilapidated vehicles, dangerously low staffing levels, excessive overtime costs, and questionable contracts for privatized services such as medical care.[9]

In a plea to the Florida Senate Criminal Justice Committee to end the culture of abuse and neglect in the Florida Department of Corrections, a former psychotherapist at Dade Correctional Institution finished his presentation with a quote from Kennedy's 2011 opinion: "A prison that deprives prisoners of basic sustenance, including adequate medical care, is incompatible with the concept of human dignity and has no place in civilized society."[10]

At the same time that the courts have stepped in to regulate deteriorating prison conditions, a group of well-connected national-level conservative Republicans began to reframe conservatives' evaluation of the
criminal justice system "in terms of cost and efficiency" rather than solely
its incapacitation effects.[11] In early 2011, Newt Gingrich and Pat Nolan
"announced a fundamental change in the conservative approach to
crime," arguing in an opinion article in the *Washington Post*,

> With nearly all 50 states facing budget deficits . . . We joined with other conser-
> vative leaders last month to announce the Right on Crime Campaign, a national
> movement urging states to make sensible and proven reforms to our criminal
> justice system—policies that will cut prison costs while keeping the public safe.

Citing a price tag of $68 billion ("300 percent more than 25 years ago")
and recidivism rates above 50 percent, Gingrich and Nolan advocated "punishing low-risk offenders through lower-cost community supervision."[12] Since
then, Right on Crime has established itself as a conservative elite movement
for criminal justice reform, signing on former architects of mass incarceration, such as Bill Bennett, Jeb Bush, Ed Meese, and George Kelling. Right
on Crime challenges parts of the carceral ethos by arguing that conservatives
should be "tough on criminal justice spending," including spending on prisons "which serve a critical role by incapacitating dangerous offenders and
career criminals but are not the solution for every type of offender."[13]

The high-profile conservative disavowal of excessive imprisonment has
opened the doors for some Republican governors and state legislators to
advocate reductions to prison populations in order to reduce costs. Many
states have drawn on available technical assistance through the Justice Reinvestment Initiative (JRI), an effort begun in 2006 by the Pew Charitable
Trusts' Center for the States and the Council for State Governments, which
helps states identify "the specific factors behind prison growth and corrections spending in the state" and the "evidence-based practices" that can
stem growth and costs.[14] As of 2015, thirty states had signed on to JRI and
many had passed policy reforms ranging from relatively minor postrelease
measures to more major sentencing reforms meant to downgrade offense
categories or remove mandatory minimum sentencing options.[15]

While Florida had not signed on to JRI, the cost of the carceral state in
the context of what I am calling *recession-era colorblind politics* sparked
three separate, and occasionally divergent, tracks of attempted penal reform in Florida between 2008 and 2016. In the legislature, moderate Re-

publican senators worked to pass a number of policy changes that would begin to reduce the prison population and create costs savings. Outside the legislature, a Republican business group and a "government watchdog" group made reducing the cost of imprisonment part of their agendas. Finally, Governor Rick Scott, a neoliberal conservative with a private business background who Floridians elected in 2010, proposed saving money by expanding the state's use of privately run prisons and prison health care.

A political developmental perspective on carceral state building helps explain the resurgence of arguably unconstitutional prison conditions *and* the Republican-initiated crack in the carceral ethos in Florida. As I discuss in more detail in the final chapter, a political developmental perspective posits that penal change is the result of policymakers' "solutions" to policy "problems," the content of which hinges on racial projects, past policy decisions, state capacity, and political context. Thus, the two developments that opened this chapter must be understood as part of a long line of penal problems and solutions over the course of the twentieth century. In fact, as I have shown, Florida state officials have continuously struggled over these same problems: how to understand the purpose of prisons, how to pay for them, and how to address the brutality that arises from caging human beings. Barney Bishop, the chief lobbyist for the Smart Justice coalition, sounding exactly like lawyers and policymakers during the 1981 recession and Governor Lawton Chiles during the 1991 recession, stated in 2010 that it was "the perfect time to focus on an issue like this, because when you don't have money, you have to start prioritizing what's the most important [and] least important to do."[16]

In the 1990s lawmakers reached a consensus under the carceral ethos that no price was too high to incapacitate criminal offenders and that once in prison, inmates could be ignored. Yet as political scientists David Dagan and Steven Teles argue, beginning in 2008, the socioeconomic and political context began to shift. The Great Recession, the reduced salience of domestic crime, and the rise of a new conservative coalition concerned with government overspending increased the political risks of large unjustified state spending programs and reduced the political benefit of tough-on-crime politics. I argue that the same political current led to policymakers' decisions to inadequately fund prisons, which, combined with the effect of the carceral ethos, caused inhumane treatment *within* prisons. Finally, the embeddedness of the dominant racial project of colorblindness in conservative recession-era politics helps explain state lawmakers' nonrecognition of both racial disparity in incarceration rates and the collateral consequences of incarceration, particularly on communities of color.

The story of Florida between 2008 and 2016 again points to the primacy of partisan politics and racial projects in determining lawmakers' penal policy decisions. While research by Peter Enns demonstrates a correlation between the decline in public punitiveness and the decreasing growth in the incarceration rate since the early 1990s, Florida's very meager progress suggests that a reduction in crime and punitiveness is not sufficient to reduce incarceration.[17] In fact, Dagan and Teles's analysis of the conservative movement for reform casts doubt on the extent to which legislators are directly responding to a rollback of punitive public sentiment. Instead, they reveal a top-down reform process that takes advantage of the decrease in the salience of crime.[18] Similarly, Philip Goodman, Michelle Phelps, and Joshua Page's reading of the Rockefeller Drug Law reforms in New York suggest that the drug reforms finally passed in 2009 because the long-term efforts of reform advocates finally met with a conducive political context.[19] Relatedly, the lack of a long-term reform movement may help explain why Florida has had little success.

To explain the developments in Florida between 2008 and 2016 and their potential impact on decarceration policies, I expand on my argument above by briefly outlining the contours of recession-era colorblind politics in the Obama era and demonstrate how within this political context, the feedback effects of the carceral state in Florida produced the conservative movement for reform and, relatedly, deplorable prison conditions. At the same time, however, recession-era colorblind politics precluded racial disparity in imprisonment or the collateral consequences of racialized imprisonment as policy problems. I then discuss the feedback effects that are sustaining the carceral state and hindering efforts at reform. In particular, I describe the persistence of the carceral ethos despite the national reform rhetoric, the complexity of penal policy after years of expansion, and the entrenched interests created by the growth of carceral capacity. In the final chapter, I conclude with recommendations toward the ultimate goal of dismantling the carceral state and its attending ethos.

Negative Feedback Effects of the Carceral State under Recession-Era Colorblind Politics

In an analysis that fits with a political developmental perspective, political scientists David Dagan and Steven Teles argue that the conservative pushback and movement for reform is a case of "negative policy feedback effects"—policy feedback effects that, instead of reinforcing or sustaining the carceral state, undermine its continued expansion.[20] First, carceral state policies have created excessive and increasing prison costs: between 1977 and 2003, state and local spending on corrections grew twice as much as health care and education spending.[21] Second, carceral state policies have done little to reduce the rate at which people come back into the criminal justice system: nationally, on average three-year recidivism rates hover around 60 percent.[22] Third, carceral state policies have created racial disparities that can no longer be ignored, in part because of public attention garnered by civil rights lawyer Michelle Alexander's 2010 book, *The New Jim Crow*, which argues that convicted felons, disproportionately African American, are effectively second-class citizens.

Of course, none of these *effects* of the carceral state are new. Most lawmakers did not consider them problems as late as 2008. As Dagan and Teles remind us, policy feedback is *constructed* within and by the larger sociopolitical context.[23] In particular, the reduced salience of domestic crime because of low crime rates, the shift to the "war on terror" as a governing theme, and the Democratic embrace of tough justice have reduced the potential political upside of tough-on-crime politics for Republicans. Arguably most important, however, was the rise of a new political coalition—the Tea Party coalition—comprising middle- and working-class white voters who fear social and demographic change, neoliberal conservatives who reflect the interests of business, and moderate Republicans.[24] The result is what I am calling *recession-era colorblind politics*, by which I mean national and state Republicans' use of white racial resentment to build a political coalition that supports cuts in state spending, while arguing that race should have no place in politics or policy. Recession-era colorblind politics has created new political risks and opportunities for both Democratic and Republican politicians that shape how they view and respond to the problems of the carceral state. Again using the story of Florida, I demonstrate how in this political context the policy feedback effects of the carceral state created the "new" problem of penal cost and efficiency, the resurgence of brutality in the prisons, and a continuing lack of concern about overrepresentation of racial minorities in the criminal justice system.

Recession-Era Colorblind Politics

In 2008, in the midst of the worst global recession since World War II, the United States elected its first African American president, Democrat

Barack Obama.[25] As Theda Skocpol and Vanessa Williamson detail in their book on the Tea Party, Obama's election and proposed policy solutions to ease the impact of the recession almost immediately set off protests by fiscal conservatives for what they saw as "the government rewarding bad behavior."[26] Over the next four years, with the concerted assistance of conservative think tanks and the conservative news media, Tea Party protests went from local rallies to a nationally organized (although still disparate) movement that joined "free-market advocacy organizations" with "grassroots activists willing to prioritize fiscal anti-government themes."[27] The rise of the Tea Party and its concern with government spending, however, was not just a response to Democratic policies or the recession, but to the new (black) face of the Democratic Party and to perceived attempts to grant amnesty to (brown) illegal immigrants. "Rather than conscious, deliberate, and publicly expressed racism, these racial resentments form part of a nebulous fear about generational societal change—fears that are crystallized in Tea Party opposition to President Obama."[28]

While white racial resentments have long fueled the conservative-liberal divide over redistributive and other government programs, Tea Party members displayed more racial resentment than traditional conservatives.[29] At the start of the Tea Party phenomena, the news media and liberal pundits pointed out the racist signs, slogans, and anti-Obama vitriol found at Tea Party protests and in online chat rooms.[30] Mainstream Republicans and Fox News, however, used these moments to effectively communicate a "colorblind" racial project.[31] The colorblind racial project has three main tenets.[32] First, the problem of race is a problem of "racial recognition." That is, as Chief Justice John Roberts wrote, "The way to stop discrimination on the basis of race, is to stop discriminating on the basis of race."[33] Second, as result, race is not a "legitimate topic or term of public discourse and public policy."[34] And third, that invoking race, recognizing racial difference, or using racial categories is in and of itself racist, and, in particular, discriminatory against whites.

The colorblind racial project worked in tandem with economic anxiety fed by the recession to generate a recession-era colorblind politics that is ironically fueled by racial commitments, while erasing race from public discourse and legitimate policy agendas.[35] As in previous conservative movements, a large part of the political rhetoric that tied racial resentment to public policy stressed white victimhood: whites as crime victims, victims of reverse discrimination, victims of immigrants who take their jobs, victims of freeloaders who use up state resources, and more recently, "victims of a politically correct and totalitarian society in which whites can't simply speak their minds."[36] Thus, recession-era colorblind politics incentivized politicians' and news pundits' continued use of racially coded appeals (what Ian Haney Lopez calls "strategic racism") *and* provided an aggressive means of deflecting critiques or observations of racism—by arguing that those that invoke race are the ones trying to "divide the country."[37]

Since 2008, Tea Party activists have organized to defeat officially endorsed GOP candidates and many who were even slightly centrist or inclined to work with Democrats, including Florida governor Charlie Crist, who lost the Republican primary for U.S. Senate to Marco Rubio. In fact, Florida's subsequent governor, Rick Scott, a businessman who self-financed his campaign, came into office in 2011 with other "hard-edged," "in-your-face" Tea Party governors who moved quickly to adopt "legislative blueprints disseminated by conservative think tanks," including attempts to curb the power of public employee unions, cut taxes, and shrink public spending.[38] In turn, "partisan racial polarization" has only worsened: in the 2012 presidential contest, 60 percent of white voters supported Republican candidate Mitt Romney, while 93 percent of African Americans, 71 percent of Latinos, and 73 percent of Asians Americans voted against him.[39]

Dagan and Teles, Hadar Aviram, and others have linked recession-era politics to the rise of a new politics of punishment policy—one that is concerned with cost and efficiency.[40] But to fully understand the effect on the carceral state, it is best to conceptualize the colorblind racial project and the new fiscal conservatism as a coherent political movement. Recession-era colorblind politics re-creates a platform (concern with the economy) for reducing public spending that disproportionately benefits African Americans and those marginalized from economic opportunity—while claiming to be race neutral. In this sense, arguments that the state should cut spending and government waste in order to give taxpayers and business back their money in order to create job growth is an extension of past arguments that welfare queens were undeserving of government largesse.[41] In this political context, many reformers constructed penal cost and inefficiency as the biggest problem of mass incarceration.

The Policy Problem: Cost and Inefficiency of Florida's Carceral State

During the recession, Florida led the country in home foreclosures and mortgage delinquency; construction sector jobs plummeted; unemployment reached a sixteen-year high; and tourism suffered.[42] General revenues from sales tax decreased by approximately $5 billion in two years, prompting the Florida legislature to significantly cut back spending. As the economy faltered, three groups of Florida Republicans launched different prison reform efforts. In the legislature, moderate Republican senators worked to pass a number of policy changes that would reduce the prison population and create cost savings.[43] In 2009, the legislature passed a multipart bill as part of the budget process designed to reduce the number of prison beds needed over the next five years by 1,250 by *requiring* judges to make a case for prison sentences for very low-level felony offenders and *allowing* judges to divert certain third-degree felons bound for prison.[44] While quite small in terms of the percentage of the prison population impacted, the legislation was notable as the first successful attempt to limit imprisonment. As part of its cost-saving efforts, the legislature decided to finance the construction of 10,200 more prison beds with lease revenue bonds instead of general revenue dollars.[45]

The prospect of new state debt prompted leaders of the Associated Industries of Florida, a Republican business group, and Florida TaxWatch, a "government watchdog" organization, to create a Public Safety Workgroup within TaxWatch's Government Cost Savings Task Force. The task force aimed to make comprehensive recommendations "to maximizing taxpayer value by facilitating a more productive, innovative, and fiscally responsible government."[46] Chaired by the former Department of Corrections secretary James McDonough, the Public Safety Workgroup argued that "with a prison population of over a hundred thousand costing taxpayers $2.4 billion this year, we can no longer afford the broken policy choices that have led to this out of control growth without making our communities any safer or offenders more accountable."[47] Their recommendations included policies and programs that would expand alternatives to incarceration, reduce time served for certain populations, and target high recidivism rates. Their work got the attention of gubernatorial candidate Rick Scott, who eventually invited members of the Public Safety Workgroup to help pick people for his criminal justice transition team.[48]

Despite comprehensive recommendations for reform by his transition team, as Aviram documents in other states, Governor Scott instead proposed expanding the state's use of privately run prisons and prison health care.[49] The prison privatization effort, in turn, had its own feedback effects that slowed the momentum of reform, splintered recession-era partnerships, and reshaped the political risks of reform in Florida. As candidate for governor, Scott campaigned on a pledge to cut $1 billion from the Department of Corrections budget—a sum that vastly exceeded the cost savings recommended by the Public Safety Workgroup. His proposal quickly drew the ire of the Florida Police Benevolent Association (PBA), which represented the state's corrections officers at the time. Working with other Scott opponents, the PBA orchestrated a radio, TV, and direct mail advertising campaign to criticize Scott on his questionable business practices, public safety issues, and his attack on state workers.[50] As one member of the Public Safety Workgroup recalled, "It was brutal. They were showing pictures of [Scott] like he was high-fiving people coming out the [prison] door."[51] After assuming office, Scott fought back, attempting to privatize prison health care and twenty-nine prisons, work camps, and work release centers in eighteen South Florida counties through a last-minute provision in the 2011 appropriations bill. The PBA sued the state, and a state judge found that the legislature "trampled on existing privatization law" by failing to run business-case studies of the pros and cons of privatization before seeking proposals from vendors.[52] The following year, with the help of Senate President Mike Haridopolos, Governor Scott tried to push privatization again—this time through the proper legislative channels. As Senator Dockery recalls, "When the bill came up and leadership was just bashing on senators to pass this, I began asking for information." Eventually she determined that the alleged cost savings didn't exist.[53] With opposition mounting from state employees' unions and a coalition of national criminal justice, civil rights, and faith-based organizations, including the ACLU of Florida, the Florida Justice Institute, and the Southern Center for Human Rights, Senator Dockery helped lead a successful effort in the Senate to defeat the privatization bills.[54] In a 21-to-19 vote, all twelve Democrats voted against the bills, joined by nine Republicans, eight of whom hailed from North and Central Florida counties with numerous prison facilities.[55]

The privatization fight splintered TaxWatch's Public Safety Workgroup. One member, Reverend Allison DeFoor, a former Republican candidate for state office and previous sheriff of Monroe County, formed his own group because he was unwilling to "get in bed with the private prison people." Using his connections in the faith-based prison movement, he decided to create the Project on Accountable Justice (PAJ) within Florida State University and join in the "national conversation . . . running around with the Koch brothers on the right and the Public Welfare Trust . . . on the left."[56] PAJ uses the language and approach of the Justice Reinvestment Initiative, styling itself as a "collaborative research institute and education center devoted to advancing public safety through evidence-based policies and practices."[57] Meanwhile, Barney Bishop, former president and CEO of Associated Industries of Florida, began the Smart Justice Alliance, which is funded primarily by nonprofit behavioral health care providers who would like the state to support "greater system-wide use of evidence-based programs that reduce costs and lower recidivism."[58] While the leaders of both organizations strongly vouch for the "conservative" nature of their initiatives, their proposals have been only minimally successful in garnering enthusiasm in the Republican-controlled legislature. As former senator Dockery told me, "We really thought when the business community came on board that it would make a difference, and I don't know why it hasn't."[59]

The Policy Problem: Corruption and Brutality in Florida's Prisons

Complicating the push for penal reform, the Florida Department of Corrections was in a perpetual state of crisis between 2000 and 2016. Although there is a consensus on the problem of corrections costs, not everyone recognizes the dysfunction in the department as a problem for lawmakers. In that time, eight secretaries have run the department—one of whom is serving time in federal prison for corruption. And in 2014, investigative reporting by the *Miami Herald* uncovered numerous inmate deaths at the hands of guards. The corruption and brutality are arguably another negative feedback effect of the carceral state and its attending ethos. As Jonathan Simon has argued about California, across the country the "new common sense" of crime control—what I call the *carceral ethos*—led to an era of inhumane conditions within prisons, where "security and control replaced education, labor and treatment almost completely."[60] More precisely, under the carceral ethos no price is too high to incapacitate criminal offenders, but this only required state legislators to fund what one Florida state legislator referred to as "bare and naked incarceration."[61] In addition, as prison building surged and the carceral ethos took over, almost everyone (except the staff who worked there and the prisoners who lived there) ignored *what was actually happening inside the prisons.* Even the field of sociology, once notable for its research documenting prison life, exited the prison as a site of investigation.[62]

Yet what has been less understood is how the new fiscal conservatism exacerbated the punitive nature of prisons and broke down the court-imposed minimum standards for professionalization, accountability, and, in particular, inmate health care. As one observer commented in 2016, "We have gone back to the pre—*Costello v. Wainwright* standards. The Department has long forgotten that settlement."[63] While some scholars place the impact of fiscal constraints after the 2007 financial crisis, in reality many states stopped or slowed their commitment to building and investing in prison maintenance after the 2001 recession, even as prison populations continued to increase (with New York a notable exception).[64] As Amy Lerman has shown, punitive prisons with few rehabilitative services and poor conditions can create a siege mentality that impacts the behavior of prisoners and corrections employees—creating "us vs. them" retaliatory violence and protection of one's own.[65] In Florida, years of neglect, the diffusion of the carceral ethos, and recession-era colorblind politics left the Florida Department of Corrections riddled with corruption, brutality, and deteriorating conditions.

In the 1980s and 1990s, Secretaries Wainwright, Dugger, and Singletary worked hard to create a culture of professionalism and accountability—even if they didn't always succeed. However, the culture changed in 1999 under Governor Bush's appointees for secretary—first, Michael Moore, a prison administrator from Texas, and then, James Crosby, a long-time FDOC employee and Bush supporter.[66] Under Moore and Crosby, the department curtailed inmate programs, let inmate health care deteriorate, promoted officers with records of violence against inmates, and gutted the Office of the Inspector General, thereby turning a blind eye to corruption and brutality.[67] By the time gubernatorial candidate Rick Scott made his pledge during the 2010 election to cut $1 billion from the corrections budget, *the state had not given officers a pay raise in three years and officer starting salaries ranked next to last among the ten largest prison systems in the country*. In addition, the average age of the prisons was nearing thirty years and the lean budget had neglected the upkeep and maintenance of prison facilities.[68] Finally, prisoner assaults on officers had increased by approximately 25 percent since 2005.[69] Over the next five years, three secretaries would cycle in and out of the top position at the FDOC, creating institutional instability, a hostile work environment, and a lack of accountability.[70]

As the research on prison violence would predict, these work conditions (which one respondent compared to a sweatshop) led to an increase in prisoner deaths and cover-ups at the hands of correctional officers.[71] In a series of over fifty articles, *Miami Herald* investigative reporter Julie K. Brown, who won a George Polk Award for Justice Reporting, detailed over a dozen prisoner deaths going back as far as 2010 and routine sexual assaults of female inmates at Lowell Correctional Institution—the largest women's prison in the United States. In tandem with a federal whistle-blower case by former FDOC investigators,[72] the *Herald* found that the department had covered up and destroyed evidence and documented its weak response after the allegations were made public.[73] After stepping down in December 2014, former Department of Corrections secretary Michael Crews told the *Miami Herald* that Governor Scott's office was "more concerned with the crafting and writing of news releases and that had little to do with the reality of what needed to be done to keep the institutions safe and secure." He blamed the crisis on years of budget cuts and neglect, noting a link between "dangerous incidents involving inmates" and "times when prisons were dangerously below minimum staffing levels."[74]

The [Non] Policy Problem: Racial Disparity and Collateral Consequences

In addition to the cost and inefficiency of penal institutions, and the corruption and brutality that take place in them, mass incarceration has two other large effects that *could* be interpreted as problems: the racial disparity in incarceration rates and the collateral consequences of incarceration, particularly on communities of color. Yet because recession-era color-blind politics renders speaking in terms of racialized groups unacceptable, lawmakers in Florida rarely define the two issues as policy problems.

First, while racial disparities have always been part of the landscape of American punishment, the expansion of carceral capacity drastically increased the proportion of black men (and women) who experience imprisonment. Bruce Western and Christopher Wildeman, the leading social scientists on the racial distribution of incarceration, find that 36 percent of black men with no college education who reached their thirties in 2005 have served time in prison (not counting jail) during their lives (compared to 6 percent of white men). Among high school dropouts, prison time has become a normal life course event. For black male dropouts born since the mid-1960s, 57 to 69 percent will spend time in prison (compared to 10 to 15 percent of white men).[75] In Florida in 2010, 1 in 39 black Floridians were in state prison or jail, compared to 1 in 160 white Floridians.[76]

Second, since the early 2000s, scholars have produced a solid body of knowledge on the negative consequences of incarceration and criminalization—consequences that reinforce inequality and marginalization of majority-black urban communities.[77] One branch of this work focuses on the difficulty of obtaining employment for people with felony convictions, especially if they are black.[78] Another highlights how removing young men from families and communities can create economic and emotional hardship for caregivers and increased emotional and behavior problems in children.[79] By 2008, 1.7 million children had a parent in state or federal prison, and 12 percent of American children had experienced the incarceration of a biological father.[80] Again the impact of incarceration is racially skewed, with one-quarter of black children estimated to experience a parent incarcerated before their eighteenth birthday.[81] Research also demonstrates that social efficacy and community capacity, which help prevent crime in the first place, are significantly diminished in neighborhoods where large groups of young men cycle in and out of prison. Thus, concentrated incarceration also produces negative outcomes for individuals in those neighborhoods who aren't involved in the criminal justice system.[82] Negative consequences extend to levels of trust, civic engagement, and political participation within a community.[83]

While some national Republicans, particularly libertarian-leaning Republicans, have reinterpreted racial disparity in the criminal justice system as a problem, the vast majority of reform rhetoric on the right ignores the fact that the money spent on incarceration has gone disproportionately toward locking up people of color. Nor have Florida policymakers defined these types of collateral consequences as policy problems. For example, although a state-level Ex-Offender Task Force under Jeb Bush acknowledged in 2006 that the prison experience did not prepare ex-offenders for law-abiding lives and that incarceration creates financial strain on inmates' families, the task force left for future "study" African Americans in prisons and the impact of their experiences "on them, their families and their communities."[84] In fact, almost none of the reports by the Coalition for Smart Justice, the Project on Accountable Justice, or the Smart Justice Alliance mention overrepresentation or collateral consequences for communities.[85] The ability of white lawmakers to ignore the devastation caused by hyperincarceration was brought home by a comment made to the press by Steve Seibert, the commissioner of community affairs under Jeb Bush. As a "leader" in the original Coalition for Smart Justice in 2009, Seibert told the *Miami Herald* that when Overtown (a historically African American

neighborhood in Miami) leaders told him that 70 percent of the neighborhood's men had felony convictions it was "an 'aha' moment" for him.[86]

The lack of public discourse on black overrepresentation dovetails with
lawmakers' priority to reduce the number of prison beds used for nonviolent drug offenders—who are increasingly thought of as white.[87] Asked
why they think reform is gaining traction, a number of respondents told
me that with "102,000 people in Florida's prison system," imprisonment impacts "everyone."[88] Allison DeFoor was most direct,

> You know why? What used to be confined to the minority community has
> now broken out into the broader community and so when I start to give these
> speeches now, I give them at the country club and I get people nodding their
> heads, because they have had a cousin, niece, nephew, daughter, son—usually
> because of drugs—who has been impacted by the system.[89]

Black Democrats in particular are careful not to talk openly about the
disparate impact of the carceral state when they propose reforms. For
example, in the first Senate Criminal Justice Committee meeting of 2016,
Senator Arthenia Joyner, a black Democrat from Manatee, presented
a proposal to revise mandatory minimums for drug trafficking without
mentioning the racially disparate impact of these laws.[90] Yet Senator Jeff
Clemens, a white Democrat from Palm Beach, commented on the legislature's willingness to address prescription drug offenses, but not de-
criminalize marijuana: "The fact of the matter is that the vast majority of
people convicted for having too many pills are white, the vast majority of
those convicted for having too much marijuana are black."[91]

Positive Feedback Effects and the Challenge of Reform

Eventually, the negative feedback effects of the carceral state in the context of recession-era colorblind politics began a conversation between
Florida legislators about prison reform. As the chair of the Senate Criminal Justice Committee, Greg Evers (R. Escambia) explained to his colleagues at the start of the 2016 Florida legislative session, "We are hearing
from a lot of people because of the expense of incarceration in the state
of Florida. It is so outlandedly [sic] expensive, *and with the problems that
we are having* (emphasis added)."[92] Yet, as of early 2016, Florida legislators had not passed any comprehensive reforms. In fact, Senator Evers's

next sentence communicates that he is disinclined to seriously disrupt the status quo: "Not that we want to re-invent the wheel, I think our predecessors did a great job, but we might want to move the spokes around, or at least move the chairs on the deck of the Titanic before it goes down."[93]

Instead, policymakers have tried (with mixed success) to pass reforms that slowly chip away at the problems they have identified. To cut costs (minimally) and reduce recidivism, the legislature has expanded the number of work release centers (under the new name of community release centers) and created a few new reentry facilities. Other legislative proposals simply attempt to mend the most egregious adverse consequences of layers of penal policy.[94] To address the problem of corruption and brutality in the Florida Department of Corrections, the Senate Criminal Justice Committee wrote a comprehensive bill (using ideas advocated by the Project on Accountable Justice) that would have created an independent monitoring and oversight commission, an outside agency to review prisoner grievances, and a new system to track use-of-force incidents.[95] Yet the more conservative House wouldn't sign on, and in the end, Governor Scott issued an executive order that provided for more internal oversight.[96]

As a result of legislative inaction, Florida civil rights lawyers urged the Department of Justice to open an investigation into whether conditions of confinement in Florida's prisons violated federal law.[97] And in January 2016, Disability Rights Florida, Florida's federally funded protection and advocacy organization for individuals with disabilities, filed a federal lawsuit against the Florida Department of Corrections for its "systemic failure to comply with federal measures intended to protect individuals with disabilities incarcerated throughout the state."[98]

Ultimately, to understand the resistance to change despite these identified problems, we need to understand the positive feedback effects of the carceral state that reinforce themselves over time, making change more difficult as the institution settles in.[99] In particular, policymakers' decisions to sustain the status quo stem from the interaction of meanings, capacities, and interests created by the carceral state. Below I outline the ways in which the continuation of the carceral ethos, carceral capacity, and the interests they create pose challenges for reform.

The Persistence of the Carceral Ethos

In chapter 6, I argue that by the turn of the twenty-first century policymakers had settled on a carceral ethos. The call for reform since 2008 has challenged three parts of the carceral ethos. Reformers argue that cost should matter, that providing services to offenders can actually *improve* public safety and reduce costs, and that therefore society does have the responsibility to rehabilitate *some* offenders. It is important, however, to distinguish the boundaries of this challenge. The few sociological studies of state-level penal reforms between 2005 and 2015 find what Christopher Seeds calls "bifurcation," where the state aims to manage certain populations of "non-violent" offenders outside of the prison in part by providing them with rehabilitative services, simultaneously managing those it deems "violent" through incapacitation inside the prison.[100] Seeds points out that 24 percent (7 of 29) of the justice reinvestment laws enacted between 2000 and 2013 were enacted *in the same legislative session* as laws that expanded life without parole sentencing options. The tendency to bifurcate offenders aids the project of cost cutting: as one Nebraska senator explained to his colleagues in 2014, "We have to understand *whether or not we're mad at them or we're scared of them.* And there's a process that we have to hone for each of those circumstances, because the process that we have right now is very expensive, when we put everyone in corrections."[101] This discourse continues to portray many, even most, offenders as unredeemable, making incarceration the "only" option. The president of Florida Tax-Watch argued, for example, that the state should "*find those prisoners who can be rehabilitated*, particularly nonviolent offenders, those that are not sexual predators, and find ways to help them from reentering the system or even preventing them from going in" (emphasis added).[102]

Thus even with these cracks in the carceral ethos, law enforcement discourse and reformers' strategies demonstrate its tenacity. Prosecutors, as I discuss in more detail below, are at the forefront of maintaining the idea that prison works to reduce crime. Testifying before the Florida Senate Criminal Justice Committee in early 2016, the president of the Florida Prosecuting Attorneys Association began,

> The one overriding consideration that I would urge on the committee is that all these mandatories [minimum sentences] are tools that your predecessors have given us over the years. Many of them were enacted when crime was rampant. Crime is at a historic low, so something must be working and somebody must be making pretty good decisions.[103]

In fact, most attempted reforms in Florida have maintained mandatory minimums while removing some categories of crimes or, in the case of drugs, increasing the weight limits. For example, in 2014 after failing to pass a bill that would remove mandatory minimums for trafficking in prescription painkillers, the legislature increased the minimum weight threshold instead, addressing "a glitch in the law" that put people in prison for three years for selling seven pills of oxycodone.[104] In critiquing the first bill, Representative Matt Gaetz (R. Shalimar), chairman of the House Criminal Justice Subcommittee, used the zero-sum logic of the carceral ethos, arguing that the bill was "only beneficial to offenders" and "did not enhance public safety."[105]

Perhaps most importantly, after years of acquiring political capital through their relationship with law enforcement and their tough-on-crime stance, lawmakers continue to believe there are strong political risks in looking soft on crime. This may be especially true for white Republican lawmakers in the Florida House, for whom being tough on crime works to signal their conservativeness and their support of (white) law-abiding citizens. Reformers intuitively understand this: for example, Barney Bishop told me that it is vital for the Smart Justice Alliance "to maintain our right-of-center reputation" to provide political cover for Republicans to support the group's initiatives.[106] Others use of the politics of fear in the service of reform. In his remarks to the Senate Criminal Justice Committee, Allison DeFoor of the Project on Accountable Justice asked senators, "Which [released inmate] do you want behind your daughter in a dark theater? The fellow who learned how to read and write, dealt with his drug and alcohol issues, learned a trade, and found his version of the Lord . . . or do you want the other one? They are coming out, the question is are they coming back in?"[107]

Carceral Capacity and the Structure of the Carceral State

In addition to producing a set of beliefs, the carceral state is a vast network of legal, technological, human, and physical resources that have developed over time to process people through arrest, prosecution, and punishment. In her comparative case study of the development of the first state prisons in the United States, Ashley Rubin argues that "proto-prisons" did not replace capital punishment as the dominant means of criminal punishment—rather lawmakers *layered* proto-prisons as a new option on top of old penal technologies. She writes, "Penal change is not a series of ruptures, but a series of accretions in which new layers are repeatedly added atop other, older layers."[108] The image of layering is particularly useful in conceptualizing the current structure of the carceral state in the United States. In 2014, Florida police officers made 865,000 arrests and the courts processed approximately 173,000 criminal defendants, of whom 30,000 were sentenced to state prison. Consider the bureaucratic institutions, people, and systems needed for this accomplishment. The carceral state is a vast multijurisdictional and multilayered network, functioning through hybrid and diffuse technologies. Four aspects of its structure in particular incentivize piecemeal reform by criminal justice insiders and exclude outsiders that might offer different visions of "justice."

First, the increasing involvement of the state and federal governments in crime control over the twentieth century has produced criminal justice policy that originates and is implemented in three different spaces—the local, state, and national levels. As punishment scholar Mona Lynch has argued, on the positive side, this means that reform efforts don't need to start at the top, but can come up through police departments, prosecutors' offices, or court circuits.[109] If the state's attorney and chief judge of the Miami Circuit Court want to create diversion programs, they can within the terms of the law. Some circuits run multiple specialized problem-solving courts (e.g., domestic violence court, drug court, and veteran's court) and diversion programs, others disproportionately use prisons.[110] However, this reform strategy is resource intensive and produces inequality across jurisdictions. Since local reforms don't necessarily impact other agencies' policies and practices, change happens only one jurisdiction at a time, and only in those jurisdictions with resourced reform coalitions. In addition, the lack of transparency around the policies and practices of law enforcement, prosecutors' offices, courts, and corrections limits outsiders' ability to develop and advocate for reforms.

Second, thirty years of state lawmakers' near constant tinkering has created complex multilayered criminal and sentencing law. Lawmakers have added hundreds of new crimes and piled on dozens of new enhancements and mandatory prison terms for various offenses and offenders. Yet most new provisions did not displace older terms; rather, they created additional optional or mandatory rules for certain crimes and/or types of offenders. Leaving aside the separate sentencing laws for juveniles, the current adult sentencing scheme in Florida falls under four different general sentencing codes, which are further complicated by multiple designations for "habitualized" defendants, statutory reclassifications of offenses, enhancements of penalties, and minimum mandatory fines and incarceration.[111] This complex layering creates amazing inefficiencies in the system, but it also empowers those who work within the system who have learned its ins and outs, including prosecutors, defense attorneys, corrections staff, court clerks, and long-term lobbyists. Outside reformers, on the other hand, face a steep learning curve that is further limited by access to system data.

Third, as punishment scholars have pointed out, carceral power and the sites of punishment have become much more diffuse over the last fifteen years. In what Katherine Beckett and Naomi Murakawa call the "shadow carceral state," punishment is carried out by "sites and actors beyond what is legally recognized as part of the criminal justice system: immigration and family courts, civil detention facilities, and even county clerk's offices."[112] They include efforts to recoup criminal justice expenditures through legal financial obligations such as fines, fees, and restitution orders. Arguably, these types of practices have a far greater reach then state incarceration—directly affecting millions of people's lives. Yet their legal hybridity (between civil and criminal law) and dispersion create significant obstacles to more fundamental change.

Fourth, the carceral state has created physical structures—prisons, reception centers, work camps—that have literally transformed the landscape and the lives in and around them. As of 2014, Florida's sixty-six counties held 145 state correctional facilities: 65 state-run prisons or prison "annexes," 7 private prisons, 31 work camps or reentry centers, 35 community release centers, 2 forestry camps, 1 boot camp, and 4 road prisons (2 of which are relics of the 1950s).[113] Together, the human and physical investments have produced sets of incentives for various groups of actors. Thus, while the system may cost billions of dollars, have a negligible impact on crime, and be inexplicable from an outside perspective, it is sustaining livelihoods, supporting communities, and growing careers—things that people are not willing to easily relinquish. Below I briefly examine the groups of people whose interests where produced by and now reproduce the carceral status quo.

Elected Law Enforcement

The current structure of sentencing policy in Florida gives state prosecutors unprecedented power with almost zero accountability.[114] Although Florida state's attorneys face reelection every four years, incumbents are rarely challenged. As of 2015, Florida's twenty state's attorneys were evenly divided between those who had served sixteen years or more (four of whom had been in office for thirty to forty years) and state's attorneys who had served eight years or less (often taking over for long serving state's attorneys).[115] This means that half of the state's attorneys were first elected during the height of the tough-on-crime era. As a group, state's attorneys and (to a lesser extent) county sheriffs still view the tough justice laws on the books as necessary and effective tools in their arsenal to fight crime, leading them to oppose even small sentencing changes.[116]

State's attorneys and sheriffs continue to maintain significant political clout—in part because they are elected officials and in part because of the belief that "a Republican running for statewide office has to be perceived as tough on crime and be able to have those commercials with law enforcement standing behind them in their uniforms."[117] As a consequence, the Florida Prosecuting Attorneys Association (FPAA) and the Florida Sheriffs Association (FSA) can exert veto power over sentencing reform initiatives. For example, in 2012 a bipartisan group of legislators supported a bill that would have reduced time served for select nonviolent offenders by diverting them at the end of their sentences into drug treatment. Despite passing the legislature almost unanimously, after consulting with the FPAA and FSA, Governor Scott vetoed the bill, stating, "The bill would permit criminals to be released after serving 50 percent of their sentences, thus creating an unwarranted exception to the rule that inmates serve 85 percent of their imposed sentences."[118]

Teamsters and Corrections Officers

As Joshua Page has persuasively illustrated, the prison boom "created a fertile environment" for the political ascent of correctional officers' unions, which "now frustrate efforts to seriously roll back hyper-incarceration."[119] While the political influence of the union Page studies, the California Correctional Peace Officers Association (CCPOA), is unique, the underlying issue is the same. States employ hundreds of thousands of people whose job it is to guard inmates in jails and prisons.[120] In Florida, one out of seven state employees works for the Department of Corrections, almost twenty thousand of whom are correctional, probation, and parole officers.[121] For many—especially in North Florida—working in the prisons is a family occupation and a source of community connection. While pay is low (starting salary in 2015 was $30,800), the job doesn't require a college degree and provides steady income and benefits. With a lack of other job opportunities in rural economies, corrections employees fight for "the future of our careers and families."[122] Responding to their decline in influence on an increasingly conservative Republican legislature that is openly hostile to public employees, in 2011 FDOC officers voted to join the Teamsters, who promised to "mobilize its members in a way that you haven't seen in Florida."[123] Since then, the political team at the Teamsters Local 2011 has fought privatization and lobbied for adequate staffing levels, pay raises, benefits, and secure pensions.[124]

While corrections officers in Florida have much less clout than corrections officers in other states (Florida is a right-to-work state), they can be expected to oppose initiatives that take resources away from the Department of Corrections. For example, in 2015 some legislators floated the idea of paying counties to house inmates with sentences under two years. The Teamsters fought the idea, saying they did "not want to see state general revenue being thrown at counties that have no proven track record in dealing with recidivism," and that "it would be better to fund the recidivism programs with the proven stewards of the state corrections system."[125] The Teamsters also indirectly weaken accountability measures by defending officers who have been fired for allegations of inmate abuse.[126] Finally, corrections officers and prison administrators have individual personal relationships with their political representatives whom they may prevail upon to intercede in hiring, promotions, and reinstatements— again limiting the effectiveness of accountability reforms.

Private Prison and Prison Services Companies

Similar to the CCPOA in California, private companies have taken advantage of an opportunity created by politicians' decision to build prisons. Aramark, Trinity Services Group, Corrections Corporation of America, GEO Group, Corizon, and others make millions of dollars providing services to and supervising federal, state, and local inmates and, increasingly, immigration detainees. Perhaps, most importantly, as of 2014, thirty-six states contracted for at least part of their prison health care services.[127] In Florida, the prevailing perception is that these companies have the ear of Republican representatives and the governor because of their lobbying prowess and campaign donations.[128] The statement released by the Private Corrections Institute in opposition to Governor Scott's privatization effort reflected the views of newspapers around the state:

> Considering there is scant evidence that private prisons in Florida have saved the state money, and the documented scandals and problems involving private

prisons in the past, the repeated efforts by the legislature to privatize Region IV
can best be explained as political payback.[129]

Yet like the FDOC, private companies are being squeezed by costly medical
services (for an older and mentally ill population) and state lawmakers' demands to provide cost savings.[130] In fact, in 2015 the largest prison
health care provider in the nation decided to *pull out* of its contract with
the Florida Department of Corrections, calling the terms too constrain-
ing.[131] Instead, as Hadar Aviram notes, private prison companies may be
revamping their business model to focus on federal detainee populations
and nonprison sanctions such as private probation and electronic monitoring.[132] Interestingly, however, the suspicion surrounding private prison
companies has spilled over to nonprofit criminal justice and treatment
providers—many of which belong to the Florida Smart Justice Alliance. As
a result, Smart Justice proposals have been tainted by accusations that
they are the brainchild of the vendors' lobbyists and are a backdoor means
of corrections privatization.[133]

Rural Communities

At the height of the prison boom, rural counties around the country at-
tracted new prisons. From the 1980s through the early 1990s, states placed
60 percent of new prisons in rural areas. In the 1990s, states added an average of twenty-six new prisons a year to nonurban areas (reaching a high
of thirty-seven in 1995).[134] While research on prison placement disputes
the notion that the presence of a prison provides economic benefits to
rural counties,[135] recent analyses by John Eason suggest that "towns that
built prisons between 1989 and 1998 experienced a less pronounced economic decline than similarly situated towns."[136] Furthermore, regardless
of documented impact on rural towns, there is the widespread perception
that the loss of a prison will wreak havoc on rural communities.

In North Florida, the economy revolves around farming, fishing, log-
ging, and prisons.[137] With a fraction of the state population, North Florida
(even excluding the Panhandle) has more prisons than Central and South
Florida combined. When the Department of Corrections announced it
would close seven prisons in 2012 (which many interpreted as a strategy to
increase reliance on private prisons), only two were located in North Florida. One of them, Jefferson Correctional Institution, is the second largest employer in Jefferson County. For employees, community members,

and businesses in the county, the news of closure was devastating.[138] Representative Alan Williams, a black Democrat whose district covers Tallahassee, where many Jefferson C.I. employees live, released the following statement at the time:

> I am saddened and disappointed with Governor Rick Scott's decision to close several correctional institutions that are economically vital to our rural communities. I care about and have great concern for the people who work at these facilities, their families, and the small businesses that have relied upon the employment and economic opportunity that these prisons have brought to these fiscally constrained areas of our state.[139]

The next day, county leaders called an emergency meeting of residents, law enforcement, corrections officers (and the Teamsters), business leaders, and local representatives to develop a strategy to stop the closure. Commenting on the successful fight to keep Jefferson C.I. open, Project on Accountable Justice's Allison DeFoor, a white Republican, was incredulous:

> I said, "Alan [Rep. Williams], how can you do this, you are the Democratic state representative, I am the former vice chairman of the Republican Party of Florida, have we gone through the looking glass? These are your people, let your people go, man!"

But as John Eason discovered in his ethnography of Forrest City, a rural prison town in Arkansas, the "prison-industrial complex" notion that white rural residents make their living by guarding black inmates is incomplete. In fact, when I visited Jefferson C.I. in 2007, 60 percent of the corrections staff were black.[140] Accordingly, Representative William's constituents are mainly working in the prison—not behind bars. This is especially the case since Florida prisoners, probationers, and parolees cannot vote. Noting this fact, but obscuring the racial dynamics in the north, Fred Grimm, a reporter for the *Miami Herald*, notes,

> [State prisoners are] the great gift urban counties ship up to state representatives in Florida's rural prison belt . . . where incarceration is a major local industry and inmates represent a sizeable chunk of the local population. . . . Those inmates—*most of them big city homies*—are counted along with the local population, making prisoners a valuable political commodity and consigning

elected officials, particularly state reps, political power out of whack with their
actual voting constituency. (emphasis added)[141]

Retaining prisons is not just in the interest of rural communities, but their
political representatives as well.

The Uncertain Future of Penal Reform

For almost three decades—the length of a generation—the carceral ethos
has dominated public policy and political strategy. In this time, it has generated new state capacities and interests. Just as the carceral state didn't
spontaneously or organically appear—it was fashioned by lawmakers'
choices—the system is unlikely to collapse under its own weight. In order to
dismantle the carceral state people will need to create new meanings, new
interests, and new state capacities. In particular, they will need to frame
the system's inefficiencies and cruelties as problems to be solved and proactive policy solutions as politically beneficial. As the political developmental perspective suggests, whether and what solutions legislators enact
to solve the new problems of the carceral state will depend upon how
they evaluate the political risks and opportunities in the current political
context. While this reframing began in many states after the Great Recession, the story of Florida between 2008 and 2016 demonstrates that local
contingencies and political realities shape reform outcomes.

In Florida, by 2016 Republicans were firmly in control of the state legislature and governor's office.[142] Most Florida Republican lawmakers still
perceived substantial political risks in penal reform, including a loss of
tough-on-crime credentials, the support of prosecutors and county sheriffs, and the votes of rural communities. Furthermore, Florida conservatives supporting reform did not speak with one voice: they split over the
role of privatization, the extent of the changes necessary, and their willingness to embrace some of the less conservative bipartisan initiatives.[143]
As a consequence, the majority of Florida lawmakers were loath to scale
back the carceral state, and reformers were left chipping away at it, one
flaw at a time.

CHAPTER EIGHT

Toward a New Ethos

Since the mid-twentieth century federal, state, and local lawmakers, bureaucrats, and other policymakers built a vast network of people, institutions, and technologies aimed at "managing" millions of people deemed criminal. The resulting carceral state was not necessary to control crime, nor was it inevitable. Rather, the U.S. carceral state developed because of a series of explicit political decisions to expand *carceral capacity* or the capacity of the state to arrest, process, supervise, and incarcerate criminal offenders.

Analyzing decisions to expand carceral capacity advances a new perspective on the causes of the carceral state. A political developmental perspective highlights how the country's evolving conflict over whether and how to incorporate African Americans into social, political, and economic life created "criminal justice policy problems" and shaped the political consequences of various "solutions." From the project to maintain white supremacy, to ameliorate racial inequality, to adequately represent racial others, to colorblindness, racial projects interacted with U.S. political and legal institutions to shape lawmakers' decisions to expand carceral capacity. In turn, each successive policy decision had a cascading effect: creating new meanings, new political interests, and new state capacities that made subsequent decisions to grow the prison state more likely.

Together, partisan politics and built carceral capacity generated a political ideology, or *carceral ethos*. The carceral ethos claims that it is better to sacrifice the liberty of a criminal offender than risk the victimization of just one person; that offenders are expendable and unredeemable; that society has no responsibility for rehabilitating people; that crime is an individual moral failing; that people should be protected from crime and criminal offenders regardless of the costs to the state or to civil liberties;

and that long fixed prison terms are the best way to respond to crime. While it began as a political ideology, the carceral ethos has intentionally and unintentionally seeped into all aspects of criminal justice practice—from policing, to prosecution, to prison conditions. As it metastasizes, the carceral ethos has reinforced the carceral state.[1]

The Florida Story

The political developmental perspective thus suggests that *the causes of the carceral state are both older and newer than previously recognized.* I began the story of Florida in the 1950s, but the real starting points are officials' decisions after the Civil War, including county officials' decision to use criminal wrongdoing to further the racial project for white supremacy, and state officials' decisions to administer state punishment for criminal wrongdoing through private and locally run convict leasing and road prisons. With changes in the sociopolitical context in the 1950s, including the growing state population, the rise of the civil rights movement, and the rise in crime rates, these starting-point decisions led reformers to characterize Florida's criminal justice system as backward, ineffective, and racist. As the conflict over the project for racial equality became intimately connected with crime and criminal justice reform, federal resources helped liberal reformers in Florida invest in new law enforcement and criminal justice capacity. The investments aimed to make the system more effective and fair, but they had feedback effects. They generated new ideas—that criminal justice bureaucratization, technology, and professionalization would reduce crime. They created and empowered new interest groups—law enforcement and victims' rights groups. And they significantly expanded state capacity to arrest and process criminal offenders. Thus, what in hindsight looks like a punitive turn in the 1970s is better characterized as a buildup of criminal justice capacity. The 1970s were dominated not by punitive rhetoric but by contestation over the role and direction of criminal punishment.

Criminal justice reformers, including Florida's secretary of corrections, pushed the legislature to spend more on prisons to address decades of racialized neglect. However, legislators' investments fell short compared to the increased flow of offenders into the system. Influenced by their experience during the civil rights movement, in the 1970s lawyers and federal judges stepped in to force the legislature to address extreme overcrowding and dangerous prison conditions. Legislators, however, resisted the court's interference—in part because of the project for white supremacy. Eventually the parties to the case agreed upon a particular stylized solution—a formal policy on prison capacity. Concerned with the cost and effectiveness of prisons, in 1983 legislators translated the court order into new policy, including sentencing guidelines to obviate the need for new prisons and an early release mechanism to keep the prisons from becoming unconstitutionally overcrowded.

In the late 1980s, however, events transpired that transformed the perceived political risks to lawmakers of spending state revenue on prisons. Nationally, conservative Republicans capitalized on and reinforced the historically constructed links between crime and African Americans. Defining drug users as criminals, the War on Drugs overwhelmed Florida's prison system. With the court looking over their shoulders, Florida Republicans actively reframed the potential solutions to prison overcrowding as a simple binary: *release inmates or build prisons.* Importantly, they constructed this binary through the media's depiction of the legislature's policy response to the overcrowding court order. In the end, despite the option to stem the influx of black nonviolent drug offenders into the prison system, legislators both built new prisons and released prisoners.

The early releases, along with media attention to violent crime, particularly at the hands of offenders recently released from prison, created new political opportunities for law enforcement in the early 1990s. By organizing crime victims, law enforcement defined early releases from prison as the government siding with criminals over law-abiding citizens. By then, prior prison building had taught policymakers that they could build prisons in rural towns as a form of economic development. In an increasingly competitive partisan environment, both Democratic and Republican leaders proposed building prisons to end the early release crisis. Ultimately, their policy proposals faced very little opposition. White liberal Democrats, following the lead of President Clinton, had moved away from the project for racial equality and embraced tough-on-crime rhetoric and policies. While some black civil rights and community leaders suggested more comprehensive solutions, they did not have access to state policymakers. Furthermore, the effort to increase the representation of black legislators also increased Republicans' political power. Thus if we are to pinpoint a punitive turn in Florida, it might better be placed in the early 1990s than the 1960s or 1970s.

By the mid-1990s, partisan competition and excess prison capacity solidified the carceral ethos. To go against the carceral ethos was to be perceived as soft on crime. Together, the built prison capacity and the carceral ethos created new symbolic policy issues for Republican officeholders, which they used to mobilize support. In turn, Republicans opened doors for prosecutors to enact a more punitive sentencing structure. In addition, the structure of legislative policymaking under Republican leadership helped propel a few key legislators to positions that enabled them to pass further sentencing enhancements—creating the need for new prisons, even as crime rates declined. Yet, ironically, the carceral ethos also limited lawmakers' responses to real problems of violence, particularly in urban communities.

The rise of Tea Party conservatism and the Great Recession in 2008 created new political imperatives to rein in corrections spending in Florida and across the country. However, the extent of reform varied substantially by state-specific political and penal dynamics. Revelations of brutality in Florida prisons, themselves a result of dramatic cuts in corrections spending, and an attempt to privatize corrections considerably slowed the potential for reform in Florida. The contestation between different groups of conservative reformers and those who support the penal status quo reveals how carceral capacity has created and sustained interests and incentives that will make dismantling the carceral state extremely difficult.

Implications for Explanations of the Carceral State

By focusing on the choices of politicians, bureaucrats, lawyers, and activists, recounting the story of Florida contributes to our understanding of how broad structural and political change interacts with state-specific variables to transform penal policy. The political developmental perspective on the carceral state thus complements an emerging understanding that "large-scale trends in the economy, politics, social sentiments, intergroup relations, demographics, and crime affect (or condition)—but do not determine—struggles over punishment and, ultimately, penal outcomes."[2] Instead, both an "agonistic" and political developmental perspective contend that penal actors' ideas, struggles and decisions matter for penal change. As Philip Goodman, Joshua Page and Michelle Phelps write, "individuals and organizations that operate within and beyond the penal field struggle over status and the ability to define and implement their conceptions of justice."[3] For example, as Ruth Wilson Gilmore and John Eason have demonstrated (in California and Arkansas), deindustrialization in rural areas impacted local officials' decisions to put prisons in rural communities.[4] In Florida, the economic benefit to rural North Florida communities provided lawmakers with an added incentive to support new prison capacity. However, the federal court order, the War on Drugs, and state partisan politics were more fundamental to their initial decision. Uncovering microdynamics such as these reveals that key actors could have made different choices.

The story of Florida further highlights that penal actors do not struggle with equal resources at their disposal. Over the second half of the twentieth century, the political and financial capital of law enforcement, prosecutors, punitively oriented interest groups, and tough-on-crime politicians grew— creating ever increasing momentum to "govern through crime."[5] What the developmental perspective adds is an attention to the accumulation of state carceral capacity and symbolic resources. Each penal policy innovation over the twentieth century has created new carceral capacity that rarely gets dismantled during the next set of fights over penal priorities. This new capacity brought new problems, new ideas, and new resources that empowered particular interest groups and fed back into policy choices. To continue the prior example, new rural prisons created new economic relationships and incentives that joined rural residents' livelihoods to the presence of prisons.

While my analysis speaks to large-scale trends such as the late modern global economy, increasing crime rates, and the rise of neoliberal and/or neoconservative political power, it more uniquely focuses on *the role of racial projects* in shaping decisions that expanded carceral capacity. My goal in engaging with the issue of race and the carceral state was not to explain the racial disparity in mass incarceration—although obviously important. Instead, I describe how the history and institutional legacy of racial inequality and racial politics is a cause of the high number of people incarcerated in the United States today—irrespective of the color of their skin. In other words, without the U.S.'s "peculiar institution" of slavery and the projects around race that followed, the system of punishment in the United States today would look different. As Naomi Murakawa has argued, the United States had a "race problem that was criminalized."[6] The early criminalization of blackness as part of the project for white supremacy facilitated liberals' and conservatives' use of the criminal justice system to address African American incorporation. Research highlights the depth and persistence of the link between blackness and criminality in the public imagination and in social institutions.[7] Policymakers, judges, and prosecutors' perception of the crime problem and ideation of potential solutions thus vary based on the salience of "black criminality" in any particular time and place. Yet the story of Florida also demonstrates that the criminalization of the U.S.'s ongoing race question was not always ill-intentioned. People working towards racial equality and racial representation also made choices that resulted in the expansion of carceral capacity.

The story of Florida sheds light on three crucial American political/legal institutions that interacted with racial projects to create the carceral state. As Lisa Miller reminds us, "Determining what conflicts reach the political agenda, as well as the scope of such conflicts, is a central feature of political power, and institutional variation shapes the nature and scope of policy proposals."[8] First, the *federalization of crime control* or the simultaneous operation of punishment at the federal, state, and local levels created policy problems, limited the types of solutions available, and created momentum for the development of the carceral ethos. National policy mandates were particularly important for initial investments in criminal justice capacity in the 1960s and 1970s. While professionalization of law enforcement was undoubtedly necessary, without the requisite investments in real crime prevention, it simply produced more arrestees, more convictions, and more people sentenced to state prison. Then, just as states began to finally grapple with overcrowded prison conditions, the federal government started waging a War on Drugs. The War on Drugs changed state lawmakers' political calculations by exacerbating overcrowding and reactivating the public's association between blackness and criminality.

In addition, national party politics "set the boundaries of political debate at the state level" and disseminated rhetorical strategies to state-level partisan actors.[9] This phenomenon was particularly important for crime control policy because, as Lisa Miller argues, "The fractured nature of the US political system drives [national] political attention to crime toward punitive policy solutions."[10] In other words, because of the long-standing racialized opposition to state-run social welfare programs first by Southern Democrats and then by Republicans, when Congress wanted to do something about crime, the only policies they could agree on were punitive (what she calls "the lowest legislative common denominator").[11] Thus the message coming from Washington implied that to be a Reagan Republican in the 1980s or a Clinton Democrat in the 1990s was to decry crime and support longer prison terms for criminal offenders.

The multijurisdictional nature of crime control policy also helped produce various competitive ratcheting-up effects. State-level control of sentencing policy privileges single-issue advocacy groups with statewide bases of political power (e.g., prosecutors) or with lobbying resources and grassroots membership (e.g., NRA, MADD). Legislators thus perceive public support for policy solutions that increase carceral capacity, but not for policy solutions that increase community capacity. Similarly, congressional representatives from more powerful states, such as Florida, Texas, and California, can influence the congressional agenda on crime control. In the 1990s, state-level policy decisions to build prisons and enact punitive sentencing laws then fed back into national crime control policy, helping to increase carceral capacity even in states that did not face prison overcrowding or high crime rates.[12]

Second, *proceduralism* in the United States has limited the solutions to both the race question and criminal justice problems. Clear and consistent rules applied equally to everyone enhance fairness, but they neither address the underlying conditions that cause inequality nor the appropriate rationale for the rules in the first place. In the mid-twentieth century liberal reformers pursued "administrative perfection" in order to remove racial bias from the criminal justice system. Most likely, professionalization did constrain the biased behavior of some criminal justice actors.[13] However, as Elizabeth Hinton makes clear, new criminal justice system rules couldn't address our selective attention to the problem of "black crime."[14] Nor could an improved criminal justice system ameliorate the generations of racial discrimination and racist policies that create the conditions that cause crime, including neighborhoods of concentrated disadvantage.[15]

Proceduralism similarly limits prison conditions litigation to the protection of prisoners' right to be free from unnecessarily brutal treatment. Yet the courts' adherence to establishing rules on prison bed capacity per facility without setting normative standards for the purpose of prison allowed prison conditions litigation to eventually increase prison capacity. Finally, legal proceduralism also individualizes public policy problems. As Michelle Alexander explains, the Supreme Court has essentially shut the courthouse door to claims of racial discrimination in the criminal justice system unless an individual defendant can prove explicit racial bias.[16] Yet when systematic bias is uncovered, judges insist that "punishments perceived as biased can be taken up with the appeals court."[17]

Third, the structure of *partisan politics* in the United States has intensified political and racial polarization and encouraged emotionally responsive rather than responsible policymaking. A survey of the literature assessing the state-level determinants of incarceration finds that "the association between Republican control of major offices in the U.S. states and increased imprisonment rates [is] difficult to dispute."[18] The story of Florida highlights that it is not the ideological grounding of a particular party per se, but the level of partisan competition, that leads to the political use of tough justice. Again, in the 1990s, a more contested period of partisan politics, Democrats (for the most part) subscribed to the carceral ethos. As Republicans took control over legislatures across the country, the effect of Republican control on incarceration rates diminished.[19]

The perceived success of partisan jockeying over punitive crime control legislation was enabled by the structure of racial politics, including the racial division in partisan identification. For Republicans, who rely on white voters to win, rhetoric on crime tapped into white racial anxieties. In what scholars have referred to as symbolic or laissez-faire racism, many white people believe that antiblack discrimination is no longer an obstacle, racial disparities are essentially deserved, and black citizens have received too much from government. These beliefs are strongly correlated with policy preferences against social welfare spending and in favor of punitive crime control.[20] For Democrats, who rely on black and other ethnic/religious/cultural minority voters, the implicit association between crime and African Americans makes crime control politics a more risky proposition. However, as Marie Gottschalk notes, increased social, economic, and political integration for the black middle class created incentives for black political leaders to avoid involvement in the problems of poor black people—including criminal violence and harsh crime control policies.[21] Furthermore, the realities of "lowest legislative common denominator politics" has led some black politicians to support tough-on-crime policies in an attempt to address the problem of crime.[22]

Together, changing racial projects, federalism, proceduralism, and partisan politics produced the carceral state and its attending carceral ethos. Policymakers and criminal justice agencies have institutionalized practices that target an imagined nonwhite offender. And while the impact of the carceral ethos crosses racial boundaries, lawmakers widely accepted its disparate impact on people of color. Taken to its extreme, as it plays out in criminal justice institutions, the carceral ethos helps to explain the policies and practices of police departments, prosecutors, and corrections agencies that arguably trample on civil liberties, human dignity, and individual rights.[23]

Beyond the Carceral Ethos

In the post–Great Recession era a new political discourse on incarceration began to emerge. Politicians across the political spectrum were no longer

willing to lock people up regardless of cost. Moreover, some began to recognize the irrationality of subjecting prisoners to harsh and degrading confinement if we want them to return to society as healthy individuals. Due
to falling crime rates, new political realities, and reform policies, states as
diverse as California, New York, Texas, and South Carolina saw their incarceration rates decrease between 15 and 30 percent between 2000 and 2014.
This decrease is not insignificant: in California, for example, fifty thousand
fewer people are in state prison.[24] However, the decrease in incarceration
rates is limited to a handful of states. Incarceration rates in thirty-three
states actually increased during this same period, despite the continuing decline in crime.[25] In addition, to roll back incarceration to 1980 levels, states
will need to reduce prison populations much further, requiring a sustained
commitment to deeper reforms, including shortening prison sentences for
violent offenders.[26]

The reasons to reduce imprisonment span the instrumental to the moral.
It is clear that we have long passed the point of diminishing returns of incarceration on crime rates. According to the best estimates, the growth of
incarceration in the United States accounted for less than one-quarter of
the crime decline since the mid-1990s.[27] In the past forty years, as prison
became "a normal life event for African American men who have dropped
out of high school," it lost much of its value as an effective deterrent.[28] In
fact, the concentration of prisoners and former prisoners in poor communities can have a criminogenic effect: producing more crime than would be
expected absent high levels of incarceration.[29] Furthermore, as criminologists have long pointed out, the propensity to commit any type of crime
significantly decreases as people age. Thus, even if we favor an incapacitation rationale for imprisonment, incarcerating people over the age of fifty
for crimes they committed in their youth delivers zero crime control value.[30]
Furthermore, high levels of incarceration create significant social costs that
contribute to cycles of poverty, crime, and imprisonment, but are in no way
limited to them. For example, social scientists and epidemiologists are only
beginning to document the health and educational effect on the ten million
children (fully one-quarter of black children) who have experienced parental incarceration.[31]

Aside from cost-benefit analyses of incarceration as a response to crime,
we need to consider our values and ideals as a society. The words of Winston Churchill are often quoted by punishment scholars to invoke society's
responsibility for the treatment of those deemed criminal. Speaking to the
House of Commons in 1910, Churchill stated that "the mood and temper

of the public in regard to the treatment of crime and criminals is one of the most unfailing tests of the civilisation of any country." What then does it say about us and our nation's strength and character that we lock millions of people behind bars, in harsh conditions, with little opportunity to better themselves, for long periods of time? What does it say about us that millions of people are tethered to systems of surveillance and referred to as problems to be managed? What does it say about our ongoing project to build a democracy, when citizens marked as felons, even after serving their time, lose voting rights (in some cases permanently), public benefits (such as food stamps and housing), and federal financing for college? Or when we allow employers, the police, landlords, and others to legally discriminate on the basis of a criminal record?[32] When considered in this light, not only does the carceral state not live up to our ideals as a nation, it violates moral principles of equality, fairness, and human dignity.

Pointing to new and growing opportunities for reform, including shrinking state budgets, reductions in crime, and the new "conservative war on prisons," optimists hope that policy entrepreneurs will keep extending reform efforts—one step at a time.[33] Reformers and optimists take heart that the effective shifts in policy and practice in some states mean that "localized, multiple, and smaller-scale interventions" can lead to lower prison populations.[34] In addition, they are encouraged that while a broad array of constituencies supported reforms, the changes did not require a mass movement.[35]

Yet skeptics point out that the cost savings justification for reform could disappear as it has done in the past, or be eclipsed by a politics of fear.[36] Some likely agree with a Nebraska ACLU lawyer that "there is a big difference between thinking that it is wrong to put that many people in prison and thinking that it is just kind of prohibitively expensive."[37] Furthermore, the notion that prison is cost-prohibitive reinforces an anti–public spending political culture that could undermine policies to address the harm caused by mass incarceration. Finally, other critical observers note that the current policy approach to decarceration says nothing of the structural links between mass incarceration and other U.S. pathologies, including political exclusion, poverty, and racial inequality.[38] Michelle Alexander, for example, has argued that if mass incarceration is a system of racialized social control, remediating penal overindulgence will require a social movement to uncover and overturn the "conscious and unconscious [racial] biases that have distorted our judgments over the years about what is fair, appropriate, and constructive" crime-control policy.[39] Others point to the exclusive focus on reducing prison populations, ignoring what Ruth Wilson Gilmore calls "the many ways in which un-freedom is enforced and continues to proliferate throughout urban and rural communities."[40]

The story of Florida poses broad lessons for decarceration reform and warnings about the potential hazards that lie ahead. First, it calls our attention to the ways that history repeats itself. Second, it speaks to the danger that reforms will expand carceral capacity. Third, it cautions us to recognize the mixed impact of the courts in prison reform movements. Fourth, it highlights that mass incarceration is a problem of politics— not just policy. Thus solutions must stem from changing the politics that sustain the carceral state. Fifth, it illuminates the hidden ways ideas about race and racial progress impact debates around criminal justice policy. And finally, it points toward the need for a new ethos that can reshape our goals and our vision of the possible.

Reframing Old Solutions

The problems of, and solutions for, prison costs and prison brutality have reoccurred repeatedly over the twentieth century and now the twenty-first. One of the most common Justice Reinvestment Initiative (JRI) proposals adopted by states, for example, is a requirement that criminal justice agencies use risk and needs assessments to determine which offenders need additional supervision or treatment.[41] Yet the idea that criminal offenders have "criminogenic needs" that can be addressed with classification, training, and treatment goes back to the Progressive vision of punishment in the 1920s and 1930s.[42] It had a resurgence in the 1950s (in places like California) and became more widespread in the 1970s with the community corrections movement.[43] Even during the 1980s and 1990s, rehabilitative practices occurred at the margins.[44] But as Garland notes, their rationales shifted from a framework of welfare and the delivery of client-centered services to a means of managing the risk the offender posed to public safety.[45] Once again, rehabilitative practices, in the form of reentry programming and drug treatment, are gaining adherents and becoming more central to state criminal punishment.[46] How this translates on the ground and in the lives of the urban poor mandated or referred to these programs is variable and complex. In his ethnography of community-based reentry programs in Chicago, Reuben Miller finds that because these programs are unable to remove the barriers former offenders "face in the labor, housing, and educational markets," program staff look to "transform" individuals through

"value re-orientation" and "personal reflection."[47] Thus, as Marie Gottschalk argues, this approach individualizes the problem of criminal justice
involvement while denying the structural features of the criminal justice
system and the political economy that constrain opportunities in the first
place.[48]

Given this, it is not surprising that for each iteration of rehabilitation,
policymakers and the public eventually become disappointed by its failures. The new enthusiasm for "evidence-based practices" and "sophisticated tools" such as "validated risk and needs assessment" portends that
we are likely to be disappointed again. According to those closest to the
research, the best "service-delivery probation" programs can reduce rear-
rests by 20 to 30 percent and a successful program inside prison reduces
a typical 40 percent recidivism rate to 34 percent. Todd Clear and Dennis
Schranz thus note that "correctional programming has a low ceiling of
possible impact on correctional populations; and whatever its long-term
impact may be, the effect will be gradual."[49] While I have focused on the
historical echoes of rehabilitation as a solution to the problems that repeatedly beset prisons, one could similarly examine other solutions that
repeat over time (such as gain-time credits). The larger point is that given
this history, it is likely that new programs and rationales will temporarily strengthen the legitimacy of the prison once again, but eventually the
problems will repeat themselves. Or as Ashley Rubin has argued, perhaps
prisons and their various iterations are bound to fail "because our understanding of prisons is flawed and our expectations about what prisons can
do are unrealistic."[50]

Carceral Capacity

The story of Florida suggests that we need to dismantle or drastically reduce the state's capacity to arrest, process, and punish. Yet it cautions that
rather than truly shrinking the carceral state, reforms could actually expand
carceral capacity, shift capacity from prisons to other forms of punishment,
or transfer it to private entities. We have already seen the carceral state
metastasize into civil and administrative arenas in what Katherine Beckett
and Naomi Murakawa call the "shadow carceral state."[51] If this continues,
reforms may create a new carceral regime that is different in form, size, or
scope, yet continues to cause substantial harm.

The transformation of the idea of "justice reinvestment" highlights the
difficulty in actually reducing carceral capacity. The original idea of jus-

tice reinvestment was to reduce spending for prisons and reinvest the savings in the communities most harmed by mass incarceration by investing
in human capital and physical infrastructure.[52] Yet when the concept was
first applied to reforms in Connecticut in 2003, it "become clear that the
'reinvestment' side of the equation was going to be tricky."[53] As the political realities set in, reinvestment in the community turned into investment
in "community corrections," such as stronger probation, halfway houses,
and drug treatment beds.[54]

Reform could also create new carceral technologies that have the effect
of "net widening" or bringing more people under the gamut of the criminal justice system than would have been otherwise.[55] In Florida, some reformers have proposed "adult civil citation" programs that would give police officers discretion to issue a civil citation instead of making an arrest
or issuing a notice to appear in court. The civil citation would not entail a
criminal charge, but would require the nonarrestee to admit to committing an offense and undergo "intervention programming"—the cost of
which (approximately $350) they must pay themselves.[56] Other new legally
hybrid tools, including criminal trespass admonishments, parks exclusion
laws, and off-limits orders, increase the state's carceral capacity by adding
new forms of social control to those already marked by the criminal justice
system.[57]

In addition, we need to be cognizant of the ways in which these new
alternative modalities, while not incarceration, are punishment nevertheless. For example, the prison population in New York has decreased in
part because New York City police have shifted from felony level arrests
to misdemeanor arrests. Yet as law professor Issa Kohler-Hausmann has
documented, these arrests—even when they don't result in conviction—
mark people as criminals, cause enormous hardship, and require a performance of self-discipline under the threat of conviction.[58] Ethnographies of
drug treatment programs and halfway houses—particularly for women—
have shown how medical notions are interweaved with carceral logics
creating systems of hidden and potentially more insidious punishment.[59]
For example, in her comparison of two female drug treatment programs
with and without a court-mandated population, Allison McKim finds that
"when deployed within the carceral state, treatment remains disciplinary
and stigmatizing."[60]

Finally, new technologies and programs may simply transfer the capacity to punish from the state to private actors and organizations. The com-
mercialization of justice has grown in low-security corrections facilities,

electronic monitoring, probation services, and reentry programming.[61] Writing about this process in New York, sociologist William Martin refers to "justice disinvestment" or the replacement of the state's direct reliance on penal institutions with "enhanced technologies and private means of supervision and control."[62] While the total percentage of prisoners in private prisons nationally is only 8 percent, between 1995 and 2005, the percentage of state prisoners in *minimum-security* private prisons grew from just over 5 percent to 25 percent.[63] Large for-profit prison companies now also provide an array of reentry and treatment services.[64] Reuben Miller similarly argues that rehabilitation, once provided by social workers inside state prisons, is now largely conducted by (nonprofit) community-based prisoner reentry organizations. "Carceral devolution" thus relieves the state of responsibility, while making "ex-offenders and the disadvantaged communities they come from. . . . responsible for their own social outcomes."[65]

Court Oversight

Since the 1960s, the federal courts have acted to both impel and constrain prison reform and, in periods of inaction, to protect the status quo. The story of Florida cautions that prison litigation is not a good tool for decreasing prison populations and can inadvertently create incentives for increasing carceral capacity. However, at the same time, litigation has played a vital role in improving prison conditions to meet basic standards of decency. Since state political systems are insufficient to protect prisoners' rights, some type of court oversight is necessary. It is not a coincidence that prison conditions across the country worsened after Congress passed the Prison Litigation Reform Act in 1996. In fact, the return of brutality and inadequate medical care shows that the courts should be more active, not less.

Given constraints of the PLRA, lawyers have become more creative in their use of litigation. After the Supreme Court's 2011 decision in *Brown v. Plata*, lawyers and reformers across the country have used the specter of federal lawsuits to advance decarcerative reform efforts and draw attention to substandard conditions.[66] Another increasingly common tactic is to combine Eighth Amendment claims with claims of discrimination under the Americans with Disabilities Act, as prison populations now include large percentages of mentally ill or disabled prisoners. Lawyers in Illinois, for example, successfully negotiated a settlement with the state to move seriously mentally ill inmates out of solitary confinement to new residential treatment facilities.[67] Yet the additional expense of three hundred new mental health providers and $40 million for new facilities comes as Illinois has cut $113.7 million in mental health services funding for communities between 2009 and 2012.[68] Thus while they are necessary to protect prisoners' lives, lawsuits that focus on adequate health care are likely to produce more carceral capacity, not less.

Cases that specifically address overcrowding, of course, have more potential to impact prison populations. And while states responded to overcrowding court orders in the 1980s and 1990s by building more prisons, there is reason to think that this time may be different. In fact, the structure of the PLRA may ironically help to integrate court ordered or negotiated solutions within a larger decarceration reform agenda. First, since the PLRA creates high entrance barriers for litigation, policymakers may be more likely to view the cases that do make it through the courts as legitimate. Second, the PLRA allows multiple stakeholders to intervene in the case and requires their participation in negotiations. As a result, the litigation process now incorporates those who are most likely to oppose decarcerative reforms (such as law enforcement), potentially increasing their commitment to reform.[69] Third, the requirement that judges consider the impact of population orders on public safety obliges parties to submit research about the impact of imprisonment on crime. Judges are likely to examine this research with a more objective eye than legislators and thus provide additional legitimacy and attention to the research that demonstrates the tenuous relationship between imprisonment and crime.

The Politics of Reform

Ever since the media dubbed Robert Martinson's review of correctional programming in 1974 as "nothing works," policy analysts, think tanks, and criminologists (including Martinson himself) have argued that we need instead to ask what works and apply evidence-based solutions to our goals to reduce violent crime, cut recidivism, and slow admissions to prison.[70] Moreover, we have recourse to a much wider menu of what works to reduce crime and imprisonment than is usually discussed. As Elliott Currie noted in his 1998 book, *Crime and Punishment in America*, the Kerner Commission's recommendations from 1967 have been confirmed by empirical social science: "in the long run, attacking violent crime meant attacking social exclusion—reducing poverty, creating opportunity for sustaining work, supporting besieged families and the marginalized young." Ultimately, as I have shown here and as Currie writes in the preface to the new edition of his book, "Our failure to take the steps we needed to end our status as both the most violent and the most punitive of advanced industrial societies was essentially a political one."[71]

This suggests that we need to change the politics of reform in addition to proposing specific policies that will work to decrease incarceration. Ultimately, the divisive structure and character of our partisan politics will need to change. In the meantime, however, we can begin to change the political incentives behind our current politics of crime. First, we need to aggressively support voting rights for all citizens. Voter-ID laws and other restrictions should be challenged. We need to continue to amend state laws that restrict people with felony convictions from voting. Relatedly, we should end prison gerrymandering, the practice of counting prisoners who cannot vote in the place where they are imprisoned for the purpose of the census and drawing political districts. In large states like California, Florida, Illinois, and New York, where the majority of prisons are located in small rural areas, prison gerrymandering systematically contributes to malapportioned legislative and congressional districts, giving less voice to the representatives of urban areas. Although the courts have not looked favorably on constitutional claims against felon voting restrictions, prison gerrymandering seems to more directly violate "one person, one vote."[72]

Second, we need to improve the social and economic prospects of rural prison towns. Dismantling the carceral state will have adverse effects on prison towns if we don't take proactive measures. Any policy proposal that reduces the need for state prisons should reinvest part of the savings in job creation in rural towns and retraining/education for corrections employees. These opportunities don't need to be exclusively available to corrections employees, but they should be framed as part of a severance benefit for anyone willing to retire from their prison job. Similarly, we can't pass policies that provide programs to formerly incarcerated people or those with criminal records without providing similar opportunities to those who haven't been convicted of a crime. It strains our sense of fairness and creates the potential for a public backlash against anything perceived as pro-offender. The public, including corrections officers and their families, need access to quality education, drug treatment, mental health care, and job training as well.

Third, we should create new participatory structures that help increase local actors' participation in state policymaking—whether they are from rural towns, suburbs, or cities. Community organizations in many areas already exist, but they run on shoestring budgets and don't have access to social media campaign strategies, communications professionals, polling data, lobbyists, or policymakers. While the country's campaign financing system will ultimately need to be overhauled, we can start by providing community organizations with the infrastructure to participate in highly professionalized and elite-driven policy processes. To be sure, popular participation in criminal justice policy can be problematic.[73] Hiding the choices around crime control policy, however, denies that punishment by its very nature is a political enterprise. As an alternative, David Green suggests creating forums for public deliberation and opportunities for public participation in restorative justice.[74] In fact, public involvement could occur in many forms—from responding to community surveys, to volunteering in correctional facilities, to court watching, to participation on a jury, restorative justice panel or a police-citizen review board. This is not to say that involvement should come at the expense of, or as an alternative to, mass mobilization or pointed critiques of policy/practice. Rather, we need both.

Fourth, in order for community organizations and the public to weigh in, the operations and deliberations of police departments, prosecutors' offices, courtrooms, and prisons need to be much more transparent and available for public consumption. As citizens we should have access to clear and timely data on crime and criminal justice processing. Transparency should include public observation of routines such as police roll calls, prosecutors' charging decisions, and judges' manner of speech. As public institutions, criminal justice agencies should be subjected to oversight by public committees, rather than solely internal systems of review. Public committees would not just provide oversight, they would be a source of advocacy when appropriate. Important to this accountability project is an independent media focused on investigation and contextualization of the issues at stake.[75]

Rethinking Race

Racial projects or the collective ways that we respond to historically determined racial inequality and hierarchies shape how we understand the problem of mass incarceration/criminalization and potential solutions. Unfortunately, neither of the two dominant racial projects of the twenty-first century, colorblindness or racial representation/diversity, provide a framework for addressing the racialized nature of the carceral state. A colorblind approach finds allegiance with technocratic solutions such as alternative sanctions for low level drug offenders, strengthening probation, reducing parole revocations and investing in reentry programs. The current reform efforts along these lines disregard the racial composition of the target population, even as they promise to disproportionately benefit poor people of color. However, colorblind drug offender diversions, for example, ignore the racialized assumptions that shaped the drug laws and continue to shape patterns of drug offense enforcement. Similarly, current reentry policy often ignores the fact that a disproportionate number of prisoners are "reentering" into racially segregated and underresourced communities. In addition, some technocratic solutions actually embed racial distinctions and discrimination within their "tools" making them likely to exacerbate racial disparity. Risk assessment measures, for example, use prior criminal justice system contact, which, as Bernard Harcourt writes, is "proxy for race." As such they increase punitive consequences for black defendants which in turn reinforces "the notion of black criminality that pervades the public imagination."[76]

Yet the project of racial representation, what could also be referred to as the "diversity" imperative, similarly fails in its analysis of the problem and solution.[77] While African American's lack of political power, and therefore, representation, helped create and sustain the carceral state, it is not clear that more black political representation would significantly alter the carceral ethos (rather than softening it at the margins). Similarly, while predominantly white environments (such as the Ferguson Police Department or the Cook County State's Attorney's office) more easily adopt cultural norms that criminalize black citizens or degrade black defendants, more racial diversity within police organizations, prosecutor's offices, and among judges is unlikely to upend the racialized carceral ethos at the core of these institutions.[78] Research findings comparing black law enforcement officers, prosecutors and judges with their white counterparts are inconsistent, potentially highlighting the conflicting and contingent pressures black criminal justice professionals face.[79] This is not to say that we should not work toward racial diversity in these places. However, even if (or as) black officials shake things up, their presence provides a means of relegitimizing the routine operation of the carceral state.

A third emergent racial project is represented by Black Lives Matter (BLM), a movement in response to the large number of incidents where police officers (predominately white) have killed black people without apparent (or justifiable) cause and without facing consequences.[80] Simply put, the movement argues that the system and people with power act as if black lives don't matter. It follows a long history of black activism against state violence (and white violence protected by the state), from antislavery abolitionists, to antilynching campaigns, to the anti–sexual violence movement, to the Black Panther Party. BLM locates the source of racial inequality in the continual and institutional devaluation of black lives, which is most dramatically symbolized by white police officers who kill black people and escape punishment. As such, its underlying analysis could usefully be applied to mass incarceration or the broader carceral state. The carceral ethos that grew out of the politics of crime and spread throughout the criminal justice system was built on policymakers' and the public's willingness to devalue, dismiss, or ignore black lives.[81] Black Lives Matter thus offers an alternative racial project to colorblindness and racial representation. It is decidedly color-conscious, rejecting the notion that racial inequality can be remedied by ignoring race, yet it does not see more black representatives as a sufficient solution.[82] Black Lives Matter rearticulates the racial project for racial equality by directly challenging the impact of supposedly race-neutral criminal justice policies. As of 2016, BLM had been very successful at calling attention to racial discrimination, especially in policing.[83] However, in part because of the lack of options, BLM activists' first demand is often the criminal prosecution of police officers who shoot or kill civilians.[84] While criminal convictions of police officers is one way to hold police departments accountable, this demand could further ingrain the idea that the criminal justice system can solve deep structural racism within society.

Toward a New Ethos

When I began studying and thinking about mass incarceration in the mid-1990s, news stories occasionally surfaced that questioned the rationality of the War on Drugs, the growth of prison populations, or the racial disparity of either. The dominant public conversation, however, was steeped in the carceral ethos. Our vision of criminal justice was to criminalize more behavior and put more people behind bars for longer periods of time. As the political theorist Albert Dzur notes, "It is hard to gainsay the late William Stuntz's quip [that] 'American criminal law's historical development has borne no relation to any plausible normative theory—unless "more" counts as a normative theory.' "[85] Yet back then it seemed futile to propose an alternative vision. Twenty years later, the public conversation began to shift toward a recognition that more is not necessarily better (or even good).

Yet while political leaders, commentators, journalists, activists, and public intellectuals have begun to identify the multiple problems with the criminal justice system, they have yet to offer a vision that replaces the carceral ethos. Quoting political philosopher Brian Barry, punishment scholars Ian Loader and Richard Sparks note that "no compilation of facts can tell us about the fairness or unfairness of particular public policies, or distributions of social goods and bads, or institutional arrangements. For that we have to have a theory."[86] We have yet to answer the questions, Upon what values should we base penal policy and practice? What is our normative rationale for criminal punishment? The lack of a new and *just* justice ethos has significant consequences. It contributes to defeatism and ongoing "lamentation"—there are so many problems, the system is so unjust, the power of the carceral state so encompassing.[87] It is easy to feel a sense of hopelessness without a vision guiding our normative critiques and political action.

In calling for a new ethos I am joining a small chorus of critical criminologists and punishment scholars who have begun to fundamentally rethink the criminal justice system and offer paths toward a new vision for policy and practice.[88] What this new vision will be is uncertain, but a few potential guiding principles are worth noting. First, it seems clear that any vision needs to go beyond the liberal democratic ideal of procedural rights. Our attention to due process and commitment to a "rights logic" has not protected us from locking millions of people behind bars in violation of our substantive values.[89] In fact, our attention to rules has justified and legitimated a broken system. Second, we need to jettison long held assumptions about the nature and purpose of our criminal justice system. The continuing failure of prisons, for example, suggests the need for a radical rethinking of sites of criminal punishment.[90] Third, a new vision should incorporate a rethinking of correctional "interventions" and how we measure "success." As Elliott Currie notes, our current rehabilitation programs "train vulnerable people to navigate what are often chronically marginal lives and stunted opportunities" and then measure success in "very minimal and essentially negative ways."[91] A different vision of intervention might instead target whole communities and prioritize outcomes such as inequality reduction or community health.[92] Fourth, a new just vision would be intertwined with the principles of a good society. Loader and Sparks, for example, argue that a just approach to crime and justice would build citizen participation, solidarity, and trust.[93] As such, it needs to stem from an inclusive social and political community that encompasses crime victims *and* people with criminal convictions, people in prison, and their families. Finally, the vision necessary to dismantle the carceral state will need to proactively value and protect the lives of black people and other marginalized groups. Under a new vision it will no longer be acceptable to give up on one child, let alone whole groups of people.

Acknowledgments

In the United States we lock millions of people behind bars, in harsh conditions, with little opportunity to better themselves—many for long periods of time. By treating people as expendable, or, alternatively, in need of constant supervision, mass incarceration and mass social control have destroyed lives, broken up families, and harmed children. Just as sadly, mass incarceration has not significantly reduced violent crime in the United States. *Building the Prison State* is my response to this man-made national tragedy. I wanted to understand how and why we built a prison state. As a sociologist, I approached the task using the tools of social science research.

Over the last ten years many people supported me in my effort to understand the origins and development of mass incarceration in Florida. I am particular grateful to the many Floridians who spoke with me about their professional decisions and their experiences in politics or corrections. Tom Blomberg, dean of Florida State University's College of Criminology and Criminal Justice, Bill Bales, and the faculty at FSU introduced me to people at the Florida Department of Corrections. I was welcomed by former corrections secretary Jim McDonough and former deputy secretary Laura Bedard, who connected me with potential interviewees. The staff of the department's research bureau provided me with data and were always available to answer my questions. Paula Bryant, the department's in-house historian, dug up old department documents for me. Former assistant secretary of institutions George Sapp arranged for me to visit various correctional facilities, where the wardens always took time to speak with me and give me extensive informational tours. These tours and frank conversations proved invaluable for grounding my interviews and archival research.

A remarkable lawyer and activist, Bill Sheppard not only opened his personal archive to me, but his home and family as well. My research also benefited from the tremendous staff at the Florida State Archives, the Florida Legislative Library, and the Criminal Justice Estimating Conference. Kristen Hazelwood Rainey supplied fun breaks during my time in in Tallahassee.

A number of institutions supported me during this project. I received financial support from the National Science Foundation and Northwestern University Department of Sociology. The Center for Comparative Studies on Race and Ethnicity at Stanford University provided me with office space during one year of writing. The Sociology Department at The Ohio State University was a fantastic place to be a new assistant professor. Zhenchao Qian, Steve Lopez, Kori Edwards, Cindy Colen, Dana Haynie, and Hui Zheng provided support, encouragement and friendship. I finished writing and researching the book while an assistant professor at the Center for Legal Studies and the School of Education and Social Policy at Northwestern University. A special thank you to Laura Beth Nielsen and Dean Penelope Peterson for their enthusiastic belief in me and this project.

The Law and Society Association has been my intellectual home away from home, providing space to receive critical feedback and recognition of my work. Most importantly, it has connected me to a wide range of scholars doing amazing research on punishment and social control. The list of people, many who have become friends, is too long to include here. Nevertheless, this book would not have been possible without their pioneering scholarship. I look forward to continuing our conversations about the penal state. A few however, deserve a special shout-out. My conversations with Vivien Miller, who documented the early history of Florida's parole and prison system in two outstanding books, helped confirm my interpretation of the archival records from Florida. I rely on her thorough research of the period in Florida before 1954. From his advice to me as an aspiring graduate student to his important scholarship to his insightful comments on draft chapters, Joshua Page strengthened this project. Likewise, I owe a large debt of gratitude to Michael Campbell, with whom I first developed some of the ideas in the book in an *American Journal of Sociology* article we wrote together. He has been extremely patient with me as we embarked on a new project while I finished this book.

A few students and former students also helped me along the way. The quantitative analysis of Florida's criminal justice data in the book would not have been possible without the tireless efforts of Rachel Durso, now an Assistant Professor of Sociology at Washington College. Amy Eisenstein,

Zach Sommers, Jenny Bates, and Tate Steidley, now an Assistant Professor at the University of Denver, all provided research assistance.

In developing my initial research ideas, I greatly benefitted from the guidance and enthusiasm of John Hagan. John is a master of scholarship that tells a good story, and his feedback helped me draw out the characters in the story of Florida. Ann Orloff pushed me to think about the parallels between punishment policy and the welfare state. Aldon Morris's insightful questions helped me refine my approach to political contention and historical scholarship. Bob Nelson, Jonathan Simon, David Garland, Mona Lynch, and Joachim Savelsberg offered me important advice, feedback, and opportunities over the years. Bill Sabol shared his criminal justice system decomposition model with me and walked me through his analysis so that I could replicate it with Florida data.

A few exceptional female scholars took time out of their busy lives to mentor me, provide feedback on my writing, and open doors for me. Ruth Peterson helped bring me to OSU and invited me to join the amazing group of scholars in the Racial Democracy Crime and Justice Network. As editor of *Law and Society Review*, Carroll Seron published the first article from my Florida research and has provided ongoing invaluable advice. Kitty Calavita read early drafts of this book and has advocated for me over the years. Marie Gottschalk read draft chapters and always encouraged me. In addition, her scholarship on the carceral state was foundational to my research. All of them inspire me to be a better scholar, teacher, and advocate.

A fabulous group of Northwestern Sociology alumni provided vital laughter, friendship, and occasional commiseration, including Elisabeth Anderson, Ellen Berrey, Michaela DeSoucey, Victor Espinosa, Gabrielle Ferrales, Corey Fields, Emily Shafer, Ron Levi, Nicole Gonzales Van Cleve, and Berit Vannebo. In addition, I am grateful to a Facebook community of academic moms who make navigating the tasks of life easier. A terrific community of scholars and friends at Northwestern University, including Shana Bernstein, Jeannette Colyvas, Mesmin Destin, Joanna Grisinger, Claudia Haase, Simon Ispa-Landa, Ann Kelchner, Quinn Mulroy, Terri Sabol, and Susan Gaunt Stearns, make every day enjoyable. All of their accomplishments continue to inspire me.

John Tryneski, formerly at University of Chicago Press, and Rodney Powell helped bring the manuscript to UCP and guided me through the review process. I greatly appreciate anonymous reviewers' time and constructive comments. The editors of UCP's Series in Law and Society, Lynn Mather and John Conley, provided helpful feedback along the way. Chuck Myers, Holly Smith, and Michael Koplow steered the book through production.

Finally, I dedicate this book to the memory my grandma, Helene Flapan. I am fortunate to have a large close family that engages in intellectual exchange and encourages my interest in scholarship. In their own lives and professions, my grandparents advocated for young people, people with chronic illness, black college students, and the environment. Their strength and compassion guide me to this day. My parents, Ellen and David, have supported me in countless ways, from caring for my children, to reading draft chapters, to providing necessary respites. I am forever thankful for their love and that of my sister Elizabeth, my brother Jonathan, my in-laws Regina and Harvey Sr., and my entire extended family. A special thank you to my lifelong friends, Jocelyn Meter, Emily Johnson and Danielle deZorzi. A big thank you to my husband, Harvey Young, for embarking on the journey of parenthood with me and, just as importantly, insisting that we get away every few months—even and especially when we had so much going on. I appreciate your unrelenting love, patience, and good humor as I finished this book. My bright and beautiful children, Mark Ezekiel and Cora Evelyn, you both mean the world to me.

Appendix

To understand the development of the carceral state, I focus on the decisions of state-level policymakers that increased our use of imprisonment, including laws and policies on sentencing and the prison system. In addition, the paradox of race and mass incarceration compelled me to look at mass incarceration in former slave states—the states that not coincidentally have the highest rates of incarceration in the country. As a historical sociologist, I examine what changed between the early part of the twentieth century and after the 1970s, when incarceration rates began to rise.

My research design consisted of four components. First, I engaged in extensive archival research. The archival material included government records, court records, and newspaper articles. I accessed government documents from the Florida State Archives and Library, the Florida Legislative Library, the Florida Supreme Court Library, and the Florida Department of Corrections in Tallahassee. After 2010, legislative material from 2006 on became available electronically, necessitating fewer trips to the archives. This material included:

- Correspondence, meeting minutes, press releases, newspaper clippings, and policy analysis on prison administration and criminal justice policy from the administration of Governors LeRoy Collins (1955–61), Cecil Farris Bryant (1961–64), Claude Roy Kirk (1967–70), Reubin Askew (1971–78), Bob Graham (1979–86), Bob Martinez (1987–90), Lawton Chiles (1991–98); and Jeb Bush (1999–2006).
- Biennial Reports of the Prison Division of the Florida Department of Agriculture (1919–56), Biennial Reports of the Florida Division of Corrections (1957–72), Annual Reports of the Florida Division of Corrections (1973–75), Annual

Reports of the Florida Department of Offender Rehabilitation (1976–77), and Annual Reports of the Florida Department of Corrections (1978–2016).

- Other published and unpublished Department of Corrections and Parole and Probation Commission reports, including secretaries' writings, monthly facility reports, and technical assistance reports.
- Law Enforcement Assistance Administration reports (1965–80) and reports from Florida's criminal justice planning agencies (1968–80).
- Correspondence, meeting minutes, newspaper clippings, policy/bill analyses, hearing transcripts, and published and unpublished reports from Florida House and Senate Committees on corrections, criminal justice, and justice appropriations (1970–2016).
- Records and reports from various state-sponsored task forces on corrections or criminal justice issues.
- Published and unpublished reports from other state agencies, including the Sentencing Guidelines Commission, the Criminal Justice Estimating Conference, and the Florida Corrections Commission.
- State Statutes, Session Laws, and Legislative Session Journals.

I accessed official court records on prison conditions litigation from the Civil Rights Clearinghouse, available online at www.clearinghouse.net. In addition, I accessed *Costello v. Wainwright* hearing transcripts, pleadings, correspondence, monitoring, and other reports from the private files of William Sheppard in Jacksonville. Finally, I also gathered newspaper articles from Florida news sources on issues of crime, crime control, prisons, sentencing, and state policy. The newspaper articles helped me catalog the public debate around the issues and the other significant events that sometimes didn't make it into the legislative record.

All three archival sources—government, court, and media—allowed me to create a historical record of key decisions concerning Florida's system of punishment between 1950 and 2016. This historical record included major organizational changes to corrections, budget allocations to build and staff prisons, changes to sentencing structure, and (to a lesser extent) changes to criminal statutes. Importantly, it also allowed me to catalog *the people* instrumental in facilitating these changes. I identified chairs of legislative committees, heads of task forces, organizations that testified at committee hearings, and those most outspoken in media accounts. In essence, the archival record helped me to determine who was (and wasn't) at the "policy table," how they defined the problems they attempted to solve, the sources of information they relied on (and didn't rely on), and their policy positions.

The archival record also uncovered some of the negotiations over policy proposals. I recorded the information about each event and person in a relational database that I designed specifically for the project.

Second, I then reached out to eighty potential interviewees who were involved in key policy decisions, including politicians, bureaucrats, lawyers, activists, and representatives of special interest groups. Although it is impossible to get inside decision makers' heads, it is possible to re-create their logic through carefully structured interviews that use the documentary evidence as a guide. Towards this goal I conducted fifty-seven interviews and a dozen more informal conversations. I conducted initial interviews in 2006 and 2007 and a second round of interviews in 2015 and 2016. I was careful to include people across key policy moments, both Republicans and Democrats, and people who were less formally involved in the policy process. Where I wasn't able to speak directly to key people, I relied on the archival data and newspaper accounts of their positions, statements, and actions. For the most part, I was able to digitally record interviews (I asked permission to record interviews and only three people declined). Where possible, I conducted interviews in person. Interviews lasted anywhere from 45 minutes to 2½ hours. Since most interviewees are public officials, are in the public eye, or were asked about their professional decisions and duties, I use interviewees' real names.

In general, I asked interviewees about their role in the decision-making process, their memory of their goals, their understandings of their choices, their thinking about their choices, what information they used to guide their decisions, their understandings of the socioeconomic and political context, who supported their decisions and who opposed their decisions, and their understandings of the consequences of their decisions. Interviewees who did not directly make policy decisions were asked about the process by which decisions were made, the information available to decision makers, or other administrative processes. Where information from interviewees conflicted or was circumspect, I triangulated the information with available documentary evidence or newspaper articles from the time.

Third, I went on field visits to a representative sample of Florida's correctional institutions, including a work release center, a road prison, and medium and maximum security facilities. I found the field visits invaluable as a reference point for my formal and informal conversations. After visits I took extensive notes, which comprise part of my data and analysis.

Finally, in order to understand the effect of policy changes on the prison population, I with the assistance of Rachel Durso, assistant professor of sociology at Washington College, performed a decomposition analysis (see chapter 6). Given that the number of people in prison per capita in any given locale is necessarily determined by the crime rate, the arrest rate, the felony conviction rate, the imprisonment rate (the proportion of prison sentences per conviction), and the time served in prison, a decomposition analysis uses these rates at different points in time for different categories of offenders to estimate the relative contribution of each stage of criminal justice processing to changes in the prison population.[1] For our decomposition analysis of Florida, we replicate former Bureau of Justice Statistics director William Sabol's 2011 analysis, which used aggregate state-level data.[2] Our analysis uses three points in time—1998, 2004, and 2010—to assess how Florida's criminal justice system responded to both declining crime rates and changes in sentencing policy brought on by the Criminal Punishment Code (which took effect October 1, 1998). While it might have been better to begin with 1997, the Florida Department of Law Enforcement's arrest data for 1997 were incomplete. In addition, I only report the decomposition between 1998 and 2010 because the 2004 prison admissions were irregularly high due to a zero-tolerance policy issued by the Department of Corrections for probation violators.[3] We chose 2010 as an ending year because this was the height of Florida's per capita incarceration rate, and the community supervision technical violators sentenced to prison as a percentage of total admissions had stabilized to approximately 20 percent per year—similar to 1998.[4]

Data Sources

- Crime data: Florida Department of Law Enforcement UCR reported offenses
  - Violent: murder, rape, robbery, aggravated assault
  - Property: burglary, larceny, motor vehicle theft
- Arrest data: Florida Department of Law Enforcement (Violent, Property, Drugs, Other)
  - Violent: same as crime data
  - Property: same as crime data
  - Drugs: possession, manufacture, sale, trafficking
  - Other: all other arrests

- Felony conviction data: Florida Courts Summary Reporting System
  - Violent: murder, sexual offense, robbery, does *not* include aggravated assault
  - Property: burglary, theft/forgery/fraud, does *not* include motor vehicle theft
  - Drugs: possession, manufacture, sale, trafficking
  - Other: other crimes against persons (including aggravated assault), other crimes against property (including motor vehicle theft)
- Prison admissions/population data: Florida Department of Corrections (these have been converted to calendar year by taking the average of the two fiscal years)
  - Violent: murder, sexual offense, robbery, aggravated assault, carjacking
  - Property: burglary, grand theft, petit theft (3rd conviction), motor vehicle theft
  - Drugs: possession, manufacture, sale, trafficking
  - Other: all other admissions
- Population data: U.S Census (rounded)

The felony conviction data include aggravated assault and motor vehicle theft in "other" rather than violent and property crime, respectively. Unfortunately, these are large offense categories. Aggravated assault accounts for between 8 and 14 percent of prison admissions for violent offenses in the years we look at. Motor vehicle theft accounts for between 7 and 14 percent of property offense admissions in the years examined. Because of this discrepancy, the analysis will understate the convictions per offense for violent crime, overstate the absolute convictions per arrest/offense for "other" crimes, overstate the absolute prison admissions rates for violent and property offenses, and understate prison admission rates for other.

Prison admissions represents all inmates who were sentenced by the courts and brought into the prison system during the year. It includes parole violators and probation violators with a new sentence to prison.

Analysis

Data were converted into rates (table 6.1):

- offense rate (O): number of reported crime per 100,000 population
- arrest rates (A): number of arrests per 100 crimes
- conviction rate (C): number of convictions per 100 arrests

- admission rate (PA): number of admissions per 100 convictions
- expected length of stay or "time served" (LOS): calculated as the number of prisoners/new commitments to prison (in years)

Expected length of stay is measured as a stock-to-flow ratio, where the stock is the number of offenders in prison at year-end and the flow is the number of new court commitments. According to Sabol, this measure of length of stay provides an estimate of the expected time served on a new court commitment, taking into account the probability that a new court commitment will return to prison as a conditional release violator and serve additional time on the original commitment. This approach to estimating time served assumes that the proportion of prison admissions that return to prison as parole violators is constant. While the proportion of probation violators sentenced to prison fluctuated over this period, the percentage of parole violators and other returns from court that did not represent new commitments remained very low—between 1.2 and 4.8 percent of all admissions.

The following is excerpted from Sabol:[5]

The analysis starts by assuming a model of stable population growth, in which the prison population at one time is determined by the flows between stages. Multiplying these transitions represented by the ratios identified in the trend analysis yields, by definition, the prison population [PP] (or incarceration rate):

$$PP_{i,t} = O_{i,t} * A_{i,t} * C_{i,t} * PA_{i,t} * LOS_{i,t}$$

where the "i" refers to the offense group [violent, property, crime, or other], and the "t" refers to the time period. The number of offenses are not available for drug and other offenses. The number of arrests for these offense categories are used to estimate the offense rate.

The difference in the incarceration rate can be decomposed into its component parts as follows:

$$PP_{i,t+n} - PP_{i,t} = O_{i,t+n} * A_{i,t+n} * C_{i,t+n} * PA_{i,t+n} * [LOS_{i,t+n} - LOS_{i,t}] +$$
$$O_{i,t+n} * A_{i,t+n} * C_{i,t+n} * [PA_{i,t+n} - PA_{i,t}] * LOS_{i,t} +$$
$$O_{i,t+n} * A_{i,t+n} * [C_{i,t+n} - C_{i,t}] * PA_{i,t} * LOS_{i,t} +$$
$$O_{i,t+n} * [A_{i,t+n} - A_{i,t}] * C_{i,t} * PA_{i,t} * LOS_{i,t} +$$
$$[O_{i,t+n} - O_{i,t}] * A_{i,t} * C_{i,t} * PA_{i,t} * LOS_{i,t}$$

The first term on the right-hand side in the first row represents the amount of change in the incarceration rate due to changes in length of stay rate. The second row represents the amount due to changes in prison admissions; the third, the amount due to changes in convictions; the fourth, arrests; and the final row, the offense rate.

Abbreviations

FDC   Florida Department of Corrections Archives, Tallahassee

FSA   Florida State Archives, Tallahassee

FSCL   Florida State Supreme Court Library, Tallahassee

GSL   Special and Area Studies Collections, George A. Smathers Libraries, University of Florida, Gainesville

HSP   Harry Singletary Papers, private collection

NUTL   Northwestern University Transportation Library, Evanston, Illinois

SLF   State Library of Florida, Tallahassee

WSP   William Sheppard Papers, private collection

Notes

Chapter 1

1. Officially called "exercise cages," they are referred to by prison staff as "dog cages" (field notes April 24, 2007).

2. As of April 2016. Personal communication with staff of Florida Criminal Justice Estimating Conference, Florida Office of Economic and Demographic Research, April 17, 2016 (email). According to a survey conducted by the Linman Program at Yale Law School, as of 2014, Florida held 2,416 in administrative segregation. "Time in Cell: The ASCA-Linman 2014 National Survey of Administrative Segregation in Prison" (August 2015), https://www.law.yale.edu/system/files/area/center/liman/document/asca-liman_administrativesegregationreport.pdf. Close management (CM) "is the confinement of prisoners, separate from the general population, for reasons of security and for the order and effective management of the institution. . . . three CM levels carry with them significant restrictions of privileges." *Osterback v. McDonough*, 549 F. Supp. 2d 1337 (M.D. Fla. 2008). At the time of the trial in 2007, the Florida Department of Corrections held 3,000 prisoners in close management units. Daniel P. Mears and Michael D. Reisig, "The Theory and Practice of Supermax Prisons," *Punishment and Society* 8 (2006): 33–57; Keramet Reiter, *23/7: Pelican Bay Prison and the Rise of Long-Term Solitary Confinement* (New Haven: Yale University Press, 2016).

3. The ultimate punishment within the Florida prison system is "disciplinary confinement," which is even more restrictive. *Osterback v. McDonough*, 1344.

4. *Osterback v. McDonough*, "Second Report of Professor Craig Haney," December 24, 2003.

5. Atul Gawande, "Hellhole," *New Yorker*, March 30, 2009; Jessica Pupovac, "StopMax: The Fight Against Supermax Prisons Heats Up," AlterNet, August 10, 2008, accessed March 23, 2015, http://www.alternet.org/story/94257/.

6. Human Rights Watch, "US: Look Critically at Widespread Use of Solitary Confinement," June 18, 2012, http://www.hrw.org/news/2012/06/18/us-look-critically

-widespread-use-solitary-confinement/. For a description of a supermax, see Gerald Berge, Jeffrey Geiger, and Scot Whitney, "Technology Is the Key to Security in Wisconsin Supermax," *Corrections Today* 63 (2001): 105–9.

7. In Florida, the sweat box lost public support between 1935 and 1950 after prisoners' deaths from this and other practices became national news. See, for example, Associated Press, "Florida Prison Guard to Appeal Conviction," *New York Times*, October 17, 1932, 34. However, their use did not completely disappear until 1958. Vivien M. L. Miller, *Hard Labor and Hard Time: Florida's "Sunshine Prison" and Chain Gangs* (Gainesville: University Press of Florida, 2012), 282.

8. Robert Lieberman, "Legacies of Slavery? Race and Historical Causation in American Political Development," in *Race and American Political Development*, eds. Joseph Lowndes, Julie Novkov, and Dorian T. Warren (New York: Routledge, 2008), 206–33.

9. Punishment scholarship has come around to this view of more gradual change. Earlier examinations of mass incarceration spoke of a punitive turn or schism. David Garland, for example, wrote that changes in the 1970s brought about a "sharp reversal" of penal policy and ideas. David Garland, *The Culture of Control: Crime and Social Order in Contemporary Society* (Chicago: University of Chicago Press, 2001), 76.

10. See Naomi Murakawa, *The First Civil Right: How Liberals Built Prison America* (Oxford: Oxford University Press, 2014), for a discussion of the effort to protect African Americans from arbitrary state violence.

11. *Osterback v. McDonough*, 1363. For example, Florida was able to show in 2006 that prisoners in the most restrictive level of close management are "authorized to receive cell-front tutoring, wellness puzzles, wellness education courses and in-cell exercise guides. CM I prisoners are provided with educational material and then someone comes by the cell to discuss the prisoner's educational progress and to answer any questions the prisoner may have." *Osterback v. McDonough*, 1362.

12. Human Rights Watch written testimony to the US Senate Committee on the Judiciary, Subcommittee on the Constitution, Civil Rights, and Human Rights, June 18, 2012.

13. For a review of the proceduralist nature of constitutional law as it applies to criminal justice see William J. Stuntz, *The Collapse of American Criminal Justice* (Harvard University Press, 2011), 196. Murakawa, *The First Civil Right*, links the "pursuit of administrative perfection" to the desire to remove racial bias from the criminal justice system (26). Charles R. Epp, *Making Rights Real: Activists, Bureaucrats, and the Creation of the Legalistic State* (Chicago: University of Chicago Press, 2010). Legalization has occurred across institutional realms and organizations. Alan David Freeman, "Legitimizing Racial Discrimination through Antidiscrimination Law: A Critical Review of Supreme Court Doctrine," in *Critical Race Theory: The Key Writings That Formed the Movement*, ed. Kimberle Crenshaw, Neil Gotanda, Gary Peller, and Kendall Thomas (New York: New Press, 1995), 29–46; John R. Sut-

ton, Frank Dobbin, John W. Meyer and W. Richard Scott, "The Legalization of the Workplace," *American Journal of Sociology* 99 (1994): 944–71.

14. The Linman Program estimates that in 2014, 80,000 to 100,000 prisoners were in restrictive housing settings in state or federal prisons. "Time in Cell: The ASCA-Linman 2014 National Survey of Administrative Segregation in Prison."

15. National Research Council, *The Growth of Incarceration in the United States: Exploring Causes and Consequences*, Committee on Causes and Consequences of High Rates of Incarceration, Jeremy Travis, Bruce Western, and Steve Redburn, eds., Committee on Law and Justice, Division of Behavioral and Social Sciences and Education (Washington, DC: National Academies Press, 2014), 33.

16. The Pew Center on the States, "One in 100: Behind Bars in America 2008" (Washington, DC: Pew Charitable Trusts, 2008).

17. Danielle Kaeble, Lauren Glaze, Anastasios Tsoutis, and Todd Minton, "Correctional Populations in the United States, 2014" (Washington, DC: Bureau of Justice Statistics, December 2015); International Centre for Prison Studies, "World Prison Population List (10th edition)" (2013), http://www.prisonstudies.org/sites/prisonstudies.org/files/resources/downloads/wppl_10.pdf.

18. In 2014, black men were incarcerated at a rate almost six times that of white men and black females at a rate twice that of white females. E. Ann Carson, "Prisoners in 2014" (Washington, DC: Bureau of Justice Statistics, 2015); Bruce Western, *Punishment and Inequality in America* (New York: Russell Sage Foundation, 2006); Michelle Alexander, *The New Jim Crow: Mass Incarceration in the Age of Colorblindness* (New York: New Press, 2009).

19. Theda Skocpol, "Bringing the State Back In: Strategies of Analysis in Current Research," in *Bringing the State Back In*, ed. Peter B. Evans, Dietrich Rueschemeyer, and Theda Skocpol (Cambridge: Cambridge University Press, 1985), 3–43.

20. In 2012, about 4.1 million people entered or exited probation and 1.25 million were admitted or released from prison. Laura M. Maruschak and Thomas P. Bonczar, "Probation and Parole in the United States, 2012" (Washington, DC: Bureau of Justice Statistics, December 2013); E. Ann Carson and Daniela Golinelli, "Prisoners in 2012: Trends in Admissions and Releases, 1991–2012" (Washington, DC: Bureau of Justice Statistics, September 2014).

21. Stephen Raphael and Michael A. Stoll, *Why Are So Many Americans in Prison?* (New York: Russell Sage Foundation, 2014), 20.

22. The Pew Charitable Trusts, "The High Cost of Corrections in America," June 12, 2012, http://www.pewtrusts.org/en/multimedia/data-visualizations/2012/the-high-cost-of-corrections-in-america/.

23. Prerna Anand, *Winners and Losers: Corrections and Higher Education in California* (California Common Sense, September 5, 2012), http://cacs.org/research/winners-and-losers-corrections-and-higher-education-in-california/#three. In 2011, 10 percent of California's general fund expenditure went to corrections and 8 percent went to higher education. The Vera Institute of Justice has calculated the true

"price of prisons" to be 13.9 percent higher when prison-related costs outside of corrections budgets are included, such as state contributions to retirees, employee benefits, capital costs, and prisoner health care expenses. Christian Henrichson and Ruth Delaney, *The Price of Prisons: What Incarceration Costs Taxpayers* (New York: Vera Institute of Justice, 2012), http://www.vera.org/sites/default/files/resources /downloads/price-of-prisons-updated-version-021914.pdf/.

24. John Eason, *Big House on the Prairie: Rise of the Rural Ghetto and Prison Proliferation* (Chicago: University of Chicago Press, 2017).

25. Author interview with Harry Singletary, former secretary of the Florida Department of Corrections, 1991–1999, May 7, 2007, Tallahassee.

26. Margo Schlanger, "Civil Rights Injunctions Over Time: A Case Study of Jail and Prison Court Orders," *New York University Law Review* 81 (2006): 550–628.

27. As I explain in chapter 7, the court oversight of "adequate" prison conditions severely waned after 1996 such that by 2016 many states are likely operating unconstitutional prison systems.

28. I focus on adult prisons and the adult criminal justice system, but my framework could be applied to the juvenile system as well.

29. Marie Gottschalk, "The Carceral State and the Politics of Punishment," in *The Sage Handbook of Punishment and Society*, ed. Jonathan Simon and Richard Sparks (Thousand Oaks, CA: Sage, 2012), 205–41. Loïc Wacquant refers to the "penal state" to signal that the criminal justice system and prisons manage poverty and act as social support systems. Loïc Wacquant, *Punishing the Poor: The Neoliberal Government of Social Insecurity* (Raleigh, NC: Duke University Press, 2009). David Garland distinguishes between "penality" or the discourses, institutions, and practices that make up criminal law, criminal justice, and penal sanctioning, on the one hand, and the "penal state," which comprises the agencies and authorities that "determine penal law and direct the deployment of the power to punish," on the other. In Garland's formulation, Gottschalk's "carceral state" is analogous to contemporary penality. David Garland, "The 2012 Sutherland Address: Penality and the Penal State," *Criminology* 51 (3) (2013): 495. Without wading into this debate, my use of "carceral state" attempts to capture the expansion of the state power and capacity to punish.

30. Marie Gottschalk, *The Prison and the Gallows: The Politics of Mass Incarceration in America* (New York: Cambridge University Press, 2006), 6; Marie Gottschalk, *Caught: The Prison State and the Lockdown of American Politics* (Princeton: Princeton University Press, 2015), 1. The 2014 count by the Bureau of Justice Statistics for "persons under the supervision of U.S. adult correctional systems" was 6.85 million or 1 in 36 adults. This includes juveniles prosecuted as adults, but not juveniles under the jurisdiction of a juvenile court or agency. Kaeble et al., "Correctional Populations in the United States," 2014.

31. Amy E. Lerman and Vesla M. Weaver, *Arresting Citizenship: The Democratic Consequences of American Crime Control* (Chicago: University of Chicago Press, 2014), 20.

32. Georg Rusche and Otto Kirchheimer, *Punishment and Social Structure* (New Brunswick, NJ: Transaction Publishers, 2003, [1939]), 5. Rusche and Kirchheimer follow in the tradition of the founding works of sociology by Emile Durkheim, Karl Marx, and W. E. B. DuBois.

33. For a review see Alessandro De Giorgi, "Punishment and Political Economy," in *The Sage Handbook of Punishment and Society*, ed. Jonathan Simon and Richard Sparks (Thousand Oaks, CA: Sage, 2012), 40–59.

34. E.g. Wacquant, *Punishing the Poor*; Garland, *The Culture of Control*, 82; Nils Christie, *Crime Control as Industry: Gulags Western Style* (London: Routledge, 1993).

35. Jonathan Simon, *Governing through Crime: How the War on Crime Transformed American Democracy and Created a Culture of Fear* (Oxford: Oxford University Press, 2007); John Hagan, *Who Are the Criminals? The Politics of Crime Policy from the Age of Roosevelt to the Age of Reagan* (Princeton: Princeton University Press, 2012).

36. Katherine Beckett, *Making Crime Pay: Law and Order in Contemporary American Politics* (New York: Oxford University Press, 1997).

37. Mona Lynch, *Sunbelt Justice: Arizona and the Transformation of American Punishment* (Palo Alto, CA: Stanford University Press, 2010); Ruth Wilson Gilmore, *Golden Gulag: Prisons, Surplus, Crisis, and Opposition in Globalizing California* (Berkeley: University of California Press, 2007); Robert Perkinson, *Texas Tough: The Rise of America's Prison Empire* (New York: Henry Holt and Company, 2010); Joshua Page, *The Toughest Beat: Politics, Punishment, and the Prison Officers Union in California* (New York: Oxford University Press, 2013).

38. Garland, *Culture of Control*, 77. My perspective on decision-making draws from a "problem-solving" model of action where state actors' goals shift with rationalized myths about the situation. Richard Biernacki, "The Action Turn? Comparative-Historical Inquiry Beyond the Classic Models of Conduct," in *Remaking Modernity: Politics, History, and Sociology*, ed. Julia Adams, Elisabeth S. Clemens, and Ann Shola Orloff (Durham: Duke University Press, 2005), 75–91.

39. Alexander L. George and Andrew Bennet, *Case Studies and Theory Development in the Social Sciences* (Cambridge: MIT Press, 2005); Dietrich Rueschemeyer and John D. Stephens, "Comparing Historical Sequences: A Powerful Tool for Causal Analysis," *Comparative Social Research* 16 (1997): 55–72.

40. Paul DiMaggio, "Culture and Cognition," *Annual Review of Sociology* 23 (1997): 263–87; Ann Shola Orloff, *The Politics of Pensions: A Comparative Analysis of Britain, Canada, and the United States* (Madison: University of Wisconsin Press, 1993); Sven Steinmo, Kathleen Thelen, and Frank Longstreth, eds., *Structuring Politics: Historical Institutionalism in Comparative Analysis* (New York: Cambridge University Press, 1992).

41. Neil Fligstein, "Social Skill and the Theory of Fields," *Sociological Theory* 19 (2001): 110. See also Garland on "habits of thought." Garland, *Culture of Control*, 77.

42. Theodore Lowi, "American Business and Public Policy: Case Studies and Political Theory" *World Politics* 16 (1964): 677–715. See also Peter B. Evans, Dietrich Rueschemeyer and Theda Skocpol, eds., *Bringing the State Back In* (Cambridge: Cambridge University Press, 1985).

43. Hugh Heclo, *Modern Social Politics in Britain and Sweden: From Relief to Income Maintenance* (New Haven: Yale University Press, 1974), 305.

44. Paul Pierson, *Politics in Time: History, Institutions, and Social Analysis* (Princeton: Princeton University Press, 2004).

45. Orloff, *The Politics of Pensions*. Theda Skocpol, *Protecting Soldiers and Mothers* (Cambridge: Harvard University Press, 1992); Margaret Weir, Ann Shola Orloff, and Theda Skocpol, eds., *The Politics of Social Policy in the United States* (Princeton: Princeton University Press, 1988).

46. Skocpol, *Protecting Soldiers and Mothers*, 58.

47. John L. Campbell, *Institutional Change and Globalization* (Princeton: Princeton University Press, 2004), 23.

48. Gottschalk, *The Prison and the Gallows*; David Jacobs and Richard Kleban, "Political Institutions, Minorities, and Punishment: A Pooled Cross-National Analysis of Imprisonment Rates," *Social Forces* 80 (2003): 725–55; Joachim Savelsberg, "Knowledge, Domination, and Criminal Punishment," *American Journal of Sociology* 99 (1994): 911–43; John R. Sutton, "The Political Economy of Imprisonment in the Affluent Western Democracies, 1960–1990," *American Sociological Review* 69 (2004): 170–89; James Q. Whitman, *Harsh Justice: Criminal Justice and the Widening Divide between America and Europe* (Oxford: Oxford University Press, 2003).

49. In addition, scholars have argued that the local election of prosecutors and judges makes them more inclined to appeal to popular punitive attitudes. Michael Tonry, *Punishing Race: A Continuing American Dilemma* (New York: Oxford University Press, 2011).

50. See, e.g., Dietrich Oberwittler and Sven Höfer, "Crime and Justice in Germany: An Analysis of Recent Trends and Research," *European Journal of Criminology* 2 (2005): 465–508.

51. Vanessa Barker, *The Politics of Imprisonment: How the Democratic Process Shapes the Way America Punishes Offenders* (New York: Oxford University Press, 2009); Lynch, *Sunbelt Justice*; Franklin Zimring, David Hawkins, and Sam Kamin, *Punishment and Democracy: Three Strikes and You're Out in California* (Oxford: Oxford University Press, 2001).

52. Barker compares Washington to the elite pragmatist democratic process of New York, which emphasizes expertise and behind-closed-door decision making, and California, which has low civic participation but institutions that buttress populist demands. Barker, *The Politics of Imprisonment*, 11; Michael C. Campbell, "Politics, Prisons, and Law Enforcement: An Examination of the Emergence of 'Law and Order' Politics in Texas," *Law and Society Review* 45 (3) (2011): 631–65.

53. Lynch, *Sunbelt Justice*, 113.

54. Malcolm Feeley and Edward Rubin, *Federalism: Political Identity and Tragic Compromise* (Ann Arbor: University of Michigan Press, 2008), 12. They define federalism as "a means of governing a polity that grants partial autonomy to *geographically* defined subdivisions of the polity." Franklin Zimring, "The Scale of Imprisonment in the United States: 20th Century Patterns and 21st Century Prospects," *Journal of Criminology and Criminal Law* 100 (3) (2010): 1225–46.

55. Raphael and Stoll, *Why Are So Many Americans in Prison?* If you count all the county- or local-level systems, the number of criminal justice systems in the United States is in the thousands.

56. Simon, *Governing through Crime*, 29.

57. Gottschalk, *The Prison and the Gallows*. The federalization of policy goes beyond crime control. Conflicts and socioeconomic changes in the twentieth century led Congress to pass a "a wide range of social and economic policies, including minimum wage, pensions and old age insurance, working conditions, the environment, civil rights, and so on" (3). Lisa L. Miller, "(Mis)Understanding American Federalism: On Constitutions, Collective Action, Competition, and Quiescence," Foundation for Law, Justice and Politics (2012), https://ora.ox.ac.uk/objects/uuid :72a4d842-8f08-4311-9c91-7d20f7bac4a6.

58. Feeley and Rubin, *Federalism*, ix.

59. Lisa L. Miller, *The Perils of Federalism: Race, Poverty, and the Politics of Crime Control* (Oxford: Oxford University Press, 2008).

60. Elliott Currie, *Crime and Punishment in America* (New York: Macmillan, 2013 [1998]).

61. Miller, *The Perils of Federalism*.

62. Pierson, *Politics in Time*, 46.

63. Loïc Wacquant, "Deadly Symbiosis: When Ghetto and Prison Meet and Mesh," *Punishment and Society* 3 (2001): 95–134; Alexander, *The New Jim Crow*.

64. Todd Clear, *Imprisoning Communities: How Mass Incarceration Makes Disadvantaged Neighborhoods Worse* (New York: Oxford University Press, 2007); Western, *Punishment and Inequality*.

65. Alexander, *The New Jim Crow*, 170.

66. Tonry, *Punishing Race*, 101.

67. This is a classic fallacy of functionalist theory: that we can always understand the causes of social phenomena by analyzing its current functions. Pierson, *Politics in Time*, 46–47; David Lee and Howard Newby, *The Problem of Sociology* (Taylor & Francis, 2012 [1983]), 258.

68. Gottschalk, *Caught*, 4.

69. Michael Omi and Howard Winant, *Racial Formation in the United States: From the 1960s to the 1990s* (New York: Routledge, 1994).

70. Many of the unique institutional features of U.S. democracy, politics, and bureaucratic structure can be traced to U.S.-specific history of racial hierarchies

and inequalities. See Joseph Lowndes, Julie Novkov, and Dorian T. Warren, eds., *Race and American Political Development* (New York: Routledge, 2008).

71. Robert C. Lieberman, *Shifting the Color Line: Race and the American Welfare State* (Cambridge: Harvard University Press, 1998).

72. Beckett, *Making Crime Pay*, 43.

73. Vesla M. Weaver, "Frontlash: Race and the Development of Punitive Crime Policy," *Studies in American Political Development* 21 (2007): 230–65.

74. Vincent L. Hutchings and Nicholas A. Valentino, "The Centrality of Race in American Politics," *Annual Review of Political Science* 7 (2004): 383–408.

75. Bernard E. Harcourt, *Against Prediction: Profiling, Policing, and Punishing in an Actuarial Age* (Chicago: University of Chicago Press, 2008); Elizabeth Hinton, *From the War on Poverty to the War on Crime: The Making of Mass Incarceration in America* (Cambridge: Harvard University Press, 2016).

76. Psychological studies continue to document people's cognitive links between blackness and crime. See Jennifer Eberhardt et al., "Seeing Black: Race, Crime and Visual Processing," *Journal of Personality and Social Psychology* 87 (2004): 876–93. See Tonry, *Punishing Race,* for a good review of this research.

77. Lawrence D. Bobo and Victor Thompson, "Unfair by Design: The War on Drugs, Race, and the Legitimacy of the Criminal Justice System," *Social Research* 73 (2) (2006): 445–72. This is similar to findings that racial resentment is correlated with policy preferences against affirmative action and social welfare spending. Hutchings and Valentino, "The Centrality of Race in American Politics."

78. Lawrence D. Bobo and Victor Thompson, "Racialized Mass Incarceration: Poverty, Prejudice, and Punishment," in *Doing Race: 21 Essays for the 21st Century,* ed. Hazel Rose Markus and Paula M. L. Moya (W. W. Norton & Company, 2010), 339, 341.

79. Black youth are disproportionately involved in violent crime because of their structural disadvantages. Ruth D. Peterson and Laurie J. Krivo, *Divergent Social Worlds: Neighborhood Crime and the Racial-Spatial Divide* (New York: Russell Sage Foundation, 2010). In earlier work, Tonry argues that it was likely obvious to policymakers that the War on Drugs would disproportionately impact African Americans, given their participation in the underground economy and the law enforcement focus of the war. Michael Tonry, *Malign Neglect: Race, Crime, and Punishment in America* (New York: Oxford University Press, 1995). See also Doris Marie Provine, "Race and Inequality in the War on Drugs," *Annual Review of Law and Social Science* 7 (2011): 41–60.

80. Tonry, *Punishing Race*, 8.

81. Murakawa, *The First Civil Right*.

82. Hinton, *From the War on Poverty to the War on Crime,* 76–77.

83. Michael C. Campbell, "The Emergence of Penal Extremism in California: A Dynamic View of Institutional Structures and Political Processes," *Law and Society Review* 48 (2014): 377–409.

84. Simon, *Governing through Crime*, 102.

85. Eduardo Bonilla-Silva, "Rethinking Racism: Toward a Structural Interpretation," *American Sociological Review* 62 (3) (1997): 465–80.

86. Omi and Winant, *Racial Formation*, 56. Robert Lieberman defines "racial order" as "the racial context underlying political action—social relations, political arrangements, and power distributions structured according to racial categories." Lieberman, "Legacies of Slavery?" 218.

87. Desmond King and Rogers Smith define "racial orders" as political actors' beliefs, commitments and aims surrounding the meanings of race. Desmond S. King and Rogers M. Smith, "Racial Orders in American Political Development," *American Political Science Review* 99 (2005): 75–92. In their more recent conceptualization, King and Smith have centered the issue of policy. Desmond S. King and Rogers M. Smith, *Still a House Divided: Race and Politics in Obama's America* (Princeton: Princeton University Press, 2011).

88. Omi and Winant, *Racial Formation*, conceptualize racial projects in terms of social movements, where action is purposeful and strategic. King and Smith, *Still a House Divided*, concede that political actors may not recognize their membership in a racial policy alliance. I try to strike a balance by focusing on actors' purposeful actions that don't rise to the level of a social movement.

89. Omi and Winant, *Racial Formation*.

90. Lieberman, *"Legacies of Slavery?"*

91. Racial divisions impact potential ideation of the problem and options through "shared understandings" or "cultural assumptions." Julia O'Connor, Ann Shola Orloff, and Sheila Shaver, *States, Markets, Families: Gender, Liberalism, and Social Policy in Australia, Canada, Great Britain, and the United States* (Cambridge: Cambridge University Press, 1999).

92. Roger Mathews, "The Myth of Punitiveness," *Theoretical Criminology* 9 (2005): 175–201; Philip Goodman, "'Another Second Chance': Rethinking Rehabilitation through the Lens of California's Prison Fire Camps," *Social Problems* 59 (2012): 437–58.

93. Between 1970 and 2000, incarceration rates grew between 150 percent (Maine) and 900 percent (Hawaii). Paige M. Harrison and Allen J. Beck, "Prisoners in 2000" (Washington, DC: Bureau of Justice Statistics, 2001).

94. There are outliers within regions. In the South, North and South Carolina's rates are historically lower. In the West, Idaho's rates are higher, Washington's are lower. Bureau of Justice Statistics, National Prisoner Statistics, 2013–2014 (Washington, DC: U.S. Census Bureau, 2014); Michelle Phelps, "The Place of Punishment: Variation in the Provision of Prisoner Services Staff across the Punitive Turn," *Journal of Criminal Justice* 40 (5) (2012): 348–57.

95. Joanne Oreskovich reports that in debates over changes to the sentencing guidelines to deal with sex offenders in the late 1980s, Minnesota public actors stated things like "However heinous their crimes, each criminal is a human being

deserving of civilized treatment." Joanne Oreskovich, "Dimensions of Sex Offender Sanctioning: A Case Study of Minnesota's Legislative Reforms, 1987–1993" (Ph.D. diss., University of Minnesota, 2001), 143. On Texas, see Michael C. Campbell, "Ornery Alligators and Soap on a Rope: Texas Prosecutors and Punishment Reform in the Lone Star State," *Theoretical Criminology* 16 (3) (2012): 289–311.

96. At the height of state prison populations in 2008, California's imprisonment rate was 467 per 100,000 residents, Florida's was 557, Arizona's was 567, and Texas's was 639. As a comparison, Louisiana's was 853 and Massachusetts's was 218. Willaim J. Sabol, Heather C. West, and Matthew Cooper, "Prisoners in 2008" (Washington, DC: Bureau of Justice Statistics, December 2009).

97. Death Penalty Information Center, Facts about the Death Penalty, May 26, 2017, https://deathpenaltyinfo.org/documents/FactSheet.pdf.

98. Erika L. Wood, *Florida: An Outlier in Denying Voting Rights* (New York: Brennan Center for Justice, 2016), 3, https://www.brennancenter.org/sites/default/files/publications/Florida_Voting_Rights_Outlier.pdf/.

99. Rapid population growth created unique problems for prison systems, which do not easily expand or contract. Michael C. Campbell and Heather Schoenfeld, "The Transformation of America's Penal Order: A Historicized Political Sociology of Punishment," *American Journal of Sociology* 118 (5) (2013): 1375–1423. In particular, the Sunbelt has been the heart of the new Republican Party and the neoconservative movement. Lisa McGirr, *Suburban Warriors: The Origins of the New American Right* (Princeton: Princeton University Press, 2001).

100. See discussion in chapters 4 and 5. Violent Crime Control and Law Enforcement Act of 1994, Title II of Pub. L. no. 103–332; Prison Litigation Reform Act of 1995, Title VIII of Pub. L. 104–134, 110 Stat. 1321.

101. *Gideon v. Wainwright*, 372 U.S. 335 (1963) overturned *Betts v. Brady*, 316 U.S. 455 (1942). For an account of Gideon and his story, see Anthony Lewis, *Gideon's Trumpet* (New York: Vintage Books, 1964).

102. David Cole, *No Equal Justice: Race and Class in the American Criminal Justice System* (New York: New Press, 1999), 16.

103. The Court held that the appropriate test of a Fourth Amendment violation is instead whether "a reasonable passenger would feel free to decline the officers' requests or otherwise terminate the encounter." *Florida v. Bostick*, 501 U.S. 429, at 433, 437.

104. *Ohio v. Robinette*, 519 U.S. 33 (1996). This approach to policing has been particularly harmful for black citizens, who, given the history of police violence, are less likely to feel free to say "no" to the police. Cole, *No Equal Justice*.

105. After the Court's decision, a judge resentenced Graham to twenty-five years in prison. Jeff Kunerth, "Life without Parole Becomes 25 Years for Terrance Graham, Subject of U.S. Supreme Court Case," *Orlando Sentinel*, February 24, 2012.

106. *Graham v. Florida*, 560 U.S. 48 (2010).

107. Lizette Alvarez, "A Florida Law Gets Scrutiny after a Teenager's Killing," New York Times, March 20, 2012.

108. Fla. Sess. Laws, ch. 2005–27 (2005).

109. As of August 2013, the *Tampa Bay Times* had identified 237 stand your ground cases in Florida. In the 134 fatal cases (involving 81 white victims, 43 black victims, and 10 Latino victims), 62.5 percent of the deaths were "justified" under the law. The youngest victims of justified deadly force were a fifteen-year-old boy involved in a gang shootout and a sixteen-year-old boy accused of bullying. Accessed on March 23, 2014, http://www.tampabay.com/stand-your-ground-law/.

110. In 2002, Florida's black/white imprisonment ratio was just below average (as is the case with Southern states). Human Rights Watch, "Race and Incarceration Backgrounder" (2003), https://www.hrw.org/legacy/backgrounder/usa/incarceration/.

111. Anna Brown and Mark Hugo Lopez, "Mapping the Latino Population, By State, County and City" (Washington, DC: Pew Research Center, 2013), http://www.pewhispanic.org/2013/08/29/mapping-the-latino-population-by-state-county-and-city/.

112. Philip Goodman, " 'It's Just Black, White, or Hispanic': An Observational Study of Racializing Moves in California's Segregated Prison Reception Centers," Law and Society Review 42 (4) (2008): 757.

113. Recognizing that those of Hispanic origin may consider themselves (or be perceived as) either black or white makes it unclear how this absence biases data on the composition of criminalized populations in Florida.

114. Pew Hispanic Center, "The Hispanic Electorate in Florida," http://www.pewhispanic.org/files/2004/10/9.pdf. Of the thirteen Cuban Americans in the Florida House and Senate in 2014, only one was a Democrat.

115. Cubans began migrating to the U.S. in large numbers beginning in 1959. Although they were encouraged to move elsewhere in the country, a majority remained in South Florida. In 1961 Congress established the Cuban Refugee Program, which provided $1 billion in funding for education, training, and other aid for Cuban migrants. In 1966, Congress passed the Cuban Refugee Adjustment Act, which made post-1958 Cuban migrants eligible for permanent residence after just one year and guaranteed their petitions would be granted. Suzanne Macartney, Alemayehu Bishaw, and Kayla Fontenot, "Poverty Rates for Selected Detailed Race and Hispanic Groups by State and Place: 2007–2011" (Washington, DC: U.S. Census Bureau, 2013), https://www.census.gov/prod/2013pubs/acsbr11-17.pdf/.

116. Carole J. Uhlander and F. Chris Garcia, "Learning Which Party Fits: Experience, Ethnic Identity, and the Demographic Foundations of Latino Party Identification," in Diversity in Democracy: Minority Representatives in the United States, ed. Gary M. Segura and Shaun Bowler (Charlottesville: University of Virginia Press, 2005), 72–101; Florida Immigrant Coalition, "Florida House Passes Anti-Immigrant Bill; Republicans Abandon Latino and Immigrant Communities," February 2016,

https://floridaimmigrant.org/?press_releases=florida-house-passes-anti-immigrant
-bill-republicans-abandon-latino-and-immigrant-communities#sthash.HZzIfehl.dpuf.

117. Skocpol, *Bringing the State Back In*, *17–18*.

118. Following the work of Gottschalk, *The Prison and the Gallows*, new schol-arship has begun to uncover the importance of criminal justice capacity building in the 1960s and 1970s. Murakawa, *The First Civil Right*; Hinton, *From the War on Poverty to the War on Crime*.

119. Robert Martinson, "What Works? Questions and Answers about Prison," *Public Interest* (Spring 1974): 22–54; Malcolm M. Feeley, "Crime, Social Order, and the Rise of Neo-conservative Politics," *Theoretical Criminology* 7 (2003): 111–30; Rick Sarre, "Beyond 'What Works?' A 25-year Jubilee Retrospective of Robert Martinson's Famous Article," *Australian and New Zealand Journal of Criminology* 34 (2001): 38–46.

120. Garland, *Culture of Control*, 62–63.

121. Garland, *Culture of Control*, 64. These include: rehabilitation was under-funded, its impact was undermined by custodial and punitive contexts, and there was a need for more staff training, better prisoner selection, more individualiza-tion, and more follow-up.

122. Lynch, *Sunbelt Justice*. Perkinson, *Texas Tough*.

123. See also Michelle S. Phelps, "Rehabilitation in the Punitive Era: The Gap between Rhetoric and Reality in US Prison Programs," *Law and Society Review* 45 (1) (2011): 33–68.

124. Stuart A. Scheingold, *The Politics of Law and Order: Street Crime and Public Policy* (New York: Longman, 1984).

125. E.g. Tonry, *Malign Neglect*; Beckett, *Making Crime Pay*.

126. Gottschalk, *The Prison and the Gallows*, 7.

127. *First Annual Report of the Justice System Improvement Act Agencies: Fis-cal Year 1980* (Washington, DC: U.S. Department of Justice, 1981), 2, NUTL; Hin-ton, *From the War on Poverty to the War on Crime*, 2.

128. Campbell, "Politics, Prisons, and Law Enforcement"; Lynch, *Sunbelt Justice*.

129. David R. Colburn and Richard K. Scher, *Florida's Gubernatorial Politics in the Twentieth Century* (Tallahassee: University Presses of Florida, 1980).

130. Campbell and Schoenfeld, "The Transformation of America's Penal Order."

131. Peter K. Enns, *Incarceration Nation: How the United States Became the Most Punitive Democracy in the World* (New York: Cambridge University Press, 2016).

132. Garland, *Culture of Control*; Anthony Giddens, *The Consequences of Mo-dernity* (Oxford: Polity Press, 1990).

133. Enns, *Incarceration Nation*; Lisa L. Miller, *The Myth of Mob Rule: Violent Crime and Democratic Politics* (New York: Oxford University Press, 2016).

134. Sara Sun Beale, "The News Media's Influence on Criminal Justice Policy: How Market-Driven News Promotes Punitiveness," *William and Mary Law Re-view* 48 (2006): 397–481; Franklin D. Gilliam and Shanto Iyengar. "Prime Suspects:

The Influence of Local Television News on the Viewing Public," *American Journal of Political Science* 44 (3) (2000): 560–73;Victor E. Kappeler and Gary W. Potter, *Constructing Crime: Perspectives on Making News and Social Problems* (Long Grove, IL: Waveland Press, 2006); Ray Surette, *Media, Crime, and Criminal Justice* (Boston: Cengage Learning, 2014).

135. Zimring, Hawkins, and Kamin, *Punishment and Democracy*; Lord Windlesham, *Politics, Punishment, and Populism* (Oxford: Oxford University Press, 1998); Joachim Savelsberg, "Knowledge, Domination, and Criminal Punishment," *American Journal of Sociology* 99 (1994): 911–43. But see Miller, *The Myth of Mob Rule*, who argues that racialized fragmented political institutions lead lawmakers to translate concern about crime into punitive policy.

136. For a review see Todd Clear and Natasha Frost, *The Punishment Imperative: The Rise and Failure of Mass Incarceration (New York: New York University Press*, 2014), 34–39.

137. Hinton, *From the War on Poverty to the War on Crime*, 24.

138. Gray Cavender, "Media and Crime Policy: A Reconsideration of David Garland's *The Culture of Control*," *Punishment and Society* 6 (3) (2004): 335–48; Jared S. Rosenberger and Valerie J. Callanan, "The Influence of Media on Penal Attitudes," *Criminal Justice Review* 36 (4) (2011): 435–55; Natasha A. Frost, "Beyond Public Opinion Polls: Punitive Public Sentiment and Criminal Justice Policy," *Sociology Compass* 4 (3) (2010): 156–68.

139. Elizabeth K. Brown, "The Dog That Did Not Bark: Punitive Social Views and the 'Professional Middle Classes,'" *Punishment and Society* 8 (3) (2006): 287–312; Mathews, "The Myth of Punitiveness."

140. Tonry, *Malign Neglect*; Beckett, *Making Crime Pay*.

141. Wacquant, *Punishing the* Poor, 3–11.

142. Beckett, *Making Crime Pay*; Michael Welch, Melissa Fenwick, and Meredith Roberts, "Primary Definitions of Crime and Moral Panic: A Content Analysis of Experts' Quotes in Feature Newspaper Articles on Crime," *Journal of Research in Crime and Delinquency* 34 (4) (1997): 474–94; Michael Welch, Melissa Fenwick, and Meredith Roberts, "State Managers, Intellectuals, and the Media: A Content Analysis of Ideology in Experts' Quotes in Feature Newspaper Articles on Crime," *Justice Quarterly* 15 (2) (1998): 219–41.

143. Hinton, *From the War on Poverty to the War on Crime*, 164.

144. David A. Green, "US Penal-Reform Catalysts, Drivers, and Prospects," *Punishment and Society* 17 (3) (2015): 271–98.

145. Michael Tonry argues that "it is the severity, not disparity, that does most of the damage" to black Americans. Tonry, *Punishing Race*, 145.

146. For the evolution of "the Negro question" postemancipation see George W. Cable, *The Negro Question* (Philadelphia: Charles Scribner's Sons, 1890); W. E. B. DuBois, *Souls of Black Folk* (Chicago: A. C. McClurg & Co., 1903); J. L. R. James, "Preliminary Notes on the Negro Question" (1939) in Scott McLemme,

C. L. R. James on the "Negro Question" (University Press of Mississippi, 1996); Gunnar Myrdal, *An American Dilemma: The Negro Problem and Modern Democracy* (New York: Harper & Row Publishers, 1944); James Baldwin, *The Fire Next Time* (New York: Dial Press, 1963). For post–civil rights era treatment see Cornel West, *Race Matters* (New York: Beacon Press, 1993); Howard Winant, "Racial Dualism at the Century's End" in *The House that Race Built*, ed. Wahneema Lubiano (New York: Vintage Books, 1998); and Ta-Nehisi Coates, *Between the World and Me* (New York: Spiegel and Grau, 2015).

147. Murakawa, *The First Civil Right*.

148. Hinton, *From the War on Poverty to the War on Crime*.

149. Gottschalk, *Caught*.

150. Michael Javen Fortner, *Black Silent Majority: The Rockefeller Drug Laws and the Politics of Punishment* (Harvard University Press, 2015).

151. Murakawa, *The First Civil Right*, 10.

152. Heather Schoenfeld, "Mass Incarceration and the Paradox of Prison Conditions Litigation," *Law and Society Review* 44 (3/4) (2010): 731–68.

153. Doris Marie Provine, *Unequal Under Law: Race in the War on Drugs* (Chicago: University of Chicago Press, 2008), 110.

154. Ann Shola Orloff, "Explaining US Welfare Reform: Power, Gender, Race, and the US Policy Legacy," *Critical Social Policy* 22 (2002): 96–118; Brian Steensland, "Cultural Categories and the American Welfare State: The Case of Guaranteed Income Policy," *American Journal of Sociology* 111 (2006): 1273–26; Joe Soss, Richard C. Fording, and Sanford F. Schram, *Disciplining the Poor: Neoliberal Paternalism and the Persistent Power of Race* (Chicago: University of Chicago Press, 2011).

155. Florida became a state in 1854. When it seceded from the Union in 1861, Florida's population (79,000 whites and 62,000 blacks) was mainly located in the northern half of the state. In 1950, the state's population reached 2.7 million.

156. For discussion on Florida's "Southernness" see Irvin D. S. Winsboro, "Image, Illusion, and Reality: Florida and the Modern Civil Rights Movement in Historical Perspective," *Old South, New South, or Down South: Florida and the Modern Civil Rights Movement*, ed. Irvin D. S. Winsboro (Morgantown: West Virginia University Press, 2009), 1–21. From 1900 to 1930 more lynching of African Americans occurred in Florida than any other state. James R. McGovern, *Anatomy of a Lynching: The Killing of Claude Neal* (Baton Rouge: Louisiana State University Press, 1982), 12; Gilbert King, *Devil in the Grove: Thurgood Marshall, the Groveland Boys, and the Dawn of a New America* (New York: Harper Collins, 2012); Danielle L. McGuire, *At the Dark End of the Street: Black Women, Rape, and Resistance: A New History of the Civil Rights Movement from Rosa Parks to the Rise of Black Power* (New York: Vintage Books, 2011).

157. Miller, *Hard Labor and Hard Time*; Heather Schoenfeld, "The Delayed Emergence of Penal Modernism in Florida," *Punishment and Society* 16 (2014): 258–84.

158. Simon, *Governing through Crime*, 100.

159. Natasha Frost quoted in E. Goode, "U.S. Prison Populations Decline, Reflect New Approach to Crime," *New York Times*, July 26, 2013.

Chapter 2

1. Hugh Douglas Price, *The Negro and Southern Politics: A Chapter of Florida History* (Westport, CT: Greenwood Press, 1973 [1957]), 95–96.

2. United States Commission on Civil Rights, "*Law Enforcement: A Report on Equal Protection in the South*" (Washington, DC: United States Commission on Civil Rights, 1965), 184.

3. Naomi Murakawa, *The First Civil Right: How Liberals Built Prison America* (New York: Oxford University Press, 2014), 57.

4. David Colburn, *From Yellow Dog Democrats to Red State Republicans: Florida and Its Politics since 1940* (Gainesville: University Press of Florida, 2007), 50, 56.

5. Elizabeth Hinton, *From the War on Poverty to the War on Crime: The Making of Mass Incarceration in America* (Cambridge: Harvard University Press, 2016); Murakawa, *The First Civil Right*.

6. Omnibus Crime Control and Safe Streets Act, Public Law 90-351; 82 Stat. 197.

7. Murakawa, *The First Civil Right*, 44.

8. Vesla M. Weaver, "Frontlash: Race and the Development of Punitive Crime Policy," *Studies in American Political Development* 21 (2007): 230–65.

9. Elizabeth Hinton's reading of this history differs from those of both Murakawa and Weaver. She argues that the Johnson administration's primary reason for the initial war on crime was to upgrade police in order to quell urban disorder, which they saw as a result of community pathology and poverty. Thus while the War on Poverty worked to address pathology, the police needed more resources in order to manage its consequences (see p. 103). In addition, after the 1967 riots the administration became increasingly worried about black radicalization. Hinton, *From the War on Poverty to the War on Crime*. Quantitative analyses of police spending during that era show that it is highly correlated with the racial composition of the city. Pamela Irving Jackson and Leo Carroll, "Race and the War on Crime: The Sociopolitical Determinants of Municipal Police Expenditures in 90 Non-Southern U.S. Cities," *American Sociological Review* 46 (3) (1981): 290–305.

10. Thomas E. Cronin, Tania Z. Cronin, and Michael E. Milakovich, *U.S. v. Crime in the Streets* (Bloomington: Indiana University Press, 1981), x.

11. Cronin, Cronin, and Milakovich, *U.S. v. Crime in the Streets*, 60.

12. Cronin, Cronin, and Milakovich, *U.S. v. Crime in the Streets*, 49–59.

13. U.S. Department of Justice, "8th Annual Report of the Law Enforcement Assistance Administration Fiscal Year 1976" (Washington, DC: U.S. Department of Justice, 1976), 4.

14. Murakawa, *The First Civil Right*; Hinton, *From the War on Poverty to the War on Crime*; Jonathan Simon, *Governing through Crime: How the War on Crime Transformed American Democracy and Created a Culture of Fear* (Oxford University Press, 2007); Vesla Weaver, "The Significance of Policy Failures in Political Development: The Law Enforcement Assistance Administration and the Growth of the Carceral State," *Living Legislation: Durability, Change, and the Politics of American Lawmaking,* ed. Jeffery Jenkins and Eric Patashnik (Chicago: University of Chicago Press, 2012): 221–54.

15. Weaver, "The Significance of Policy Failures in Political Development."

16. Numerous internal policy evaluations were written during the life of LEAA. For reviews, see S. R. Allinson, "LEAA's Impact on Criminal Justice: A Review of the Literature" (Washington, DC: National Council on Crime and Delinquency, 1979); John K. Hudzik, ed., *Federal Aid to Criminal Justice: Rhetoric, Results, Lessons* (Washington, DC: National Criminal Justice Association, 1984). A few monographs evaluating LEAA appeared in the early 1980s. See, e.g., Malcolm Feeley and Austin Sarat, *The Policy Dilemma: Federal Crime Policy and the Law Enforcement Assistance Administration* (Minneapolis: University of Minnesota Press, 1980); Cronin, Cronin, and Milakovich, *U.S. v. Crime in the Streets.*

17. Hinton, *From the War on Poverty to the War on Crime*, 306.

18. Daniel L. Skoler, "Standards for Criminal Justice Structure and Organization: the Impact of the National Advisory Commission," *Criminal Justice Review* 2 (1977): 1–13, also finds that although the National Advisory Commission on Criminal Justice Standards and Goals influenced state reorganization in the 1970s, state action was as much a result of state-level pressures for standards throughout the 1960s.

19. David Colburn and Lance deHaven-Smith, *Government in the Sunshine State* (Gainesville: University Press of Florida, 1999), 78.

20. Tom Wagy, *Governor LeRoy Collins of Florida: Spokesman of the New South* (Montgomery: University of Alabama Press, 1985).

21. State of Florida, Executive Department, "A Proclamation by the Governor," Tallahassee, July 20, 1956, Fla. Sess. Laws (1956), 19.

22. Florida, Office of the Attorney General, *Amicus Brief of the Attorney General* (Tallahassee, 1954), as cited in Joseph A. Tomberline, "Florida and the School Desegregation Issue, 1954–1959: A Summary View," *Journal of Negro Education* 43 (1974): 457–67.

23. *Journal of the Senate*, State of Florida, April 22, 1955, 183.

24. *Hawkins v. Board of Control*, 93 So 2d 354 (Fla. 1957), FSCL.

25. See Phillip J. Campanella, "Constitutional Law—Equal Protection—Pupil Placement Statutes," *Western Reserve Law Review* 6 (1964): 800–808. The law reserved the right of county school boards to assign students to schools based on a host of "sociological, psychological and intangible social scientific factors." Fla. Sess. Laws, ch. 31380. 2 (1956).

26. Fla. Sess. Laws, House Concurrent Resolution No. 174 (1957). Collins's handwritten note is available at http://www.floridamemory.com/FloridaHighlights /collins/collins_9.cfm.

27. "A Proclamation by the Governor," July 20, 1956. Fla. Sess. Laws, Special Extraordinary Session, ch. 31389, ch. 31390, ch 31400, ch. 31397 (1956).

28. William C. Havard and Loren P. Beth, *The Politics of Mis-representation: Rural-Urban Conflict in the Florida Legislature* (Baton Rouge: Louisiana State University Press, 1962).

29. Colburn, *From Yellow Dog Democrats to Red State Republicans*, 52.

30. Havard and Beth, *The Politics of Mis-representation*, 58.

31. See for example, Associated Press, "Shackles Needed Sometimes Raiford Head Tells Ohio Court," *Palm Beach Times*, September 9, 1949; Jack Bell, "The Town Crier," *Miami Herald*, September 21, 1949; Vivien M. L. Miller, *Hard Labor and Hard Time: Florida's "Sunshine Prison" and Chain Gangs* (Gainesville: University Press of Florida, 2012), 274.

32. Alex Lichtenstein, *Twice the Work of Free Labor: The Political Economy of Convict Labor in the New South* (New York: Verso, 1996); Matthew Mancini, *One Dies, Get Another: Convict Leasing in the American South, 1866–1928* (Columbia: University of South Carolina Press, 1996).

33. George Brown Tindall, *The Emergence of the New South, 1913–1945* (Baton Rouge: Louisiana State University Press, 1967), 212.

34. Miller, *Hard Labor and Hard Time*; Heather Schoenfeld, "The Delayed Emergence of Penal Modernism in Florida," *Punishment and Society,* 16 (2014): 258–84.

35. Miller, *Hard Labor and Hard Time*, 108. By the 1930s Raiford, while small compared to plantation prisons like Parchman Farm (in Mississippi) and Angola (in Louisiana), supported the cultivation of 4,200 acres of grain, soybeans, corn, rice, cotton, and timber and the pasture of milk cows, beef cows, and pigs. In addition, state officials brought a variety of small-scale industrial work to the prison (shirt, shoe, and license plate factories). Prison industrial labor was reserved for white male prisoners; black prisoners "dug ditches and worked in the fields"; "scrubbing, sewing, laundry, and cultivating vegetable patches remained the mainstays of female prison labor." Miller, *Hard Labor and Hard Time*, 111, 112, 118.

36. Associated Press, "Shackles Needed Sometimes Raiford Head Tells Ohio Court;" Jack Bell, "The Town Crier."

37. The percentage of state prisoners who were black had been decreasing since the mid-1940s from 63 percent to 45 percent in 1954.

38. Sen. Rodgers letter to Gov. Collins, July 16 1956, S776, Box 20, FSA.

39. Gov. Collins letter to Commissioner Mayo, September 4, 1956, S776, Box 20, FSA.

40. Culver, "Report on Conditions at Belle Glade Prison Farm," July 21, 1957, S776, Box 92, FSA.

41. See Sen. Johns's letter to Gov. Collins, November 6, 1958, S776, box 93, FSA, where he berates Culver for accusing him of "running the prison system."

42. Harvie J. Besler, letter to the Board of Commissioners of State Institutions, November 14, 1958, S776, Box 93, FSA.

43. Miller, *Hard Labor and Hard Time*, 282–85.

44. Editorial, W. C. Baggs, "Untie Culver's Hands," *Miami News*, December 22, 1958, 8A.

45. Unanimous Statement of Members of the Board of Commissioners of State Institutions, April 15, 1959, S776, Box 92, FSA.

46. Constituent to Gov. Collins, December 19, 1959, S776, Box 93, 6, FSA.

47. Abel A. Bartley, *Keeping the Faith: Race, Politics and Social Developments in Jacksonville, Florida, 1940–1970* (Westport, CT: Greenwoods Press, 2000); Glenda Alice Rabby, *The Pain and the Promise: The Struggle for Civil Rights in Tallahassee Florida* (Athens: University of Georgia Press, 1999).

48. Taylor Branch, *Pillar of Fire: America in the King Years 1963–65* (New York: Simon & Schuster, 1998).

49. David J. Garrow, *Bearing the Cross: Martin Luther King Jr., and the Southern Christian Leadership Conference* (New York: William Morrow and Company, Inc., 1986), 329.

50. David R. Colburn, *Racial Change and Community Crisis: St. Augustine, Florida 1877–1980* (New York: Columbia University Press, 1985).

51. *Johnson v. Davis*, 9 Race Rel. L. Representative 814 (M.D. Fla. 1964).

52. United States Commission on Civil Rights, "Law Enforcement: A Report on Equal Protection in the South" (Washington, DC: United States Commission on Civil Rights, 1965).

53. Colburn, *Racial Change and Community Crisis*, 49.

54. Adam Fairclough, *To Redeem the Soul of America: The Southern Christian Leadership Conference and Martin Luther King, Jr.* (Athens: University of Georgia Press, 1987).

55. Fairclough, *To Redeem the Soul of America*, 182.

56. United States Commission on Civil Rights, "Law Enforcement: A Report on Equal Protection in the South."

57. Colburn, *Racial Change and Community Crisis*, 96; Fairclough, *To Redeem the Soul of America*, 183; Garrow, *Bearing the Cross,* 328; United States Commission on Civil Rights, "Law Enforcement: A Report on Equal Protection in the South," 74.

58. Colburn, *Racial Change and Community Crisis*, 105; Fairclough, *To Redeem the Soul of America*, 185.

59. The departure of King and the SCLC from St. Augustine was in reality quite complicated. There was a sense by some SCLC activists that no progress had been made because the city remained opposed to the appointment of a biracial commission. In addition, King and the SCLC wanted to move on to an Alabama campaign.

They were able to save face when Governor Bryant announced the appointment of a biracial committee that never convened. Fairclough, *To Redeem the Soul of America*; Garrow, *Bearing the Cross*.

60. Fairclough, *To Redeem the Soul of America*, 190. In addition, Judge Bryan Simpson, whom some observers have credited for finally changing white practices, also issued injunctions against the Klan's intimidation of white businesses that served black patrons. Garrow, *Bearing the Cross*, 341.

61. Colburn, *Racial Change and Community Crisis*, 187.

62. Colburn, *Racial Change and Community Crisis*, offers a fairly dismal portrait of the improvement in life for black St. Augustinians between 1965 and 1980. Although schools finally desegregated in 1971 (due to the efforts of President Nixon, the Department of Health, Education, and Welfare, and the courts), the economic and political status of black residents did not improve. Median income for white families was still more than 150 percent that of blacks. In addition, white city leaders remained "unwilling to grant black residents full access to power and equal status with whites." Colburn, *Racial Change and Community Crisis*, 217.

63. Colburn, *Racial Change and Community Crisis*, 122.

64. Appropriations were for $22.5 million, funded grants totaled approximately $19 million. Third Annual Report to the President and the Congress on Activities under the Law Enforcement Assistance Act of 1965 (Department of Justice, 1968) 2, NUTL; Lyndon B. Johnson, "Statement by the President Following the Signing of Law Enforcement Assistance Bills," September 22, 1965, Gerhard Peters and John T. Woolley, *The American Presidency Project*, http://www.presidency.ucsb.edu/ws/?pid=27270.

65. In 1963, the Florida legislature attempt to comply with *Baker v. Carr*, 369 U.S. 186 (1962) by adding more members to highly populated Senate and House districts. This plan was found insufficient by the Court in *Swann v. Adams* 385 U.S. 440 (1967). A new system was written into the 1968 Constitutional revision and implemented in the 1972 election, based on the 1970 census. Karl H. Dixon, "Reapportionment and Reform: The Florida Example," *National Civic Review* 62 (1973): 548.

66. By the 1966 primary, almost 17 percent of Florida's electorate was black.

67. Frederick B. Karl, *The 57 Club: My Four Decades in Florida Politics* (Gainesville: University Press of Florida, 2010), 190. Burns beat High in the 1964 Democratic primary by over 500,000 votes, securing him the governorship. David R. Colburn and Richard K. Scher, *Florida's Gubernatorial Politics in the Twentieth Century* (Tallahassee: University Press of Florida, 1980), 81.

68. Florida State Committee on Law Enforcement and Administration of Justice, *Final Report* (Tallahassee: Attorney General of the State of Florida, 1968), 11, NUTL.

69. Office of Law Enforcement Assistance, "LEAA Grants and Contracts, Fiscal 1966–1968" (Washington, DC: U.S. Department of Justice, 1968), 11, NUTL.

OLEA provided Florida Committee on Law Enforcement and the Administration of Justice a grant of $22,000.

70. Statement by Rep. Ralph Turlington, *Journal of the House of Representatives*, State of Florida, April 4, 1967, 5, FSA.

71. Remarks by Chesterfield Smith, *Journal of the House of Representatives*, State of Florida, January 10, 1967, 19, FSA.

72. Statement by Sen. Verle Pope, *Journal of the Senate*, State of Florida, April 4, 1967, 4, FSA.

73. Linda K. Kerber, *No Constitutional Right to Be Ladies: Women and the Obligations of Citizenship* (New York: Macmillan, 1999), 153–55.

74. Florida State Committee on Law Enforcement and Administration of Justice 1968, 11, FSA.

75. Murray Dubbin, "Local Police Due Major Credit for Trying to Help Standards," *Miami News*, March 11, 1967, 2A.

76. Warren E. Headlough, "Development Police Training and Education in Florida: LEAA Grant 350 Final Project Report" (Tallahassee: Florida Police Standards Council, 1969); "Higher Standards Sought," *Daytona Beach Morning Journal*, October 21, 1958, 9.

77. Roland J. Chilton and James R. Jorgenson, "Municipal Police Departments in Florida: Problems and Prospects" (Tallahassee: Institute for Social Research Florida State University, 1969), 40–41, NUTL. Police reformers believed that every police department needed upgrading because a police department can only be as good as its neighboring departments. Address by Attorney General Ramsey Clark to the International Chiefs of Police, September 11, 1967, http://www.justice.gov/sites/default/files/ag/legacy/2011/08/23/09-11-1967.pdf/.

78. Chilton and Jorgenson, "Municipal Police Departments in Florida."

79. Police Standards Council Act, Florida Statutes 1967, as reprinted in Florida Police Standards Council, "First Annual Report: October 1967–December 1968" (Tallahassee, 1968), 13–17, NUTL.

80. Statement by Gov. Claude Kirk, *Journal of the House of Representatives*, State of Florida, April 4, 1967, 23, FSA.

81. Statement by Representative Ralph Turlington, *Journal of the House of Representatives*, State of Florida, April 4, 1967, 5, FSA.

82. Earl Faircloth, "Florida Future #1" (radio clip), http://ufdc.ufl.edu/UF00081886/00001/.

83. Florida Police Standards Council, "First Annual Report: October 1967–December 1968" (Tallahassee, 1968), 6.

84. State of Florida Police Standards Board, "1969 Annual Report" (Tallahassee, 1970), 17, NUTL. The report states that 2,952 men had completed the basic training (out of approximately 13,000 employed statewide).

85. Headlough, "Development Police Training and Education in Florida"; State of Florida Police Standards Board, "1969 Annual Report" (Tallahassee, 1970), 8.

86. Law Enforcement Assistance Administration Annual Reports, 1969–1979. Calculated by author.

87. Florida State Committee on Law Enforcement and Administration of Justice, *Final Report*, 1.

88. Florida State Committee on Law Enforcement and Administration of Justice, *Final Report*, 5. In creating the Division of Youth Services, legislators renamed old "industrial schools," focusing instead on education and treatment. Youth Services administrators opened eleven regional "aftercare" offices and five halfway houses between 1967 and 1971. Florida Governor's Council on Criminal Justice, "Florida's Comprehensive Plan 1971" (Tallahassee 1971), 270–72, SLF.

89. Christian Parenti, *Lockdown America: Police and Prisons in the Age of Crisis* (New York: Verso, 1999), 14–26.

90. Martin Waldron, "Florida's Governor Sets Up Private Police Force," *New York Times*, January 8, 1967, 56.

91. Colburn and Scher, *Florida's Gubernatorial Politics in the Twentieth Century*, 269; Martin Waldron, "Florida's Governor Sets Up Private Police Force," *New York Times,* January 8, 1967, 52. Wackenhut Corporation went on to become one of the top private security firms in the country. In 2002 it was purchased by Danish security firm G4S, which also later purchased Sunshine Youth Services, a for-profit juvenile justice facility operator.

92. Faircloth, "Florida Future #1."

93. Fla. Sess. Laws, ch. 69-23.086 (1969).

94. Florida State Committee on Law Enforcement and Administration of Justice, *Final Report*, 4.

95. Florida Governor's Council on Criminal Justice, "Florida's Comprehensive Plan 1971," 497; Martin Waldron, "Mafia Again Issue in Florida Politics," *New York Times*, October 26, 1969, 78; Timothy Griffin and Monica K. Miller, "Child Abduction, AMBER Alert, and Crime Control Theater," *Criminal Justice Review* 33 (2008): 159–76.

96. Florida Governor's Council on Criminal Justice, "Florida's Comprehensive Plan 1971," 648.

97. Florida Governor's Council on Criminal Justice, "Florida's Comprehensive Plan 1971," 648–49.

98. Fla. Sess. Laws, ch. 70-95 (1970). By 1979, appropriations had increased to over $21 million for 730 positions. Fla. Sess. Laws, ch. 79-212 (1979). By 1979, appropriations had increased to over $21 million for 730 positions. Fla. Laws, ch. 79-212 (1979).

99. Florida Governor's Council on Criminal Justice, "Florida's Comprehensive Plan 1971," 498; LEAA Annual Reports 1970, 1971, 1972; State of Florida Governor's Council on Criminal Justice, "1973 Program Areas LEAA Program Part 'C' and 'E' Funds" (Tallahassee, 1973), SLF.

100. Prior to his appointment, Wainwright was superintendent at Avon Park, Florida's first "honor" prison farm designed for minimum security prisoners who couldn't work.

101. Author interview with Louie Wainwright (Secretary of Department of Corrections, 1957–88), April 17, 2007 (Tallahassee).

102. Florida Division of Corrections, Press Release, August 26, 1965, S131, Box 31, File 5, FSA.

103. Louie Wainwright to Gov. Kirk, March 30, 1967, S923, Box 58, File 6, FSA.

104. Wainwright did this through the division's employee newsletter, *Correctional Compass*.

105. See Florida Laws 1963, ch. 63-450.

106. "Florida's Modern Correctional Institutions," *American Journal of Corrections* (August 1967): 18–22.

107. See for example Wainwright's letter to Gov. Burns, September 21, 1965, S 131, Box 31, File 5, FSA, denying the speaker of the House's request to transfer an employee. After stating that the employee would not have a job if not for the speaker, Wainwright writes that the employee would not be appropriate for Sumter Correctional Institution given "the type of program we are going to try to develop there."

108. "Florida's Modern Correctional Institutions," *American Journal of Correction*.

109. In 1966, President Johnson appointed a National Advisory Council on Correctional Manpower and Training. See Wainwright's statement in support of establishing the council, May 7, 1965, S131, Box 32, 1, FSA.

110. Office of Law Enforcement Assistance, "LEAA Grants and Contracts, Fiscal 1966–1968," 81. Also advertised in the *Correctional Compass*, official newsletter of the Florida Division of Corrections, April 1969, NUTL.

111. Florida Bureau of Criminal Justice Planning and Assistance, "Florida's 1978 State Comprehensive Plan for Criminal Justice," Criminal Justice Systems (Tallahassee: Department of Administration, 1978), 78.

112. For example, at Apalachee Correctional Institution (70 percent white), 70 percent of the white prisoners participated in some type of educational programming, while only 6 percent of black prisoners did. Monthly Report, Apalachee Correctional Institution, April 12, 1963, S756, Box 63, 4.

113. Florida Division of Corrections, "Second Biennial Report" (Tallahassee, 1961) 15, FDC.

114. Minutes from the meeting of the Cabinet Committee on Corrections, September 26, 1967, S923, Box 23, File 7, FSA, state that areas at Florida State Prison and Avon Park are still segregated, but the rest of the main facilities have integrated.

115. Florida Division of Corrections, "8th Biennial Report" (Tallahassee, 1972), 14. FDC.

116. See, for example, the handwritten note from a Pasco County jail inmate to Gov. Burns, September 5, 1965, S131, Box 31, File 5, FSA, that states that prisoners are treated like "we are not human" and "have no constitutional rights" and are fed "like pigs," and that "we sleep in filth and dirt."

117. *Johnson v. Davis,* 9 Race Rel. L. Representative 814 (M.D. Fla. 1964), cited in United States Commission on Civil Rights, *"Law Enforcement,"* 83.

118. Louie Wainwright to Sheriff L. O. Davis, July 29, 1964, S756, Box 64, File 1, FSA. See also Rich Oppel, "Prison Chief Laments Good Ole Days," *Orlando Sentinel,* February 11, 1968, S923, Box 59, File 4, FSA.

119. Fla. Sess. Laws, ch. 67-241 (1967).

120. Florida Division of Corrections, "8th Biennial Report" (Tallahassee, 1972), 8.

121. Simon, *Governing through Crime,* 77.

122. Hinton, *From the War on Poverty to the War on Crime;* Murakawa, *The First Civil Right;* Weaver, "The Significance of Policy Failures in Political Development."

123. Weaver, "The Significance of Policy Failures in Political Development," 234.

124. Eleanor Chelimsky, "Primary Source Examination of the Law Enforcement Assistance Administration (LEAA), and Some Reflections on Crime Control Policy," *Journal of Police Science and Administration* 3 (2) (1975): 218. She writes that there were "pages and pages of [LEAA] hearing appendices filled with letters of support" [from mayors, county executives, governors, criminal justice system personnel, educators, researchers, planners, and evaluators] and "these, of course, have been extremely useful in bolstering bureau claims for project excellence or popularity."

125. Lisa L. Miller, *The Perils of Federalism: Race, Poverty, and the Politics of Crime Control* (Oxford University Press, 2008).

126. Elizabeth Bernstein, "Militarized Humanitarianism Meets Carceral Feminism: The Politics of Sex, Rights, and Freedom in Contemporary Anti-trafficking Campaigns," *Signs* 36 (1) (2010): 45–71; Marie Gottschalk, *The Prison and the Gallows: The Politics of Mass Incarceration in America* (New York: Cambridge University Press, 2006).

127. Jay N. Varon, "A Reexamination of the Law Enforcement Assistance Administration," *Stanford Law Review* 27 (1975): 1303–24; Cronin, Cronin, and Milakovich, *U.S. v. Crime in the Streets.*

128. Feeley and Sarat, *The Policy Dilemma,* 6. Crime rates in the late 1960s and 1970s may have been inflated by new reporting systems and local governments responding to monetary incentives. See John Hagan, *Who Are the Criminals? The Politics of Crime Policy from the Age of Roosevelt to the Age of Reagan* (Princeton: Princeton University Press, 2012), 23–24.

129. This does not include spending on juvenile justice, which was taken over by the Office of Juvenile Justice and Delinquency Prevention in 1974. In 1979,

the office awarded $22 million in grants to support "deinstitutionalization, diversion, prevention, restitution, and model programs." U.S. Department of Justice, "11th Annual Report of the Law Enforcement Assistance Administration" (Washington, DC: Department of Justice, 1979), 3.

130. Robert F. Diegelman, "Federal Financial Assistance for Crime Control: Lessons of the LEAA Experience," *Journal of Criminal Law and Criminology* 73 (1982): 1001; Weaver, "The Significance of Policy Failures in Political Development," 227.

131. Morris Cobern, "Manpower Implications of New Legislation and New Federal Programs; Manpower Needs in State and Local Public Safety Activities: The Impact of Federal Programs" (National Planning Association, 1971), 17.

132. Allen E. Liska, Joseph J. Lawrence, and Michael Benson, "Perspectives on the Legal Order: The Capacity for Social Control," *American Journal of Sociology* 87 (2) (1981): 413–26; Mahesh K. Nalla, "Perspectives on the Growth of Police Bureaucracies, 1948–1984: An Examination of Three Explanations." *Policing and Society* 3 (1992): 51–61; William P. McCarty, Ling Ren, and Jihong "Solomon" Zhao, "Determinants of Police Strength in Large U.S. Cities during the 1990s: A Fixed-Effects Panel Analysis," *Crime and Delinquency* 58 (3) (2012): 397–424; Robert Vargas and Philip McHarris, "Race and State in City Police Spending Growth: 1980 to 2010," *Sociology of Race and Ethnicity* 3 (2016): 96–112.

133. U.S. Department of Justice, "First Annual Report of the Justice System Improvement Act Agencies" (Washington, DC 1981), 23, NUTL.

134. Hinton, *From the War on Poverty to the War on Crime*, 218–49.

135. Florida Governor's Council on Criminal Justice, "Florida's Comprehensive Plan 1971," 722–50.

136. Florida Council on Criminal Justice, "1980 Annual Report" (Tallahassee: Bureau of Criminal Justice Assistance, 1980), 45, SLF.

137. Florida Governor's Council on Criminal Justice, "Florida's Comprehensive Plan 1971," 351–58. For example, in a thirteen-county area in northwest Florida, thirty-one out of thirty-five local police agencies had ten or fewer officers. Bureau of Criminal Justice Planning and Assistance, "1977 Annual Report: Input into the Law Enforcement Assistance Administration's 9th Annual Report" (Tallahassee: Florida Department of Administration, 1977), 31, SLF.

138. According to reports by region, local police and sheriff expenditures for 1970 totaled $47.5 million. Florida Governor's Council on Criminal Justice, "Florida's Comprehensive Plan 1971," 46.

139. U.S. Department of Justice, "3rd Annual Report of the Law Enforcement Assistance Administration Fiscal Year 1971" (Washington, DC: U.S. Department of Justice, 1971), 292. Other large grant allocations went toward small grants to local agencies for buying and installing communications equipment and training officers in its use. Florida Governor's Council on Criminal Justice, "1973 Program Areas," 3–4.

140. Florida Governor's Council on Criminal Justice, "Florida's Comprehensive Plan 1971," 610.

141. Florida Bureau of Criminal Justice Planning and Assistance, "Florida's 1978 State Comprehensive Plan for Criminal Justice," Law Enforcement Improvement, 39.

142. The 1970 numbers are from Florida Governor's Council on Criminal Justice, "Florida's Comprehensive Plan 1971," 49, 30. The 1976 numbers are from Florida Bureau of Criminal Justice Planning and Assistance, "Florida's 1978 State Comprehensive Plan for Criminal Justice," Law Enforcement, 25, 28.

143. U.S. Department of Justice, "First Annual Report of the Law Enforcement Assistance Administration" (Washington, DC: U.S. Department of Justice, 1969); U.S. Department of Justice, "Second Annual Report of the Law Enforcement Assistance Administration" (Washington, DC: U.S. Department of Justice, 1969), 101.

144. Bureau of Justice Statistics, *Enhancing Capacities and Confronting Controversies in Criminal Justice: Proceedings of the 1993 National Conference* (Washington, DC: U.S. Department of Justice, 1994), 66.

145. Florida Bureau of Criminal Justice Planning and Assistance, "Florida's 1978 State Comprehensive Plan for Criminal Justice," Law Enforcement, 125–27.

146. Florida Council on Criminal Justice, "1980 Annual Report"; Diegelman, "Federal Financial Assistance for Crime Control," 1006.

147. Florida Council on Criminal Justice, "1980 Annual Report," 18.

148. U.S. Department of Justice, "11th Annual Report of the Law Enforcement Assistance Administration" (Washington, DC: U.S. Department of Justice 1979), 5.

149. Law Enforcement Assistance Administration, Annual Reports, 1970–1973.

150. U.S. Department of Justice, "4th Annual Report of the Law Enforcement Assistance Administration Fiscal Year 1972" (Washington, DC: U.S. Department of Justice, 1972), 36.

151. Florida Governor's Council on Criminal Justice, "1973 Program Areas."

152. Florida Bureau of Criminal Justice Planning and Assistance, "Florida's 1978 State Comprehensive Plan for Criminal Justice," Law Enforcement, 42. In 1976 alone, the state funded organized crime control programs in forty-four localities, including small cities like Belle Glade in south Florida and Deland in central Florida. In 1977, the SPA provided another million dollars to city and county agencies for specific crime control units. U.S. Department of Justice, "9th Annual Report of the Law Enforcement Assistance Administration Fiscal Year 1977" (Washington, DC: U.S. Department of Justice, 1977), 49.

153. Hinton, *From the War on Poverty to the War on Crime*, 199.

154. Bruce Porter and Marvin Dunn, *The Miami Riot of 1980: Crossing the Bounds* (Lexington, MA: Lexington Books, 1984).

155. Florida Governor's Council on Criminal Justice, "Florida's Comprehensive Plan 1971," 391.

156. Florida Governor's Council on Criminal Justice, "Florida's Comprehensive Plan 1971," 64.

157. Public defenders in each judicial circuit were to be elected in a manner similar to state's attorneys. Talbot D'Alemberte, *The Florida State Constitution* (New York: Oxford University Press, 2011), 17.

158. Florida Senate Ways and Means Committee, "Fiscal Analysis in Brief Based on 1972 Passed Legislation," 15, 2; Florida Senate Ways and Means Committee, "Fiscal Analysis in Brief Based on 1980 Legislation," 2.

159. LEAA grant allocations for courts averaged approximately 6 percent of Florida's block grant per year.

160. Training included both sending judges and administrators to the National College of Trial Judges in Reno, Nevada, and more local workshops and sessions. Florida Governor's Council on Criminal Justice, "1973 Program Areas," 25.

161. Florida Bureau of Criminal Justice Planning and Assistance, "Florida's 1978 State Comprehensive Plan for Criminal Justice," Courts.

162. Florida Bureau of Criminal Justice Planning and Assistance, "Florida's 1978 State Comprehensive Plan for Criminal Justice," Courts, 106.

163. Florida Governor's Council on Criminal Justice, "Florida's Comprehensive Plan 1971," 392.

164. In 1976, LEAA selected Florida, along with ten other states, for a grant to develop a statewide judicial information system. U.S. Department of Justice, "8th Annual Report of the Law Enforcement Assistance Administration," 32. In 1980 Florida reported $1 million in LEAA grants for sixteen projects with the "on-going objective" of implementing information systems in county, circuit, and state jurisdictions in line with the state master plan. Florida Council on Criminal Justice, "1980 Annual Report," 42.

165. See, for example, Florida Division of State Planning, "The Florida Annual Action Plan for Criminal Justice, 1974" (Tallahassee: Department of Administration), 65, SLF.

166. Florida Bureau of Criminal Justice Planning and Assistance, "Florida's 1978 State Comprehensive Plan for Criminal Justice," Courts.

167. U.S. Department of Justice, "3rd Annual Report of the Law Enforcement Assistance Administration Fiscal Year 1971" (Washington, DC: U.S. Department of Justice, 1972), 377.

168. U.S. Department of Justice, "3rd Annual Report of the Law Enforcement Assistance Administration Fiscal Year 1971," 319.

169. Florida Governor's Council on Criminal Justice, "1973 Program Areas."

170. Florida Bureau of Criminal Justice Planning and Assistance, "Florida's 1978 State Comprehensive Plan for Criminal Justice," Courts, 146.

171. Florida Bureau of Criminal Justice Planning and Assistance, "Florida 1974 State Comprehensive Plan for Criminal Justice" (Tallahassee: Department of Administration, 1974).

172. Florida Council on Criminal Justice, "1980 Annual Report," 9.

173. U.S. Department of Justice, "8th Annual Report of the Law Enforcement Assistance Administration Fiscal Year 1976" (Washington, DC: U.S. Department of Justice, 1976), 49.

174. Florida Bureau of Criminal Justice Planning and Assistance, "Florida's 1978 State Comprehensive Plan for Criminal Justice," Courts, 145.

175. National Legal Data Center, "Career Criminal Program: An Overview" (Thousand Oaks, CA, 1977), 9, http://www.ncjrs.gov.

176. U.S. Department of Justice, "9th Annual Report of the Law Enforcement Assistance Administration," 49.

177. In 1967 at the urging of Wainwright, the legislature authorized the Division of Corrections to establish a furlough and conditional release program, and required the division to provide "treatment and rehabilitation" to mentally disordered sex offenders. Florida Laws 1967, ch. 67-59, 67-421. Louie Wainwright to Gov. Kirk, March 30, 1967, S923, Box 58, File 6, FSA.

178. Florida Department of Offender Rehabilitation, 1975–1976 Annual Report (Tallahassee FL, 1976), 15, FDC. Parole officials complained that their caseloads were too high to be effective.

179. Bureau of Criminal Justice Planning and Assistance, "1977 Annual Report: Input into the Law Enforcement Assistance Administration's 9th Annual Report," 22.

180. Bureau of Criminal Justice Planning and Assistance, "1977 Annual Report: Input into the Law Enforcement Assistance Administration's 9th Annual Report," 22.

181. Florida Council on Criminal Justice, "1980 Annual Report," 19.

182. Florida Governor's Council on Criminal Justice, "Florida's Comprehensive Plan 1971," 625.

183. Morris Cobern, "Manpower Implications of New Legislation and New Federal Programs," 2.

184. Florida Bureau of Criminal Justice Planning and Assistance, "Florida's 1978 State Comprehensive Plan for Criminal Justice," 1. The local planning agencies recognized this limitation as well. For example, half of Broward County's Plan included "crime prevention" goals that were not fundable by LEAA. "Florida Comprehensive Plan for Criminal Justice," Vol II (Tallahassee 1974), 660, SLF.

185. Florida Bureau of Criminal Justice Planning and Assistance, "Florida's 1978 State Comprehensive Plan for Criminal Justice," 2.

186. Chelimsky, "Primary Source Examination of The Law Enforcement Assistance Administration," 211.

187. Florida Inter-agency Law Enforcement Planning Council, "Responsibility of the Task Forces," FSA, n.d.

188. U.S. Department of Justice, "6th Annual Report of the Law Enforcement Assistance Administration" (Washington, DC: U.S. Department of Justice, 1974).

189. For example, in 1971 the National Crime Prevention Institute was established with a LEAA grant to train citizens and police in practices to reduce opportunities for crime.

190. Florida Governor's Council on Criminal Justice, "Florida's Comprehensive Plan 1971," 376.

191. U.S. Department of Justice, "6th Annual Report of the Law Enforcement Assistance Administration," 95–97. One of the first victim/witness programs funded by LEAA, in Milwaukee, Wisconsin, included access to social services, an alert system to reduce time waiting in court, an advocacy unit to change laws and practices in the interest of victims/witnesses, and a sensitive crime unit to provide specialized services to rape victims.

192. U.S. Department of Justice, "6th Annual Report of the Law Enforcement Assistance Administration," 99–100.

193. Florida Bureau of Criminal Justice Planning and Assistance, "Florida's 1978 State Comprehensive Plan for Criminal Justice," 38.

194. U.S. Department of Justice, "8th Annual Report of the Law Enforcement Assistance Administration," 78.

195. U.S. Department of Justice, "11th Annual Report of the Law Enforcement Assistance Administration," 3.

196. Florida Bureau of Criminal Justice Planning and Assistance, "Florida's 1978 State Comprehensive Plan for Criminal Justice," 35.

197. Florida Council on Criminal Justice, "1980 Annual Report," 9, 22–23.

198. Earl Black and Merle Black, *Politics and Society in the South* (Cambridge: Harvard University Press, 1987), 194.

199. Morris Cobern, "Manpower Implications of New Legislation and New Federal Programs."

200. Hinton, *From the War on Poverty to the War on Crime*, 229.

201. Hagan, *Who Are the Criminals?*

202. Gottschalk, *The Prison and the Gallows.*

203. Florida Bureau of Criminal Justice Planning and Assistance, "Florida's 1978 State Comprehensive Plan for Criminal Justice," 35.

Chapter 3

1. *Costello v. Wainwright*, 397 F. Supp. 20, 38, 34 (M.D. Fla. 1975).

2. Margo Schlanger, "Beyond the Hero Judge: Institutional Reform Litigation as Litigation," *Michigan Law Review* 97 (1999): 2030.

3. Stephen Steinberg, *Turning Back: The Retreat from Racial Justice in American Thought and Policy* (Boston: Beacon Press, 1995).

4. Malcolm M. Feeley and Edward L. Rubin, *Judicial Policy Making and the Modern State* (Cambridge: Cambridge University Press, 1998).

5. Schlanger, "Beyond the Hero Judge," 2004. Forty-four percent of the country's jail inmates were housed in jails under court order.

6. Ben Crouch and J. W. Marquart, *An Appeal to Justice: Litigated Reform of Texas Prisons* (Austin: University of Texas Press, 1980); John J. DiIulio Jr., editor, *Courts, Corrections, and the Constitution: The Impact of Judicial Intervention on Prisons and Jails* (New York: Oxford University Press, 1990); Steve Martin and Sheldon Ekland-Olson, *Texas Prisons: The Walls Come Tumbling Down* (Austin: Texas Monthly Press, 1987); Feeley and Rubin, *Judicial Policy Making and the Modern State*; Larry W. Yackle, *Reform and Regret: The Story of Federal Judicial Involvement in the Alabama Prison System* (New York: Oxford University Press, 1989). Also see Susan P. Sturm, "The Legacy and Future of Corrections Litigation," *University of Pennsylvania Law Review* 142 (1993): 639–738.

7. W. E. B. DuBois, "The Spawn of Slavery: The Convict Lease System in the South," *Missionary Review of the World* 24 (1901): 737–45; Alex Lichtenstein, *Twice the Work of Free Labor: The Political Economy of Convict Labor in the New South* (New York: Verso, 1996); Matthew Mancini, *One Dies, Get Another: Convict Leasing in the American South, 1866–1928* (Columbia: University of South Carolina Press, 1996); David M. Oshinsky, *Worse Than Slavery: Parchman Farm and the Ordeal of Jim Crow Justice* (New York: Free Press, 1996).

8. Schlanger, "Beyond the Hero Judge," n151.

9. Feeley and Rubin, *Judicial Policy Making and the Modern State*, 159. It is important to note that prison conditions litigation was not exclusive to the South. Early conditions cases were also brought in Ohio, New York, and Rhode Island. Schlanger, "Beyond the Hero Judge," 2028.

10. Malcolm Feeley and Van Swearingen, "The Prison Conditions Cases and the Bureaucratization of American Corrections: Influences, Impacts, and Implications," *Pace Law Review* 24 (2004): 466.

11. Schlanger, "Beyond the Hero Judge," n19, commenting on Feeley and Rubin, *Judicial Policy Making and the Modern State*.

12. Joshua Guetzkow and Eric Schoon, "If You Build It, They Will Fill It: The Unintended Consequences of Prison Overcrowding Litigation," *Law and Society Review* 49 (2015): 401–32.

13. Margo Schlanger, "Civil Rights Injunctions over Time: A Case Study of Jail and Prison Court Orders," *New York University Law Review* 81 (2006): 560.

14. Paul Frymer, *Uneasy Alliances: Race and Party Competition in America* (Princeton: Princeton University Press, 2010 [1999]).

15. Edward G. Carmines and James A. Stimson, *Issue Evolution: Race and the Transformation of American Politics* (Princeton: Princeton University Press, 1989),

xiii; John Hagan, *Who Are the Criminals? The Politics of Crime Policy from the Age of Roosevelt to the Age of Reagan* (Princeton: Princeton University Press, 2010); Ruy A. Teixeira and Joel Rogers, *America's Forgotten Majority: Why the White Working Class Still Matters* (New York: Basic Books, 2000).

16. Katherine Beckett, *Making Crime Pay: Law and Order in Contemporary American Politics* (New York: Oxford University Press, 1997).

17. Michelle Alexander, *The New Jim Crow: Mass Incarceration in the Age of Colorblindness* (New York: New Press, 2010), 44.

18. Earl Black and Merle Black, *Politics and Society in the South* (Cambridge: Harvard University Press, 1989), 266.

19. Warren E. Miller and J. Merrill Shanks, *The New American Voter* (Cambridge: Harvard University Press, 1996).

20. David R. Colburn and Richard K. Scher, *Florida's Gubernatorial Politics in the Twentieth Century* (Tallahassee: University Presses of Florida, 1980).

21. David R. Colburn, *From Yellow Dog Democrats to Red State Republicans: Florida and Its Politics Since 1940* (Gainesville: University of Florida Press, 2007), 75.

22. Colburn, *From Yellow Dog Democrats to Red State Republicans*, 86.

23. See *Baker v. Carr*, 369 U.S. 186 (1962) and *Reynolds v. Sims*, 377 U.S. 533 (1964).

24. Karl H. Dixon, "Reapportionment and Reform: The Florida Example," *National Civic Review* 62 (1973): 548–53.

25. Michael A. Maggiotto, Manning J. Dauer, Steven G. Koven, Joan S. Carver, and Joel Gottlieb, "The Impact of Reapportionment on Public Policy: The Case of Florida, 1960–1980," *American Politics Research* 13 (1985): 101–21.

26. Robert Lieberman, "Legacies of Slavery? Race and Historical Causation in American Political Development" in *Race and American Political Development*, ed. Joseph Lowndes, Julie Novkov, and Dorian T. Warren (New York: Routledge, 2008), 206–33.

27. Buddy MacKay and Rick Edmonds, *How Florida Happened: The Political Education of Buddy MacKay* (Gainesville, FL: University Press of Florida, 2010), 34–35.

28. MacKay and Edmonds, *How Florida Happened*, 43.

29. Jack Greenberg, *Crusaders in the Courts: Legal Battles of the Civil Rights Movement* (New York: Twelve Tables Press, 1985 [2004 edition]).

30. Schlanger, "Civil Rights Injunctions over Time." In addition, local lawyers (and occasionally the Department of Justice) brought prison and jail desegregation cases to the federal courts as part of an overall push to desegregate public institutions. Schlanger, "Beyond the Hero Judge," 2034.

31. *Fullwood v. Clenner*, 206 F. Supp. 370 (D.D.C. 1962). Bill Sheppard, a Jacksonville attorney who later took over as plaintiff's counsel in *Costello*, recalls his first prison case was in 1969 representing Black Muslims in the Florida system

who were trying to obtain the Koran, appropriate meals, and access to a minister. *Mason v. Wainwright,* 417 F.2d 769 (5th Cir. 1969). Author interview with William Sheppard, attorney, Sheppard & White, February 21, 2008, Jacksonville.

32. In 1971 the Eighth Circuit Court of Appeals affirmed that the whole prison system in Arkansas constituted cruel and unusual punishment. *Holt v. Sarver,* 442 F.2d 304 (1971). In 1972, the Northern District Court for Ohio entered a consent decree for the Ohio prison system. *Taylor v. Perini,* 365 F. Supp. 557 (N.D. Ohio 1972).

33. John Irwin, *Prisons in Turmoil* (Boston: Little, Brown and Company, 1980), 105.

34. *Gideon v. Wainwright,* 372 U.S. 335 (1963).

35. *Costello v. Wainwright,* Amended Complaint, December 11, 1972, WSP.

36. "U.S. Judge Charles R. Scott; Ruled on Busing and Prisons," *New York Times,* May 14, 1983.

37. Department of Justice resources made possible a complete medical survey of the prison system by assigning two federal employees with significant experience in this area to the survey team. The lead doctor's expenses were funded by the Florida Governor's Council on Criminal Justice (itself a LEAA-funded project).

38. Author interview with Jack Greenberg, former director, NAACP Legal Defense Fund, February 8, 2008 (phone).

39. Greenberg, *Crusaders in the Courts,* 479.

40. Gideon was probably mentally ill and later refused ACLU's help after having sought it, instead asking the court for a local lawyer. Anthony Lewis, *Gideon's Trumpet* (New York: Vintage Books, 1964), 239.

41. Associated Press, "King Seized in Florida Cafe Protest: Aide, 12 Others Also Jailed after Integration Try," *Los Angeles Times,* June 12, 1964, 3.

42. *Robinson v. California* 370 U.S. 660 (1962).

43. Greenberg, *Crusaders in the Courts,* 106.

44. Greenberg, *Crusaders in the Courts,* 479; *Adderly v. Wainwright* 272 F. Supp. 530 (M.D. Fla. 1972).

45. *Adderly v. Wainwright,* 58 F.R.D. 389, 400 (M.D. Fla. 1972).

46. Chesterfield Smith, "Development of Florida Legal Services, Inc," *Florida Bar Journal* 48 (1974): 733; Chesterfield Smith, interview by Oral History Project, videocassette (Washington, DC: National Equal Justice Library, 2002).

47. Eventually, after the creation of the Legal Services Corporation in 1974 to provide ongoing federal grants to local legal services agencies, the Prison Project became Florida Institutional Legal Services Inc. and received funding from the State of Florida under Judge Scott's order in *Hooks v. Wainwright* 352 F. Supp. 163 (1972). Richard A. Belz, "Legal Services for Florida's Inmates: Expanding Access to the Courts by *Hooks* and *Bounds,*" *Florida Bar Journal* (February 1982): 183–85.

48. Greenberg, *Crusaders in the Courts,* 395.

49. Schlanger, "Beyond the Hero Judge," 2018.

50. *Arias v. Wainwright*, T.C.A. 79-0792 (N.D. Fla. 1979).

51. *Costello v. Wainwright*, Amended Complaint, December 11, 1972.

52. *Costello v. Wainwright*, 397 F. Supp. 20, 38 (1975).

53. Heather Schoenfeld, "The Delayed Emergence of Penal Modernism in Florida," *Punishment and Society* 16 (2014): 258–84; Mancini, *One Dies, Get Another.*

54. Howard Ohmart and Harold Bradley, "Overcrowding in the Florida Prison System: A Technical Assistance Report" (Washington, DC: American Justice Institute, 1972), S19, Box 123, A-1, FSA.

55. Author interview with Elisabeth DuFresne, attorney, September 21, 2009 (phone).

56. On the disproportionate impact of legal services see Greenberg, *Crusaders in the Courts*; Martha F. Davis, *Brutal Need: Lawyers and the Welfare Rights Movement, 1960–1973* (New Haven: Yale University Press, 1995).

57. Calculations by author from Florida Division of Corrections Annual Reports.

58. Sumter Correctional Institution opened in 1965 (pop. 776), North Florida Reception Center opened in 1968 (pop. 1,100), DeSoto Correctional Institution opened in 1969 (pop. 575). The Division also opened a road prison (pop. 65) and work release center (pop. unknown). Florida Division of Corrections, "8th Biennial Report, Fiscal Year 1970–1972" (Tallahassee 1973). Data on facilities available at http://www.dc.state.fl.us/pub/annual/1213/facil.html. Ohmart and Bradley, "Overcrowding in the Florida Prison System."

59. Schoenfeld, "The Delayed Emergence of Penal Modernism in Florida."

60. Florida Division of Corrections, "8th Biennial Report, Fiscal Year 1970–1972" (Tallahassee 1973), 27.

61. Florida Division of Corrections "First Annual Report, Fiscal Year 1972–1973" (Tallahassee 1974), 45.

62. Author interview with David Bachman, former deputy director of the Florida Division of Corrections, March 28, 2007, Tallahassee.

63. Ohmart and Bradley, "Overcrowding in the Florida Prison System," A-1.

64. Ohmart and Bradley, "Overcrowding in the Florida Prison System," A-10.

65. In January 1971 in his inaugural address, Askew stated "we are aware of the conditions in our prisons . . . we can take the occasion of criticism as an opportunity to look at ourselves objectively and honestly . . . and correct the errors." Office of the Governor, "Inaugural Address by Reubin Askew," *Reubin O'Donovan Askew Speeches*, January 5, 1971, Box 1, File 7, GSL.

66. Ohmart and Bradley, "Overcrowding in the Florida Prison System," A-1.

67. Horace Gosier, "Wainwright Denies Report that Crisis Exists for Black Inmates," *Tallahassee Democrat*, June 28, 1973.

68. James B. Jacobs, "The Prisoner's Rights Movement and Its Impacts," *Crime and Justice: An Annual Review of Research*, ed. Norval Morris and Michael Tonry (Chicago: University of Chicago Press, 1980), 429–70. I have not been able to lo-

cate any Florida organization (or Florida branch of a national organization) that supported prisoners' rights during this time period (except legal organizations such as the ACLU). None of my interviewees could remember any either.

69. *Journal of the Senate*, State of Florida, April 6, 1971, 6–7.

70. The preface to the proposed reform states that "it is unlikely that the majority of offenders can be effectively socialized in the coercive environment of large prisons. Consequently, emphasis has been placed on the development of pretrial programs and the sentencing alternative concept." Florida House of Representatives, Committee on Corrections, "Goals of the Adult Correctional Reform System" (Tallahassee: Florida House of Representatives, 1973).

71. Author interview with Rep. Jim Tillman, former vice vhair, Crime and Law Enforcement Committee, Florida House of Representatives, May 10, 2007, Tallahassee.

72. Author interview with Rep. Don Hazelton, former chair, Corrections Committee, Florida House of Representatives, May 3, 2007, Tallahassee.

73. *Costello v. Wainwright*, Pretrial stipulation, December 6, 1974, WSP.

74. *Costello v. Wainwright*, 397 F. Supp. 20, 22, 34 (1975).

75. Author interview with William Sherrill, attorney, formerly with the Florida Department of Legal Affairs, April 2, 2008 (phone). Sherrill also remembers the attorney general not being happy about the pretrial stipulation. Sherrill noted, however, "but I think it was accurate. It was truly an honest stipulation. But it did put a fire to the case."

76. The experts included Dr. Babcock, expert special master and author of the earlier medical care survey, Dr. Walls, a FDOC psychiatrist, Dr. Alderete, Chief Medical Officer at the U.S. Penitentiary in Atlanta.

77. *Costello v. Wainwright*, 397 F. Supp. 20, 25 (1975).

78. *Costello v. Wainwright*, 397 F. Supp. 20, 32 (1975).

79. *Costello v. Wainwright*, 397 F. Supp. 20, 31 (1975).

80. Ohmart and Bradley, "Overcrowding in the Florida Prison System," C-6; emphasis added.

81. *Costello v. Wainwright*, 397 F. Supp. 20, 35 (1975).

82. *Costello v. Wainwright*, 397 F. Supp. 20, 22 (1975).

83. *Costello v. Wainwright*, 397 F. Supp. 20, 22 (1975). The following correctional institutions had opened since 1970: Cross City CI (1973), Quincy Annex (1973), and Lake CI (1973). Plans were underway for facilities in Brevard, Hillsborough, Indian River, and Broward/Dade Counties. Florida Division of Corrections, "Annual Report 1974–75" (Tallahassee, 1975), 27.

84. *Costello v. Wainwright*, Second amended complaint, February 26, 1973, denied April 24.

85. *Costello v. Wainwright*, 397 F. Supp. 20, 43 (1975).

86. Ohmart and Bradley, "Overcrowding in the Florida Prison System," B-12, B-14.

87. *Gates v. Collier*, 501 F.2d 1291 (5th Cir 1974).

88. Author interview with Tom Herndon, former budget director and chief of staff for Gov. Graham, May 7, 2007, Tallahassee.

89. Sherrill interview.

90. Sherrill interview. At issue is the italicized phrase in 28 U.S.C.A §2281, which states that only a three-judge panel can issue an injunction "restraining the enforcement, operation or execution of any State statute by restraining the action of any officer of such State . . . upon the ground of the unconstitutionality of such statute." Judge Scott had originally rejected the defendant's argument: "[the order] . . . has not and will not require the defendant Wainwright to refuse to accept prisoners lawfully committed to his custody. He may use whatever means within his control, consistent with his constitutional and statutory obligations, to comply with this Court's injunction." *Wainwright v. Costello*, 397 F. Supp. 20, 36 (M.D. Fla. 1975).

91. *Costello v. Wainwright*, 525 F.2d 1239 (Crt. of App. 5th Cir. 1976, affirmed), 539 F.2d 547 (en banc), reversed and remanded, 430 U.S. 325 (1977). Relying almost completely on the lack of challenge to the constitutionality of the law in question, the court clarified that the "temporary suspension of an otherwise valid state statute" in order to comply with court-ordered relief is *not* "equivalent to finding that statute unconstitutional."

92. Press Release, "Governor Askew Task Force on Corrections," December 2, 1975, S966, Box 1, File 20, FSA; Florida House of Representatives, Committee on Corrections, Probation and Parole, "A Report Submitted to the House Committee on Corrections, Probation and Parole" (Tallahassee: Florida House of Representatives, 1978).

93. Fla. Sess. Laws, ch. 75-49 (1975). The purpose of the "new" department was to "integrate the delivery of all offender rehabalitation and incarceration services that are deemed necessary for the rehabalitation of offenders and protection of society . . . (Sec. 2)" and "protect society through incarceration as deterrent . . . by substituting for retributive punishment methods of training and treatment which correct and rehabilitate offenders."

94. *Journal of the House of Representatives*, State of Florida, April 11, 1978. When crime rates actually decreased between the 1976 and 1977 legislative session, there was concern among the governor's staff that lower crime rates would undermine his tough justice stance. Memo to Gov. Askew, March 2, 1977, S92, Box 2, 6.

95. Sherrill interview.

96. Rep. Eric Smith to Rayman Hamlin, Jacksonville, February 5, 1975, S18, Box 89, FSA.

97. Sen. Dempsey Barron (D. Washington Co.), for example, claimed that the amount of funding for corrections wasn't the problem—the problem was waste by the bureaucracy. Dempsey Barron, "Address to Florida Sheriffs Association," January 24, 1975, FSA.

98. Fla. Sess. Laws, ch. 77-465 (1977); Fla. Sess. Laws, ch. 78-401 (1978); Fla. Sess. Laws, ch. 79-212 (1979). Gov. Askew had asked for $100 million in 1976 and another $38 million in 1977–78. Deposition of Joseph Kresse, January 31, 1977, exhibit 1, WSP; Motion for an Evidentiary Hearing Due to Changed Circumstances, June 6, 1977, 17, WSP. Gov. Askew's budget proposal for 1977–78 included funding for three new facilities, the expansion of another four facilities, and the completion of two facilities already under way (in Baker and Dade County). State of Florida "Recommended Budget for the Fiscal Year 1977–1978," March 3, 1977, *Reubin O'Donovan Askew Speeches*, Box 5, GSL.

99. Fla. Sess. Laws, chs. 78-304, 78-318, 78-84, 78-417, 78-420 (1978).

100. Florida House of Representatives, "A Report Submitted to the House Committee on Corrections, Probation and Parole." Interestingly, legislators did not ever cite (then or now) racial discrimination as a reason for these reforms, as some scholars have suggested about reform in other states. Pamala L. Griset, *Determinate Sentencing: The Promise and the Reality of Retributive Justice* (Albany: State University of New York Press, 1991). While this may have been a hidden agenda for the few black legislators and some urban Democrats, the problem of discretion was mainly one of regional disparities, political influence, and individual idiosyncrasies. Governor's Task Force on Criminal Justice System Reform, "Final Report" (Tallahassee: State of Florida, 1982).

101. Fla. Sess. Laws, ch. 74-112 (1974).

102. Florida Division of Corrections, "Annual Report 1974–1975," 7.

103. Bachman interview.

104. Author interview with Louie Wainwright, former secretary of the Department of Corrections, April 17, 2007, Tallahassee.

105. Herndon interview.

106. Florida Department of Offender Rehabilitation, Bureau of Planning Research and Staff Development, "Analysis of the Effects of the *Costello v. Wainwright* Court Order," February 5, 1976, S966, Box 1, FSA.

107. Sherrill interview.

108. *Costello v. Wainwright*, 489 F. Supp. 1100 (M.D. Fla. 1980).

109. Roger Schindler, telephone communication with author, March 20, 2007; Transcripts of Hearing on the Overcrowding Settlement Agreement, October 23, 1979, WSP.

110. "Prisoners Forum," *Prison Law Monitor* (January 1980): 170. After advertising the settlement to prisoners across the state, the court received only thirty-four written objections from prisoners. Transcripts of Hearing on the Overcrowding Settlement Agreement, February 1, 1980, 22, WSP.

111. Roger Schindler communication; Transcripts of Hearing on the Overcrowding Settlement Agreement, October 23, 1979, 31–33, WSP. In May 1979 the Supreme Court held in *Bell v. Wolfish*, 441 U.S. 520 (1979) that lower courts should defer to the expertise of correction officials and that double-celling was not

in violation of Eighth Amendment. And, in fact, the court's (and lower courts') subsequent rulings trended away from comprehensive federal court intervention in prison conditions cases.

112. Transcripts of Hearing on the Overcrowding Settlement Agreement, October 23, 1979, 34, WSP.

113. Transcripts of Hearing on the Overcrowding Settlement Agreement, February 1, 1980, 7, 15, WSP.

114. *Costello v. Wainwright*, 489 F. Supp. 1100, 1111 (M.D. Fla. 1980).

115. Transcripts of Hearing on the Overcrowding Settlement Agreement, February 1, 1980, 11–12, WSP.

116. *Costello v. Wainwright*, 489 F. Supp. 1100, 1102. See "Summary of Capacities . . . as of May 7, 1979."

117. Sherrill interview.

118. See *Arias v. Wainwright*, T.C.A. 79-0792, (N.D. Fla. 1979); author interview with John Middleton, attorney, formerly with Florida Institutional Legal Services, April 25, 2007, Melrose. See, e.g., *Vann v. Graham*, 394 So. 2d 176 (1981).

119. *Costello v. Wainwright*, 489 F. Supp. 1100, 1111 (M.D. Fla. 1980). Ironically, the prototype dormitory institutions built in the late 1980s did include separate buildings for educational and other activities; however, budget cuts in 2006 for correctional education and other programming left them unused. Author interview with Richard Dugger, March 22, 2007, Monticello.

120. Office of the Governor, Press Release, November 12, 2008, S1215, Box 4, FSA.

121. For the argument that developments in civil rights law led to prisoner rights litigation, see also Greenberg, *Crusaders in the Courts*; Jim Thomas, *Prisoner Litigation: The Paradox of the Jailhouse Lawyer* (Lanham, MD: Rowman & Littlefield Publishers, Inc, 1988).

122. Sharon B. Jacobs, "The Inmate Grievance Procedure Pilot Project," *Florida Bar Journal* 57 (1983): 229–32.

123. Louie Wainwright to Gov. Kirk, March 30, 1967, S923, Box 58, File 6, FSA. He writes: "Florida must expand its programs of academic education, vocational training, religious training, and other modern concepts which help to change attitudes and prepare the offender to re-enter society as a contributing tax-paying citizen."

124. Donald Horowitz, *The Courts and Social Policy* (Washington, DC: Brookings Institution, 1977), 56–61.

125. Bill Sherrill told me that when he and Joe Kresse began presenting the draft agreement to officials and legislators in Tallahassee, the speaker of the House and the Senate president did not have any objections, but that if Sen. Dempsey Barron (D. Washington Co.) objected, it would have been a problem. Sen. Barron, a law-and-order proponent, had considerable sway in the legislature and frequently

fought with Gov. Askew. Dempsey Barron, "Address to Florida Sheriffs Association," January 24, 1975, FSA; Craig Basse and Lucy Morgan, "Dempsey Barron Dead at 79," *St. Petersburg Times*, July 8, 2001.

126. Schoenfeld, "The Delayed Emergence of Penal Modernism in Florida."

127. The percentage of voting-age blacks registered in Florida went from 15 percent in 1947 to 63 percent in 1964 and held steady until dipping slightly in 1980s. This is a sharp contrast to neighboring Alabama, where only 23 percent of voting-age blacks were registered by 1964. John Sutton, *Law/Society: Origins, Interactions, and Change* (Thousand Oaks, CA:Pine Forge Press, 2001), 166.

128. Colburn, *From Yellow Dog Democrats to Red State Republicans*, 102.

129. By 1980 the typical black student could expect to go to a school with 50 percent white student enrollment. Hispanic students were actually more segregated by 1980 due to demographic changes in the state, including the growth of the Cuban population in South Florida. Gary Orfield, "Public School Desegregation in the United States, 1968–1980" (The Civil Rights Project, 1983), http://escholar ship.org/uc/item/85w788b9.

Chapter 4

1. Transcripts of Hearing on the Overcrowding Settlement Agreement, October 23, 1979, 34, WSP.

2. Author interview with John Mills, former speaker of the Florida House of Representatives, April 26, 2007, Gainesville.

3. Joan Mullen, Kenneth Carlson, and Bradford Smith, "American Prisons and Jails, Volume 1—Summary and Policy Implications of a National Survey" (Washington, DC: National Institute of Justice, 1980), http://www.ncjrs.gov/App/publica tions/abstract.aspx?ID=75752, 61–66.

4. Heather Schoenfeld, "Mass Incarceration and the Paradox of Prison Conditions Litigation," *Law and Society Review* 44 (3/4) (2010): 731–68.

5. Katherine Beckett, *Making Crime Pay: Law and Order in Contemporary American Politics* (New York: Oxford, 1997); John Hagan, *Who Are the Criminals? The Politics of Crime Policy from the Age of Roosevelt to the Age of Reagan* (Princeton: Princeton University Press, 2010); Craig Reinarman and Harry G. Levine, *Crack in America: Demon Drugs and Social Justice* (Berkeley: University of California Press, 1997).

6. Thomas B. Edsall and Mary D. Edsall, *Chain Reaction: The Impact of Race, Rights, and Taxes on American Politics* (New York: W. W. Norton, 1992), 129. Pat O'Malley describes the New Right as the pairing of neoconservative ideologists with neoliberals. On the one hand, neoconservatives emphasized the value of order, discipline, and traditional institutions such as marriage and the family. They believed in the state's responsibility to restore order and reinforce morality through

severe sanctions and retributive punishments. On the other hand, neoliberals emphasized the market as the model for social order and the individual as the site of choice and responsibility. Pat O'Malley, "Volatile and Contradictory Punishment," *Theoretical Criminology* 3 (1999): 175–96.

7. Paul Pearson, *Dismantling the Welfare State: Reagan, Thatcher, and the Politics of Retrenchment* (New York: Cambridge University Press, 1994).

8. Hagan, *Who Are the Criminals?*

9. For more on President Ford and President Carter's approach to federal crime control policy, see Elizabeth Hinton, *From the War on Poverty to the War on Crime: The Making of Mass Incarceration in America* (Cambridge: Harvard University Press, 2016).

10. Hagan, *Who Are the Criminals?* 144.

11. Hagan, *Who Are the Criminals?* 116.

12. John R. Petrocik, "Issue Ownership in Presidential Elections, with a 1980 Case Study," *American Journal of Political Science* 40 (3) (1996): 825–50.

13. Chris Hale, "Economy, Punishment and Imprisonment," *Contemporary Crises* 13 (1989), 342, as quoted in Beckett, *Making Crime Pay*, 50.

14. Ronald Reagan, "Radio Address to the Nation on Federal Drug Policy," October 2, 1982, online at Gerhard Peters and John T. Woolley, *The American Presidency Project*, http://www.presidency.ucsb.edu/ws/?pid=43085.

15. Michael Tonry, *Malign Neglect: Race, Crime, and Punishment in America* (New York: Oxford University Press, 1995), 91.

16. The FBI's antidrug budget increased from $8 to $95 million between 1980 and 1984. Beckett, *Making Crime Pay*, 52.

17. Kenneth R. Feinberg, "Introduction," *American Criminal Law Review* 22 (1984–1985): 705; Ted Gest, *Crime and Politics: Big Government's Erratic Campaign for Law and Order* (New York: Oxford, 2001), 57. See also Joseph E. diGenova and Constance L. Belfiore, "An Overview of the Comprehensive Crime Control Act of 1984—The Prosecutor's Perspective," *American Criminal Law Review* 22 (1984–1985): 707–36.

18. Gest, *Crime and Politics*, 54–57.

19. Beckett, *Making Crime Pay*, 56.

20. Beckett, *Making Crime Pay*, 56.

21. Doris Marie Provine, *Unequal under Law: Race in the War on Drugs* (Chicago: University of Chicago Press, 2008), 108.

22. Provine, *Unequal Under Law*, 114.

23. Naomi Murakawa, *The First Civil Right: How Liberals Built Prison America* (Oxford: Oxford University Press, 2014), 117.

24. The 1988 Anti-Drug Abuse Act also denied student loans to anyone with a drug conviction, provided for the death penalty for major drug dealers, and established a five-year mandatory minimum sentence for simple possession of crack, even for first-time offenders.

25. National Institute of Justice, *National Assessment of the Byrne Formula Grant Program: A Policy Maker's Overview* (Washington, DC: U.S. Department of Justice, 1996), 25.

26. Bruce L. Benson, David W. Rasmussen, and David L. Sollars, "Police Bureaucracies, Their Incentives, and the War on Drugs," *Public Choice* 83 (1–2) (1995): 21–45; Eric Blumenson and Eva Nilsen, "Policing for Profit: The Drug War's Hidden Economic Agenda," *University of Chicago Law Review* (1998): 35–114.

27. Roger Simon, "How a Murderer and Rapist Became the Bush Campaign's Most Valuable Player," *Baltimore Sun*, November 11, 1990.

28. Simon, "How a Murderer and Rapist Became the Bush Campaign's Most Valuable Player."

29. Tali Mendelberg, *The Race Card: Campaign Strategy, Implicit Messages, and the Norm of Equality* (Princeton: Princeton University Press, 2001).

30. Shanto Iyengar, *Is Anyone Responsible? How Television Frames Political Issues* (Chicago: University of Chicago Press, 1991).

31. Katherine Beckett and Theodore Sasson, *The Politics of Injustice: Crime and Punishment in America* (New York: Sage, 2004), 79.

32. Beckett and Sasson, *The Politics of Injustice*, 76.

33. Iyengar, *Is Anyone Responsible?*

34. Beckett, *Making Crime Pay*, 52.

35. As early as 1980, Sen. Joseph Biden (D. Delaware) is reported to have urged Democrats to take over the crime issue. Gest, *Crime and Politics*, 45.

36. Charles S. Bullock and Mike J. Rozell, eds., *The New Politics of the Old South: An Introduction to Southern Politics* (New York: Rowman & Littlefield Publishers, 2013).

37. David R. Colburn and Richard K. Scher, *Florida's Gubernatorial Politics in the Twentieth Century* (Tallahassee: University Presses of Florida, 1980), 87.

38. Colburn and Scher, *Florida's Gubernatorial Politics*, 88.

39. Florida Office of the Governor, Press Release, November 12, 1980, S1236, Box 2, FSA.

40. Office of the Governor, Executive Order No. 80-109, December 9, 1980.

41. Louie Wainwright to Gov. Graham, January 13, 1981, S1215, Box 4, FSA.

42. Florida House of Representatives, Committee on Corrections, "Corrections Issues Orientation Package" (Tallahassee: Florida House of Representatives, 1996). The House Corrections Committee issued a scathing report in 1980 accusing Wainwright of mismanagement and nepotism. Lanny Larson, Memo on Final Report of Ad Hoc Subcommittee on Management Oversight, November 6, 1980, S1215, Box 4, FSA. In June 1981, a Florida state inmate won the first ever civil damages against a corrections officer in a jury trial. Joseph Verrengia, "Inmate Awarded $26,500in damages," *Florida Times-Union*. Jacksonville, June 19, 1981, A1. See also *Vann v. Graham*, 394 So. 2d 176 (1981), which found conditions at Florida State Prison that "daily imperil [inmates] lives and safety."

43. Louie Wainwright letter to Gov. Graham, January 13, 1981, S1215, Box 4, FSA.

44. Transcript of Hearing on Violation of Settlement Agreements, July 6, 1982; Report to the Court Pursuant to the Order of May 12, 1982, May 17, 1982, WSP.

45. Transcript of Hearing on Violation of Settlement Agreements, July 6, 1982, 189, WSP; *Costello v. Wainwright*, Order, July 14, 1982, 8–9, WSP.

46. Stephen K. Doig, "Jammed Prisons to be Tackled by Legislature," *Miami Herald*, June 18, 1982, 8A. Associated Press, "Lawmakers OK $25 million for Prisons," *Miami Herald* June 23, 1982. The legislature had also funded 1500 permanent beds during the regular session, which were expected to take a few years to come online.

47. Corrections Overcrowding Task Force, "Final Report and Recommendations" (Tallahassee: State of Florida, 1983), SLF.

48. Florida Office of Management and Budget, "Department of Corrections Long Term Male Bed Needs," Revised May 6, 1982, WSP.

49. Governor's Advisory Committee on Corrections, Minutes of September 2, 1982, WSP.

50. Attorney General Jim Smith, Statement to the Task Force on Prison Overcrowding, February 24, 1983, WSP.

51. Attorney General Jim Smith, Statement to the Task Force on Prison Overcrowding, February 24, 1983, WSP.

52. Judge Ralph Nimmons, Jr., Memo to Members of the Task Force on Prison Overcrowding, November 1, 1982, WSP.

53. Corrections Overcrowding Task Force, Minutes, August 4, 1982, WSP.

54. Edward Hammock, Chairman New York Division of Parole, "Determinate Sentencing, Not a Disaster . . . Yet!" (unpublished paper, 1980), WSP.

55. Robert Mathias and Diane Steelman, Controlling Prison Populations: An Assessment of Current Mechanisms (Fort Lee, NJ: National Council on Crime and Delinquency, 1982).

56. Milo Geyelin, "Legislators to Reform Prison System," *St. Petersburg Times*, March 25, 1983.

57. Corrections Overcrowding Task Force, "Final Report," 79.

58. A group of senators submitted an alternative bill that would have made alternatives to incarceration mandatory for certain offenses, and some legislators favored maintaining a role for the Parole Commission. House Committee on Corrections, Probation, and Parole Report on SB644, May 1, 1983, S19, Box 1488, FSA.

59. The Parole and Probation Commission had been beset by controversy since the mid-1960s and legislators had been trying to abolish it (or move it under the Division of Corrections) ever since. Critics thought release decisions were too arbitrary, political, or conservative. In 1978 a compromise was reached requiring the commission to establish "objective parole guidelines" that would determine a presumptive parole date for each inmate. In addition, the law required the com-

mission to give prisoners a definition of "unsatisfactory conduct" and details of release terms and conditions. Fla. Sess. Laws, 1978, ch. 78-417 (1978). The abolition of parole in 1983 was also due to a change in thinking about the efficacy of correctional rehabilitation. Governor's Task Force on Criminal Justice Reform, Final Report, June 1982, SLF.

60. Fla. Sess. Laws, ch. 83-87 (1983).

61. Corrections Overcrowding Task Force, "Final Report," iii.

62. Corrections Overcrowding Task Force, "Final Report," 70.

63. Florida had a history of controlling population via gain-time. The first gain-time laws came about as part of the large overhaul of the Division of Corrections in 1957. Fla. Sess. Laws, ch. 57-121.25 (1957). At the time, gain-time credits were given to well-behaved inmates at the discretion of the individual warden or prison supervisor. In 1963, the legislature spelled out a more generous, but uniform, schedule of gain-time credits—awarding each inmate a certain number of days credit for each month served. Fla. Sess. Laws, ch. 63-243 (1963). In 1978, legislators returned discretion to the Department of Corrections to award gain-time for each prisoner (from zero to ten days per month), plus special gain-time for "outstanding deeds." Fla. Sess. Laws, ch. 78-304 (1978).

64. Fla. Sess. Laws, ch. 83-131 (1983).

65. Fla. Sess. Laws, ch. 83-131 (1983). See Governor's Advisory Committee on Corrections, Minutes of September 2, 1982, WSP.

66. *Mason v. Wainwright, 417* F.2d 769 (5th Cir. 1969).

67. Author interview with William Sheppard, attorney, Sheppard & White, February 2, 2008 (phone).

68. *Miller v. Carson*, 392 F. Supp. 515 (M.D. Fla. 1975); *Arias v. Wainwright*, TCA 79-0792 (N.D. Fla, 1979).

69. Letter to Bill Sheppard from Sharon Jacobs, February 24, 1981, WSP.

70. Sheppard interview.

71. Dictation of phone message from Bill Sherrill in "Notes RE Exhibits," October 10, 1982, WSP.

72. Sheppard interview.

73. Motion for Hearing to Determine Whether the Defendant's Proposed Building of Plywood Tents to House Inmates Violates the Federal Constitution, the Laws of the State of Florida, or This Court's Order of February 11, 1980, July 6, 1982, WSP.

74. Letter to Sheppard from John Dale, chief, Bureau of Planning, Research, and Statistics, September 28, 1983, WSP. In addition, Sheppard filed motions on violation of the health care agreement that had been reached in 1981.

75. Mark Dykstra, "Apart from the Crowd: Florida's New Prison Release Program," *Florida State University Law Review* 14 (1986): 799–810. The prison population decreased from 27,717 in June 1983 to 26,471 in June 1984, but then rose again to 28,310 by June 1985.

76. *Costello* Opinion and Order Preamble, August 22, 1985, 4, 29.

77. *Costello v. Wainwright*, Opinion and Order, August 22, 1985, and December 6, 1985, WSP. Author interview with Linda Hudson, former law clerk, Federal District Court, Middle District of Florida, February 18, 2008 (phone).

78. Francis A. Allen, "Transcript of Address at Memorial Service for Dean Joseph R. Julin, August 7, 1993," *Florida Law Review* 45 (1993): xii. Bill Sheppard referred to Julin as a "heavyweight" among Florida's governing class.

79. *Costello v. Wainwright*, Transcript of Status Hearing, August 22, 1985, 11–12, WSP.

80. Sheppard interview.

81. *Costello* Opinion, October 9, 1992. According to Richard Dugger, the warden of Florida State Prison at the time, even the temporary wooden tents were often not used to house inmates, but were constructed in order to count the space when determining maximum capacity. Author interview with Richard Dugger, former secretary of the Florida Department of Corrections, March 22, 2007, Monticello.

82. *Costello v. Wainwright*, Civil Docket, 72-109-Civ-J, WSP.

83. To enhance his tough justice image, Graham presided over the reintroduction of the death penalty in Florida—signing the first death warrant since 1964 and fifteen more in his eight years in office. In addition, he signed Florida's 1979 mandatory minimum drug sentence law.

84. Fla. Sess. Laws, ch. 86-46 (1986).

85. Louie Wainwright to Gov. Graham, June 11, 1986, S 1349, Box 2, FSA.

86. Florida Department of Corrections, "2006–2007 Annual Report" (Tallahassee, 2007), http://www.dc.state.fl.us/pub/annual/0607/facil.html.

87. Notice of Violation of Overcrowding Settlement Agreement and Motion for Order to Show Cause, March 27, 1985, WSP. The notice included a letter from a prisoner in Union CI's West Unit who wrote, "There is not enough security personnel to properly supervise these men living like this, so, a rule has been made to keep them locked inside . . . often with no officer at all present. Living like this breeds violence, as it is; when no officer is provided for supervision, minor irritants could lead to violence and with summer coming on . . ."

88. Michael Moline, "Graham Seeks Contract with Shands to Manage Troubled Prison Health System," *United Press International*, November 6, 1985.

89. The variety of beds slated to come online demonstrates the department's scramble to put together enough bed space. They included 480 "quick construction beds" (dormitory style) just appropriated, 200 beds in a former EconoLodge in Osceola County, two 150-bed community corrections centers (Orange and Pinellas Counties), and another in Dade County for which the department had been unable to locate a site. *Costello v. Wainwright*, Status Conference, June 10, 1986, 35, WSP.

90. George Stein, "War on Drugs: Results Mixed, But Residents' Outlook Brightens," *Miami Herald*, March 21, 1983, A1.

91. Christian Parenti, *Lockdown America: Police and Prisons in the Age of Crisis* (New York: Verso, 1999), 47.

92. Miami Herald Staff, "Renew Drug War," *Miami Herald*, February 14, 1984, 22A.

93. Itabari Njeri, "Freebasing: Just Six Seconds from Hit to Trouble," *Miami Herald*, August 22, 1982, 7G.

94. Herbert Buchsbaum, "Arrests Crack Two-County Burglary Ring, Police Say," *Miami Herald*, November 16, 1985, 2TC; Ray Huard, "Cocaine a Cheap High, Hotline Finding," *Miami Herald*, November 21, 1985, 1PB; Jeff Leen, "Freebase Coke Use Sweeping South Florida," *Miami Herald*, December 30, 1985, 1B.

95. R. W. Apple Jr., "Drugs Dominating Florida Campaign," *New York Times*, October 5, 1986, 35.

96. Status Report on Governor's Crack Cocaine Action Plan, August 13, 1986, S1349, Box 2, FSA.

97. Tammerlin Drummond, "Police Deaths on Rise in Florida, Officials Blame Transients, Drugs, Gun Law for Increase," *St. Petersburg Times*, January 11, 1988, 1B; Jacquee Petchel, "Mother's Nightmare: Innocent Daughter Killed in Drug Fight," *Miami Herald*, August 30 1988, 1BR; Lauren Ritchie and Kristen Gallagher, "Drug Buy Becomes Deadly Deal: Woman Was Victim of Rising Cocaine Violence in Orlando," *Orlando Sentinel*, June 26, 1988, B1.

98. Martinez was further helped by support among Cuban Floridians in South Florida and support by traditional South Florida Democrats. In addition, a very close Democratic primary left Democrats vulnerable. David R. Colburn, *From Yellow Dog Democrats to Red State Republicans: Florida and Its Politics since 1940* (Gainesville: University Press of Florida, 2007).

99. The 1986 primary campaigns for the Democratic and Republican candidate for governor was described as devoid of "debate on issues other than crime," and the emphasis on crime and capital punishment as reaching "obsessive heights." Jon Nordheimer, "Florida Race Underscores Changes," *New York Times*, September 2, 1986, D16.

100. Dugger interview.

101. *Journal of the House of Representatives*, State of Florida, February 4, 1987, 1.

102. David Dahl, "Martinez Will Seek Special Legislative Session on Prisons," *St. Petersburg Times*, January 30, 1987, 1A.

103. Fla. Sess. Laws, Special Session, ch. 87-1 (1987). Only ten Senate Democrats voted against the bill, as they didn't feel comfortable giving all release decision power to the Department of Corrections and would have instead involved the Parole Commission.

104. Fla. Sess. Laws, Special Session, ch. 87-2 (1987). On June 30, 1988 the Department of Corrections held 8,314 inmates serving mandatory minimum sentences (25 percent of the total prison population). Approximately 2,500 of these were

drug offenders. Florida House of Representatives, Committee on Criminal Justice, "Habitual Offender and Minimum Mandatory Sentencing in Florida: A Focus on Sentencing Practices and Recommendations for Legislative Reform," Florida House of Representatives, November 11, 1991, S 19, Box 2266, FSA.

105. David Dahl, "Are Prisons Holding Florida Hostage?" *St. Petersburg Times*, February 1, 1987, 1B.

106. A poll commissioned by one of Gov. Martinez's political opponents in May 1988 found that only 15 percent of respondents favored the construction of new prisons. "Eckerd Says Poll Backs Alternatives to New Prisons," *St. Petersburg Times*, May 20, 1988, 6B.

107. Author interview with Bobby Brantley, former lieutenant governor of Florida, April 12, 2007, Tallahassee.

108. "Real Prison Solutions," *St. Petersburg Times*, December 19, 1986.

109. David Dahl, "Prison Time Dips to 20% of Sentence," *St. Petersburg Times*, November 4, 1987, quoting Sen. Wayne Hollingsworth (D. Lake City).

110. Brantley interview.

111. David Dahl and Tim Nickens, "Plan Approved to Release Inmates to Ease Crowding," *St. Petersburg Times*, February 5, 1987, 2B.

112. Randall Berg, "Florida Does Not Need More Prisons," *Florida Forum*, June 1, 1987. See also John Irwin, "It's about Time" (San Francisco: National Council on Crime and Delinquency, 1987), which Sec. Dugger passed on to Lt. Gov. Brantley, January 12, 1988, S 1322, Box 2, FSA.

113. Author interview with Robert Trammell, former Florida representative, May 2, 1007, Tallahassee.

114. Herald Staff, "Florida's 'Willie Horton,'" *Miami Herald*, November 30, 1988, 24A.

115. David Dahl, "The Prison Crisis Series: For a Better Florida," *St. Petersburg Times*, March 5, 1989, 1A.

116. Dugger interview.

117. Author interview with Al Lawson, former Florida legislator, May 14, 2007, Tallahassee.

118. Author interview with Samuel P. Bell, former Florida representative, May 30, 2007, Tallahassee.

119. Lawson interview.

120. Dugger interview. See, for example, correspondence between Lt. Gov. Brantley and the town of Century, suggesting that Century would be more "competitive" in its bid to attract a new prison with the donation of funds to purchase land. May 27 1987, S 1322, Box 2, FSA.

121. Trammell interview.

122. Dugger interview.

123. Dugger interview.

124. Florida Department of Corrections, "1988 Update of February 1, 1984 report entitled: Comprehensive Statewide Study to Determine the Current and

Future Needs for all Types of Correctional Facilities in the State," February 1, 1988, WSP.

125. Mills interview, emphasis added.

126. Florida House of Representatives, "Corrections Issues Orientation Package" (Tallahassee: Florida House of Representatives, 1996), SLF.

127. Fla. Stat. § 893.13 (1991).

128. Fla. Sess. Laws, ch. 88-131 (1988).

129. Florida Sentencing Guidelines Commission Report, May 1, 1989, FSCL.

130. Author interview with Buddy Ferguson, Florida Department of Corrections, March 30, 2007, Tallahassee.

131. Task Force for the Review of the Criminal Justice and Corrections Systems, Interim Report, 1994, 14, SLF.

132. Andrew H. Malcolm, "Florida's Jammed Prisons, More In Means More Out," *New York Times*, July 3, 1989, 1.

133. The sales tax already supported 70 percent of the state's budget. Jon Nordheimer, "Florida Legislators Vote to Repeal Tax on Advertising and Services," *New York Times*, December 11, 1987.

134. The CMA also indirectly monitored overcrowding through its oversight of FDOC's Office of Health Services, which could certify housing occupancy. Satisfied with this arrangement and the CMA's capabilities by the end of 1990, the court relinquished the "physical health care survey and monitoring responsibilities" to the CMA. *Costello v. Singletary*, Special Master's Report and Recommendation on Case Closure (M.D. Fla. October 9, 1992).

135. Parties Request to the Special Master May 30, 1991, WSP.

136. *Costello v. Singletary*, Special Master's Report and Recommendation on Case Closure (M.D. Fla. October 9, 1992).

137. Hudson interview; Sheppard interview.

138. Sheppard interview.

139. Author interview with Jason E. Vail, attorney, February 18, 2008 (phone).

140. Vail interview.

141. *Costello v. Singletary*, Final Order (M.D. Fla. March 30, 1993).

142. "Letter to the Editor," *St. Petersburg Times*, March 26, 1993.

143. Doug Nurse, "Canady Urges Limiting Judges' Power over Prisons." *Tampa Tribune*, June 13, 1993, 10A; Mona Lynch, *Sunbelt Justice: Arizona and the Transformation of American Punishment* (Palo Alto, CA: Stanford University Press, 2009), 190; Margo Schlanger and Giovanna Shay, "Preserving the Rule of Law in American's Prisons: The Case for Amending the Prison Litigation Reform Act" (Washington, DC: American Constitution Society for Law and Policy, 2007).

144. Michael C. Campbell, "Politics, Prisons, and Law Enforcement: An Examination of the Emergence of 'Law and Order' Politics in Texas," *Law and Society Review* 45 (2011): 631–65; Lynch, *Sunbelt Justice*.

145. Interview with Dave Bachman, former Florida Department of Corrections assistant secretary, March 28, 2007, Tallahassee.

146. Ruth Wilson Gilmore, *Golden Gulag: Prisons, Surplus, Crisis, and Opposition in Globalizing California* (Berkeley: University of California Press, 2007), 87–127.

147. Blumstein and Beck find that across all states 33 percent of the growth in incarceration rates between 1980 and 1993 is attributable to drug offenses. Drug arrests increased approximately 4.8 percent a year, while prison commitments to prison for drug offenses increased by 8.8 per year. They did not have data on convictions per arrest. Alfred Blumstein and Allen J. Beck, "Population Growth in U.S. Prisons, 1980 to 1996," in *Crime and Justice: Prisons*, ed. Michael Tonry and Joan Petersilia (Chicago: University of Chicago, 1999), 17–62.

148. Dorothy Roberts, "Punishing Drug Addicts Who Have Babies: Women of Color, Equality, and the Right of Privacy," in *Critical Race Theory: The Key Writings That Formed the Movement*, ed. Kimberle Crenshaw, Neil Gotanda, Gary Peller, and Kendall Thomas (New York: New Press, 1995), 385–426; Alan David Freeman, "Legitimizing Racial Discrimination through Antidiscrimination Law: A Critical Review of Supreme Court Doctrine," in *Critical Race Theory: The Key Writings That Formed the Movement*, ed. Kimberle Crenshaw, Neil Gotanda, Gary Peller, and Kendall Thomas (New York: New Press, 1995), 29–46.

149. This finding has interesting implications for what Lisa Miller calls the "myth of mob rule," where public punitive sentiment forces legislators to pass punitive crime control policy. On the one hand, it confirms findings that public punitive sentiment was growing during the 1980s. However, it also demonstrates that policymakers don't necessarily act based on public sentiment. In fact, similar to Lisa Miller's finding that politicians are slow to respond to public concerns about crime, the historical record in Florida doesn't suggest a generalized concern about crime among legislators between 1983 and 1988, when violent crime was rising. However, they were focused on improving primary and secondary education, which can help prevent crime. Instead, the real tough talk on crime appeared only after the Charlie Street incident in 1988. Lisa L. Miller, *The Myth of Mob Rule: Violent Crime and Democratic Politics* (New York: Oxford University Press, 2016).

150. In addition to eighteen people losing their lives, newspapers reported $200 million in damaged property. A more accurate estimate of the damage, while still quite large, is $80 million. Bruce Porter and Marvin Dunn, *The Miami Riot of 1980: Crossing the Bounds* (Lexington, MA: Lexington Books, 1984), 130.

151. Edward Schumacher, "Retarded People and Criminals Are Included in Cuban Exodus," *New York Times*, May 10, 1980, 1.

152. *Journal of the House of Representatives*, State of Florida, April 8, 1980, 7.

153. The Task Force on Criminal Justice System Reform cited "questions regarding the ability of the State to rehabilitate most offenders, injustices resulting from a treatment model of correctional response, and mixed signals concerning the goals of rehabilitation and punishment to corrections personnel," all of which had contributed to the failure to "produce the desired results." Task Force on

Criminal Justice System Reform, "Final Recommendations: Reforming the Florida Criminal Justice System" (Tallahassee, 1982), 46, SLF.

154. The Task Force on Criminal Justice System Reform stated that "treatment and rehabilitation would not be abolished under the Task Force proposal. Rather, the concept of treatment would return to its classical definition and treatment interventions would be provided to only those offenders diagnosed as needing such intervention—through standard clinical evaluations." Task Force on Criminal Justice System Reform, 49.

155. Task Force on Criminal Justice System Reform, 46.

Chapter 5

1. Florida House of Representatives, Press Release, "Speaker Appoints Task Force on Sentencing Practices," October 7, 1991, S19, Box 2266, FSA. Opa-locka is majority black city within Maimi-Dade County.

2. Quoted in Miami Herald Staff, "Kendall Statewide Attack on Crime Sought," *Miami Herald*, October 27, 1993, 2A. Kendall is a census designated area within Miami-Dade that in 1990 was 80 percent white and Hispanic (mainly Cuban).

3. On the rise of the Sunbelt in national politics see William Frey, "The Electoral College Moves to the Sunbelt" (Washington, DC: Brookings Institution, 2005), and Adam Nagourney, "The Sunbelt, Eclipsed," *New York Times*, August 26, 2012.

4. One pamphlet was later expanded into a book: John Irwin and James Austin, *It's about Time: America's Imprisonment Binge* (Belmont, CA: Wadsworth Publishing Co., 1994). See also John Irwin and James Austin, "It's about Time: Solving America's Prison Crowding Crisis" (National Council on Crime and Delinquency, 1987); James Austin and John Irwin, "Who Goes to Prison?" (National Council on Crime and Delinquency, 1990); James Austin and John Irwin, "Does Imprisonment Reduce Crime?: A Critique of 'Voodoo' Criminology" (National Council on Crime and Delinquency, 1993).

5. The Sentencing Project, "Young Black Men and the Criminal Justice System: A Growing National Problem" (Washington, DC: The Sentencing Project, 1990).

6. Ed Johnson, "More Prisons Offer More Proof of Failure," *Daily Commercial*, March 12, 1990.

7. Florida Supreme Court Racial and Ethnic Bias Study Commission, "Where the Injured Fly for Justice: Reforming the Practices Which Impede the Dispensation of Justice to Minorities in Florida" (Tallahassee: Florida Supreme Court, 1991), FSCL.

8. The Florida population grew from 9.7 million in 1980 to 12.9 million in 1990. Much of that growth occurred in the suburbs, which tended to attract more conservative voters. In 1990, when Gov. Chiles was elected, Republicans added two

seats in the state House of Representatives and three seats in the state Senate. The gain in the Senate gave the Republicans equal representation in the Senate for the first time in state history. David Colburn, *From Yellow Dog Democrats to Red State Republicans: Florida and Its Politics since 1940* (Gainesville: University Press of Florida, 2007), 139.

9. David Garland, *The Culture of Control: Crime and Social Order in Contemporary Society* (Chicago: University of Chicago Press, 2001), 10.

10. Jonathan Simon, *Governing through Crime: How the War on Crime Transformed American Democracy and Created a Culture of Fear* (Oxford: Oxford University Press, 2007), 100.

11. Franklin Zimring, David Hawkins, and Sam Kamin, *Punishment and Democracy: Three Strikes and You're Out in California* (New York: Oxford University Press, 2001).

12. Joshua Page, *The Toughest Beat: Politics, Punishment, and the Prison Officers Union in California* (New York: Oxford University Press, 2011), 108.

13. Katherine Beckett, *Making Crime Pay: Law and Order in Contemporary American Politics* (Oxford: Oxford University Press, 1997).

14. Zimring, Hawkins, and Kamin, *Punishment and Democracy*, 231.

15. Philip A. Klinkner and Rogers M. Smith, *The Unsteady March: The Rise and Decline of Racial Equality in America* (Chicago: University of Chicago Press, 2002), 306–12.

16. Frey, "The Electoral College Moves to the Sunbelt," 3.

17. Ann Chih Lin, "The Troubled Success of Crime Policy," in *The Social Divide: Political Parties and the Future of Activist Government*, ed. Margaret Weir (Washington, DC: Brookings Institution Press, 1998), 314.

18. The idea that President Clinton was the first black president came from Toni Morrison, writing in a 1998 *New Yorker* essay defending Clinton during the Monica Lewinsky debacle. This notion both offended and resonated with black Americans (for a critique, see Jabari Asim, "Bill Clinton Isn't Black!" *Salon*, February 26, 2001 accessed June 2, 2013, http://www.salon.com/2001/02/26/black_6/). Morrison wrote that Clinton "displays almost every trope of blackness: single-parent household, born poor, working-class, saxophone-playing, McDonald's-and-junk-food-loving boy from Arkansas." It resonated because Clinton was the first president to signal a taste for and comfort with black culture, style, and people. He legitimately had black friends, and spoke with people from all walks of life with an ease that had not been found before in the White House. See DeWayne Wickham, *Bill Clinton and Black America* (New York: One World, 2004).

19. Paul Frymer, *Uneasy Alliances: Race and Party Competition in America* (Princeton: Princeton University Press, 2010 [1999]), 5.

20. Clinton very publically did not stop the execution of Rickey Ray Rector, a severely brain-damaged African American. L. F. Williams, "Race and the Politics of Social Politics," in *The Social Divide: Political Parties and the Future of Activist*

Government, ed. Margaret Weir (Washington, DC: Brookings Institution Press, 1998), 417–63.

21. Frymer, *Uneasy Alliances*, 5.

22. In 1996 President Clinton signed a welfare reform bill that eliminated the entitlement to social support for poor mothers, linked social assistance to participation in the labor market, and gave states new leeway to enact hurdles for the poor. Ann Shola Orloff, "Explaining US Welfare Reform: Power, Gender, Race, and the US Policy Legacy," *Critical Social Policy* 22 (2002): 96–118.

23. Simon, *Governing through Crime*, 102.

24. The original bill introduced in August 1993 by Senators Phil Gramm (R. Texas), Connie Mack (R. Florida), and Pete Domenici (R. New Mexico) (along with thirteen others) provided for a system of regional prisons and grants for state prison construction and operation. To qualify for the regional prison system, states had to impose truth in sentencing, which required that prisoners serve 85 percent of their imposed sentences and that sentences for violent offenders had to be "at least as long" as those imposed under federal law. 103d Congress, 1st session, S.1356. Representative Bill McCollum (R. Florida) proposed similar bills in the House. 103d Congress, 1st session, H.R.2892, H.R.2872.

25. A coalition of civil rights organizations, including the NAACP and the Black Police Officers Association opposed the president's crime bill. Steven Holmes, "Prominent Blacks Meet to Search for an Answer to Mounting Crime," *New York Times*, January 7, 1994, A1. President Clinton managed to snub the Congressional Black Caucus on a number of occasions, but most notably around the proposed inclusion of the Racial Justice Act in the crime bill which would have allowed death penalty defendants to use statistical evidence to demonstrate that race was a significant factor in their prosecution. Williams, "Race and the Politics of Social Politics," 430.

26. On the move from black liberation to representation, see Cedric Johnson, *Revolutionaries to Race Leaders: Black Power and the Making of African American Politics* (Minneapolis: University of Minnesota Press, 2007).

27. Claire Jean Kim, "Managing the Racial Breach: Clinton, Black-White Polarization, and the Race Initiative," *Political Science Quarterly* 117 (2002): 55–79; Sarah Wilson, "Appellate Judicial Appointments during the Clinton Presidency: An Inside Perspective," *Journal of Appellate Practice and Process* (2003): 29–48.

28. Editorial Board, "Poised for a Good Year Ahead," *Miami Times*, December 31, 1992, 4A.

29. Fredrick Harris, *The Price of the Ticket: Barack Obama and Rise and Decline of Black Politics* (New York: Oxford University Press, 2012); 128; Robert C. Smith, *We Have No Leaders: African Americans in the Post–Civil Rights Era* (Albany: State University of New York Press, 1996), 88–89.

30. Smith, *We Have No Leaders*, 3.

31. Quoted in Smith, *We Have No Leaders*, 83.

32. Alex Kotlowitz, "A Bridge Too Far? Benjamin Chavis," *New York Times Magazine*, June 12, 1994. It is important to note that the NAACP still spent considerable resources on legal strategies to fight discrimination during this time. Michelle Alexander, *The New Jim Crow: Mass Incarceration in the Age of Color-blindness* (New York: New Press, 2010).

33. "N.A.A.C.P. Invites Farrakhan," *New York Times*, February 20, 1994. The Million Man March took place in October 1995 and created a lot of controversy over its focus, its perceived exclusionary politics, and its leader.

34. Early release was first implemented as administrative gain-time in February 1987, replaced by provisional credits in July 1988, and by control release in November 1990. While they all had slightly different criteria, the basic goal—to regulate the prison population by releasing prisoners before the expiration of their sentences—remained the same.

35. Sean Holton and Mark Vosburgh, "About This Report," *Orlando Sentinel*, August 13, 1989, A14.

36. Sean Holton and Mark Vosburgh, "8 Taps and Computer Decides Who Gets Out," *Orlando Sentinel*, August 14, 1989, A1.

37. Florida Office of Economic and Demographic Research, "An Alternative to Florida's Current Sentencing Guidelines" (Tallahassee: Florida State Legislature, 1991), S19, Box 2266, 9, FSA.

38. Sean Holton and Mark Vosburgh, "The Irony: Getting Tougher on Crime Favors the Bad Guys," *Orlando Sentinel*, August 15, 1989, A1.

39. Holton and Vosburgh, "The Irony: Getting Tougher on Crime Favors the Bad Guys."

40. Author interview with former state senator Al Lawson, May 14, 2007 (Tallahassee).

41. For example, in three months in the summer of 1989, Broward County sent 491 people to prison for possessing small amounts of cocaine. At the time, Broward County had only thirty-five state-funded residential treatment beds. Jean Dubail, "Broward Drug Busts Swamp State Prisons," *Sun Sentinel* (Fort Lauderdale), September 10, 1989.

42. Florida House of Representatives, Committee on Criminal Justice, *Habitual Offender and Minimum Mandatory Sentencing in Florida: A Focus on Sentencing Practices and Recommendations for Legislative Reform* (Tallahassee, 1991) S19, Box 2266, FSA. By 1991 prisoners with mandatory minimum sentences made up 30 percent of the prison population and habitual offenders 10 percent. Florida Office of Economic and Demographic Research, "An Alternative to Florida's Current Sentencing Guidelines," 12, 14. Some evidence suggests that this practice by state's attorneys was itself a result of the early release policy; by charging offenders as habitual offenders (or under mandatory minimum laws) prosecutors could avoid the possibility of offenders' early release from prison.

43. Fla. Sess. Laws, ch. 91-239 (1991).

44. The proposal consisted of ten offense ranking categories and assigned point values for each rank for primary, additional, and prior offenses. Judges would then use the point value to determine the recommended sentence. Rankings were initially generated by the actual sentences received since 1993 (with some changes based on a survey of judges). The decision to use actual sentences may have inadvertently embedded judges' overcompensation for early release policies during the late 1980s, leading to unrealistic guideline ranges.

45. For example, purchase of cocaine within one thousand feet of a public school (formerly a mandatory minimum sentence) would be put in offense category 6 (along with aggravated assault.) This category would get a score of thirty-six points, plus any prior offense would add two to eight points. If the total number of points was below forty, the recommended sentence was to be no state prison. Florida Sentencing Guidelines Commission, "A Proposal to Revise the Statewide Sentencing Guidelines" (Tallahassee: Florida Sentencing Guidelines Commission, 1992) FSCL.

46. Letter from Gov. Chiles to Rep. Willie Logan, November 4, 1991, S19, Box 2266, FSA. It should be noted that as a United States Senator, Chiles was a strong proponent of using federal prisons for drug offenders. Doris Marie Provine, *Unequal under Law: Race in the War on Drugs* (Chicago: University of Chicago Press, 2008), 115.

47. Florida House of Representatives, *Habitual Offender and Minimum Mandatory Sentencing in Florida*, Florida Supreme Court Racial and Ethnic Bias Study Commission 1991, FSCL.

48. *House Committee on Corrections Bill Analysis of SB* 1088, n.d., S18, Box 1908, FSA.

49. *Truth in Sentencing Act of 1992*, Florida Legislature, 24th Regular Session, CS/SB 1088 and CS/HB 411.

50. Kate Pursell, "STOP Takes Stand Statewide Against Inmates' Early-Release," *Bradenton Herald*, May 18, 1991, B1.

51. Matt Schudel, "Kathleen Finnegan's Closed-Door Policy," *Orlando Sentinel*, August 28, 1994, A8. As evidence of MADD's influence, the 1993 sentencing legislation, which was aimed at making more space available in prison, added DUI manslaughter to the categories of offenders not eligible for control release. Fla. Sess. Laws, ch. 93-406 (1993).

52. The sheriffs lost the case at the trial and on appeal. *Wells v. Dugger*, 589 So. 2d 342 (Fla. Dist. Ct. App., 1991).

53. Chris Downey, "Prisoner Gain Time Besieged," *Bradenton Herald*, February 18, 1990, B1. For example, because Broward County paid a $1,000-a-day fine for exceeding its jail capacity, Broward County Prosecuting Attorney Michael Satz gave drug offenders probation sentences, with the threat of state prison if they failed. According to Satz, "the certainty of going to prison if the offender fails is an added incentive to reform. . . . Besides, the county jail already is crowded. . . .

You can't put all those people in the county jail, there is not enough room." Jean Dubail, "Broward Drug Busts Swamp State Prisons," *Sun Sentinel*, September 10, 1989.

54. The victim was likely black as well. Carlos Galarza, "Early-Release Convict Charge with Killing Teen," *Bradenton Herald*, March 8, 1991, A1; Kate Pursell, "Crime Infuriates Manatee Sheriff," *Bradenton Herald*, March 8, 1991, A1.

55. David Ballingrud, "Prosecutors in Florida Welcome Drug Plan," *St. Petersburg Times*, September 7, 1989, A1.

56. Author interview with Brian Berkowitz, executive director, Task Force for Review of Criminal Justice and Corrections, May 14, 2007, Tallahassee.

57. Stephen Koff, "Prosecutors Fight Score-Sheet Sentencing," *St. Petersburg Times*, July 25, 1989, 3B.

58. Author interview with Ed Austin, former state's attorney and former mayor of Jacksonville, September 21, 2008, Jacksonville.

59. John East, "Guidelines for Justice," *St. Petersburg Times*, January 5, 1992, 1D.

60. Maria Douglas, "Early Release in Group's Sights," *Bradenton Herald*, May 31, 1991, 1.

61. Ellen Moses, "Wells New Chairman of Sheriffs Group," *Bradenton Herald*, July 18, 1991, B6.

62. Ellen Moses, "Early Release Opponents Organize Locally," *Bradenton Herald*, July 24, 1991, B2.

63. Diane Sears, "Citizens Lobby against Early Release," *Orlando Sentinel*, January 12, 1993, B6.

64. See, e.g., "Group Opposing Early Releases to Meet," *Palm Beach Post*, May 12, 1992, 2B. See also, e.g., "Demonstrators Protest Shortening Prison Time," *Orlando Sentinel*, January 28, 1992, B3.

65. Diane Sears, "Activist Works from the Heart to Keep Criminals Behind Bars," *Orlando Sentinel*, January 21, 1993, B1.

66. "Junny's Mom to Appear on '60 Minutes' Tonight," *Orlando Sentinel*, April 11, 1993, B3.

67. In an attempt to verify Wells's statement, I conducted a search of local newspapers in 1992 to see how many chapters were specifically mentioned. I found six chapters: Manatee/Sarasota (known as the first local chapter), St. Lucie, Martin, Indian River, Hillsborough, and Pinellas/Pasco. Three had explicit ties to the states attorney's office.

68. In one particularly notorious case, Attorney General Bob Butterworth responded to STOP's lobbying efforts by blocking the release of Donald McDougall, who was sentenced to thirty-one years in prison in 1983 for the torture and murder of a five-year-old girl. In addition, Butterworth signed an opinion authorizing the retroactive revocation of all previously awarded provisional credits to prisoners sentenced for murder. As a result, the Department of Corrections had to reincar-

cerate more than a dozen previously released offenders. Author interview with Buddy Ferguson, March 30, 2007. The U.S. Supreme Court later ruled that Butterworth's action violated the ex post facto clause of the federal constitution. *Lynce v. Mathis*, 117 U.S. 981 (1997).

69. Marty Rosen, "Prison Sentences Often Don't Mean Much," *St. Petersburg Times*, July 18, 1992, 3D.

70. Beth Muniz, "Convicted Molester Out Soon," *Bradenton Herald*, September 4, 1992, B1.

71. Darryl E. Owens, "Shorter Sentences Create More Victims, Protestors Say," *Orlando Sentinel*, April 26, 1992, B3. See also Sandra Mathers, "STOP: Felons Should Stay In," *Orlando Sentinel*, April 25, 1993, B1.

72. "Demonstrators Protest Shortening Prison Time," *Orlando Sentinel*, January 28, 1992, B3.

73. Belinda Gomez, "Clair-Mel," *Tampa Tribune*, April 18, 1992, 10.

74. Florida 12th Legislative Session, SB1088 (died in Appropriations Committee), HB411 (died on House Calendar).

75. "Senate Staff Analysis and Economic Impact Statement," May 1, 1992, Box 1088, FSA, noting that there was a problem in the low percentage of offenders available for early release. S18, Box 1908, FSA.

76. Associated Press, "Rule Change May Free Inmates Earlier," *Tampa Tribune*, May 27, 1992, 4.

77. David Olinger, "Prisons: A Prison System Nobody Points to with Pride," *St. Petersburg Times*, January 10, 1993, 1D.

78. John Kennedy, "Prison System Near Gridlock," *Sun Sentinel*, March 7, 1993, A1.

79. The 21,000 prison bed plan was actually a revision of Chiles's original proposal, which included only 3,600 new prison beds. This plan was quickly criticized by sheriffs and state's attorneys as not building enough new space for prisoners, and Chiles just as quickly modified his proposal. Olinger, "Prisons: A Prison System Nobody Points to with Pride," 1D; Diane Rado, "Chiles Now Wants Big Expansion of Prisons," *St. Petersburg Times*, February 17, 1993, 1B.

80. Rado, "Chiles Now Wants Big Expansion of Prisons," 1B.

81. Gov. Chiles letter to Fraternal Order of Police, March 26, 1992, S1946, 16, FSA.

82. See, for example, Beth Muniz, "Rapist to Be Freed Early," *Bradenton Herald*, April 28, 1993, B1.

83. Laura Cassels, "Early Release Boosts Crime, Study Shows 481 Inmates Released," *Fort Pierce Tribune*, May 8, 1993, B1.

84. Sandra Mathers, "STOP: Felons Should Stay In," *Orlando Sentinel*, April 25, 1993, B1.

85. Monica Davey, "Prison Bed Expansion Focus of Marchers," *St. Petersburg Times*, May 9, 1993, 1.

86. The widow of the Metro-Dade police officer killed by Charlie Street also lobbied on behalf of the cigarette tax. Charlotte Sutton, "Keep Convicts In, Officer's Widow Pleads," *St. Petersburg Times*, March 31, 1993, 4B.

87. Laura Griffin, "Governor Solicits Solutions on Prisons," *St. Petersburg Times*, January 30, 1993, 1B.

88. Colburn, *From Yellow Dog Democrats to Red State Republicans*, 134.

89. Florida Senate Staff Analysis and Economic Impact Statement for Committee Substitute for House Bill 1824, March 17, 1993, S18, Box 1979, FSA.

90. Michael Griffin, "Wanted: New Taxes for Jails—Chiles and the Host of 'America's Most Wanted' Rally Supporters in Orlando for the Governor's Prison Building Program," *Orlando Sentinel*, May 23, 1993, B1.

91. Bill Moss, "Question Now Is How to Pay for Prisons," *St. Petersburg Times*, May 29, 1993, 1B.

92. *Journal of the Senate*, State of Florida, April 1993, 11.

93. Fla. Sess. Laws, ch. 93-406 (1993), 2919.

94. The bill repealed mandatory minimums for *purchase* or *possession* of drugs one thousand feet from a school, violence against law enforcement, assault on an older person, and use of a destructive device. But it retained mandatory minimum of three and eight years for possession of firearms during commission of felony (Fla. Stat. § 775.087 [1995]), three years for *sale* of drugs within one thousand feet of a school (Fla. Stat. § 893.13 [1995]), and fifteen and twenty-five years for drug trafficking (Fla. Stat. § 893.135 [1995]). The habitual offender laws were tightened by taking out drug crimes as qualifying offenses and requiring state's attorneys to develop uniform standards for application. Finally, the new law required that released drug offenders be put in treatment programs (but money for drug treatment was not funded on an ongoing basis).

95. Fla. Sess. Laws, ch. 93-406 (1993), 2968. In 1989 the legislature had passed a law that allowed the state to use contract prisons, but the 1993 law created the mechanism to move forward. The law required that privately contracted prisons provide 7 percent savings. In 1994, the Correctional Privatization Commission contracted with the Correctional Corporation of America and Wackenhut to build and operate three prisons.

96. Fla. Sess. Laws, ch. 93-406 (1993), 2922.

97. The Correctional Privatization Commission (CPC) issued three bonds (Certificates of Participation) for a total of $72 million for lease purchase agreements with Corrections Corporation of America and Wackenhut to build three prisons. The agreements give the bond proceeds to the companies to build the prisons. The debt service is paid by the state through annual appropriations. At the end of the term of the lease the CPC owns the facilities.

98. Editorial, "A Test for Gov. Chiles," *St. Petersburg Times*, August 28, 1991, 12A.

99. Author interview with Wilson Barnes, Tallahassee branch of the NAACP, March 23, 2007 (Tallahassee).

100. For example, the Community Crusade Against Drugs was established in the Miami area in 1982, but its main goal was education about the problems of drug use. In March 1990 the NAACP Southeast Regional Conference in Orlando made a point of recognizing the problem of the disproportionate number of black men in prison, but blamed it on those young men's "lack of respect and pride." Ines Davis Parrish, "Speakers Fear for Futures of Young Blacks," *Orlando Sentinel*, March 30, 1990, B1.

101. Tom Davidson, "Program Stresses Self-Help Blacks Seek to Solve Community Problems," *Sun Sentinel*, September 11, 1990, 3B.

102. Mohamed Hamaludin, "Tough Love Is at the Center of Urban League's 10-Year Focus on Kids," *Miami Times*, July 2, 1992, 1A.

103. Hamaludin, "Tough Love Is at the Center of Urban League's 10-Year Focus on Kids." In doing so, Fair may have furthered stereotypes about poor black families (and mothers). The *Miami Times* quotes Fair: "Many parents spend their income in the first few days on alcohol or very expensive food and, a few days later, have nothing to eat and their children go hungry." And "We must tell [girls] if they get pregnant, they will go to hell, not COPE [a public school for pregnant teenagers]."

104. Editorial, "Political Pawns," *Miami Times*, February 20, 1992, 4A.

105. Colburn, *From Yellow Dog Democrats to Red State Republicans*, 141.

106. Editorial, "White Stranglehold," *Miami Times*, February 6, 1992, 4A. Colburn, *From Yellow Dog Democrats to Red State Republicans*, 141, quotes State Senator Tom Slade (R. Jacksonville) as saying "the creation of every black Democratic district creates two Republican districts. Now, as far as the eye can see, Republicans will control both Houses in Florida."

107. Associated Press, "Black Students in Need of NAACP Help, Speaker Says," *St. Petersburg Times*, May 13, 1989, 2B.

108. "Senator Meek Draws Warm Praise as FAMU Confers Honorary Degree," *Miami Times*, April 30, 1992, 3A.

109. Lisa Jacques, "Liberty City Told of 'Safe Streets' Plan," *Miami Times*, May 20, 1993, 1A.

110. In 1989 a white Miami police officer had killed two young black men on Martin Luther King Day. A jury found him guilty, but an appeals court set aside the verdict because they found that the jury felt pressured because of fear that an acquittal would cause a riot. Mohamed Hamaludin, "Churches: Our Demand Is for Justice," *Miami Times*, May 14, 1992, 1A. Similarly, in 1993, the Ft. Lauderdale NAACP reported that complaints of police brutality in Broward County doubled from the prior year. Stories cataloged included everything from verbal harassment to beatings to shootings. Barry Hercules, "Lauderdale Residents Speak Out against Brutality by Area Police," *Miami Times*, January 27, 1994, 3A. Since the beating of Rodney King by Los Angeles police officers in March 1991, the historical and continued strained relationship between police officers and black citizens

had become a national topic of conversation. See National Association for the Advancement of Colored People, "Beyond Rodney King: An NAACP Report on Police Conduct and Community Relations" (Baltimore: NAACP, 1993).

111. Jacques, "Liberty City Told of 'Safe Streets' Plan," 1A; Lisa Jacques, "Killing of Tourist Sparks Crime Crackdown," *Miami Times*, September 16, 1993, 1A.

112. Lisa Jacques, "Stunned Community Outraged at Killing," *Miami Times*, April 8, 1993, 1A.

113. Jacques, "Killing of Tourist Sparks Crime Crackdown," 1A.

114. Jacques, "Killing of Tourist Sparks Crime Crackdown," 1A.

115. Lisa L. Miller, *The Perils of Federalism: Race, Poverty, and the Politics of Crime Control* (New York: Oxford University Press, 2008).

116. While the NAACP had branches in Florida as early as 1915 and was active in the civil rights movement, there was no state field office with paid staff starting in 1972. In the early 1980s, the national office attempted a recruiting drive in Florida because its statewide membership was at a low of ten thousand (compared to fifteen thousand in the less populated state of Georgia). See Walter T. Howard and Virginia M. Howard, "Family, Religion, and Education: A Profile of African-American Life in Tampa, Florida, 1900–1930," *Journal of Negro History* 79 (1994): 1–17, and "NAACP Meeting Set Tonight," *Daytona Beach Morning Journal*, April 6, 1972, 7.

117. PULSE demanded a lot from the police and also supported taking a hardline approach to crime. In 1993 after a long violent summer, the Rev. Rommie Loudd, president of PULSE, kicked off an anticrime campaign, stating: "It's time for the citizens of our community to put the heat on criminals. It's time to hold ourselves and the police department accountable for the rampant crime and fear that we face daily. We no longer can allow crime to go on unchallenged." As part of this campaign, PULSE created a system in which people could report crime anonymously directly to the organization (who would then give it to the police). This addressed both people's mistrust of going directly to the police and fear of reprisals. See "PULSE Is Seeking Support in Campaign against Crime," *Miami Times*, August 26, 1993, 1A.

118. Miller, *The Perils of Federalism*, 103.

119. Lisa L. Miller, "The Invisible Black Victim: How American Federalism Perpetuates Racial Inequality in Criminal Justice," *Law and Society Review* 44 (2010): 805–42.

120. "First Annual Report of the Florida Commission on African American Affairs" (Tallahassee, 1994), SLF.

121. Author interview with Tom Herndon, former legislative and gubernatorial staff, May 7, 2007.

122. Author interview with Harry Singletary, former Secretary of the Florida Department of Corrections, May 7, 2007.

123. "Cities Calling for More Prison Beds," *St. Petersburg Times*, January 6, 1994, 4B; In September, a British tourist was shot to death at a rest stop on Inter-

state 10, about thirty-five miles east of Tallahassee, becoming the ninth foreign tourist killed in Florida in 1993. Larry Rohter, "Tourist Is Killed in Florida Despite Taking Precautions," *New York Times*, September 9, 1993. Data later showed that the violent crime rate had gone down slightly in 1993, although it was still 159 percent higher than the national average. FBI Uniform Crime Report Data online, 1994, http://ucrdatatool.gov. The murder rate was actually down by 25 percent since the late 1980s. Florida Department of Law Enforcement, "Crime in Florida, 1971–2015" (Tallahassee: FDLE, 2016).

124. *Journal of the House of Representatives*, State of Florida, Regular Session, February 1994, 5.

125. Gallagher's proposal relied on a penny sales tax increase that would bring in $1.7 billion more in revenue a year. Bush's $786 million prison construction program, which would allow offenders to serve 85 percent of their sentences, did not raise taxes.

126. *Journal of the House of Representatives*, State of Florida, February 1994, 5.

127. The State Republican Committee ran TV advertisements rebuking Governor Chiles for "devoting only 6 percent of total state spending to the prisons." Bill Cotterell, "Polls Don't Speak Volumes to Lawmakers," *Tallahassee Democrat*, April 6, 1994, B4.

128. Jill Jorden Spitz, "Group's Goal Is to End Prisoners' Early Release," *Orlando Sentinel*, July 3, 1993, 1.

129. "Tell Officials to Stop Turning Out Criminals," *Orlando Sentinel*, August 25, 1993, 4.

130. For example, in a meeting in Gainesville in July 1993, the victim assistance administrator for the Department of Corrections told the local STOP chapter that offenders were still eligible for too much gain-time—despite the fact that offenders sentenced to prison after January 1994 would not receive any basic gain-time. Donya Currie, "STOP Aims to Keep Prisoners Behind Bars," *Ocala Star-Banner*, July 30, 1993, 2B.

131. Associated Press, "Mack Calls for End to Early Prison Releases," *Bradenton Herald*, December 10, 1993, A8. The number of 85 percent was in part motivated by a federal crime bill under consideration (supported by Senator Mack) that would allow states to send prisoners to a regional prison system if they required offenders to serve 85 percent of their sentences.

132. "Cities Calling for More Prison Beds," *St. Petersburg Times*, January 6, 1994, 4B.

133. Author interview with Al Shopp, business and services director, Florida Police Benevolent Association, May 9, 2007 (Tallahassee); author interview with former State Representative Robert Trammell, D. Marianna, May 2, 2007 (Tallahassee).

134. Bill Cotterell, "Can Lawmakers Stop Talk to 'Walk the Walk'?" *Tallahassee Democrat*, March 4, 1994, 5C.

135. Sen. Ron Silver, D. North Miami Beach, chairman of the Senate Criminal Justice Committee as quoted in Bill Cotterell, "Polls Don't Speak Volumes to Lawmakers," *Tallahassee Democrat*, April 6,1994, B4.

136. Letter from Brian Berkowitz to Patsy Palmer, October 22, 1993, S1566, Box 1, FSA. The Task Force for Review of the Criminal Justice and Corrections Systems, appointed by Governor Chiles in 1993, attempted to look at the issue from all sides. However, their ultimate recommendation was to build more prisons. Author interview with Brian Berkowitz. The task force heard testimony from Dr. James Austin that discredited the connection between increased incarceration and lower crime rates. And they heard testimony from Dr. John DiIulio, who argued that the only thing known to lower crime is locking up more offenders. Task Force on Criminal Justice and Corrections, Meeting Agenda and Minutes, August 19, 1993. The task force also read a report by Sven Johnson, "The Relationship between Crime Rates and Incarceration Rates" (Tallahassee: Leroy Collins Center for Public Policy, 1994), and the Ben Wattenberg editorial, "Crime Solution—Lock 'Em Up," *Washington Post*, December 17, 1993, S1566, Box 1, FSA.

137. Garland, *Culture of Control*, 136. Senate staff recommended that the chair of the task force read Wilson and Herrnstein's book. S1566, Box 1, FSA.

138. Dana Peck, "Work is Held Up by Senate's Bid to Teach Morality," *Tallahassee Democrat*, March 31, 1994, 4B.

139. Task Force for the Review of the Criminal Justice and Corrections Systems, Interim Report (Tallahassee, 1994), SLF.

140. Dana Peck and Bill Cotterell, "Session Ends But Doubts Remain, the Legislature Has Made Promises, but Found Few Ways to Fulfill Them," *Tallahassee Democrat*, April 17, 1994, A1; Trammell interview.

141. Florida Department of Corrections, *1993–1994 Annual Report* (Tallahassee, 1994), 15, FDC.

142. The department instituted an accelerated prison building program using prefabricated concrete prison cells in 1993 that reduced the time it took to construct a new prison from twelve to five months. Florida Department of Corrections, *1994–1995 Annual Report* (Tallahassee, 1995), 2, FDC.

143. Florida Department of Corrections, *1994–1995 Annual Report*. In a preliminary report on the impact of Sentencing Guidelines (which went into effect January 1, 1994), the Department of Corrections found they were having the desired impact: overall, judges were sentencing less people to prison, but more violent offenders, and all offenders were serving more of their sentences. Florida Department of Corrections, Bureau of Planning, Research and Statistics, "Statistical Analysis for the Sentencing Guidelines Commission" (Tallahassee, 1995), FSA.

144. Associated Press, "Early Release Is History," *Bradenton Herald*, December 9, 1994, F1.

145. Diane Hirth, "Chiles Bars Early Outs for Inmates." *Orlando Sentinel*, December 9, 1994, A1.

146. The effort to create more black legislative districts "gained black Democrats legislative members but lost them influence over public policy" by helping to facilitate the rise of Republican political power at the state level. Colburn, *From Yellow Dog Democrats to Red State Republicans*, 141.

147. Malcolm M. Feeley, "Crime, Social Order, and the Rise of Neo-conservative Politics," *Theoretical Criminology* 7 (2003): 111–30. As evidence, Gov. Chiles cited voters' approval of a constitutional amendment that limited the growth of state spending. Article 7, section 1 of the Florida Constitution limits each year's state revenue above the previous year to the average annual growth in Floridians' personal income during the previous twenty quarters.

148. Gov. Chiles budget proposal increased state spending by less than 3 percent—the smallest increase in spending in twenty years. It included $96.5 million to increase prison capacity to allow violent offenders to serve, on average, 85 percent of their sentences. Bill Cotterell and Mickey Higginbotham, "Chiles' Budget Places Crime over Education," *Tallahassee Democrat*, January 20, 1995, A1.

149. The court ruled that "at worst, it misleads voters into believing that the amendment is ironclad," but could instead lead to renewed federal lawsuits or new executive forms of early release. Associated Press, "Court Rejects Prison Terms Amendment," *Orlando Sentinel*, July 8, 1994, C1.

150. Florida Department of Corrections, "Report on Increasing Lawful Capacity to 150%," January 11, 1995, S18, Box 2162, FSA.

151. Associated Press, "Early Release is History," F1.

152. Charlie Crist, "Voters' Frustration with Crime Will Guide Reform," *St. Petersburg Times*, February 5, 1995, 2.

153. Charlie Crist, "Voters' Frustration with Crime Will Guide Reform."

154. Lawmakers would have pushed for a 100 percent time-served requirement, but the Department of Corrections insisted that it needed to be able to award some incentive for good behavior. Singletary interview; author interview with former state senator Victor Crist (R. Tampa), September 9, 2008, Tampa.

155. Sabrina Miller, "More Prisons and Tougher Time," *St. Petersburg Times*, May 5, 1995, 1A.

156. Rep. Alex Villalobos (R. Miami), who worked as a defense attorney, recalled that the early release program had "gotten so bad" that defense attorneys would carry a slip of paper around with them that calculated the actual time an offender would serve if they pled to a certain sentence. He campaigned on the issue, he said, because felt that the system should be honest. Author interview with former House representative Alex Villalobos, September 25, 2008, Miami.

157. Florida House of Representatives, "Florida's Criminal Justice System: What Shapes Policy? What Would Enhance Accountability?" (1995), 6, SLF.

158. Adam Yeomans, "STOP Bill Goes to Chiles," *Tallahassee Democrat*, May 5, 1995, 6B.

159. Author interview with Representative Al Lawson (D. Tallahassee), May 14, 2007, Tallahassee.

160. Author interview with former state representative Robert Trammell, May 2, 2007, Tallahassee.

161. Author interview with Richard Stevens, former director, Florida Criminal Justice Estimating Conference, May 10, 2007, Tallahassee. In the end, the legislature funded approximately 3,500 new beds for 1995–1996.

162. Between 1996 and 2001, Florida received federal grants of $237 million for 1,751 juvenile and 5,922 adult prison bed spaces. Bureau of Justice Assistance, VOITIS Projects by State and Territory, https://www.bja.gov/Programs/voitis/Florida.pdf.

163. Associated Press, "Chiles Vetoes Total $100-million," *St. Petersburg Times*, June 17, 1995, A1.

164. Author interview with Ray Wilson, former staff director, Senate Corrections Committee (1974–1994), May 16, 2007, Tallahassee.

165. Mark Silva and Tim Nickens, "State Budget Hits Poor Most, Helps Prisons," *Miami Herald*, May 11, 1995, A1.

166. Miami Herald Staff, "No New Taxes, Lots of New Prison Beds," *Miami Herald*, May 12, 1995, 1A.

167. Since 1990, the percentage of the state budget that went to universities had decreased by over 5 percent. In 1995, the budget for 200,000 university students was $1.1 billion, versus $1.4 billion for 60,000 state prisoners. Stephen Hegarty, "Lawmakers 'Investing in Failure,' Chancellor Says," *St. Petersburg Times*, May 23, 1995, 6B.

168. By cutting social services and education, the legislature was able to fund 3,552 new prison beds ($80 million), operating costs for the 17,000 prison beds expected to come on line in 1995–96 ($219.5 million), 2,942 new Department of Corrections positions, and a 6 percent pay raise for corrections officers (teachers received only a 3 percent raise). Mark Silva and Tim Nickens, "Prisons, Courts Top Spending List," *Miami Herald*, April 7, 1995, A28.

169. For example, the state's attorney for Miami-Dade County worked to establish the Miami Drug Treatment Court in 1989.

170. For example, in the 1989 *Sun Sentinel* series mentioned at the beginning of the chapter, of the twenty-three offenders pictured, fourteen were identifiable as black. Research on media portrayal of offenders and victims find that these disparities are greater for TV news. Robert Reiner, Sonia Livingstone, and Jessica Allen, "From Law and Order to Lynch Mobs: Crime News since the Second World War," *Criminal Visions: Media Representations of Crime and Justice*, ed. Paul Mason (New York: Routledge, 2013), 13–32. In a content analysis of evening news programs in Tallahassee in 1995, Florida State University criminologists found that

the most common TV news victim was a white female. Ted Chiricos, Sarah Es-chholz, and Marc Gertz, "Crime, News and Fear of Crime: Toward an Identifica-tion of Audience Effects," *Social Problems* 44 (3) (1997): 353.

171. Jacques, "Killing of Tourist Sparks Crime Crackdown," 1A.

172. Jacques, "Stunned Community Outraged at Killing" *Miami Times*, April 8, 1993, 1A; Michael Javen Fortner, *Black Silent Majority: The Rockefeller Drug Laws and the Politics of Punishment* (Cambridge: Harvard University Press, 2015).

173. Frymer, *Uneasy Alliances*.

174. Alexander, *The New Jim Crow*, 212.

175. For example, the two white Democrats who I interviewed who were active during this time both told me that the one black legislator in the room was the only one who brought up the issue of black overrepresentation during conversations and meetings about legislation.

176. Florida House of Representatives, "Florida's Criminal Justice System: What Shapes Policy? What Would Enhance Accountability?" (Tallahassee, 1995).

177. Wilson interview.

178. Loïc Wacquant, *Punishing the Poor: The Neoliberal Government of Social Insecurity* (Raleigh, NC: Duke University Press, 2009), 58.

179. Ken Kopczynski, *Private Capitol Punishment: The Florida Model* (Bloom-ington, IN: Ken Kopczynski, 2004).

Chapter 6

1. Author interview with Ray Wilson, former Staff Director, Senate Corrections Committee, May 16, 2007, Tallahassee, FL.

2. David Garland, *The Culture of Control: Crime and Social Order in Contem-porary Society* (Chicago: University of Chicago Press, 2001), 192.

3. Jonathan Simon documents how the carceral ethos spread to other policy domains, such as family relations, education, and even work conditions. Jonathan Simon, *Governing through Crime: How the War on Crime Transformed American Democracy and Created a Culture of Fear* (Oxford: Oxford University Press, 2007).

4. Philip Goodman, Joshua Page, and Michelle Phelps, "The Long Struggle: An Agonistic Perspective on Penal Development," *Theoretical Criminology* 19 (3) (2014): 315–35.

5. Simon, *Governing through Crime*.

6. Joshua Page, *The Toughest Beat: Politics, Punishment, and the Prison Officers Union in California* (New York: Oxford University Press, 2011); Michael C. Camp-bell, "Ornery Alligators and Soap on a Rope: Texas Prosecutors and Punishment Reform in the Lone Star State," *Theoretical Criminology* 16 (3) (2011): 289–311.

7. Charlie Crist, "Voters' Frustration with Crime Will Guide Reform," *St. Pe-tersburg Times*, February 5, 1995, 2.

8. Bill Moss, "Chiles' Budget Bows to 'Realities,'" *St. Petersburg Times*, January 20, 1995, 1B.

9. Crist, "Voters' Frustration with Crime Will Guide Reform." At the time, three-fourths of work-eligible prisoners had work or program assignments. Florida House of Representatives Committee on Corrections, "Corrections Issues Orientation Package" (Tallahassee: Florida House of Representatives, 1996), SLF; author interview with Wilson Bell, former deputy director of the Florida Department of Corrections, April 25, 2007, Gainesville.

10. Florida Legislature, 28th Regular Session, SB 2944.

11. In the eight Florida newspapers with the largest circulation, Charlie Crist and his chain gang proposal were mentioned in over one hundred news stories in 1995. Calculated from Newsbank.

12. Curtis Krueger, "In Race for Senate, a Battle of Opposites—Charlie Crist," *St. Petersburg Times*, October 12, 1998, 1A.

13. Mireya Navarro, "Florida to Resume Chain Gangs; Rules on Shackles Are Criticized," *New York Times*, November 21, 1995.

14. Author interview with Jim Tillman, former state representative, May 10, 2007, Tallahassee.

15. Bill Cotterell, "Chain Gang Spat Erupts," *Tallahassee Democrat*, September 19, 1995, A1.

16. Harry Singletary, *Correctional Compass*, July 1994, HSP.

17. Nicole Winfield, "State's Prisoners Step Back in Time," *Tallahassee Democrat*, November 22, 1995, 1A.

18. Democrat News Services, "Legislator Wants Links Added to Chain-Gang Law," *Tallahassee Democrat*, August 8, 1996, 6B. Florida Legislature, 29th Regular Session, SB122.

19. Author interview with Allen Trovillion, former state representative, January 8, 2008, Maitland.

20. Trovillion interview.

21. Shirsh Date, "Committee Kills Idea to Have Felons Do Road Work," *Tallahassee Democrat*, May 1, 1997, 3B.

22. Brent Kallestad, "Long-shot Crist Challenges Graham." *Tallahassee Democrat*, August 10, 1997, 3B.

23. Sen. Malcolm Beard, chair of the Senate Committee on Corrections, to Harry Singletary, August 4, 1994, S18, Box 2090, FSA.

24. Florida Legislature, 26th Regular Session, CS/SB1320.

25. Singletary interview.

26. Florida Legislature, 28th Regular Session, SB400, SB390, HB95 (the Prison Safety Act of 1996). The legislature had earlier also banned the department from purchasing weight equipment for prisoners from the Inmate Welfare Trust Fund.

27. Louis Lavelle, "Lawmakers Aim to Make Prisons Safer, Tougher," *Tampa Tribune*, February 27, 1996, A1.The other complaint I heard in my interviews from

lawmakers (and from corrections administrators complaining about lawmakers) was about prisoners having color televisions.

28. Author interview with Al Shopp, business and services director, Florida Police Benevolent Association, May 9, 2007, Tallahassee.

29. Florida Department of Corrections, Annual reports from 1994/1995 to 1997/ 1998 (Tallahassee, FL).

30. Florida Department of Corrections, "Corrections in Florida: What the Public, News Media and DC Staff Think," http://www.dc.state.fl.us/pub/survey/index.html.

31. David Colburn, *From Yellow Dog Democrats to Red State Republicans: Florida and Its Politics since 1940* (Gainesville: University Press of Florida, 2007), 142. In the Florida House of Representatives, Republicans held sixty-three seats to Democrats' fifty-seven. In the Florida Senate, Republicans held twenty-three seats to Democrats' seventeen.

32. Florida Prosecuting Attorneys Association to Senate Committee on Criminal Justice, January 4, 1995, S18, Box 2162, FSA.

33. Author interview with Brian Berkowitz, former executive director, Task Force for Review of Criminal Justice and Corrections, May 14, 2007, Tallahassee.

34. Author interview with committee staff, September 24, 2008, Tallahassee.

35. For example, level 8 sentences mandated prison time, but in 1994 less than 60 percent of offenders convicted of level 8 crimes actually received a prison sentence. Florida House of Representatives, "Florida's Criminal Justice System: What Shapes Policy? What Would Enhance Accountability?" (Tallahassee: Florida House of Representatives, 1995).

36. Florida Prosecuting Attorneys Association to Senate Committee on Criminal Justice, January 4, 1995, S18, Box 2162, FSA.

37. Louis Lavelle, "Prisons to Refund Surplus, Admissions Drop-off Leads to Give-back." *Tampa Tribune*, January 17, 1996, A6.

38. Associated Press, "Prison Growth Rate Dropping." *Tampa Tribune*, March 12, 1997, 4.

39. Lavelle, "Prisons to Refund Surplus."

40. President of Florida Sheriffs Association to Rep. Randy Ball, January 15, 1997, S19, Box 2911, FSA.

41. Trovillion interview.

42. Author interview with Arthur "Buddy" Jacobs, lobbyist, Florida Prosecuting Attorneys Association, September 19, 2008 (phone).

43. Florida Legislature, 99th Regular Session, HB241.

44. The bill analysis cited a United States Department of Justice study that found that structured sentencing reduced sentencing disparities across similarly situated offenders. "House Committee on Crime and Punishment Bill Analysis and Economic Impact Statement of HB241," April 30, 1997, S19, Box 2909, FSA.

45. Florida House of Representatives Criminal Justice Appropriations Committee, Record of Meeting, April 11, 1997, S19, Box 2909, FSA.

46. Rep. Fred Lippman (D. Hollywood) argued that "if you're going to have judges, they should have the responsibility to deal with justice the way they were taught to deal with it." Lavelle, "Lawmakers Aim to Make Prisons Safer, Tougher."

47. According to the House Committee on Crime and Punishment Bill Analysis, under the 1994 Guidelines an offender would receive seven convictions for possession of cocaine and five for sale before being sentenced to state prison (assuming no other prior offenses). "House Committee on Crime and Punishment Bill Analysis and Economic Impact Statement of HB241."

48. Jacobs interview.

49. Quoted in Pamala L. Griset, "New Sentencing Laws Follow Old Patterns: A Florida Case Study," *Journal of Criminal Justice 30* (2002): 296.

50. The House Committee on Crime and Punishment Bill Analysis reports that many judges opposed guidelines because they "reduce issues of justice and fairness to a mathematical formula." However, no judge testified before the committee.

51. "House Committee on Crime and Punishment Bill Analysis and Economic Impact Statement of HB241."

52. *Calamia v. Singletary*, 694 So 2d 733 (1997).

53. Shirish Date, "Bill Targets Repeat Offenders," *Tallahassee Democrat*, March 19, 1997, 3B.

54. Margaret Talev, "House Plan Calls for Judges to Issue Full Sentences for Repeat Offenders," *Tampa Tribune*, March 19, 1997, 6.

55. *Prison Releasee Reoffender Act*, Florida Legislature, 99th Regular Session, HB1371.

56. Griset, "New Sentencing Laws Follow Old Patterns," 287–301.

57. Talev, "House Plan Calls for Judges to Issue Full Sentences for Repeat Offenders."

58. Margaret Talev, "Crime Bills Target Expansion of Prisons," *Tampa Tribune*, May 4, 1997, 6.

59. T. Christian Miller, "Tough Crime Measure Sent to Governor," *St. Petersburg Times*, May 3, 1997, 4B.

60. *Journal of the House of Representatives*, State of Florida, May 2, 1997, 1891; *Journal of the Senate*, State of Florida, May 1, 1997, 1262.

61. "New Laws Tough on Criminals, Teens," *Sarasota Herald-Tribune*, May 30, 1997, 3B. The Democrats did not completely lose out during the legislative session. The approved budget added approximately $2.5 billion more than the previous year, allowing Democrats to appropriate money to some of their priorities, including increased per-pupil school spending and an additional $20 million for both Chiles's "Healthy Kids" insurance program for the poor and programs to address juvenile crime. Bill Cotterell, "GOP Legislature Pats Itself on Back," *Tallahassee Democrat*, May 3, 1997, A1.

62. Author interview with Frank Messersmith, lobbyist, Florida Sheriffs Association, September 22, 2008, Tallahassee.

63. Mary Ellen Klas, "Legislators Propose Increasing Term Limits," *Miami Herald*, November 20, 2015.

64. Author interview with Alex Villalobos, former chair, House Criminal Justice Appropriations Committee, September 25, 2008, Miami.

65. Author interview with anonymous legislative committee staff, September 24, 2008, Tallahassee.

66. Tom Feeney, "Principles Matter: Policy Making Based on First Principles," *Notre Dame Journal of Law Ethics and Public Policy* 20 (2006): 365.

67. Author interview with Victor Crist, former chair, Florida Legislature Justice Council, September 29, 2008, Tampa.

68. Author interview with Amanda Cannon, staff director, Senate Criminal Justice Committee, May 14, 2007, Tallahassee.

69. Colleen J. Shogan, "Anti-intellectualism in the Modern Presidency: A Republican Populism," *Perspectives on Politics* 5 (2) (2007): 295–303.

70. Author interview with Richard Stevens, former director, Criminal Justice Estimating Conference, May 10, 2007, Tallahassee. Stevens recalls a particular incident in 2006 when an academic journal asked him to participate in a panel on "the research used by the state in deciding to implement electronic monitoring." He had to decline the invitation because "as far as we knew . . . the Florida legislature didn't review the research." Instead, electronic monitoring passed because it sounded good and could be done within the legal structure of the 85 percent law.

71. Anonymous interview.

72. Cannon interview.

73. Stevens interview.

74. Loïc Wacquant, *Punishing the Poor: The Neoliberal Government of Social Insecurity* (Raleigh, NC: Duke University Press, 2009), 306–7; Katherine Beckett, *Making Crime Pay: Law and Order in Contemporary American Politics* (New York: Oxford University Press, 1997).

75. This is not to suggest that actors' motivations are single, unchanging, or entirely discernable. Richard Biernacki, "The Action Turn? Comparative-Historical Inquiry beyond the Classic Models of Conduct," in *Remaking Modernity: Politics, History, and Sociology*, ed. Julia Adams, Elisabeth S. Clemens, and Ann Shola Orloff (Durham: Duke University Press, 2005), 75–91.

76. Timothy Griffin and Monica K. Miller, "Child Abduction, AMBER Alert, and Crime Control Theater," *Criminal Justice Review* 33 (2008): 159–76.

77. Joseph R. Gusfield, *Symbolic Crusade: Status Politics and the American Temperance Movement* (Urbana: University of Illinois Press, 1963). Governor Bush also engaged in symbolic politics when he interfered in the case of Terri Schiavo, a Florida woman in a persistent vegetative state whose husband wanted to take her off life support after over ten years. Governor Bush used his office to keep Schiavo alive as a symbol of his ideological commitments. Colburn, *From Yellow Dog Democrats*, 212.

78. Colburn, *From Yellow Dog Democrats*, 165.

79. Molly Ball, "Is This What Post-partisanship Looks Like?" *Atlantic*, March 11, 2014.

80. David R. Colburn, "Take-charge Charlie," *Orlando Sentinel*, February 25, 2007, http://articles.orlandosentinel.com/2007-02-25/news/COLBURN25_1_charlie -crist-jeb-bush-observed.

81. Hugh Heclo, *Modern Social Politics in Britain and Sweden: From Relief to Income Maintenance* (New Haven: Yale University Press, 1974). Some of the information used by Florida legislators came from sources with neoliberal agendas, such as the American Legislative Exchange Council (ALEC). Crist interview.

82. Simon, *Governing through Crime*, 155.

83. John Matthews, "Wilson Vetoes Ban on Cheap Handguns," *Sacramento Bee*, September 27, 1997, A1.

84. According to one newspaper account, the Bush campaign discussed his proposal and how to sell it to the public with Mike Reynolds, who told reporters that "the plan appeals to Republicans who fear upsetting powerful special interests such as the National Rifle Association but want to look tough on crime." Peter Wallsten, "Bush Targets Gun Use in Crime," *St. Petersburg Times*, September 23, 1998, 1A.

85. Peter Wallsten, "Spot Check," *St. Petersburg Times*, October 24, 1997, 8B.

86. Crist interview. This statement contradicts others Crist made during the interview, such as that most juveniles are capable of change.

87. House Committee on Crime and Punishment, Minutes, January 6, 1999, S19, Box 2982, FSA.

88. Florida Department of Corrections, *10-20-Life Criminals Sentenced to Florida's Prisons* (Tallahassee, 2007), http://www.dc.state.fl.us/pub/10-20-life/index .html.

89. House Committee on Corrections, Minutes, January 20 1999, S19, Box 2979, FSA.

90. The bill included a reporting requirement for state's attorneys similar to one passed under the Prison Releasee Reoffender Act. The original bill analysis for 10-20-life makes clear that the reporting requirement was meant to ensure that state's attorneys charge people under the law and make them "more accountable" if they didn't: "since the state attorneys are elected officials, the reports could be used by political opponents to show a lack of willingness to impose the minimum mandatory sentences." "House Committee on Crime and Punishment Bill Analysis and Economic Impact Statement of HB113," S19, Box 2982, FSA.

91. Author interview with anonymous legislative committee staff, September 24, 2008, Tallahassee, FL.

92. Governor's Office of Policy and Budget, "Legislative Bill Analysis of HB113," March 13, 1999, S2104, FSA.

93. Messersmith interview.

94. Trovillion interview.

95. Governor's Office of Policy and Budget, "Legislative Bill Analysis of HB113"; Colburn, *From Yellow Dog Democrats to Red State Republicans*, 162.

96. Nancy C. Roberts and Paula J. King, "Policy Entrepreneurs: Their Activity Structure and Function in the Policy Process," *Journal of Public Administration Research and Theory* 1 (1991): 147–75.

97. T. Christian Miller, "Lawmakers Split on Juvenile Crime," *St. Petersburg Times*, April 18, 1997, 7B.

98. Villalobos interview.

99. At the time his counterpart in the Senate, Sen. Ron Silver (D. North Miami Beach) is quoted as saying, "If we had extra dollars, we could deal with prevention, but I don't think people want these kids on the street." Miller, "Lawmakers Split on Juvenile Crime."

100. In 2004, Villalobos supported a ballot initiative for a constitutional amendment that limited class size even though Governor Bush opposed the amendment. At the time, Florida ranked forty-third in the nation in per-student funding, and Villalobos believed that public education needed more resources. Kids Count Data Center, "Per-pupil Educational Expenditures Adjusted for Regional Cost Differences," http://datacenter.kidscount.org/data/tables/5199-per-pupil-educational -expenditures-adjusted-for-regional-cost-differences#ranking/2/any/true/15/any /11678. When Governor Bush attempted to weaken the class-size amendment approved by voters, Villalobos actively opposed his initiative. As a result, Bush stripped Villalobos of his election to the majority leader's position in the Senate and campaigned against him. Colburn, *From Yellow Dog Democrats to Red State Republicans*, 209. Villalobos told me that overnight they had moved his office into "a closet."

101. Villalobos interview. The *Miami Herald* "Naked Politics" blog confirms the use of Bundy in an attack mailer. "Naked Politics: Move Over Hillary, Here's Bundy," *Miami Herald*, July 31, 2006.

102. Villalobos interview.

103. Villalobos interview.

104. Crist interview. The brand they developed was the name "suitcase city," which dramatized the claim that the transient nature of the population had caused the area's decline in quality of life for all residents.

105. Crist interview.

106. The Justice Council was established in 1998 as the umbrella committee for all substantive justice committees. The council prioritized all the criminal justice bills for the session.

107. Crist interview.

108. Governor's Office of Policy and Budget, "Legislative Bill Analysis of HB121," June 8, 1999, S2104, FSA.

109. Fla. Sess. Laws, ch. 99-188 (1999).

110. Crist interview.

111. *Journal of the Florida House of Representatives*, State of Florida, April 26, 1999, 1129.

112. Governor's Office of Policy and Budget, "Legislative Bill Analysis of HB 121."

113. Peter W. Greenwood et al., "Three Strikes Revisited: An Early Assessment of Implementation and Effects" (Santa Monica: RAND, 1998).

114. "House Committee on Corrections Bill Analysis and Economic Impact Statement of HB 121," S19, Box 2979, FSA. In 2005, the California Legislative Analyst's Office estimated that three strikes *cost* the state $500 million per year. Solomon Moore, "The Prison Overcrowding Fix." *New York Times*, February 11, 2009.

115. Crist interview.

116. Crist interview.

117. Crist interview.

118. Marie Gottschalk, *Caught: The Prison State and the Lockdown of American Politics* (Princeton: Princeton University Press, 2015), 196.

119. Wacquant, *Punishing the Poor*, 214.

120. David Krajicek, "The Abduction of Carlie Brucia," http://murderpedia.org/male.S/s/smith-joseph-peter.htm.

121. Tatiana Morales, "Mechanic Charged in Carlie's Death," *CBS News*, February 6, 2004.

122. Curtis Krueger, Richard Raeke, and Dong-Phuong Nguyen, "The Problem with Probation," *St. Petersburg Times*, June 13, 2004.

123. House of Representatives Staff Analysis, HB 1877 CS, April 15, 2005.

124. Kevin Graham, "Sheriff: Sex Offender Says He Killed Teen," *Tampa Bay Times*, April 18, 2005.

125. Stephen Majors, "Bill Targets Probation Offenders," *Bradenton Herald*, March 10, 2005, 1C.

126. Florida Legislature, 37th Regular Session, HB451 and CS/SB608. Both bills died in Justice Appropriations. They cited the $350 to $630 million costs in additional court and prison resources.

127. Miami-Dade Circuit judge Stanford Blake, quoted in Scott Hiaasen, "Costly Bill Targets Violent Felons," *Miami Herald*, April 4, 2005, 1B.

128. Adam Smith, "Crist Sets Off Race for governor," *St. Petersburg Times*, May 10, 2005, 1B.

129. Steve Bousquet, "Crist Sticking to His Theme," *St. Petersburg Times*, June 22, 2006, 1B.

130. "The Anti-Murder Act," *St. Petersburg Times*, April 27, 2006, 14A; Charlie Crist, "Anti-Murder Act Is a Sound Way to Protect State Residents," *St. Petersburg Times*, May 3, 2006, 10A.

131. Bousquet, "Crist Sticking to His Theme."

132. Bousquet, "Crist Sticking to His Theme."

133. Steve Bousquet, "Crist, the NRA's Choice," *St. Petersburg Times: Blogs*, August 8, 2006.

134. Colburn, *From Yellow Dog Democrats*, 214.

135. Senate Democratic leader Steve Geller (D. Hallandale Beach) stated to a reporter after the election, "I have now spent about three hours discussing issues with Governor Crist—that's about 2½ hours more than I ever spent with Governor Bush in eight years." Mary Ellen Klas, "Crist Setting Early Bipartisan Tone," *Miami Herald*, December 31, 2006, 1B. Two months into his term, the same reporter wrote that in Crist's first address to the legislature, in addition to "familiar populist themes of property taxes, crime and education," Crist "embraced a host of Democratic ideas traditionally shunned by Florida's GOP leaders," including paying for limited class sizes, teacher salary hikes, and climate change. Mary Ellen Klas, "Crist: Progress, Not Politics," *Miami Herald*, March 7, 2007, 1A. In April, Crist also streamlined the process to restore voting rights to many nonviolent former felons. Erika L. Wood, *Florida: An Outlier in Denying Voting Rights* (New York: Brennan Center for Justice, 2016), https://www.brennancenter.org/sites/de fault/files/publications/Florida_Voting_Rights_Outlier.pdf.

136. Shannon Colavecchio-Van Sickler, "Crist's Hard Line on Crime Pricey," *Tampa Bay Times*, March 3, 2007; Michael Echter, "Crist Faces 'Gnawing Issues'— Property Taxes, Insurance Urgent," *Tampa Tribune*, January 2, 2007, 10.

137. "Anti-Murder Bill a Political Hit That Killers Will Not Notice," *Tampa Tribune*, February 8, 2007, 14.

138. Office of the Governor, State of Florida, "Press Release: Governor Crist Signs Anti-Murder Act," March 12, 2007.

139. Fla. Stat. § 948.06 (2008).

140. Florida Senate, Criminal and Civil Justice Appropriations Committee, Staff Analysis and Economic Impact Statement on CS/CS/SB 146, February 23, 2007.

141. Author interview with Ecitrym LaMarr, executive director, Florida Conference of Black State Legislators, June 1, 2007, Tallahassee.

142. I found no evidence that any civil rights, community organization, or national advocacy organization testified or advocated against the 1997 guideline changes, 10-20-life, or three strikes. ACLU staff did question the wisdom of the Anti-Murder Act given the required new bed commitment. Florida ACLU, 2007 Florida Legislative Session Summary, June 1, 2007, https://aclufl.org/2007/. The black caucus looked for supportive allies in sympathetic judges, but many insisted on staying out of political debates. LaMarr interview.

143. Marc Mauer, *The Crisis of Young African American Male and the Criminal Justice System* (Washington, DC: Sentencing Project, 2000).

144. The U.S. Leadership Conference on Civil Rights, *Justice on Trial: Racial Disparities in the American Criminal Justice System* (Washington D.C., 2000), http://www.civilrights.org/publications/justice-on-trial/.

145. "House Committee on Corrections Bill Analysis and Economic Impact Statement of HB121," S19, Box 2979, FSA.

146. Governor's Office of Policy and Budget, "Legislative Bill Analysis of HB121."

147. Governor's Office of Policy and Budget, "Legislative Bill Analysis of HB113."

148. Colburn, *From Yellow Dog Democrats*, 160.

149. Desmond S. King and Rogers M. Smith, *Still a House Divided: Race and Politics in Obama's America* (Princeton: Princeton University Press, 2011).

150. Andrea Robinson, "Blacks Spurred to Rally against Policy Changes," *Miami Herald*, January 20, 2000, 11A.

151. Peter T. Kilborn, "Jeb Bush Roils Florida on Affirmative Action," *New York Times*, February 4, 2000.

152. Florida House of Representatives, Floor Debate, May 4, 2000, FSA.

153. Author interview with Bobby Brantley, former lieutenant governor of Florida, April 12, 2007, Tallahassee.

154. Victor Crist explained that the state had lowered the legal driving limit so low that he and I could receive a DUI after a few beers. He characterized the DUI laws as draconian. Other legislators or corrections officials expressed a similar sentiment in interviews. As of June 30, 2007, white prisoners were 85 percent of those in prison for DUI injury and 90 percent of those in prison for DUI no injury. Florida Department of Corrections, *2006–2007 Annual Report* (Tallahassee, 2007).

155. Florida Department of Corrections, *2006–2007 Annual Report*.

156. Ajowa Nzinga Ifateyo, "Community Leaders Spread the Word about New Gun Law," *Miami Herald*, July 1, 1999, 3NW.

157. Florida Legislature, Senate Staff Analysis and Economic Impact Statement, SB1548, March 15, 2000, FSA.

158. Jim Defede, "The Enigma," *Miami New Times*, March 8, 2001; Florida Legislature, 102nd Regular Session, SB1548, 3rd Engrossed; Governor's Office, "Talking Points: 10-20-Life for 16 and 17-Year Old Violent Criminals," n.d., FSA. Rep. Tony Suarez (D. Orlando) (a Puerto Rican lawyer originally from New York) and Rep. Alzo J. Reddick (D. Orlando) (the first African American state legislator from Orlando) proposed an unsuccessful amendment that would have required youth sentenced under the law to receive appropriate treatment and education. *Journal of the House of Representatives*, State of Florida, May 4, 2000, 1554.

159. Senate bill 1548 was passed in the Senate by a 31-to-7 vote, in the House by 96-to-20. http://www.archive.flsenate.gov.

160. Scott Fingerhut and Robert N. Scola, Jr., "Tough Times in the Sunshine State," *Florida Bar Journal* 73 (November 1999): 28; Florida Senate Criminal Justice Committee, Meeting Packet, January 19, 2016, http://www.flsenate.com.

161. William J. Stuntz, "The Pathological Politics of Criminal Law," *Michigan Law Review* 100 (3) (2001): 505–600.

162. William J. Sabol, "Implications of Criminal Justice System Adaptation for Prison Population Growth and Corrections Policy" (2011) (unpublished manuscript), http://www.albany.edu/scj/documents/Sabol_ManagingPopulations_000.pdf.

163. The decomposition analysis also reveals that the number of convictions per arrest increased during this time period for violent and property offenders, while decreasing for drugs and other offenses. While the ratio is skewed by the crime categories included in the conviction data (see appendix), the trend suggests that prosecutors used surplus resources (from reduced violent and property crime) to pursue more convictions for those crimes. Alternatively, the CPC, new mandatory minimums and habitual offender laws gave them more leverage to obtain convictions in borderline cases. In addition, it may be possible that as serious crime went down, police arrested people for less serious drug and other offenses, which prosecutors declined to prosecute.

164. Florida Department of Corrections, *Florida's Criminal Punishment Code: A Comparative Assessment, October 2000* (Tallahassee, 2000), 6.

165. Matthew S. Crow and Marc Gertz, "Sentencing Policy and Disparity: Guidelines and the Influence of Legal and Democratic Subcultures," *Journal of Criminal Justice* 36 (4) (2008): 368.

166. I use Uniform Crime Report crime categories. Violent crime includes murder, forcible sex offenses, robbery, and aggravated assault. Property crime includes burglary, larceny, and motor vehicle theft. All other non–drug related crimes fall into the "other" category. "Criminal Justice System Process" offenses (approximately 800 admissions in 2010) includes jury tampering, failure to appear, failure to register as a sex offender, probation and parole violations, smuggling contraband and perjury, among others.

167. A lack of detailed conviction data and arrest categories that align with FDOC "other" offense categories makes it difficult to separate the impact of arrests and convictions on prison admissions for specific "other" offenses.

168. Office of Economic and Demographic Research, Criminal Justice Estimating Conference, "Criminal Justice Trends," December 17, 2005 (Tallahassee), 53–54.

169. By 2000, the state was using five private prisons (3,700 beds). The facilities were beset with problems getting off the ground and did not realize the mandated 7 percent savings initially. Office of Program Policy Analysis and Government Accountability, "Follow-up Report on the Review of Correctional Privatization," September 1997, http://www.oppaga.state.fl.us/Summary.aspx?reportNum=97-06 During that time, staff and consultants for the Correctional Privatization Commission, which oversaw the contracts, were found to have violated state ethics laws by not disclosing their financial relationships or consulting positions with private prison companies or other municipalities engaged in privatization. Ken Kopczynski, *Private Capitol Punishment: The Florida Model* (Ken Kopczynski, 2004). Florida did not add any new private adult correctional facilities again until 2007.

170. FDOC, Annual Reports 1999–2000 to 2007–2008 (Tallahassee).

171. Vera Institute of Justice, "The Price of Prisons, Florida," January 2012, http://www.vera.org/files/price-of-prisons-florida-fact-sheet.pdf; Numbers are for 2009–10 appropriations. Florida Department of Education, "2009–2010 Education Budget," May 19, 2009.

172. Todd Clear, *Imprisoning Communities: How Mass Incarceration Makes Disadvantaged Neighborhoods Worse* (New York: Oxford University Press, 2007).

173. Joseph Murray, David P. Farrington, and Ivana Sekol, "Children's Antisocial Behavior, Mental Health, Drug Use, and Educational Performance after Parental Incarceration: A Systematic Review and Meta-analysis," *Psychological Bulletin* 138 (2) (2012): 175.

Chapter 7

1. Governor-Elect Rick Scott Law and Order Transition Team, *Department and Policy Review: Florida Department of Corrections*, December 2010, 2.

2. The PLRA requires inmates to fully exhaust administrative remedies before filing in federal court, limits the number of claims inmates can file, imposes new special hurdles for population orders, and caps attorney fees. Margo Schlanger, "Trends in Prisoner Litigation, as the PLRA Enters Adulthood," *University of California Irvine Law Review* 5 (1) (2015): 153–79.

3. *Brown v. Plata*, 563 U.S. 493 (2011).

4. These states are Arizona, Alabama, Illinois, Louisiana, Massachusetts, Mississippi, Nevada, Pennsylvania, Virginia, Washington, and Wisconsin. The data on lawsuits was culled from a search of PACER, Bloomberg Law, and Westlaw for Sec. 1983 8th Amendment claims that involve overcrowding, health care, or mental health care. Not included are cases that only tangentially mention overcrowding, cases challenging segregation practices, cases against private prisons, or cases where only the correctional officer or warden is being sued in their personal capacity.

5. *Flynn v. Doyle*, 672 F. Supp. 2d 858 (E.D. Wis. 2009), 866.

6. *Boyd v. Godinez*, No. 3:12-cv-704-JPG-PMF, 2013 WL 5230238 (S.D. Ill. 2013), 1.

7. *Hicks v. Hetzel*, 2:09-cv-00155-WKW-WC (M.D. Al.).

8. See, for example, DOJ Investigation of the Julia Tutwiler Prison for Women (Alabama), January 17, 2014, findings letter https://www.justice.gov/sites/default/files/crt/legacy/2014/01/23/tutwiler_findings_1-17-14.pdf, accessed on June 14, 2017.

9. Paula Dockery, "Privatizing Prisons Could Be Governor's End Game," *Tampa Tribune*, February 26, 2015.

10. George Mallinckrodt testimony to the Florida Senate Criminal Justice Committee, January 5, 2015.

11. David Dagan and Steven M. Teles, "The Social Construction of Policy Feedback: Incarceration, Conservatism, and Ideological Change," *Studies in American Political Development* 29 (2015): 127–53.

12. Newt Gingrich and Pat Nolan, "Prison Reform: A Smart Way for States to Save Money and Lives," *Washington Post*, January 7, 2011.

13. Right on Crime "Statement of Principles," http://www.rightoncrime.com /the-conservative-case-for-reform/statement-of-principles/, accessed on September 25, 2014.

14. The JRI was originally conceptualized by the Soros Foundation and in 2016 was run through both the Bureau for Justice Assistance and Council for State Governments (with continued funding from Pew Charitable Trusts) with technical assistance provided by CSG, the Vera Institute of Justice, and other research organizations. Nancy LaVigne et al. *Justice Reinvestment Initiative State Assessment Report* (Washington, DC: Urban Institute, 2014).

15. Council of State Governments, "States Receiving Technical Assistance from the CSG Justice Center," https://csgjusticecenter.org/jr/, accessed December 2015.

16. Suevon Lee, "Reformers: Council Vital to Change Sentencing Laws," *Ocala Star Banner*, April 26, 2010.

17. Peter K. Enns, *Incarceration Nation: How the United States Became the Most Punitive Democracy in the World* (New York: Cambridge University Press, 2016).

18. David Dagan and Steven Teles, *Prison Break: Why Conservatives Turned against Mass Incarceration* (New York: Oxford University Press, 2016).

19. Philip Goodman, Joshua Page, and Michelle Phelps, *Breaking the Pendulum: The Long Struggle over Criminal Justice* (New York: Oxford University Press, 2017).

20. David Dagan and Steven M. Teles, "Locked In? Conservative Reform and the Future of Mass Incarceration," *Annals of the American Academy of Political and Social Science* 651 (1) (2014): 266–76.

21. But see Marie Gottschalk, *Caught: The Prison State and the Lockdown of American Politics* (Princeton: Princeton University Press, 2015), chapter 2, which argues that corrections costs are still only 2 to 3 percent of states' total expenditures.

22. But see John Pfaff, *Locked In: The True Causes of Mass Incarceration and How to Achieve Real Reform* (New York: Basic Books, 2017), 66–68.

23. Dagan and Teles, "The Social Construction of Policy Feedback"; Gottschalk, *Caught*; and David Garland, *The Culture of Control: Crime and Social Order in Contemporary Society* (Chicago: University of Chicago Press, 2001), demonstrate that in past fiscal crises politicians constructed crackdowns on crime to ease recession-induced social anxiety.

24. Vanessa Williamson, Theda Skocpol, and John Coggin, "The Tea Party and the Remaking of Republican Conservatism," *Perspectives on Politics* 9 (1) (2011): 25–43.

25. For analysis of the financial crisis and recession see Andrew W. Lo, "Reading about the Financial Crisis: A Twenty-One-Book Review," *Journal of Economic Literature* 50 (March 2012): 151–78; Joseph E. Stiglitz, *Freefall: America, Free Markets, and the Sinking of the World Economy* (New York: W. W. Norton, 2010).

26. Theda Skocpol and Vanessa Williamson, *The Tea Party and the Remaking of Republican Conservatism* (New York: Oxford University Press, 2012), 7.

27. Skocpol and Williamson *The Tea Party and the Remaking of Republican Conservatism*, 9.

28. Williamson, Skocpol, and Coggin, "The Tea Party and the Remaking of Republican Conservatism"; Matt A. Barreto et al. "The Tea Party in the Age of Obama: Mainstream Conservatism or Out-Group Anxiety?" *Political Power and Social Theory* 22 (2011): 105–37.

29. Daniel Tope, Justin T. Pickett, and Ted Chiricos, "Anti-minority Attitudes and Tea Party Movement Membership," *Social Science Research* 51 (2015): 322–37.

30. Matthew W. Hughey and Gregory S. Parks, *The Wrongs of the Right: Language, Race, and the Republican Party in the Age of Obama* (New York: NYU Press, 2014).

31. Desmond S. King and Rogers M. Smith, "'Without Regard to Race': Critical Ideational Development in Modern American Politics," *Journal of Politics* 76 (4) (2014): 958–71.

32. King and Smith, "Without Regard to Race." For statements of the colorblind racial project see Stephan Thernstrom and Abigail Thernstrom, *America in Black and White* (New York: Simon & Schuster, 1997); Richard Herrnstein and Charles Murray, *Bell Curve: Intelligence and Class Structure in American Life* (New York: Free Press, 1994); *Gratz v. Bollinger*, 539 U.S. 244 (2003).

33. *Parents Involved in Community Schools v. Seattle School District No. 1*, 551 U.S. 701 (2007).

34. Darrel Enck-Wanzer, "Barack Obama, the Tea Party, and the Threat of Race: On Racial Neoliberalism and Born Again Racism," *Communication, Culture and Critique* 4 (2011): 23–30.

35. King and Smith, "Without Regard to Race," 958.

36. Hughey and Parks. *The Wrongs of the Right*, 7, 53.

37. Hughey and Parks, *The Wrongs of the Right*, 61; Joe R. Feagin, *White Party, White Government: Race, Class, and U.S. Politics* (New York: Routledge, 2012).

38. Skocpol and Williamson, *The Tea Party and the Remaking of Republican Conservatism*, 192.

39. Ian Haney Lopez, *Dog Whistle Politics: How Coded Racial Appeals Have Reinvented Racism and Wrecked the Middle Class* (Oxford: Oxford University Press, 2014), 167.

40. Hadar Aviram, *Cheap on Crime: Recession-Era Politics and the Transformation of American Punishment* (Berkeley: University of California Press, 2015); Dagan and Teles, "The Social Construction of Policy Feedback."

41. See, for example, Rick Scott, "It's Your Money Tax Cut Budget Announcement," n.d., http://www.flgov.com/wp-content/uploads/2014/01/Remarks1.pdf.

42. Lynne Holt and David Colburn, "Florida and Orlando: Choosing the Future after Recession," *Florida Focus* 7 (2) (May 2011).

43. In 2008 the Florida legislature passed a bill that established a Correctional Policy Advisory Council to examine alternatives to imprisonment, but it was never funded. Florida Legislature, 40th Regular Session, SB2000. They also passed legislation necessary to take advantage of American Recovery and Reinvestment Act funds to expand drug courts in four judicial districts. Florida Legislature, 41st Regular Session, CS/SB 1726. Florida Office of the State Courts Administrator, "Drug Courts in Florida," updated March 2015.

44. Florida Legislature, 41st Regular Session, CS/SB 1722; Florida Office of Economic and Demographic Research, Summary of Final Actions: 2009 Criminal Justice Impact Conference Bills, http://edr.state.fl.us/Content/conferences/criminaljusticeimpact/archives/2009/2009%20CJIC%20Final%20Actions.pdf.

45. Florida Department of Corrections, Office of Legislative Affairs, 2009 Legislative Review, 8, http:// www.dc.state.fl.us/orginfo/leg/2009session/2009legislativereview.doc; Florida Legislature, Fiscal Analysis in Brief: 2009 Legislative Session, September 2009, 53, http://edr.state.fl.us/Content/revenues/reports/fiscal-analysis-in-brief/FiscalAnalysisInBrief2009.pdf.

46. Florida TaxWatch, *Report and Recommendation of the Florida TaxWatch Government Cost Savings Task Force to Save More Than $3 Billion* (Tallahassee, March 2010), iv, http://www.floridataxwatch.org/resources/pdf/03042010fullreport.pdf; author interview with Barney Bishop, executive director, Smart Justice Alliance, February 5, 2016 (phone); author interview with Allison DeFoor, founding chairman, Project on Accountable Justice, February 2, 2016 (phone).

47. Florida TaxWatch, *Report and Recommendation of the Florida TaxWatch Government Cost Savings Task Force for Fiscal Year 2011–12* (Tallahassee, December 2010), 29, http://www.floridataxwatch.org/resources/pdf/12082010gctsf.pdf.

48. DeFoor interview.

49. Aviram, *Cheap on Crime*, 99–109.

50. Jim Baiardi, "President's Message," *Florida PBA Corrections Review* 24 (2) (September 2011).

51. DeFoor interview.

52. Steve Bousquet, "Florida Judge to Call Prison Outsourcing Unconstitutional," *Miami Herald*, September 30, 2011.

53. Author interview with Paula Dockery, February 4, 2016 (phone).

54. Letter to Sen. Mike Haridopolos, "Groups Oppose Unprecedented Private Prison Expansion and Encourage Adoption of Policies that Reduce Reliance on Incarceration," January 31, 2012, https://www.privateci.org/letters.html.

55. Florida Legislature, 44th Regular Session, SB2036 and SB2038.

56. DeFoor interview.

57. Newsletter of the FSU Project on Accountable Justice, December 2012, http://www.iog.fsu.edu/paj/documents/PAJ%20December%20Newsletter.pdf.

58. Smartjusticealliance.org, accessed on February 10, 2016.

59. Dockery interview.

60. Jonathan Simon, *Mass Incarceration on Trial: A Remarkable Court Decision and the Future of Prisons in America* (New York: New Press, 2014), 41. Michelle Phelps finds a substantial decline in service staff to inmate ratios and the rate of inmates who report participation in educational programming between 1990 and 2005. Michelle S. Phelps, "Rehabilitation in the Punitive Era: The Gap between Rhetoric and Reality in US Prison Programs," *Law and Society Review* 45 (1) (2011): 33–68; Michelle S. Phelps, "The Place of Punishment: Variation in the Provision of Inmate Services Staff across the Punitive Turn," *Journal of Criminal Justice* 40 (5) (2012): 348–57.

61. Steven Bousquet and Katie Sanders, "Edwin Buss Abruptly Resigns as Florida's Prison Chief," *Tampa Bay Times*, November 24, 2011.

62. Loïc Wacquant, "The Curious Eclipse of Prison Ethnography in the Age of Mass Incarceration," *Ethnography* 3 (4) (2002): 371–97.

63. Elsa Whitlock, testimony to the Florida Senate Criminal Justice Committee, January 5, 2015.

64. Simon, *Mass Incarceration on Trial*, 113. According to the U.S. Census Bureau data on state government finances, state capital spending on prisons decreased by 24 percent between 2005 and 2010.

65. Amy Lerman, *The Modern Prison Paradox: Politics, Punishment, and Social Community* (Cambridge: Cambridge University Press, 2013), 66.

66. More than one interviewee and numerous news reports claim that Governor Bush looked the other direction when told what was going on. See, for example, editorial, "Culture of Corruption," *St. Petersburg Times*, July 7, 2006, 14A; Trovillion interview.

67. Between FY 2000–2001 and FY 2005–2006, funding for educational programming decreased by 24 percent and the number of drug treatment slots decreased from 4,569 to 2,235, even though the prison population increased from 72,000 to 88,500. Florida Senate Committee on Criminal Justice, Issue Brief 2009-13, October 2008; Florida Department of Corrections, *2006–2007 Annual Report* (Tallahassee, 2007), 2; McAndrews interview; Lise Fisher, "Tentative Settlement Research in Valdes Case," *Gainesville Sun*, January 19, 2007.

68. Florida Legislature, Office of Program Policy Analysis and Government Accountability (OPPAGA), "Study of Operations of the Florida Department of Corrections," November 2015.

69. The number of staff assaults increased from 6.2 per 1,000 inmates in FY 2005–2006 to 7.9 in FY 2010–2011. OPPAGA, "Corrections Experiences Turnover and Vacancies, But Performance Not Diminished," February 2007, 5; OPPAGA 2015, 38.

70. Secs. Edwin Buss (January 2011–August 2011), Ken Tucker (August 2011–December 2012), and Michael Crews (January 2013–December 2014).

71. Commission on Safety and Abuse in America's Prisons, *Confronting Confinement* (New York: Vera Institute of Justice, 2006).

72. Julie K. Brown, "Inmate's Gassing Death Detailed in Florida DOC Whistle-blower Complaint," *Miami Herald*, July 7, 2014.

73. At hearings before the Senate Criminal Justice committee in March 2015, current and former FDOC investigators "cited cases where they were told to with-hold information from prosecutors, to close investigations into staffers who were politically connected, and to avoid bringing criminal charges no matter how much evidence they had." Julie K. Brown, "Florida Prisons Riddled with Corruption, Staffers Tell Senators," *Miami Herald*, March 10, 2015; Julie K. Brown and Mary Ellen Klas, "Florida Prison Inspectors Turn Over Rocks, Find Little Wrongdo-ing," *Miami Herald*, February 7, 2015.

74. Julie K. Brown and Mary Ellen Klas, "Former Florida Prison Chief Says Gov. Rick Scott Ignored Crisis in Corrections System," *Miami Herald*, January 31, 2015.

75. Bruce Western and Christopher Wildeman, "The Black Family and Mass Incarceration," *Annals of the American Academy of Political and Social Science* 621 (1) (2009): 221–42.

76. Based on 2010 Census data, U.S. Census Bureau, 2011 American Com-munity Survey (Washington, DC, 2012). Prison Policy Initiative, "Breaking Down Mass Incarceration in the 2010 Census: State-by-State Incarceration Rates by Race/Ethnicity," May 28, 2014, http://www.prisonpolicy.org/reports/rates.html.

77. Robert J. Sampson, "The Incarceration Ledger: Toward a New Era in As-sessing Societal Consequences," *Criminology and Public Policy* 10 (2011): 819–28; Kristin Turney, "Incarceration and Social Inequality: Challenges and Directions for Future Research," *Annals of the American Academy of Political and Social Science* 651 (1) (2014): 97–101.

78. William J. Sabol and James P. Lynch, "Assessing the Longer-run Effects of Incarceration: Impact on Families and Employment," in *Crime Control and Social Justice: The Delicate Balance*, ed. Darnell Hawkins, Samuel Myers, Jr., and Ran-dolph Stine (Westport, CT: Greenwood Press, 2003), 3–26; Devah Pager, "The Mark of a Criminal Record," *American Journal of Sociology* 108 (5) (2006): 937–75.

79. A meta-analysis of studies on the impact of parental incarceration on children finds that parental incarceration is associated with higher risk for children's anti-social behavior, but not for mental health problems, drug use, or poor educational performance. Joseph Murray, David P. Farrington, and Ivana Sekol, "Children's Antisocial Behavior, Mental Health, Drug Use, and Educational Performance af-ter Parental Incarceration: A Systematic Review and Meta-analysis," *Psychologi-cal Bulletin* 138 (2) (2012): 175–210. See also Amanda Geller, Carey E. Cooper, Irwin Garfinkel, Ofira Schwartz-Soicher, and Ronald B. Mincy, "Beyond Absen-teeism: Father Incarceration and Child Development." *Demography* 49 (2012): 49–76; Beth M. Huebner and Regan Gustafson, "The Effect of Maternal Incar-ceration on Adult Offspring Involvement in the Criminal Justice System," *Journal of Criminal Justice* 35 (2007): 283–96.

80. Lauren E. Glaze and Laura M. Maruschak, *Parents in Prison and Their Minor Children* (Washington, DC: U.S. Department of Justice, Office of Justice Programs, 2008); Holly Foster and John Hagan, "The Mass Incarceration of Parents in America: Issues of Race/Ethnicity, Collateral Damage to Children, and Prisoner Reentry," *Annals of the American Academy of Political and Social Science* 623 (2009): 179–94.

81. Christopher Wildeman, "Parental Imprisonment, the Prison Boom, and the Concentration of Childhood Disadvantage," *Demography*, 46 (2009): 265–80.

82. Robert J. Sampson, Stephen W. Raudenbush, and Felton Earls, "Neighborhoods and Violent Crime: A Multilevel Study of Collective Efficacy," *Science* 227 (1997): 916–24; Todd R. Clear, *Imprisoning Communities: How Mass Incarceration Makes Disadvantaged Neighborhoods Worse* (New York: Oxford University Press, 2007).

83. Hedwig Lee, Lauren C. Porter, and Megan Comfort, "Consequences of Family Member Incarceration: Impacts on Civic Participation and Perceptions of the Legitimacy and Fairness of Government," *Annals of the American Academy of Political and Social Science* 651 (2014): 44–73; Amy E. Lerman and Vesla M. Weaver, *Arresting Citizenship: The Democratic Consequences of American Crime Control* (Chicago: University of Chicago Press, 2014); Traci R. Burch, *Trading Democracy for Justice: Criminal Convictions and the Decline of Neighborhood Political Participation* (Chicago: University of Chicago Press, 2013).

84. Final Report of the Ex-Offender Task Force, November 2006 (Tallahassee, Florida), 26.

85. In Gov. Scott's criminal justice transition team's 260-page report, overrepresentation comes up three times: twice in the report of the 2006 Ex-Offender Task Force and once in a summary of the 2008 Juvenile Justice Blue Print Commission. Governor-Elect Rick Scott Law and Order Transition Team, *Department and Policy Review*, 131, 154, 262.

86. Carol Marbin Miller, "Change Sought in Florida Prison System," *Miami Herald*, June 24, 2009.

87. See, e.g., Jeffrey Sparshott, "The Great Recession May Have Worsened Drug Abuse, Especially among Whites," *Wall Street Journal*, March 1, 2016.

88. Dockery interview.

89. DeFoor interview.

90. Sen. Arthenia Joyner, Senate Criminal Justice Committee Meeting, January 19, 2016, http://thefloridachannel.org/videos/11916-senate-criminal-justice-committee/.

91. Sen. Jeff Clemens, Senate Criminal Justice Committee Meeting, January 19, 2016. Sen. Audrey Gibson, a black Democrat from Duval County similarly responds to a comment by a state's attorney that "not everyone is treated the same way," without explicitly mentioning race.

92. Sen. Greg Evers, Senate Criminal Justice Committee Meeting, January 19, 2016.

93. Sen. Greg Evers, Senate Criminal Justice Committee Meeting, January 19, 2016.

94. Sen. Arthenia Joyner (D. Tampa) repeatedly proposed a bill that would exempt first-time drug trafficking defendants from mandatory minimums because low-level drug dealers who have no information to leverage with prosecutors face stiffer penalties than more connected drug dealers. Sen. Joyner, Senate Criminal Justice Committee Meeting, January 19, 2016. Proposed reforms in the juvenile justice system have been much more successful, however.

95. Florida Legislature, 46th Regular Session, CS/SB7020.

96. State of Florida, Office of the Governor, Executive Order No. 15-102, May 8, 2015.

97. Request for CRIPA Investigation into the Florida Department of Corrections, October 15, 2015, https://www.floridajusticeinstitute.org/wp-content/uploads/2015/10/florida-coalition-letter-to-usdoj.pdf.

98. Florida Justice Institute Press Release, January 26, 2016; *Disability Rights Florida v. Julie Jones* (N.D. Fla. 2014).

99. Paul Pierson, *Politics in Time: History, Institutions, and Social Analysis* (Princeton: Princeton University Press, 2004), 146.

100. Christopher Seeds, "Bifurcation Nation: American Penal Policy in Late Mass Incarceration," *Punishment and Society*, first published online October 19, 2016, doi: 10.1177/1462474516673822; Katherine Beckett, Anna Reosti, and Emily Knaphus, "The End of an Era? Understanding the Contradictions of Criminal Justice Reform," *Annals of the American Academy of Political and Social Science* 664 (1) (2016): 238–59.

101. Nebraska senator Heath Mello quoted in Heather Schoenfeld, "A Research Agenda on Reform: Penal Policy and Politics across the States," *Annals of the American Academy of Political and Social Science* 664 (1) (2016): 155–74.

102. Collins Center for Public Policy, "Smart Justice: Findings and Recommendations for Florida Criminal Justice Reform," February 2010.

103. Bill Cervone, Florida State's Attorney 8th Judicial District, testimony to the Senate Criminal Justice Committee, January 19, 2016.

104. Florida Legislature, 44th Regular Session, HB159; Florida Legislature, 45th Regular Session, SB360.

105. Mary Ellen Klas, "Push for Leniency in Drug Sentencing Has Been a Hard Sell in Florida," *Miami Herald*, August 18, 2013.

106. Bishop interview.

107. Allison DeFoor testimony to the Senate Criminal Justice Committee, January 5, 2015.

108. Ashley Rubin, "Penal Change as Penal Layering: A Case Study of Proto-Prison Adoption and Capital Punishment Reduction, 1785–1822," *Punishment and Society* 18 (4): 420–41.

109. Mona Lynch, "Mass Incarceration, Legal Change, and Locale," *Criminology and Public Policy* 10 (3) (2011): 673–98.

110. This is true in other states as well. Anjuli Verma, "A Turning Point in Mass Incarceration? Local Imprisonment Trajectories and Decarceration under California's Realignment," *Annals of the American Academy of Political and Social Science* 664 (1) (2016): 108–35.

111. William H. Burgess, preface to 2015–16 ed., *Florida Sentencing*, vol. 16, West's Florida Practice Series (Eagan, MN: Thomson-West, 2015).

112. Katherine Beckett and Naomi Murakawa, "Mapping the Shadow Carceral State: Toward an Institutionally Capacious Approach to Punishment," *Theoretical Criminology* 16 (2) (2012): 222.

113. "Annexes" are prisons built on the site of a previous prison, a common practice in Florida. They hold on average a slightly smaller population. Florida Department of Corrections, *2013–2014 Annual Report* (Tallahassee, 2015).

114. William J. Stuntz, *The Collapse of American Criminal Justice* (Cambridge: Harvard University Press, 2011).

115. Data on the State's Attorneys compiled from judicial circuit websites (accessed January 2016).

116. Bill Cervone testimony to the Senate Criminal Justice Committee, January 19, 2016; Dockery interview. According to Dockery, the sheriffs opposed removing prison as an option for driving on a suspended license if the underlying crime was failure to pay a fine. Dockery told me, "I cannot impress on you how the sheriffs went ballistic on the suspended license thing."

117. Bishop interview.

118. Bishop interview; Steve Bousquet, "Rick Scott's Veto of Prison Bill Misses Point," *Tampa Bay Times*, April 9, 2012.

119. Joshua Page, *The Toughest Beat: Politics, Punishment, and the Prison Officers Union in California* (New York: Oxford University Press, 2013), 7.

120. Bureau of Labor Statistics, Occupational Employment Statistics, May 2014.

121. Project on Accountable Justice, "Recommendations to Advance Public Safety through Increased Transparency, Accountability, and Oversight of the Florida Department of Corrections," November 2014.

122. Baiardi, "President's Message."

123. Brandon Larrabee, "Florida Department of Corrections Vote to Join Teamsters," *News Service of Florida*, November 18, 2011.

124. Jeff Burlew, "Correctional Officers Say Pay Not Keeping Up with Peers," *Tallahassee Democrat*, April 9, 2014; Teamsters Local 2011, Legislative Update, April 27, 2015.

125. Teamsters Local 2011, Legislative Update, March 20, 2015. In fact, this was the original rationale for moving prisoners with sentences over one year to the state prison system in the late 1960s. Fla. Sess. Laws 67-241 (1967).

126. "CCI Officers Reach Settlement to Get Jobs Back after Death of Inmate," WINK News, December 3, 2014.

127. David Royse, "Medical Battle behind Bars: Big Prison Healthcare Firm Corizon Struggles with Contracts," *Modernhealthcare.com*, April 11, 2015.

128. Between 2010 and 2012, GEO Group spent $2.3 million on lobbyists in the state. In addition, GEO Group's political action committee contributed $1.6 million mainly, but not exclusively, to Republican political candidates and political party organizations, contributing another $25,000 to Gov. Rick Scott's inauguration ceremony. Dan Christensen, "GEO Group Spends Big on Politicians, Lobbyists, as Lucrative State Contract Goes Out for Bids," *Florida Bulldog*, July 28, 2011; Pat Beall, "Money at the Statehouse? Prison Firms Are on It," *Palm Beach Post*, November 16, 2013.

129. "Florida Senate Rejects Privatization of 27 State Prisons—But Just Barely," *Prison Legal News* (April 2012): 38.

130. Royse, "Medical Battle behind Bars."

131. Mary Ellen Klas, "Private Prison Healthcare in Doubt as Contract with Florida Collapses," *Miami Herald*, November 30, 2015.

132. Aviram, *Cheap on Crime*, 103–9.

133. Holly Kirby, "Will 'Smart Justice' in Florida Mean Prison Privatization?" *Grassrootsleadership.org*, January 23, 2013.

134. John Eason, "Mapping Prison Proliferation: Region, Rurality, Race, and Disadvantage in Prison Placement," *Social Science Research* 39 (6) (2010): 1015–28.

135. E.g., Ryan S. King, Marc Mauer, and Tracy Huling, "Big Prisons, Small Towns: Prison Economy in Rural America" (Washington, DC: Sentencing Project, 2003).

136. John Eason, *Big House on the Prairie: Rise of the Rural Ghetto and Prison Proliferation* (Chicago: University of Chicago Press, 2017).

137. Erica Bough, "Tourism, Farming, Prisons Power North Florida's Rural Economy," *Gainesville Sun*, September 16, 2012.

138. Julie Montanaro, WCTV News, 6:30 PM broadcast, January 12, 2012.

139. Julie Montanaro, WCTV News, 6:30 PM broadcast, January 12, 2012.

140. Author, field notes, March 22, 2007.

141. Fred Grimm, "Putting the Con in Constituent," *Miami Herald*, September 28, 2013.

142. In 2016, Republicans held 81 of 120 House seats and 26 of 40 Senate seats. Republican governors have held office since 1999. Nevertheless, the governorship is more contested than the legislature. In both 2010 and 2014, Rick Scott beat his opponent by only 1 percent of the vote.

143. Such as civil asset forfeiture reforms. The Coalition for Public Safety is one of the new bipartisan national reform organizations (sponsored by both the Ford Foundation and Koch Industries Inc.) that have made civil asset forfeiture

reform one of their main issues; see http://www.coalitionforpublicsafety.org/issue
/civil-asset-forfeiture/, accessed August 2015.

Chapter 8

1. Marie Gottschalk, *Caught: The Prison State and the Lockdown of American Politics* (Princeton: Princeton University Press, 2015), 2. See also Jonathan Simon, *Governing through Crime: How the War on Crime Transformed American Democracy and Created a Culture of Fear* (Oxford: Oxford University Press, 2007).

2. Philip Goodman, Joshua Page, and Michelle Phelps, *Breaking the Pendulum: The Long Struggle over Criminal Justice* (New York: Oxford University Press, 2017), 13.

3. Goodman, Page, and Phelps, *Breaking the Pendulum*, 9.

4. Ruth Wilson Gilmore, *Golden Gulag: Prisons, Surplus, Crisis, and Opposition in Globalizing California* (Berkeley: University of California Press, 2007); John Eason, *Big House on the Prairie: Rise of the Rural Ghetto and Prison Proliferation* (Chicago: University of Chicago Press, 2017).

5. Simon, *Governing through Crime*.

6. Naomi Murakawa, *The First Civil Right: How Liberals Built Prison America* (New York: Oxford University Press, 2014), 3.

7. Khalil Gibran Muhammad, *The Condemnation of Blackness* (Cambridge: Harvard University Press, 2010); Christopher Muller, "Northward Migration and the Rise of Racial Disparity in American Incarceration, 1880–1950," *American Journal of Sociology* 118 (2) (2012): 281–326.

8. Lisa L. Miller, *The Myth of Mob Rule: Violent Crime and Democratic Politics* (New York: Oxford University Press, 2016), 198, citing E. E. Schattschneider, *The Semi-sovereign People: A Realist's View of Democracy in America* (New York: Hold, Rinehart, and Winston, 1960). See also Goodman, Page, and Phelps, *Breaking the Pendulum*, 12.

9. Michael C. Campbell and Heather Schoenfeld, "The Transformation of America's Penal Order: A Historicized Political Sociology of Punishment," *American Journal of Sociology* 118 (5) (2013): 1388.

10. Miller, *The Myth of Mob Rule*, 121.

11. For an empirical examination of the racialized opposition to social welfare see Joe Soss, Sanford F. Schram, Thomas P. Vartanian, and Erin O'Brien, "Setting the Terms of Relief: Explaining State Policy Choices in the Devolution Revolution," *American Journal of Political Science* 45 (2) (2001): 378–95.

12. Campbell and Schoenfeld, "The Transformation of America's Penal Order."

13. Murakawa, *The First Civil Right*, 26.

14. Elizabeth Hinton, *From the War on Poverty to the War on Crime: The Making of Mass Incarceration in America* (Cambridge: Harvard University Press, 2016).

15. Ruth D. Peterson and Laurie J. Krivo, *Divergent Social Worlds: Neighborhood Crime and the Racial-Spatial Divide* (New York: Russell Sage Foundation, 2010).

16. Michelle Alexander, *The New Jim Crow: Mass Incarceration in the Age of Colorblindness* (New York: New Press, 2009).

17. Josh Salman, Emily Le Coz, and Elizabeth Johnson, "Florida's Broken Sentencing System," *Sarasota Herald Tribune*, December 8, 2016.

18. David Jacobs and Aubrey L. Jackson, "On the Politics of Imprisonments: A Review of Systematic Findings," *Annual Review of Law and Social Science* 6 (2010): 137.

19. Michael C. Campbell, Matt Vogel, and Joshua Williams, "Historical Contingencies and the Evolving Importance of Race, Violent Crime, and Region in Explaining Mass Incarceration in the United States," *Criminology* 53 (2015): 180–203.

20. Christopher Tarman and David Sears, "The Conceptualization and Measurement of Symbolic Racism," *Journal of Politics* 67 (3) (2005): 731–61.

21. Gottschalk, *Caught.*

22. Michael Javen Fortner, *Black Silent Majority: The Rockefeller Drug Laws and the Politics of Punishment* (Cambridge: Harvard University Press, 2015).

23. Kitty Calavita and Valerie Jenness, *Appealing to Justice: Prisoner Grievances, Rights, and Carceral Logic* (Berkeley: University of California Press, 2014); Nicole Gonzalez Van Cleve, *Crook County: Racism and Injustice in America's Largest Criminal Court* (Palo Alto: Stanford University Press, 2016); Issa Kohler-Hausmann, "Managerial Justice and Mass Misdemeanors," *Stanford Law Review* 66 (3) (2014); Charles R. Epp, Steven Maynard-Moody, and Donald P. Haider-Markel, *Pulled Over: How Police Stops Define Race and Citizenship* (Chicago: University of Chicago Press, 2014).

24. Bureau of Justice Statistics, Imprisonment Rate of Sentenced Prisoners under the Jurisdiction of State or Federal Correctional Authorities per 100,000 U.S. Residents, December 31, 1978–2014, generated using the Corrections Statistical Analysis Tool at www.bjs.gov/index.cfm?ty=daa; Public Policy Institute of California, "California's Changing Prison Population," April 2015, http://www.ppic.org/main/publication_show.asp?i=702.

25. Fifteen states' incarceration rates grew 2 percent or more between 2008 and 2014. Bureau of Justice Statistics, Imprisonment Rate of Sentenced Prisoners under the Jurisdiction of State or Federal Correctional Authorities per 100,000 U.S. residents (Department of Justice, 2015).

26. The aggregate state incarceration rate in 2014 was 412, the rate in 1980 was 129. Ryan King, Bryce Peterson, Brian Ederbroom, and Elizabeth Pelletier, "Reducing Mass Incarceration Requires Far-Reaching Reforms" (Urban Institute, 2015), http://webapp.urban.org/reducing-mass-incarceration/index.html.

27. William Spelman, "Jobs or Jails? The Crime Drop in Texas," *Journal of Policy Analysis and Management* 24 (2005): 133–65. See John Donohue, "Assessing

the Relative Benefits of Incarceration: The Overall Change over the Previous Decades and the Benefits on the Margin," in *Do Prisons Make Us Safer? The Benefits
and Costs of the Prison Boom*, ed. Stephen Raphael and Michael A. Stoll (New
York: Russell Sage Foundation, 2009). But see a critique and discussion of the
methodological problems of determining the causal relationship between incarceration and crime rates. Steven F. Durlauf and Daniel S. Nagin, "The Deterrent Effect of Imprisonment," in *Controlling Crime: Strategies and Tradeoffs*, ed. Philip J.
Cook, Jens Ludwig, and Justin McCrary (Chicago: University of Chicago Press,
2011).

28. Bruce Western and Becky Pettit, "Incarceration and Social inequality," *Daedalus*, Summer 2010, 8–19.

29. Todd Clear, *Imprisoning Communities: How Mass Incarceration Makes
Disadvantaged Neighborhoods Worse* (New York: Oxford University Press, 2007).

30. Long-serving prisoners in state prison have drastically increased given truth
in sentencing, natural life (eighty-plus year) sentences, and life without parole.
Many states dismantled their discretionary parole systems in the 1980s and thus
have no way of statutorily releasing older prisoners. In Illinois, for example, the
number of prisoners over fifty years of age grew from 1,030 in 1990 to 7,162 in 2014,
and the number of prisoners who have served over twenty-five years in prison has
grown from 32 in 1990 to 1,009. "Illinois House Bill 3668 Talking Points," *Statev-
ille Speaks 2014 Special Edition*, http://www.illinoisprisontalk.org/pdf/SS2014spe
cialv4.pdf/, p. 4.

31. Holly Foster and John Hagan, "The Mass Incarceration of Parents in America: Issues of Race/Ethnicity, Collateral Damage to Children, and Prisoner Reentry," *Annals of the American Academy of Political and Social Science*, 623 (2009):
179–94; Christopher Wildeman, "Parental Imprisonment, the Prison Boom, and
the Concentration of Childhood Disadvantage," *Demography* 46 (2009): 265–80;
Bruce Western and Christopher Wildeman, "The Black Family and Mass Incarceration," *Annals of the American Academy of Political and Social Science* 621 (1)
(2009): 221–42.

32. Legal Action Center, *After Prison: Roadblocks to Reentry, A Report on
State Legal Barriers Facing People with Criminal Convictions* (Legal Action Center, 2004), accessed March 23, 2015, http://lac.org/roadblocks-to-reentry/.

33. David Dagan and Steven Teles, "The Conservative War on Prisons," *Washington Monthly*, November/December 2012. Dagan and Teles cite the momentum
of reform in Georgia. David Dagan and Steven Teles, *Prison Break: Why Conservatives Turned against Mass Incarceration* (New York: Oxford University Press,
2016), 111–34.

34. Mona Lynch, "Mass Incarceration, Legal Change, and Locale," *Criminol-
ogy and Public Policy* 10 (3) (2011): 673–98. See also, e.g., Luke Mogelson, "Prison
Break: How Michigan Managed to Empty Its Penitentiaries While Lowering Its
Crime Rate," *Washington Monthly* November/December 2010; Sentencing Project,

"Fewer Prisoners, Less Crime: A Tale of Three States" (Washington, DC: Sentencing Project, 2015), http://sentencingproject.org/wp-content/uploads/2015/11/Fewer-Prisoners-Less-Crime-A-Tale-of-Three-States.pdf.

35. Nevertheless, strong political coalitions, such as the Drop the Rock campaign in New York, are likely significant. The Drop the Rock coalition included "faith groups, allies in the criminal justice field, service providers who run alternatives to incarceration, communities in Harlem, families and individuals directly affected by the laws, the public defender community, labor unions, college and law student groups." Katrina vanden Heuvel, "Drop the Rock," *Nation*, February 19, 2009.

36. Gottschalk, *Caught*.

37. Author interview, Nebraska ACLU staff attorney Joel Donahue, September 12, 2014 (phone).

38. Marie Gottschalk, "Democracy and the Carceral State in America," *Annals of the American Academy of Political and Social Science* 651 (1) (January 1, 2014): 288–95; Bruce Western, "Incarceration, Inequality, and Imagining Alternatives," *Annals of the American Academy of Political and Social Science* 651 (1) (2014): 302–6; Ruth Wilson Gilmore, "The Worrying State of the Anti-prison Movement," *Social Justice*, February 2015, http://www.socialjusticejournal.org/?p=2888.

39. Michelle Alexander, *The New Jim Crow: Mass Incarceration in the Age of Colorblindness* (New York: New Press, 2010), 225.

40. Gilmore, "The Worrying State of the Anti-prison Movement." See also Heather Ann Thompson, "Dodging Decarceration: The Shell Game of 'Getting Smart' on Crime," *Huffington Post*, September 8, 2014.

41. Nancy LaVigne et al., *Justice Reinvestment Initiative State Assessment Report* (Washington, DC: Urban Institute, 2014). For example, Kentucky now requires that "the terms and intensity of [parole and probation] supervision shall be based on an individual's level of risk to public safety, criminal risk factors, and the need for treatment and other interventions." Kentucky Legislature, 2011, HB 463, Sec. 31 and 36.

42. David J. Rothman, *Conscience and Convenience: The Asylum and Its Alternatives in Progressive America* (Boston: Little, Brown, 1980).

43. Jonathan Simon, *Poor Discipline: Parole and the Social Control of the Underclass, 1890–1990* (Chicago: University of Chicago Press, 1993).

44. Goodman, Page, and Phelps, *Breaking the Pendulum*.

45. David Garland, *The Culture of Control: Crime and Social Order in Contemporary Society* (Chicago: University of Chicago Press, 2001), 176.

46. Bruce Western, "Reentry: Reversing Mass Imprisonment," *Boston Review*, July 1, 2008.

47. Reuben Jonathan Miller, "Devolving the Carceral State: Race, Prisoner Reentry, and the Micro-Politics of Urban Poverty Management," *Punishment and Society* 16 (3) (2014): 305–35.

48. Gottschalk, *Caught*, 81.

49. Todd R. Clear and Dennis Schranz, "Strategies for Reducing Prison Populations," *Prison Journal* 91 (3) (2011): 151S.

50. Ashley T. Rubin, "The Birth of the Penal Organization: Why Prisons Were Born to Fail," in *The Legal Process and the Promise of Justice, ed.* Jonathan Simon, Hadar Aviram, and Rosann Greenspan (forthcoming).

51. Gottschalk, *Caught*; Katherine Beckett and Naomi Murakawa, "Mapping the Shadow Carceral State: Toward an Institutionally Capacious Approach to Punishment," *Theoretical Criminology* 16 (2) (2012): 221–44.

52. Eric Cadora and Susan Tucker, "Justice Reinvestment: To Invest in Public Safety by Reallocating Justice Dollars to Refinance Education, Housing, Healthcare, and Jobs," *Ideas for an Open Society* (New York: Open Society Institute, 2003), https://www.opensocietyfoundations.org/sites/default/files/ideas_reinvestment.pdf.

53. Dagan and Teles, *Prison Break*, 69.

54. Heather Schoenfeld, "A Research Agenda on Reform: Penal Policy and Politics across the States," *Annals of the American Academy of Political and Social Sciences* 664 (1) (2016): 155–74.

55. Thomas G. Blomberg and Julie Mestre, "Net-Widening," in *The Encyclopedia of Theoretical Criminology* (West Sussex, UK: Wiley & Sons Inc., 2014). While the use of "risk assessment" technology may help guard against this potentiality, in practice criminal justice actors on the ground can resist these types of tools because they deny their "professional expertise" and limit their discretion. Sarah M. Smith, Marisa K. Omori, Susan F. Turner, and Jesse Jannetta, "Assessing the Earned Discharge Pilot Project," *Criminology and Public Policy* 11, 2 (2012): 385–410.

56. Albert M. Kopak, J. Jordan Coward, Greg Frost, and Ashley Ballard, "The Adult Civil Citation Network: An Innovative Pre-charge Program for Misdemeanor Offenders," *Journal of Community Corrections* (Fall 2015): 14.

57. Beckett and Murakawa, "Mapping the Shadow Carceral State."

58. Kohler-Hausmann, "Managerial Justice."

59. Rebecca Tiger, *Judging Addicts: Drug Courts and Coercion in the Justice System* (New York: New York University Press, 2012); Teresa Gowan and Sarah Whetstone, "Making the Criminal Addict: Subjectivity and Social Control in a Strong-Arm Rehab," *Punishment and Society* 14 (1) (2012): 69–93; Lynne A. Haney, *Offending Women: Power, Punishment, and the Regulation of Desire* (Berkeley: University of California Press, 2010).

60. Allison McKim, "Roxanne's Dress: Governing Gender and Marginality through Addiction Treatment," *Signs: Journal of Women in Culture and Society* 39 (2) (2014): 456; Allison McKim, *Addicted to Rehab: Race, Gender, and Drugs in the Era of Mass Incarceration* (New Brunswick: Rutgers University Press, 2017).

61. David Garland, *Culture of Control*, 116.

62. William G. Martin, "Decarceration and Justice Disinvestment: Evidence from New York State," *Punishment and Society* 18 (4) (2016): 479–504.

63. Brett C. Burkhardt, "Who Punishes Whom? Bifurcation of Private and Public Responsibilities in Criminal Punishment," *Journal of Crime and Justice* (2016), doi: 10.1080/0735648X.2016.1174619.

64. Sarah Stillman, "Get Out of Jail, Inc.: Does the Alternatives-to-Incarceration Industry Profit from Injustice?" *New Yorker*, June 23, 2004.

65. Miller, "Devolving the Carceral State," 328.

66. Interview with staff at the John Howard Association, Chicago, September 16, 2014. See also statement by Alan Mills of the Uptown People's Law Center, quoted in Bruce Rushton, "State Sued over Prison Conditions," *Illinois Times* (Springfield), June 28, 2012. The Nebraska ACLU issued a white paper entitled "The Tipping Point: Have Nebraska's Prisons Crossed into Unconstitutional Territory?" a week before the legislature's debate on a reform package in order to "convince the legislature that we were headed down a path that was unsustainable." Donahue interview. In both Illinois and Nebraska, state legislators picked up on these arguments and used them when trying to convince colleagues to pass reform legislation.

67. *Rasho v. Walker* (C.D. Illinois, 2015).

68. Deni Kamper, "Illinois Prisons Act as Mental Health Facilities for the State," *DePaulia*, April 15, 2016, http://depauliaonline.com/2016/04/15/illinois-prisons -mental-health/.

69. Margo Schlanger, "*Plata v. Brown* and Realignment: Jails, Prisons, Courts, and Politics," *Harvard Civil Rights–Civil Liberties Law Review* 48 (2013): 165–215.

70. Robert Martinson, "What Works? Questions and Answers about Prison," *Public Interest* (Spring 1974): 22-54. See, for example, Edward Latessa, Francis Cullen, and Paul Gendreau, "Beyond Correctional Quackery—Professionalism and the Possibility of Effective Treatment," *Federal Probation* 66 (2) (2002): 43–49; Doris MacKenzie and David Farrington, "Preventing Future Offending of Delinquents and Offenders: What Have We Learned from Experiments and Meta-analyses?" *Journal of Experimental Criminology* 11 (4) (2015): 565–95.

71. Elliott Currie, *Crime and Punishment in America* (New York: Macmillan, 2013 [1998]), 179, xvi.

72. The District Court of the Northern District of Florida found prison gerrymandering in Jefferson County unconstitutional. *Calvin v. Jefferson County Board of Commissioners*, No. 4:15-cv-00131-MW-CAS (N.D. Fla. 2016).

73. Franklin Zimring, David Hawkins, and Sam Kamin, *Punishment and Democracy: Three Strikes and You're Out in California* (Oxford: Oxford University Press, 2001); Nicola Lacey, *The Prisoner's Dilemma: Political Economy and Punishment in Contemporary Democracies* (Cambridge: Cambridge University Press, 2008).

74. David A. Green, "Penal Populism and the Folly of 'Doing Good by Stealth.'" *Good Society* 23 (1) (2014): 73–86.

75. The Marshall Project, www.themarshallproject.org, is one such news organization that is attempting "to elevate the criminal justice issue to one of national urgency, and to help spark a national conversation about reform." Accessed May 11, 2016.

76. Bernard E. Harcourt, "Risk as a Proxy for Race: The Dangers of Risk Assessment." *Federal Sentencing Reporter* 27 (4) (2015): 237–43.

77. Ellen Berrey, *The Enigma of Diversity: The Language of Race and the Limits of Racial Justice* (Chicago: University of Chicago Press, 2015).

78. Van Cleve, *Crook County*. United States Department of Justice Civil Rights Division, *Investigation of the Ferguson Police Department*, March 4, 2015.

79. Although taken together it seems that black decision makers have the potential to reduce some of the racial disparity in criminal justice outcomes. Johnson, Brian D. "The Multilevel Context of Criminal Sentencing: Integrating Judge- and County-Level Influences," *Criminology* 44 (2) (2006): 259–98. Robert A. Brown and James Frank, "Race and Officer Decision Making: Examining Differences in Arrest Outcomes between Black and White Officers," *Justice Quarterly* 23 (1) (2006): 96–126. Darrell Steffensmeier and Chester L. Britt, "Judges' Race and Judicial Decision Making: Do Black Judges Sentence Differently?" *Social Science Quarterly* 82 (4) (2001): 749–64. Amy Farrell, Geoff Ward, and Danielle Rousseau, "Race Effects of Representation among Federal Court Workers: Does Black Workforce Representation Reduce Sentencing Disparities?" *Annals of the American Academy of Political and Social Science* 623 (1) (2009): 121–33.

80. BLM originated as twitter hashtag after the shooting death in 2012 of Trayvon Martin, a black teenager, in Sanford, Florida, by George Zimmerman, a self-proclaimed "neighborhood watchman" who thought Martin looked "suspicious." The movement grew in 2014 after Darren Wilson, a white Ferguson, Missouri, police officer, shot and killed Michael Brown, a black teenager suspected of stealing cigarillos. The Michael Brown shooting led to large protests in Ferguson and other cities. Brown was initially reported to have had his hands up in the air when shot. Later investigation by the Department of Justice found that Officer Wilson shot Brown after Brown had "punched and grabbed" Wilson. Although Brown walked away from Wilson after the initial altercation, witnesses reported that Brown was moving back toward Wilson when Wilson shot and killed him. A grand jury decided not to bring charges against Wilson. "Department of Justice Report Regarding the Criminal Investigation Into the Shooting Death of Michael Brown by Ferguson, Missouri Police Officer Darren Wilson" (United States Department of Justice, March 4, 2015).

81. The lack of public figures standing up for black lives felt especially palpable (especially to young people) toward the end of President Obama's first term, as it became increasingly clear that the nation's first black president could not even successfully invoke race, let alone challenge our "broad sympathy toward some and broader skepticism toward others." President Obama's reaction to Trayvon Martin's killing and the arrest of Professor Henry Louis Gates in his own home

created significant backlash for comments he made sympathizing with Martin and Gates, in part over their shared racial identity. Ta-Nehisi Coates, "Fear of a Black President," *Atlantic*, September 2012.

82. As evidence of the dominance of the racial project of racial representation, mayors in cities with besieged police departments have been quick to appoint black police officers to leadership positions.

83. BLM activists pushed Democratic and (to a lesser extent) Republican presidential candidates to address racial profiling and mass incarceration. In 2015, for the first time since the Pew Research Center began polling people in 2009, a majority of white respondents said that the country needed to continue making changes to give blacks equal rights. Pew Research Center, "Across Racial Lines, More Say Nation Needs to Make Changes to Achieve Racial Equality," August 5, 2015, http://www.people-press.org/2015/08/05/across-racial-lines-more-say-nation-needs-to-make-changes-to-achieve-racial-equality/.

84. The vast majority of police officers are not held legally accountable, although some local BLM branches have been more successful. For example, in Chicago, after the video of the police killing of Laquan McDonald, an unarmed black man, was released protesters successfully prompted the dismissal of the Chicago Police Department's superintendent. In addition, BLM provided momentum to an effort to remove the Cook County state's attorney, who had not pressed charges against the officer who killed McDonald (the officer was subsequently indicted).

85. Albert Dzur, "An Introduction: Penal Democracy," *The Good Society* 23, 1 (2014): 1–5 quoting William J. Stuntz, "The Pathological Politics of Criminal Law," *Michigan Law Review* 100, 3 (2001): 505–600.

86. Brian Barry, *Why Social Justice Matters* (Cambridge: Polity Press, 2005), quoted in Ian Loader and Richard Sparks, "Beyond Lamentation: Towards a Democratic Egalitarian Politics of Crime and Justice," *Edinburgh School of Law Research Paper* 2012/23 (2012): 13.

87. Loader and Sparks, "Beyond Lamentation."

88. See contributions to a 2014 issue of *The Good Society* 23 (1) of papers from a "Good Society Symposium on 'Democratic Theory and Mass Incarceration.'" See also two issues from the *International Journal for Crime, Justice, and Social Democracy* 2 (2013).

89. Calavita and Jenness, *Appealing to Justice.*

90. See, e.g., Jonathan Simon, "The New Gaol Seeing Incarceration Like a City," *Annals of the American Academy of Political and Social Science* 664 (1) (2016): 280–301.

91. Elliott Currie, "Consciousness, Solidarity, and Hope as Prevention and Rehabilitation," *International Journal for Crime, Justice, and Social Democracy* 2 (2) (2013): 3–11.

92. Pat Carlan, "Against Rehabilitation, for Reparative Justice," in *Crime, Justice, and Social Democracy: International Perspectives, ed.* Kerry Carrington, Matthew

Ball, Erin O'Brien, and Juan Tauri (Houndsmill, UK: Palgrave Macmillan, 2013), 101.

93. Loader and Sparks, "Beyond Lamentation."

Appendix

1. Todd R. Clear and James Austin, "Reducing Mass Incarceration: Implications of the Iron Law of Prison Populations," *Harvard Law and Policy Review* 3 (2009): 307–24.

2. William J. Sabol, "Implications of Criminal Justice System Adaptation for Prison Population Growth and Corrections Policy" (2011) (unpublished manuscript), *available at* http://www.albany.edu/scj/documents/Sabol_ManagingPopulations_000.pdf. See also Alfred Blumstein and Allen J. Beck, "Population Growth in U.S. Prisons, 1980–1996," in *Crime and Justice: Prisons*, ed. Michael Tonry and Joan Petersilia (Chicago: University of Chicago Press, 1999), 17–62; Alfred Blumstein and Allen J. Beck, "Reentry as a Transient State between Liberty and Recommitment," in *Prisoner Reentry and Crime in America*, ed. Jeremy Travis and Christy Visher (Cambridge: Cambridge University Press, 2005), 50–79.

3. Florida Office of Economic and Demographic Research, Criminal Justice Estimating Conference, February 16, 2004, 1, http://edr.state.fl.us/content/conferences/criminaljustice/archives/040216criminaljustice.pdf.

4. Florida Office of Economic and Demographic Research, "Criminal Justice Trends," December 17, 2015, http://edr.state.fl.us/content/conferences/criminaljustice/trends.pdf.

5. Sabol, "Implications of Criminal Justice System Adaptation for Prison Population Growth and Corrections Policy," 28–29. Please note that I've changed some of Sabol's notation to uppercase or subscript and redefined and reabbreviated some of his variables.

Selected Bibliography

Adams, Julia, Elisabeth S. Clemens, and Ann Shola Orloff. *Remaking Modernity: Politics, History, and Sociology*. Durham: Duke University Press, 2005.

Alexander, Michelle. *The New Jim Crow: Mass Incarceration in the Age of Colorblindness*. New York: New Press, 2009.

Aviram, Hadar. *Cheap on Crime: Recession-Era Politics and the Transformation of American Punishment*. Berkeley: University of California Press, 2015.

Baldwin, James. *The Fire Next Time*. New York: Dial Press, 1963.

Barker, Vanessa. *The Politics of Imprisonment: How the Democratic Process Shapes the Way America Punishes Offenders*. New York: Oxford University Press, 2009.

Beale, Sara Sun. "The News Media's Influence on Criminal Justice Policy: How Market-Driven News Promotes Punitiveness." *William and Mary Law Review* 48 (2006): 397–481.

Beckett, Katherine. *Making Crime Pay: Law and Order in Contemporary American Politics*. New York: Oxford University Press, 1997.

Beckett, Katherine, and Naomi Murakawa. "Mapping the Shadow Carceral State: Toward an Institutionally Capacious Approach to Punishment." *Theoretical Criminology* 16 (2) (2012): 221–44.

Beckett, Katherine, Anna Reosti, and Emily Knaphus. "The End of an Era? Understanding the Contradictions of Criminal Justice Reform." *Annals of the American Academy of Political and Social Science* 664 (1) (2016): 238–59.

Beckett, Katherine, and Theodore Sasson. *The Politics of Injustice: Crime and Punishment in America*. New York: Sage, 2004.

Benson, Bruce L., David W. Rasmussen, and David L. Sollars. "Police Bureaucracies, Their Incentives, and the War on Drugs." *Public Choice* 83 (1–2) (1995): 21–45.

Bernstein, Elizabeth. "Militarized Humanitarianism Meets Carceral Feminism: The Politics of Sex, Rights, and Freedom in Contemporary Anti-trafficking Campaigns." *Signs* 36 (1) (2010): 45–71.

Berrey, Ellen. *The Enigma of Diversity: The Language of Race and the Limits of Racial Justice*. Chicago: University of Chicago Press, 2015.

Black, Earl, and Merle Black. *Politics and Society in the South*. Cambridge: Harvard University Press, 1989.

Blumenson, Eric, and Eva Nilsen. "Policing for Profit: The Drug War's Hidden Economic Agenda." *University of Chicago Law Review* (1998): 35–114.

Bobo, Lawrence D., and Victor Thompson. "Unfair by Design: The War on Drugs, Race, and the Legitimacy of the Criminal Justice System." *Social Research* 73 (2) (2006): 445–72.

Bonilla-Silva, Eduardo. "Rethinking Racism: Toward a Structural Interpretation." *American Sociological Review* 62 (3) (1997): 465–80.

Branch, Taylor. *Pillar of Fire: America in the King Years 1963–65*. New York: Simon & Schuster, 1998.

Brown, Elizabeth K. "The Dog That Did Not Bark: Punitive Social Views and the 'Professional Middle Classes.'" *Punishment and Society* 8 (3) (2006): 287–312.

Brown, Robert A., and James Frank. "Race and Officer Decision Making: Examining Differences in Arrest Outcomes between Black and White Officers." *Justice Quarterly* 23 (1) (2006): 96–126.

Bullock, Charles S., and Mike J. Rozell, eds. *The New Politics of the Old South: An Introduction to Southern Politics*. New York: Rowman & Littlefield Publishers, 2013.

Burch, Traci R. *Trading Democracy for Justice: Criminal Convictions and the Decline of Neighborhood Political Participation*. Chicago: University of Chicago Press, 2013.

Burkhardt, Brett C. "Who Punishes Whom? Bifurcation of Private and Public Responsibilities in Criminal Punishment." *Journal of Crime and Justice* (2016), doi: 10.1080/0735648X.2016.1174619.

Cable, George W. *The Negro Question*. Philadelphia: Charles Scribner's Sons, 1890.

Calavita, Kitty, and Valerie Jenness. *Appealing to Justice: Prisoner Grievances, Rights, and Carceral Logic*. Berkeley: University of California Press, 2014.

Campbell, John L. *Institutional Change and Globalization*. Princeton: Princeton University Press, 2004.

Campbell, Michael C. "The Emergence of Penal Extremism in California: A Dynamic View of Institutional Structures and Political Processes." *Law and Society Review* 48 (2014): 377–409.

Campbell, Michael C. "Ornery Alligators and Soap on a Rope: Texas Prosecutors and Punishment Reform in the Lone Star State." *Theoretical Criminology* 16 (3) (2012): 289–311.

Campbell, Michael C. "Politics, Prisons, and Law Enforcement: An Examination of the Emergence of 'Law and Order' Politics in Texas." *Law and Society Review* 45 (3) (2011): 631–65.

Campbell, Michael C., and Heather Schoenfeld. "The Transformation of America's Penal Order: A Historicized Political Sociology of Punishment." *American Journal of Sociology* 118 (5) (2013): 1375–1423.

Campbell, Michael C., Matt Vogel, and Joshua Williams. "Historical Contingencies and the Evolving Importance of Race, Violent Crime, and Region in Explaining Mass Incarceration in the United States." *Criminology* 53 (2015): 180–203.

Carmines, Edward G., and James A. Stimson. *Issue Evolution: Race and the Transformation of American Politics*. Princeton: Princeton University Press, 1989.

Carrington, Kerry, Matthew Ball, Erin O'Brien, and Juan Tauri, eds. *Crime, Justice, and Social Democracy: International Perspectives*. Houndsmill, UK: Palgrave Macmillan, 2013.

Cavender, Gray. "Media and Crime Policy: A Reconsideration of David Garland's *The Culture of Control*." *Punishment and Society* 6 (3) (2004): 335–48.

Chiricos, Ted, Sarah Eschholz, and Marc Gertz. "Crime, News and Fear of Crime: Toward an Identification of Audience Effects." *Social Problems* 44 (3) (1997): 353.

Christie, Nils. *Crime Control as Industry: Gulags Western Style*. London: Routledge, 1993.

Clear, Todd R. *Imprisoning Communities: How Mass Incarceration Makes Disadvantaged Neighborhoods Worse*. New York: Oxford University Press, 2007.

Clear, Todd R., and Natasha Frost. *The Punishment Imperative: The Rise and Failure of Mass Incarceration. New York: New York University Press*, 2014.

Coates, Ta-Nehisi. *Between the World and Me*. New York: Spiegel and Grau, 2015.

Colburn, David R. *From Yellow Dog Democrats to Red State Republicans: Florida and Its Politics Since 1940*. Gainesville: University Press of Florida, 2007.

Colburn, David R. *Racial Change and Community Crisis: St. Augustine, Florida 1877–1980*. New York: Columbia University Press, 1985.

Colburn, David R., and Lance deHaven-Smith. *Government in the Sunshine State*. Gainesville: University Press of Florida, 1999.

Colburn, David R., and Richard K. Scher. *Florida's Gubernatorial Politics in the Twentieth Century*. Gainesville: University Press of Florida, 1980.

Cole, David. *No Equal Justice: Race and Class in the American Criminal Justice System*. New York: The New Press, 1999.

Crenshaw, Kimberle, Neil Gotanda, Gary Peller, and Kendall Thomas, eds. *Critical Race Theory: The Key Writings That Formed the Movement*. New York: New Press, 1995.

Cronin, Thomas E., Tania Z. Cronin, and Michael E. Milakovich. *U.S. v. Crime in the Streets*. Bloomington: Indiana University Press, 1981.

Crouch, Ben, and J. W. Marquart. *An Appeal to Justice: Litigated Reform of Texas Prisons*. Austin: University of Texas Press, 1980.

Crow, Matthew S., and Marc Gertz. "Sentencing Policy and Disparity: Guidelines and the Influence of Legal and Democratic Subcultures." *Journal of Criminal Justice* 36 (4) (2008): 368.

Cullen, Francis T., Bonnie S. Fisher, and Brandon K. Applegate. "Public Opinion About Punishment and Corrections." *Crime and Justice: A Review of Research* 27 (2000): 1–79.

Currie, Elliott. "Consciousness, Solidarity, and Hope as Prevention and Rehabilitation." *International Journal for Crime, Justice, and Social Democracy* 2 (2) (2013): 3–11.

Currie, Elliott. *Crime and Punishment in America*. New York: Macmillan, 2013 [1998].

Dagan, David, and Steven M. Teles. "Locked In? Conservative Reform and the Future of Mass Incarceration." *Annals of the American Academy of Political and Social Science* 651 (1) (2014): 266–76.

Dagan, David, and Steven M. Teles. *Prison Break: Why Conservatives Turned Against Mass Incarceration*. New York: Oxford University Press, 2016.

Dagan, David, and Steven M. Teles. "The Social Construction of Policy Feedback: Incarceration, Conservatism, and Ideological Change." *Studies in American Political Development* 29 (2015): 127–53.

Davis, Martha F. *Brutal Need: Lawyers and the Welfare Rights Movement, 1960–1973*. New Haven: Yale University Press, 1995.

DiIulio, John J., Jr., ed. *Courts, Corrections, and the Constitution: The Impact of Judicial Intervention on Prisons and Jails*. New York: Oxford University Press, 1990.

DiMaggio, Paul. "Culture and Cognition." *Annual Review of Sociology* 23 (1997): 263–87.

DuBois, W. E. B. *Souls of Black Folk*. Chicago: A. C. McClurg & Co., 1903.

DuBois, W. E. B. "The Spawn of Slavery: The Convict Lease System in the South." *Missionary Review of the World* 24 (1901): 737–45.

Dzur, Albert. "An Introduction: Penal Democracy." *Good Society* 23 (1) (2014): 1–5.

Eason, John. *Big House on the Prairie: Rise of the Rural Ghetto and Prison Proliferation*. Chicago: University of Chicago Press, 2017.

Eason, John. "Mapping Prison Proliferation: Region, Rurality, Race, and Disadvantage in Prison Placement." *Social Science Research* 39 (6) (2010): 1015–28.

Eberhardt, Jennifer, et al. "Seeing Black: Race, Crime, and Visual Processing." *Journal of Personality and Social Psychology* 87 (2004): 876–93.

Edsall, Thomas B., and Mary D. Edsall, *Chain Reaction: The Impact of Race, Rights, and Taxes on American Politics*. New York: W. W. Norton, 1992.

Enck-Wanzer, Darrel. "Barack Obama, the Tea Party, and the Threat of Race: On Racial Neoliberalism and Born Again Racism." *Communication, Culture, and Critique* 4 (2011): 23–30.

Enns, Peter K. *Incarceration Nation: How the United States Became the Most Punitive Democracy in the World*. New York: Cambridge University Press, 2016.

Epp, Charles R. *Making Rights Real: Activists, Bureaucrats, and the Creation of the Legalistic State*. Chicago: University of Chicago Press, 2010.

Epp, Charles R., Steven Maynard-Moody, and Donald P. Haider-Markel. *Pulled Over: How Police Stops Define Race and Citizenship*. Chicago: University of Chicago Press, 2014.

Evans, Peter B., Dietrich Rueschemeyer, and Theda Skocpol, eds. *Bringing the State Back In*. Cambridge: Cambridge University Press, 1985.

Fairclough, Adam. *To Redeem the Soul of America: The Southern Christian Leadership Conference and Martin Luther King, Jr.* Athens: University of Georgia Press, 1987.

Farrell, Amy, Geoff Ward, and Danielle Rousseau. "Race Effects of Representation among Federal Court Workers: Does Black Workforce Representation Reduce Sentencing Disparities?" *Annals of the American Academy of Political and Social Science* 623 (1) (2009): 121–33.

Feagin, Joe R. *White Party, White Government: Race, Class, and U.S. Politics*. New York: Routledge, 2012.

Feeley, Malcolm M. "Crime, Social Order, and the Rise of Neo-conservative Politics." *Theoretical Criminology*, 7 (2003): 111–30.

Feeley, Malcolm M, and Edward L. Rubin. *Federalism: Political Identity and Tragic Compromise*. Ann Arbor: University of Michigan Press, 2008.

Feeley, Malcolm M., and Austin Sarat. *The Policy Dilemma: Federal Crime Policy and the Law Enforcement Assistance Administration*. Minneapolis: University of Minnesota Press, 1980.

Feeley, Malcolm M., and Van Swearingen. "The Prison Conditions Cases and the Bureaucratization of American Corrections: Influences, Impacts, and Implications." *Pace Law Review* 24 (2004): 433–75.

Fligstein, Neil. "Social Skill and the Theory of Fields." *Sociological Theory* 19 (2001): 105–25.

Fortner, Michael Javen. *Black Silent Majority: The Rockefeller Drug Laws and the Politics of Punishment*. Cambridge: Harvard University Press, 2015.

Foster, Holly, and John Hagan. "The Mass Incarceration of Parents in America: Issues of Race/Ethnicity, Collateral Damage to Children, and Prisoner Reentry." *Annals of the American Academy of Political and Social Science* 623 (2009): 179–94.

Frost, Natasha A. "Beyond Public Opinion Polls: Punitive Public Sentiment and Criminal Justice Policy." *Sociology Compass* 4 (3) (2010): 156–68.

Frymer, Paul. *Uneasy Alliances: Race and Party Competition in America*. Princeton: Princeton University Press, 2010 [1999].

Garland, David. *The Culture of Control: Crime and Social Order in Contemporary Society*. Chicago: University of Chicago Press, 2001.

Garland, David. "The 2012 Sutherland Address: Penality and the Penal State." *Criminology* 51 (3) (2013): 475–517.

Garrow, David J. *Bearing the Cross: Martin Luther King Jr. and the Southern Christian Leadership Conference*. New York: William Morrow and Company, Inc., 1986.

Geller, Amanda, Carey E. Cooper, Irwin Garfinkel, Ofira Schwartz-Soicher, and Ronald B. Mincy. "Beyond Absenteeism: Father Incarceration and Child Development." *Demography* 49 (2012): 49–76.

Gest, Ted. *Crime and Politics: Big Government's Erratic Campaign for Law and Order*. New York: Oxford University Press, 2001.

Gilliam, Franklin D., and Shanto Iyengar. "Prime Suspects: The Influence of Local Television News on the Viewing Public." *American Journal of Political Science* 44 (3) (2000): 560–73.

Gilmore, Ruth Wilson. *Golden Gulag: Prisons, Surplus, Crisis, and Opposition in Globalizing California*. Berkeley: University of California Press, 2007.

Gilmore, Ruth Wilson. "The Worrying State of the Anti-prison Movement." *Social Justice* (2015), available at http://www.socialjusticejournal.org/?p=2888.

Goodman, Philip. "'Another Second Chance': Rethinking Rehabilitation through the Lens of California's Prison Fire Camps." *Social Problems* 59 (2012): 437–58.

Goodman, Philip. "'It's Just Black, White, or Hispanic': An Observational Study of Racializing Moves in California's Segregated Prison Reception Centers." *Law and Society Review* 42 (4) (2008): 735–70.

Goodman, Philip, Joshua Page, and Michelle Phelps. *Breaking the Pendulum: The Long Struggle over Criminal Justice*. New York: Oxford University Press, 2017.

Goodman, Philip, Joshua Page, and Michelle Phelps. "The Long Struggle: An Agonistic Perspective on Penal Development." *Theoretical Criminology* 19 (3) (2014): 315–35.

Gottschalk, Marie. *Caught: The Prison State and the Lockdown of American Politics*. Princeton: Princeton University Press, 2015.

Gottschalk, Marie. "Democracy and the Carceral State in America." *Annals of the American Academy of Political and Social Science* 651 (1) (2014): 288–95.

Gottschalk, Marie. *The Prison and the Gallows: The Politics of Mass Incarceration in America*. New York: Cambridge University Press, 2006.

Gowan, Teresa, and Sarah Whetstone, "Making the Criminal Addict: Subjectivity and Social Control in a Strong-Arm Rehab." *Punishment and Society* 14 (1) (2012): 69–93.

Green, David A. "Penal Populism and the Folly of 'Doing Good by Stealth.'" *Good Society* 23 (1) (2014): 73–86.

Green, David A. "US Penal-Reform Catalysts, Drivers, and Prospects." *Punishment and Society* 17 (3) (2015): 271–98.

Greenberg, Jack. *Crusaders in the Courts: Legal Battles of the Civil Rights Movement*. New York: Twelve Tables Press, 1985 [2004 edition].

Griffin, Timothy, and Monica K. Miller. "Child Abduction, AMBER Alert, and Crime Control Theater." *Criminal Justice Review* 33 (2008): 159–76.

Griset, Pamala L. *Determinate Sentencing: The Promise and the Reality of Retributive Justice* Albany: State University of New York Press, 1991.

Guetzkow, Joshua, and Eric Schoon. "If You Build It, They Will Fill It: The Unintended Consequences of Prison Overcrowding Litigation." *Law and Society Review* 49 (2015): 401–32.

Gusfield, Joseph R. *Symbolic Crusade: Status Politics and the American Temperance Movement*. Urbana: University of Illinois Press, 1963.

Hagan, John. *Who Are the Criminals?: The Politics of Crime Policy from the Age of Roosevelt to the Age of Reagan.* Princeton: Princeton University Press, 2012.

Haney, Lynne A. *Offending Women: Power, Punishment, and the Regulation of Desire.* Berkeley: University of California Press, 2010.

Haney Lopez, Ian. *Dog Whistle Politics: How Coded Racial Appeals Have Reinvented Racism and Wrecked the Middle Class.* New York: Oxford University Press, 2014.

Harcourt, Bernard E. *Against Prediction: Profiling, Policing, and Punishing in an Actuarial Age.* Chicago: University of Chicago Press, 2008.

Harcourt, Bernard E. "Risk as a Proxy for Race: The Dangers of Risk Assessment." *Federal Sentencing Reporter* 27 (4) (2015): 237–43.

Harris, Fredrick. *The Price of the Ticket: Barack Obama and Rise and Decline of Black Politics.* New York: Oxford University Press, 2012.

Havard, William C., and Loren P. Beth. *The Politics of Mis-representation: Rural-Urban Conflict in the Florida Legislature.* Baton Rouge: Louisiana State University Press, 1962.

Hawkins, Darnell, Samuel Myers, Jr., and Randolph Stine, eds. *Crime Control and Social Justice: The Delicate Balance.* Westport, CT: Greenwood Press, 2003.

Heclo, Hugh. *Modern Social Politics in Britain and Sweden: From Relief to Income Maintenance.* New Haven: Yale University Press, 1974.

Hinton, Elizabeth. *From the War on Poverty to the War on Crime: The Making of Mass Incarceration in America.* Cambridge: Harvard University Press, 2016.

Horowitz, Donald. *The Courts and Social Policy.* Washington, DC: Brookings Institution, 1977.

Huebner, Beth M., and Regan Gustafson. "The Effect of Maternal Incarceration on Adult Offspring Involvement in the Criminal Justice System." *Journal of Criminal Justice* 35 (2007): 283–96.

Hughey, Matthew W., and Gregory S. Parks. *The Wrongs of the Right: Language, Race, and the Republican Party in the Age of Obama.* New York: NYU Press, 2014.

Hutchings, Vincent L., and Nicholas A. Valentino. "The Centrality of Race in American Politics." *Annual Review of Political Science* 7 (2004): 383–408.

Irwin, John. *Prisons in Turmoil.* Boston: Little, Brown and Company, 1980.

Irwin, John, and James Austin. *It's about Time: America's Imprisonment Binge.* Belmont, CA: Wadsworth Publishing Co., 1994.

Iyengar, Shanto. *Is Anyone Responsible? How Television Frames Political Issues* Chicago: University of Chicago Press, 1991.

Jackson, Pamela Irving, and Leo Carroll. "Race and the War on Crime: The Sociopolitical Determinants of Municipal Police Expenditures in 90 Non-Southern U.S. Cities." *American Sociological Review* 46 (3) (1981): 290–305.

Jacobs, David, and Aubrey L. Jackson. "On the Politics of Imprisonments: A Review of Systematic Findings." *Annual Review of Law and Social Science* 6 (2010): 129–49.

Jacobs, David, and Richard Kleban. "Political Institutions, Minorities, and Pun-ishment: A Pooled Cross-National Analysis of Imprisonment Rates." *Social Forces* 80 (2003): 725–55.

Jacobs, James B. "The Prisoner's Rights Movement and Its Impacts." In *Crime and Justice: An Annual Review of Research*, edited by Norval Morris and Michael Tonry, 429–70. Chicago: University of Chicago Press, 1980.

James, C. L. R. "Preliminary Notes on the Negro Question" (1939). In *C. L. R. James on the "Negro Question,"* edited by Scott McLemee. Jackson: University Press of Mississippi, 1996.

Johnson, Brian D. "The Multilevel Context of Criminal Sentencing: Integrating Judge- and County-Level Influences." *Criminology* 44 (2) (2006): 259–98.

Johnson, Cedric. *Revolutionaries to Race Leaders: Black Power and the Making of African American Politics*. Minneapolis: University of Minnesota Press, 2007.

Kappeler, Victor E., and Gary W. Potter. *Constructing Crime: Perspectives on Mak-ing News and Social Problems*. Long Grove, IL: Waveland Press, 2006.

Karl, Frederick B. *The 57 Club: My Four Decades in Florida Politics*. Gainesville: University Press of Florida, 2010.

Kim, Claire Jean. "Managing the Racial Breach: Clinton, Black-White Polariza-tion, and the Race Initiative." *Political Science Quarterly* 117 (2002): 55–79.

King, Desmond S., and Rogers M. Smith. "Racial Orders in American Political Development." *American Political Science Review* 99 (2005): 75–92.

King, Desmond S., and Rogers M. Smith. *Still a House Divided: Race and Politics in Obama's America*. Princeton: Princeton University Press, 2011.

King, Desmond S., and Rogers M. Smith, " 'Without Regard to Race': Critical Ide-ational Development in Modern American Politics." *Journal of Politics* 76 (4) (2014): 958–71.

King, Gilbert. *Devil in the Grove: Thurgood Marshall, the Groveland Boys, and the Dawn of a New America*. New York: Harper Collins, 2012.

Klinkner, Philip A., and Rogers M. Smith. *The Unsteady March: The Rise and De-cline of Racial Equality in America*. Chicago: University of Chicago Press, 2002.

Kohler-Hausmann, Issa. "Managerial Justice and Mass Misdemeanors." *Stanford Law Review* 66 (3) (2014).

Lacey, Nicola. *The Prisoner's Dilemma: Political Economy and Punishment in Con-temporary Democracies*. Cambridge: Cambridge University Press, 2008.

Latessa, Edward, Francis Cullen, and Paul Gendreau. "Beyond Correctional Quackery—Professionalism and the Possibility of Effective Treatment." *Fed-eral Probation* 66 (2) (2002): 43–49.

Lee, David, and Howard Newby. *The Problem of Sociology*. New York: Taylor & Francis, 2012 [1983].

Lee, Hedwig, Lauren C. Porter, and Megan Comfort. "Consequences of Family Member Incarceration: Impacts on Civic Participation and Perceptions of the Legitimacy and Fairness of Government." *Annals of the American Academy of Political and Social Science* 651 (2014): 44–73.

Lerman, Amy E. *The Modern Prison Paradox: Politics, Punishment, and Social Community*. New York: Cambridge University Press, 2013.

Lerman, Amy E., and Vesla M. Weaver. *Arresting Citizenship: The Democratic Consequences of American Crime Control*. Chicago: University of Chicago Press, 2014.

Lewis, Anthony. *Gideon's Trumpet*. New York: Vintage Books, 1964.

Lichtenstein, Alex. *Twice the Work of Free Labor: The Political Economy of Convict Labor in the New South*. New York: Verso, 1996.

Lieberman, Robert C. *Shifting the Color Line: Race and the American Welfare State*. Cambridge: Harvard University Press, 1998.

Liska, Allen E., Joseph J. Lawrence, and Michael Benson. "Perspectives on the Legal Order: The Capacity for Social Control." *American Journal of Sociology* 87 (2) (1981): 413–26.

Loader, Ian, and Richard Sparks. "Beyond Lamentation: Towards a Democratic Egalitarian Politics of Crime and Justice." *Edinburgh School of Law Research Paper* 2012/23 (2012).

Lowi, Theodore. "American Business and Public Policy: Case Studies and Political Theory." *World Politics* 16 (1964): 677–715.

Lowndes, Joseph, Julie Novkov, and Dorian T. Warren, eds. *Race and American Political Development*. New York: Routledge, 2008.

Lubiano, Wahneema, ed. *The House that Race Built*. New York: Vintage Books, 1998.

Lynch, Mona. "Mass Incarceration, Legal Change, and Locale." *Criminology and Public Policy* 10 (3) (2011): 673–98.

Lynch, Mona. *Sunbelt Justice: Arizona and the Transformation of American Punishment*. Palo Alto, CA: Stanford University Press, 2010.

MacKenzie, Doris, and David Farrington. "Preventing Future Offending of Delinquents and Offenders: What Have We Learned from Experiments and Meta-analyses?" *Journal of Experimental Criminology* 11 (4) (2015): 565–95.

Mancini, Matthew. *One Dies, Get Another: Convict Leasing in the American South, 1866–1928*. Columbia: University of South Carolina Press, 1996.

Martin, Steve, and Sheldon Ekland-Olson. *Texas Prisons: The Walls Come Tumbling Down*. Austin: Texas Monthly Press, 1987.

Martinson, Robert. "What Works? Questions and Answers about Prison." *Public Interest* (Spring 1974): 22–54.

Mason, Paul, ed. *Criminal Visions: Media Representations of Crime and Justice*. New York: Routledge, 2013.

Mathews, Roger. "The Myth of Punitiveness." *Theoretical Criminology* 9 (2005): 175–201.

McCarty, William P., Ling Ren, and Jihong "Solomon" Zhao. "Determinants of Police Strength in Large U.S. Cities during the 1990s: A Fixed-Effects Panel Analysis." *Crime and Delinquency* 58 (3) (2012): 397–424.

McGirr, Lisa. *Suburban Warriors: The Origins of the New American Right*. Princeton: Princeton University Press, 2001.

McGovern, James R. *Anatomy of a Lynching: The Killing of Claude Neal.* Baton Rouge: Louisiana State University Press, 1982.

McGuire, Danielle L. *At the Dark End of the Street: Black Women, Rape, and Resistance: A New History of the Civil Rights Movement from Rosa Parks to the Rise of Black Power.* New York: Vintage Books, 2011.

McKim, Allison. "Roxanne's Dress: Governing Gender and Marginality through Addiction Treatment." *Signs: Journal of Women in Culture and Society* 39 (2) (2014): 433–58.

McKim, Allison. *Addicted to Rehab: Race, Gender, and Drugs in the Era of Mass Incarceration.* New Brunswick: Rutgers University Press, 2017.

Mears, Daniel P., and Michael D. Reisig, "The Theory and Practice of Supermax Prisons." *Punishment and Society* 8 (2006): 33–57.

Mendelberg, Tali. *The Race Card: Campaign Strategy, Implicit Messages, and the Norm of Equality.* Princeton: Princeton University Press, 2001.

Miller, Lisa L. *The Myth of Mob Rule: Violent Crime and Democratic Politics.* New York: Oxford University Press, 2016.

Miller, Lisa L. *The Perils of Federalism: Race, Poverty, and the Politics of Crime Control.* Oxford: Oxford University Press, 2008.

Miller, Reuben Jonathan. "Devolving the Carceral State: Race, Prisoner Reentry, and the Micro-politics of Urban Poverty Management." *Punishment and Society* 16 (3) (2014): 305–35.

Miller, Vivien M. L. *Hard Labor and Hard Time: Florida's "Sunshine Prison" and Chain Gangs.* Gainesville: University Press of Florida, 2012.

Miller, Warren E., and J. Merrill Shanks. *The New American Voter.* Cambridge: Harvard University Press, 1996.

Muhammad, Khalil Gibran. *The Condemnation of Blackness.* Cambridge: Harvard University Press, 2010.

Muller, Christopher. "Northward Migration and the Rise of Racial Disparity in American Incarceration, 1880–1950." *American Journal of Sociology* 118 (2) (2012): 281–326.

Murakawa, Naomi. *The First Civil Right: How Liberals Built Prison America.* Oxford: Oxford University Press, 2014.

Murray, Joseph, David P. Farrington, and Ivana Sekol. "Children's Antisocial Behavior, Mental Health, Drug Use, and Educational Performance after Parental Incarceration: A Systematic Review and Meta-analysis." *Psychological Bulletin* 138 (2) (2012): 175–210.

Myrdal, Gunnar. *An American Dilemma: The Negro Problem and Modern Democracy.* New York: Harper & Row Publishers, 1944.

Nalla, Mahesh K. "Perspectives on the Growth of Police Bureaucracies, 1948–1984: An Examination of Three Explanations." *Policing and Society* 3 (1992): 51–61.

National Research Council, *The Growth of Incarceration in the United States: Exploring Causes and Consequences.* Committee on Causes and Consequences of

High Rates of Incarceration, Jeremy Travis, Bruce Western, and Steve Redburn, eds. Committee on Law and Justice, Division of Behavioral and Social Sciences and Education. Washington, DC: National Academies Press, 2014.

Oberwittler, Dietrich, and Sven Höfer, "Crime and Justice in Germany: An Analysis of Recent Trends and Research." *European Journal of Criminology* 2 (2005): 465–508.

O'Connor, Julia, Ann Shola Orloff, and Sheila Shaver. *States, Markets, Families: Gender, Liberalism, and Social Policy in Australia, Canada, Great Britain, and the United States.* Cambridge: Cambridge University Press, 1999.

O'Malley, Pat. "Volatile and Contradictory Punishment." *Theoretical Criminology* 3 (1999): 175–96.

Omi, Michael, and Howard Winant. *Racial Formation in the United States: From the 1960s to the 1990s.* New York: Routledge, 1994.

Oreskovich, Joanne. "Dimensions of Sex Offender Sanctioning: A Case Study of Minnesota's Legislative Reforms, 1987–1993." Ph.D. diss., University of Minnesota, 2001.

Orloff, Ann Shola. "Explaining US Welfare Reform: Power, Gender, Race, and the US Policy Legacy." *Critical Social Policy* 22 (2002): 96–118.

Orloff, Ann Shola. *The Politics of Pensions: A Comparative Analysis of Britain, Canada, and the United States.* Madison: University of Wisconsin Press, 1993.

Oshinsky, David M. *Worse than Slavery: Parchman Farm and the Ordeal of Jim Crow Justice.* New York: Free Press, 1996.

Page, Joshua. *The Toughest Beat: Politics, Punishment, and the Prison Officers Union in California.* New York: Oxford University Press, 2011.

Pager, Devah. "The Mark of a Criminal Record." *American Journal of Sociology* 108 (5) (2006): 937–75.

Parenti, Christian. *Lockdown America: Police and Prisons in the Age of Crisis.* New York: Verso, 1999.

Pearson, Paul. *Dismantling the Welfare State: Reagan, Thatcher, and the Politics of Retrenchment.* New York: Cambridge University Press, 1994.

Perkinson, Robert. *Texas Tough: The Rise of America's Prison Empire.* New York: Henry Holt and Company, 2010.

Peterson, Ruth D., and Laurie J. Krivo. *Divergent Social Worlds: Neighborhood Crime and the Racial-Spatial Divide.* New York: Russell Sage Foundation, 2010.

Petrocik, John R. "Issue Ownership in Presidential Elections, with a 1980 Case Study." *American Journal of Political Science* 40 (3) (1996): 825–50.

Pfaff, John. *Locked In: The True Causes of Mass Incarceration and How to Achieve Real Reform.* New York: Basic Books, 2017.

Phelps, Michelle S. "The Place of Punishment: Variation in the Provision of Inmate Services Staff across the Punitive Turn." *Journal of Criminal Justice* 40 (5) (2012): 348–57.

Phelps, Michelle S. "Rehabilitation in the Punitive Era: The Gap between Rhetoric and Reality in US Prison Programs." *Law and Society Review* 45 (1) (2011): 33–68.

Pierson, Paul. *Politics in Time: History, Institutions, and Social Analysis.* Princeton: Princeton University Press, 2004.

Porter, Bruce, and Marvin Dunn. *The Miami Riot of 1980: Crossing the Bounds.* Lexington, MA: Lexington Books, 1984.

Price, Hugh Douglas. *The Negro and Southern Politics: A Chapter of Florida History.* Westport, CT: Greenwood Press, 1973 [1957].

Provine, Doris Marie. "Race and Inequality in the War on Drugs." *Annual Review of Law and Social Science* 7 (2011): 41–60.

Provine, Doris Marie. *Unequal under Law: Race in the War on Drugs.* Chicago: University of Chicago Press, 2008.

Rabby, Glenda Alice. *The Pain and the Promise: The Struggle for Civil Rights in Tallahassee, Florida.* Athens: University of Georgia Press, 1999.

Raphael, Stephen, and Michael A. Stoll, eds. *Do Prisons Make Us Safer? The Benefits and Costs of the Prison Boom.* New York: Russell Sage Foundation, 2009.

Raphael, Stephen, and Michael A. Stoll. *Why Are So Many Americans in Prison?* New York: Russell Sage Foundation, 2014.

Reinarman, Craig, and Harry G. Levine. *Crack in America: Demon Drugs and Social Justice.* Berkeley: University of California Press, 1997.

Reiter, Keramet. *23/7: Pelican Bay Prison and the Rise of Long-Term Solitary Confinement.* New Haven: Yale University Press, 2016.

Rosenberger, Jared S., and Valerie J. Callanan, "The Influence of Media on Penal Attitudes." *Criminal Justice Review* 36 (4) (2011): 435–55.

Rothman, David J. *Conscience and Convenience: The Asylum and Its Alternatives in Progressive America.* Boston: Little, Brown, 1980.

Rubin, Ashley T. "Penal Change as Penal Layering: A Case Study of Proto-prison Adoption and Capital Punishment Reduction, 1785–1822." *Punishment and Society* 18 (4): 420–41.

Sabol, William J. "Implications of Criminal Justice System Adaptation for Prison Population Growth and Corrections Policy" (2011) (unpublished manuscript). Available at http://www.albany.edu/scj/documents/Sabol_ManagingPopulations_000.pdf.

Sampson, Robert J. "The Incarceration Ledger: Toward a New Era in Assessing Societal Consequences." *Criminology and Public Policy* 10 (2011): 819–28.

Sampson, Robert J., Stephen W. Raudenbush, and Felton Earls. "Neighborhoods and Violent Crime: A Multilevel Study of Collective Efficacy." *Science* 227 (1997): 916–24.

Sarre, Rick. "Beyond 'What Works?' A 25-year Jubilee Retrospective of Robert Martinson's Famous Article." *Australian and New Zealand Journal of Criminology* 34 (2001): 38–46.

Savelsberg, Joachim. "Knowledge, Domination, and Criminal Punishment." *American Journal of Sociology* 99 (1994): 911–43.

Scheingold, Stuart A. *The Politics of Law and Order: Street Crime and Public Policy*. New York: Longman, 1984.

Schlanger, Margo. "Beyond the Hero Judge: Institutional Reform Litigation as Litigation." *Michigan Law Review* 97 (1999): 1994–2036.

Schlanger, Margo. "Civil Rights Injunctions over Time: A Case Study of Jail and Prison Court Orders." *New York University Law Review* 81 (2006): 550–628.

Schlanger, Margo. "*Plata v. Brown* and Realignment: Jails, Prisons, Courts, and Politics." *Harvard Civil Rights–Civil Liberties Law Review* 48 (2013): 165–215.

Schoenfeld, Heather. "The Delayed Emergence of Penal Modernism in Florida." *Punishment and Society* 16 (2014): 258–84.

Schoenfeld, Heather. "Mass Incarceration and the Paradox of Prison Conditions Litigation." *Law and Society Review* 44 (3/4) (2010): 731–68.

Schoenfeld, Heather. "A Research Agenda on Reform: Penal Policy and Politics across the States." *Annals of the American Academy of Political and Social Science* 664 (1) (2016): 155–74.

Seeds, Christopher. "Bifurcation Nation: American Penal Policy in Late Mass Incarceration." *Punishment and Society*. First published online October 19, 2016. doi: 10.1177/1462474516673822.

Shogan, Colleen J. "Anti-intellectualism in the Modern Presidency: A Republican Populism." *Perspectives on Politics* 5 (2) (2007): 295–303.

Simon, Jonathan. *Governing through Crime: How the War on Crime Transformed American Democracy and Created a Culture of Fear*. Oxford: Oxford University Press, 2007.

Simon, Jonathan. *Mass Incarceration on Trial: A Remarkable Court Decision and the Future of Prisons in America*. New York: New Press, 2014.

Simon, Jonathan. "The New Gaol: Seeing Incarceration like a City." *Annals of the American Academy of Political and Social Science* 664 (1) (2016): 280–301.

Simon, Jonathan. *Poor Discipline: Parole and the Social Control of the Underclass, 1890–1990*. Chicago: University of Chicago Press, 1993.

Simon, Jonathan, and Richard Sparks, eds. *The Sage Handbook of Punishment and Society*. Thousand Oaks, CA: Sage, 2012.

Skocpol, Theda. *Protecting Soldiers and Mothers*. Cambridge: Harvard University Press, 1992.

Skocpol, Theda, and Vanessa Williamson. *The Tea Party and the Remaking of Republican Conservatism*. New York: Oxford University Press, 2012.

Smith, Robert C. *We Have No Leaders: African Americans in the Post–Civil Rights Era*. Albany: State University of New York Press, 1996.

Smith, Sarah M., Marisa K. Omori, Susan F. Turner, and Jesse Jannetta. "Assessing the Earned Discharge Pilot Project." *Criminology and Public Policy* 11 (2) (2012): 385–410.

Soss, Joe, Richard C. Fording, and Sanford F. Schram. *Disciplining the Poor: Neo-liberal Paternalism and the Persistent Power of Race.* Chicago: University of Chicago Press, 2011.

Soss, Joe, Sanford F. Schram, Thomas P. Vartanian, and Erin O'Brien. "Setting the Terms of Relief: Explaining State Policy Choices in the Devolution Revolution." *American Journal of Political Science* 45 (2) (2001): 378–95.

Spelman, William. "Jobs or Jails? The Crime Drop in Texas." *Journal of Policy Analysis and Management* 24 (2005): 133–65.

Steensland, Brian. "Cultural Categories and the American Welfare State: The Case of Guaranteed Income Policy." *American Journal of Sociology* 111 (2006): 1273–1326.

Steffensmeier, Darrell, and Chester L. Britt. "Judges' Race and Judicial Decision Making: Do Black Judges Sentence Differently?" *Social Science Quarterly* 82 (4) (2001): 749–64.

Steinberg, Stephen. *Turning Back: The Retreat from Racial Justice in American Thought and Policy.* Boston: Beacon Press, 1995.

Steinmo, Sven, Kathleen Thelen, and Frank Longstreth, eds. *Structuring Politics: Historical Institutionalism in Comparative Analysis.* New York: Cambridge University Press, 1992.

Stuntz, William J. *The Collapse of American Criminal Justice.* Cambridge: Harvard University Press, 2011.

Stuntz, William J. "The Pathological Politics of Criminal Law." *Michigan Law Review* 100 (3) (2001): 505–600.

Sturm, Susan P. "The Legacy and Future of Corrections Litigation." *University of Pennsylvania Law Review* 142 (1993): 639–738.

Surette, Ray. *Media, Crime, and Criminal Justice.* Boston: Cengage Learning, 2014.

Sutton, John R. "The Political Economy of Imprisonment in the Affluent Western Democracies, 1960–1990." *American Sociological Review* 69 (2004): 170–89.

Sutton, John R., Frank Dobbin, John W. Meyer, and W. Richard Scott. "The Legalization of the Workplace." *American Journal of Sociology* 99 (1994): 944–71.

Tarman, Christopher, and David Sears. "The Conceptualization and Measurement of Symbolic Racism." *Journal of Politics* 67 (3) (2005): 731–61.

Teixeira, Ruy A., and Joel Rogers. *America's Forgotten Majority: Why the White Working Class Still Matters.* New York: Basic Books, 2000.

Thomas, Jim. *Prisoner Litigation: The Paradox of the Jailhouse Lawyer.* Lanham, MD: Rowman & Littlefield Publishers, Inc., 1988.

Tiger, Rebecca. *Judging Addicts: Drug Courts and Coercion in the Justice System.* New York: New York University Press, 2012.

Tonry, Michael. *Malign Neglect: Race, Crime, and Punishment in America.* New York: Oxford University Press, 1995.

Tonry, Michael. *Punishing Race: A Continuing American Dilemma.* New York: Oxford University Press, 2011.

Tonry, Michael, and Joan Petersilia, eds. *Crime and Justice: Prisons*. Chicago: University of Chicago Press, 1999.

Tope, Daniel, Justin T. Pickett, and Ted Chiricos. "Anti-minority Attitudes and Tea Party Movement Membership." *Social Science Research* 51 (2015): 322–37.

Turney, Kristin. "Incarceration and Social Inequality: Challenges and Directions for Future Research." *Annals of the American Academy of Political and Social Science* 651 (1) (2014): 97–101.

Van Cleve, Nicole Gonzalez. *Crook County: Racism and Injustice in America's Largest Criminal Court*. Palo Alto, CA: Stanford University Press, 2016.

Vargas, Robert, and Philip McHarris. "Race and State in City Police Spending Growth: 1980 to 2010." *Sociology of Race and Ethnicity* 3 (2016): 96–112.

Verma, Anjuli. "A Turning Point in Mass Incarceration? Local Imprisonment Trajectories and Decarceration under California's Realignment." *Annals of the American Academy of Political and Social Science* 664 (1) (2016): 108–35.

Wacquant, Loïc. "Deadly Symbiosis: When Ghetto and Prison Meet and Mesh." *Punishment and Society* 3 (2001): 95–134.

Wacquant, Loïc. *Punishing the Poor: The Neoliberal Government of Social Insecurity*. Raleigh, NC: Duke University Press, 2009.

Wagy, Tom. *Governor LeRoy Collins of Florida: Spokesman of the New South*. Montgomery: University of Alabama Press, 1985.

Weaver, Vesla. "Frontlash: Race and the Development of Punitive Crime Policy." *Studies in American Political Development* 21 (2007): 230–65.

Weaver, Vesla. "The Significance of Policy Failures in Political Development: The Law Enforcement Assistance Administration and the Growth of the Carceral State." In *Living Legislation: Durability, Change, and the Politics of American Lawmaking*, edited by Jeffery Jenkins and Eric Patashnik, 221–54. Chicago: University of Chicago Press, 2012.

Weir, Margaret, ed. *The Social Divide: Political Parties and the Future of Activist Government*. Washington, DC: Brookings Institution Press, 1998.

Weir, Margaret, Ann Shola Orloff, and Theda Skocpol, eds. *The Politics of Social Policy in the United States*. Princeton: Princeton University Press, 1988.

Welch, Michael, Melissa Fenwick, and Meredith Roberts. "Primary Definitions of Crime and Moral Panic: A Content Analysis of Experts' Quotes in Feature Newspaper Articles on Crime." *Journal of Research in Crime and Delinquency* 34 (4) (1997): 474–94.

Welch, Michael, Melissa Fenwick, and Meredith Roberts. "State Managers, Intellectuals, and the Media: A Content Analysis of Ideology in Experts' Quotes in Feature Newspaper Articles on Crime." *Justice Quarterly* 15 (2) (1998): 219–41.

West, Cornel. *Race Matters*. New York: Beacon Press, 1993.

Western, Bruce. "Incarceration, Inequality, and Imagining Alternatives." *Annals of the American Academy of Political and Social Science* 651 (1) (2014): 302–6.

Western, Bruce. *Punishment and Inequality in America*. New York: Russell Sage Foundation, 2006.

Western, Bruce, and Becky Pettit. "Incarceration and Social Inequality." *Daedalus*, Summer 2010, 8–19.

Western, Bruce, and Christopher Wildeman. "The Black Family and Mass Incarceration." *Annals of the American Academy of Political and Social Science* 621 (1) (2009): 221–42.

Whitman, James Q. *Harsh Justice: Criminal Justice and the Widening Divide between America and Europe*. Oxford: Oxford University Press, 2003.

Wickham, DeWayne. *Bill Clinton and Black America*. New York: One World, 2004.

Wildeman, Christopher. "Parental Imprisonment, the Prison Boom, and the Concentration of Childhood Disadvantage." *Demography* 46 (2009): 265–80.

Williamson, Vanessa, Theda Skocpol, and John Coggin. "The Tea Party and the Remaking of Republican Conservatism." *Perspectives on Politics* 9 (1) (2011): 25–43.

Wilson, Sarah. "Appellate Judicial Appointments during the Clinton Presidency: An Inside Perspective." *Journal of Appellate Practice and Process* 5 (2003): 29–48.

Windlesham, Lord. *Politics, Punishment, and Populism*. Oxford: Oxford University Press, 1998.

Winsboro, Irvin D. S., ed. *Old South, New South, or Down South: Florida and the Modern Civil Rights Movement*. Morgantown: West Virginia University, 2009.

Yackle, Larry W. *Reform and Regret: The Story of Federal Judicial Involvement in the Alabama Prison System*. New York: Oxford University Press, 1989.

Zimring, Franklin. "The Scale of Imprisonment in the United States: 20th Century Patterns and 21st Century Prospects." *Journal of Criminology and Criminal Law* 100 (3) (2010): 1225–46.

Zimring, Franklin, David Hawkins, and Sam Kamin. *Punishment and Democracy: Three Strikes and You're Out in California*. Oxford: Oxford University Press, 2001.

Index

The Chicago Series in Law and Society

EDITED BY JOHN M. CONLEY AND LYNN MATHER

Series titles, continued from front matter: